Ken Wilber
in Dialogue

Ken Wilber
in Dialogue

Conversations
with Leading
Transpersonal
Thinkers

edited by **Donald Rothberg** *and* **Sean Kelly**

A publication supported by
THE KERN FOUNDATION

Quest Books
Theosophical Publishing House

Wheaton, Illinois ◆ Chennai (Madras), India

The Theosophical Publishing House
P.O. Box 270
Wheaton, IL 60189-0270

A publication of the Theosophical Publishing House,
a department of the Theosophical Society in America

Library of Congress Cataloging-in-Publication Data

Ken Wilber in dialogue: conversations with leading transpersonal
    thinkers / edited by Donald Rothberg and Sean Kelly. -- 1st
    Quest ed.
    p.   cm.
    Includes bibliographical references and index.
    ISBN 0-8356-0766-6
    1. Transpersonal psychology.   I. Rothberg, Donald Jay.
    II. Kelly, Sean M., 1957-   .
BF204.7.K46   1998
150.19'8—dc21   97-35286
                                                        CIP

    5   4   3   2   1   *   98   99   00   01   02   03   04

Printed in the United States of America

Contents

Foreword

Stanley Krippner, Ph.D.

 THE TERM "TRANSPERSONAL STUDIES" REFERS TO THE DISCIPLINED study of observed or reported human behaviors and experiences in which an individual's sense of identity appears to extend beyond its ordinary limits to encompass wider, broader, or deeper aspects of life or the cosmos—including divine elements of creation. Transpersonal studies may center on the ethical and moral implications of such behaviors and experiences; cultural and text-related themes; developmental and evolutionary processes; applications to education, health care, social change, and other areas; or a host of other topics.

Pioneering books written from transpersonal perspectives have been published in Europe, North America, South America, Asia, and Africa by Roberto Assagioli (1965), Stanislav Grof (1975), Aldous Huxley (1945), Hiroshi Motoyama (1971), Abraham Maslow (1970), Frances Vaughan (1979), Alan Watts (1961), J. H. M. Whiteman (1961), and Pierre Weil (1977), among many others. The word "transpersonal" seems to have been independently introduced early in this century by William James and C. G. Jung (Vich 1988), and later by Gardner Murphy (1949).

However, no one has written more comprehensively on this topic than Ken Wilber, whose publications comprise a Grand Theory of human consciousness and its evolution toward what Wilber refers to as "Spirit," the animating and unifying force and intelligence of the universe that humans may know in many ways, for instance, through love, recognition of the commonality of the other, or mystical experience. If Wilber is even partially correct, one can understand why transpersonalists focus their studies on those observed and reported behaviors and experiences that appear to transcend a person's everyday activities. One's identity plunges more deeply, extends more widely, or expands more broadly (depending on which descriptive metaphor is used). "Spirit" is encountered, and the nature of this encounter provides profound meaning and direction for one's life.

Wilber does not promise transpersonal travelers an easy journey. There are hazards at each step of the individual's evolution as well as that of the species. But there are spiritual technologies and psychotherapies appropriate to each of these difficulties, and Wilber's description of them makes his work relevant to mental health practitioners as well as to the philosophers and social scientists who were among his first readers.

   Ken Wilber in Dialogue: Conversations with Leading Transpersonal Thinkers is a pivotal book. Its contributors include not only Wilber but also men and women from the fields of anthropology, psychology, psychiatry, religious studies, and from spiritual disciplines. The book's splendid organizational schema allows its readers to read it straight through in a linear manner, if they wish. Nonlinear readers, on the other hand, can select individual writers or chapters that pique their interest (from Parts I-IV), skip to Wilber's response (in Part V), and then read the appropriate rejoinder (in Part VI).

   I find the dialogical quality of this book quite engaging. The dialogues revolve around current unresolved issues in the transpersonal field, issues that many commentators on spiritual matters do not discuss seriously, whether because of their beliefs in "revealed teachings" and "final truths" or because of their ambivalence toward critical inquiry. Instead of the pitched battles that make a mockery of the term "religion" and the common lack of questioning and critical intelligence in many spiritual quarters, the participants in these dialogues seem to dance in an interaction marked for the most part by grace, style, and insight.

   Having been a contributor to one of Wilber's books (Krippner 1982) and having frequently cited his ideas in my own writing (e.g., Feinstein and Krippner 1988), I am aware of the depth of his knowledge and the breadth of his scholarship. For example, Wilber's recent (1997) article in the prestigious *Journal of Consciousness Studies* is a tour-de-force in which he describes a dozen competing theories of consciousness, their assignment to one of four "quadrants of existence," the delineation of each quadrant's "dimensions" (or "levels"), an assessment of the validity claims of each quadrant, and a listing of the methodologies and agendas that will assist each theory's integration into a larger synthesis.

   One notable aspect of this book is its extremely reader-friendly quality. It could serve the uninitiated as an articulate introduction to Wilber's thought, especially in regard to some of the wider issues to which it is related, such as: (1) the core concepts and major paradigms of transpersonal theory; (2) transpersonal theory and its treatment of what is typically devalued in Western (and much of Asian) culture—namely, nature, women, and indigenous peoples; (3) theoretical and practical concerns related to "regression"; and (4) transpersonal approaches to disciplined inquiry.

   In my view, the essays in this collection represent a distinguished body of work that will instruct the future of transpersonal studies for decades. This is an important endeavor because there is an urgent need in today's fractious world for integrative transpersonal perspectives, especially if presented in ways that are self-critical and able to be linked to contemporary scientific and practical concerns. If a dissonant humanity is to avoid further carnage, it needs to transcend the economic, ethnic, religious, and political conflagrations that have polarized and shattered it.

Tribal people rarely insisted that their "truth" was applicable to their neighbors; even when locked in battle, there was a respect for their opponents' courage and bravery that is sadly lacking in modern times. Respect for diversity, empathy for other human beings, and concern for other life forms are not only adaptive traits that will help human survival but are conduits to behaviors and experiences that may help humanity participate in whatever "Spirit" can be uncovered in this skeptical age.

Ken Wilber in Dialogue: Conversations with Leading Transpersonal Thinkers represents the cutting edge of a growing and provocative field. One might disagree with the focus, assumptions, or epistemology of this field, but one can no longer disregard it. Furthermore, the contributors point in a number of important new directions; there are many implications in these dialogues for future theory, research, and practice. Finally, there is an amenable willingness for new voices to join in future dialogues. Let us hope that these voices will be heard, and that this book will evoke their wisdom.

References

Assagioli, R. 1965. *Psychosynthesis: A manual of principles and procedures.* New York: Hobbs Dorman.

Feinstein, D., and S. Krippner. 1988. *Personal mythology: The psychology of your evolving self.* Los Angeles: Tarcher.

Grof, S. 1975. *Realms of the human unconscious: Observations from LSD research.* New York: Viking Press.

Huxley, A. 1945. *The perennial philosophy.* New York: Harper & Row.

Krippner, S. 1982. Holonomy and parapsychology. In *The holographic paradigm and other paradoxes: Exploring the leading edge of science*, edited by K. Wilber. Boulder: Shambhala.

Maslow, A. 1970. *Religions, values, and peak experiences.* New York: Viking Press.

Motoyama, H. 1971. *Hypnosis and religious superconsciousness.* Tokyo: Institute for Religious Psychology.

Murphy, G. 1949. Psychical research and personality. *Proceedings of the Society for Psychical Research* 49: 1-15.

Vaughan, F. 1979. *Awakening intuition.* Garden City, N.Y.: Anchor Books.

Vich, M. 1988. Some historical sources of the term "transpersonal." *Journal of Transpersonal Psychology* 20(2): 107-10.

Watts, A. 1961. *Psychotherapy East and West.* New York: Pantheon Books.

Weil, P. 1977. *A consciencia cosmica* (The cosmic consciousness). Petropolis, Brazil: Vozes.

Whiteman, J. 1961. *The mystical life.* London: Faber and Faber.

Wilber, K. 1997. An integral theory of consciousness. *Journal of Consciousness Studies* 4 (1): 71-92.

Preface

The Nature of the Conversation and the Structure of this Book

THIS CONVERSATION ABOUT KEN WILBER'S WORK AND THE ISSUES OF THE transpersonal field (and contemporary spirituality) was initially inspired by the recognition that, despite the widespread appeal and popularity of transpersonal psychology (and more generally of transpersonal studies), there has been little sustained discussion of this work. We wanted to examine Wilber's writings particularly, because of their scope and influence, yet we hoped to combine a focus on his work with attention to general issues and new horizons in transpersonal theory and practice. We intended the conversation to be both appreciative of the basic intentions of Wilber's work and of the field, as well as critical, in the sense of examining core assumptions and claims.

We thought it crucial to encourage significant dialogue among participants to provide energy to help the field develop—to spur insights and explore major differences. We also hoped to contribute to new models of transpersonal inquiry and scholarly practice that are in keeping with transpersonal values. Specifically, it was our intention that the dialogue format provide an alternative to more combative "debates" and critiques, all too common in the academic and political worlds, that are often short on sympathetic listening and collaborative learning, particularly when differences surface. The reader may judge how well we have succeeded.

The book's five sections reflect our goal of dialogue and respectful exchange:

> (1) Donald Rothberg's introduction (chapter 1) establishes the basis of the conversation. He identifies briefly some of the challenges of our contemporary cultural and social context. He then gives an overview of the transpersonal movement, of Ken Wilber's life and work, and of the main themes in Wilber's writings. He concludes with an outline of the main questions that have arisen in relation to Wilber's writing, an outline closely linked to the organization of the chapters of this book.

> (2) The twelve chapters in Parts I-IV have been authored by leading transpersonal thinkers; one of the chapters

(chapter 7) includes conversations with three additional authors, giving a total of fifteen contributors. Each contributor is introduced by an account of his or her life and work, along with a short summary of the chapter or conversation. These are intended to provide the personal and cultural contexts for the ideas being presented and to help connect practice and theory. Reading these introductions may both remind the reader that "ideas don't fall from the sky" (as Latin American liberation theologians phrase it), and underscore the common patterns of passionate intellectual and spiritual quest that is evident in the lives of all of the contributors. These chapters are organized around four main themes:

• *The Spirit of Evolution*—Part I, chapters 2-3, including a broad overview of Wilber's recent work by Roger Walsh in chapter 2

• *Alternative Paradigms of Transpersonal Theory*—Part II, chapters 4-7, including chapters by Michael Washburn and Stanislav Grof, who have developed the main alternative approaches to transpersonal studies

• *Transpersonal Theory and the "Other": Nature, Women, Indigenous Traditions, and Relationships*—Part III, chapters 8-11, treating these themes in the context of Wilber's work

• *How Do We Inquire Spiritually?*—Part IV, chapters 12-13, concerning the process of transpersonal inquiry

(3) In Part V (chapter 14) Ken Wilber responds to these chapters. Although the length of Wilber's responses to the chapters varies considerably, he has something to say about every chapter. By and large, Wilber discusses the contributions in more or less the same order as they are presented in the book, except for those chapters which are treated more briefly, which appear at the end of his response.

(4) In Part VI (chapter 15), twelve of the contributors respond to Ken Wilber and, in some cases, to other contributors, again in the same order as the initial chapters.

(5) Finally, in Part VII (chapters 16 and 17), Ken Wilber reflects on the entire conversation, followed by the editors' own retrospective and suggestions for further inquiry and dialogue.

Despite the many topics examined, we do want to acknowledge that even this book-length treatment is necessarily selective in terms of themes and authors. We might well have included chapters on a number of other areas. For example, the conversation would benefit by chapters on Wilber's treatment of physics, systems theory, modernity and postmodernity, philosophy since Kant, multiculturalism and cultural pluralism, and comparative religion, among others, and by many authors in the transpersonal field who did not contribute to this volume. In some cases, fine chapters on Wilber's work came to our attention only after decisions about what would be published had been made.

Most of the chapters in this volume first appeared in three issues of the journal *ReVision* (Spring, Summer, and Fall 1996), also edited by Donald Rothberg and Sean M. Kelly. The chapters by Michael Murphy (chapter 3) and Kaisa Puhakka (chapter 13) are new, as are Wilber's responses to them (in chapters 14 and 16) and their responses to him (in chapter 15). The introduction and the editors' closing reflections have been substantially revised and expanded from the versions published in *ReVision*. The introductions to each chapter are also new.

Our hope is that this volume (and others) might contribute to a kind of turning point in the transpersonal field—a growing capacity for critical discussion and exploration; a closer connection between theory and practice and between theory and empirical work; a deeper engagement of the field with mainstream thinking and institutions; a willingness to discuss new themes and to hear new voices, particularly those of women and people of color; and a greater openness and respectful dialogue (particularly when exploring differences) among transpersonal colleagues. We invite our readers to join us—in developing chapters, classes, conferences, Web sites, forums, study and/or practice groups, and other vehicles—in following these intentions.

Acknowledgments

A number of wonderful transpersonal persons helped in major ways with this project, and the editors wish to thank them! First of all, we thank the contributors, whose timeliness and skill in articulating often complex ideas and whose cooperation provided the foundation of our work together. We thank those many colleagues who gave feedback on the the individual essays and who are generally named in acknowledgements at the end of some of the chapters. We also want very much to thank our editor at Quest Books, Brenda Rosen, for her careful and very cooperative work with us, her enthusiasm for the project, and for her skillful editing. We give many kudos to Trena Cleland, who helped to assemble the entire manuscript on computer disk, gave a number of editing suggestions, and provided all-around support at many crucial moments. We thank Adele Mujal, the managing editor of the journal *ReVision*, who worked steadily to help craft most of the essays, and Richard Tarnas, who initially suggested that *ReVision* devote an issue (which later grew to three issues) to a consideration through dialogue of Ken Wilber's work. We also appreciate the generosity of Stanley Krippner in writing the foreword to the book, and the wonderful art of Elly Simmons, whose image graces our cover and re-appears throughout the book. Lastly, the editors respectively want to express their gratitude to Mary Anne Cutaia and Alison Armstrong-Webber for their editorial, moral, and spiritual support and manifold contributions during the sometimes difficult period of the book's composition.

This book is dedicated

To my parents Simon and Bernice (DR)

and

To the spirit of dialogue (DR, SK).

Introduction

Donald Rothberg

Ken Wilber and the Future
of Transpersonal Inquiry:
An Introduction to the Conversation

 WE LIVE AT A TIME OF CRISIS AND TRANSITION. MANY OF THE fundamental understandings of self, society, and nature that have guided Western experience for 2500 years stand questioned and criticized, if not condemned and rejected. In the emergence of the "modern" world, religious and metaphysical approaches that have historically provided the core images, norms, and worldviews for Western traditions have lost much of their former legitimacy. Similar changes have occurred recently and in rapid fashion in virtually the whole rest of the world.

Yet modern approaches often suffer from having lost the integrative power of tradition. The hallmarks of modernity—the rise of natural sciences, democratic values, and emphasis on the individual—have, despite their many virtues, often brought on uncertainty, confusion, and incoherence, coexisting at times with vast devastation. The awesome growth of science and our ability to manipulate the natural world through technology have seemingly obeyed their own internal logic, separate from the values and wisdom that might temper and guide their development. Free choice and self-determination have often given rise to more cacophony than harmony, threatening the coherence of society and the possibility of sustainable families and relationships. In fact, contemporary authors often describe a fragmented and "disenchanted" world, bereft of commonly shared values other than those of material prosperity. With the recent increasing polarization of rich and poor, even the social and cultural coherence provided by prosperity may be undermined (Head 1996).

Yet alternatives to the modern world are, at the present time, neither clearly articulated nor obviously preferable. While many defend modern worldviews rooted in scientific, rational, democratic, or individualistic values, others (whom we sometimes call "fundamentalists") press for a return to traditional religious or metaphysical worldviews often in explicit conflict with modern values. Yet history shows clearly the limitations and negative features of societies organized around religious worldviews.

Others who find little value in the modern Western world look instead to non-Western images, practices, and traditions, whether Asian, African, or indigenous, or to what they can reconstruct from "pre-patriarchal" Western traditions. Still others (representing some versions of "postmodernism") champion the rejection of modernity and its basic ideals in the name of pluralism and difference. They suspect, it seems, that an integrative worldview is, by its very nature, oppressive and totalitarian and typically profess an unwillingness to suggest coherent alternatives to the modern world. For an increasing number, particularly among the young, there remains only the painful presence of the failed ideals and promises of civilization and the growing anger, confusion, and suffering that follow fallen gods.

Reflecting on these contemporary challenges helps us to appreciate the contributions of Ken Wilber and establish the context for the dialogues in this book. Wilber's aspiration for his work is to help provide a new integrative vision for our times. This vision would be capable of showing us more clearly the insights and the blindness of modernists and anti-modernists, fundamentalists and postmodernists, primitivists and Orientalists, idealists and cynics. For Wilber and the other contributors, what is at stake is not narrowly theoretical or academic, but rather central to our cultural and individual survival. The goal is nothing less than discovering how to guide, in a visionary way, the collective and individual healing our culture so desperately needs.

AN OVERVIEW OF WILBER'S WORK

Wilber's integrative vision is both spiritual and, in a broad sense, rational. His intuition and claim are, as Jim Wallis (1994, xvii) has written, that we find common ground only by moving to "higher" ground and, further, that this new common ground includes room for the sciences and for rationality in political and individual life. In this sense, Wilber's vision is continuous with both the best of modernity and what is arguably the core philosophical and religious lineage of Western culture—what we might call a "rational mysticism" (Findlay 1970).

This lineage has its origins in the work of Pythagoras, Parmenides, Socrates, Plato, and Aristotle, and then passes through Augustine and Aquinas, Maimonides and Spinoza, Hegel and Heidegger, echoing in many ways the lineages of the Buddha and Nagarjuna, Shankara and Aurobindo, Fa-Tsang and Chu Hsi, Ibn Sina and Ibn al-Arabi.

The Transpersonal Movement

Wilber speaks of a "transpersonal" vision, reflecting his own more specific lineage of "transpersonal psychology" (and what we might call more generally "transpersonal studies"). Transpersonal psychology, with its initial intellectual roots in the work of William James, Carl Jung, humanistic psychology (particularly the work of Abraham Maslow), and early studies of Asian contemplative traditions, was self-consciously forged as a separate discipline in the late 1960s. The initial impetus was to bring into psychology the study of a variety of experiences not commonly examined in mainstream psychology and to develop wider conceptions of the nature of the mind, consciousness, human nature, and reality than were found in behaviorist, psychoanalytic, and humanistic approaches.

The *Journal of Transpersonal Psychology*, founded in 1969, took as its subject matter the study of "unitive consciousness, metaneeds, peak experiences, ecstasy, mystical experience, being, essence, bliss, awe, wonder, transcendence of self. . . ." Roger Walsh (one of the contributors to this volume) and Frances Vaughan, two leaders in the field, speak more recently (1993, 3) of *transpersonal experiences* as "experiences in which the sense of identity or self extends beyond (*trans*) the individual or personal to encompass wider aspects of humankind, life, *psyche*, and cosmos," and *transpersonal disciplines* as directed to the study of "transpersonal experiences and related phenomena." The intention of the field has been to make sense of experiences which traditionally would have been called "religious" within a more "scientific" framework—without bringing in traditional religious language, yet treating many of the same concerns of meaning, the unity of life, and the depths of insight, wisdom, and love.

Transpersonal psychology in North America and Europe also had many of its roots among those whom we might call the "spiritual counterculture," and its development since the late 1960s has paralleled some of this counterculture's directions of development. The initial emphasis on "altered states of consciousness" and nonordinary experiences (notably those states catalyzed by psychedelic drugs) gave way to an exploration of contemplative (and sometimes shamanic or psychotherapeutic) disciplines and practices (mostly Asian, sometimes Western or indigenous) that evoke such extraordinary experiences. More recent approaches have often focused on integrating such experiences and practices with everyday life in the West—with the mainstream disciplines of psychology, psychotherapy, philosophy, medicine, and physics, among others; and with exploration of pressing contemporary issues, such as those related to gender, ecology, and social justice.

Ken Wilber's Life and Work

Ken Wilber is probably the most prominent contemporary theorist in transpersonal studies. His work, published starting in 1975, represents all three phases of the transpersonal movement. He has distinguished himself by his prolific output (some fourteen books and many articles already published, although he is only forty-nine years old), by the multidisciplinary, cross-cultural, systematic, integrative, visionary, and scholarly aspirations of his work, and by the powerful impact of his work on many readers.

Born in 1949, Wilber moved frequently while young, his father a career officer in the Air Force. Still, he reports being outwardly successful in sports and academics and was elected student body president at two different schools. He was also obsessed by science. He wrote later (1982a, 58): "My true passion, my inner daemon, was for science. I fashioned a self that was built on logic, structured by physics, and moved by chemistry. . . . My mental youth was an idyll of precision and accuracy, a fortress of the clear and evident."

Following a chance reading of Lao Tzu while a student at Duke University, his life shifted radically in many ways. He began consuming books on Asian and Western spiritual traditions and on Western psychology and philosophy. He soon dropped out of Duke, returning to Nebraska, where his father was stationed. Because of the Vietnam War and the threat of being drafted, he enrolled at the University of Nebraska, eventually moving on to graduate school there in biochemistry and biophysics, all the while following a rigorous extracurricular study of spiritual, psychological, and philosophical texts.

After a short time in graduate school, however, Wilber married, left school and, in a three-month period in the winter of 1973, wrote his first book, *The Spectrum of Consciousness* (1977). Rejected by some twenty publishers over three years, it was finally published by Quest Books. The book displays many of the characteristics of Wilber's more mature work. Deeply synthetic, it suggests that psychology, psychotherapy, and philosophy needn't be seen as mutually competing and mutually exclusive, as if they were all attempting the same tasks. Rather, it outlines an integrative approach to the "full spectrum" of consciousness and experience, in which the different schools and theories—mainstream academic as well as spiritual or transpersonal—can be understood as focused primarily on one or another part of the same spectrum. As in Wilber's later work, the scholarship is immensely creative and original, at times unconventional, reflecting Wilber's process of intensive self-education and relative isolation, as well as the presence of his "daemon."

Over the next years, Wilber continued a life of intensive reading and writing, supported himself through part-time manual work, and deepened his practice of Zen with several hours of daily meditation as well as monthly short retreats. A series of essays and books followed in quick succession, further developing the approach in *Spectrum*. Many essays and parts of books to come were first published in the journal *ReVision*, which Wilber cofounded with Jack Crittenden. Wilber later became editor of the journal for several years. From 1979 to 1984, Wilber published books and essays articulating integrative models of individual development (1980, 1981); cultural and social evolution (1983a, originally 1981); epistemology and philosophy of science (1982b, 1990a, originally 1983, 1984); sociology (1983b); and the varieties of psychopathology and psychotherapy (Wilber, Engler, and Brown 1986, with Wilber's contributions originally published in 1984).

In 1983, Wilber met Terry (later Treya) Killam, and they were married in the same year. (His earlier marriage had ended in 1981, he later reported, with a friendly separation.) Some ten days after the marriage, his wife was diagnosed with breast cancer. His life changed profoundly, and there would be little writing at all for over five years. Dedicating himself in large part to his wife's well-being, and for a time becoming very sick himself, he learned to function, as he later wrote, as a full-time "support person" (Wilber 1988), traveling extensively with his wife for medical treatment. She died in 1989. The powerful and moving story of their life together is told by Wilber, accompanied by his wife's journal entries, in *Grace and Grit* (1991).

After a period of mourning and the writing of *Grace and Grit*, Wilber returned to the life of intensive study, writing, and meditation, this time by himself in Boulder, Colorado, where he and his wife had lived their last few years together. The daemon and the inspiration, which since his marriage had sometimes seemed absent, evidently returned. In 1995, Wilber published what he regards as his first "mature" work, *Sex, Ecology, Spirituality: The Spirit of Evolution* (1995a), the first volume of a planned three-volume trilogy (the Kosmos trilogy). A brief, informal version of that volume appeared a year later, structured as an interview with himself, under the suitably modest title, *A Brief History of Everything* (1996a). All of the basic themes of his earlier work are brought together in these two works, along with a number of conceptual innovations and extensive treatment of a number of areas not previously treated in depth in his earlier work, including systems theory, evolutionary theory, feminism, ecological thinking, and philosophical work on modernity and postmodernity. (For a helpful overview of *Sex, Ecology, Spirituality*, see Roger Walsh's essay in this book.)

While Wilber has been working on the second and third volumes of his trilogy, he has also managed to complete two further books and a number of articles. In *The Eye of Spirit* (1997a), he brings together a number of essays, many of them exploring the nature of his integrative approach to various fields, including psychology, philosophy, cognitive science and consciousness studies (see also Wilber 1997b), anthropology, art, and literary theory. He also presents his responses to a variety of critics and commentators on his work; a version (1996b) of this set of responses was first published in *ReVision* in 1996 and forms the basis for Wilber's essay, "A More Integral Approach," which appears in this book with two new sections. A further book, *The Marriage of Sense and Soul: Integrating Science and Religion* (Wilber 1998), has just been finished.

A Contemporary Updating of the Perennial Philosophy

Despite such prodigious output on such varied themes, it is still possible to characterize Wilber's main themes in fairly simple terms.[1] His work is unified, as are the writings of many other "grand theorists" and systematic thinkers, by a relatively simple general idea, which he uses to integrate in a very plausible way a number of disparate authors, viewpoints, and areas of study.

Wilber's core idea (or intuition) is this: There is a profound drive in humans, as well as in all life and even matter, to evolve toward what he usually calls "Spirit." All evolution at any time, whether physical, biological, or cultural, whether individual or collective, follows such a movement. The final terminus, as it were, of all evolution is the self-realization of Spirit in "nondual" mystical "experience."

Like Huston Smith (1976) and others, such as Aldous Huxley (1945), Frithjof Schuon (1984), and Seyyed Nasr (1981), Wilber takes his work, and this core idea, to be in the tradition of the "perennial philosophy" (or what Smith calls the "primordial tradition"), although Wilber's interpretation of the perennial philosophy is, to be sure, more psychological and much more contemporary than the "perennialists" mentioned above. For all perennialists, however, there is an identifiable mystical "common core" to all great "wisdom" traditions, especially as found in the world religions, such that there are common underlying understandings of the nature of reality, knowledge, ethics, and spiritual life, despite the great surface variety of doctrines, practices, and cultures. The claim is that the wisest of Jewish mystics, Christian contemplatives, Buddhist or Hindu meditators, and Taoist sages, were they able to dialogue with each other, would eventually get beyond their surface differences and come to agree, "Yes, we share the same understandings; we live our lives with the same basic intentions."[2]

Like Smith and other perennialists, one of Wilber's fundamental claims is that reality and the psyche have a clearly *hierarchical* structure. There are "levels" of reality and development, and the "higher" levels are "superior" to the "lower" levels in the logical and theoretical sense that Wilber finds clearly articulated in the work of Hegel, Piaget, and Habermas, among others, as well as in biology and systems theory. A given "level" or "stage" of development shows newly differentiated, emergent qualities in relation to the previous level or stage, qualities that make possible new properties or achievements.

So, for example, in Piaget's theory of cognitive development, there are four basic stages. In a first stage, there is primarily sensory experiencing of the world (the sensory-motor stage), out of which emerge, in three successive stages, the ability to represent experiences through words and images (the pre-operational stage), the ability to work with representations concretely (the concrete operations stage), and, lastly, the ability to represent representations abstractly (the formal operations stage). Each ability depends on the earlier achievements.

Yet with each stage there are also new systematic "problems" or difficulties that are only resolved by further development to a new level of integration, made possible by new differentiations. In Habermas' theory of the evolution of cultural worldviews, to give another example, the development of religious worldviews starts with what Habermas calls the "systems problem" of making sense of undeserved suffering, a problem that in itself signals a way of thinking beyond mythical worldviews (1984, 194ff.). Concern with this problem can be seen in the Asian notion of karma, in the story of Job, and in the struggle with the problem of "evil." Habermas believes that attempting to resolve this problem leads, in all traditions, toward the "rationalization" of worldviews, toward a "disenchanted" understanding of the world further purified of magical thinking—in other words, toward the development of a "modern" worldview. Yet this process of rationalization itself eventually requires new differentiations; for example, the "external" world must be increasingly seen in an "objective" way and differentiated from theology, metaphysics, and ethical concerns. This process, generated from within religious worldviews, paradoxically leads, according to Habermas, to a new (i.e., modern) and increasingly secular worldview and to the rise of the natural sciences and other modern institutions.

The claim by Wilber (and Hegel, Piaget, and Habermas, among others), however, is that each new stage is not merely a substitute for the old stage but, as in Hegel's notion of *Aufhebung*, both integrates earlier properties and achievements and transcends its limitations. (Wilber, following developmental psychologists in the tradition of Piaget,

sometimes speaks of this process of combining transcendence and integration as *holarchical integration*.) Like Hegel, Wilber finds this basic
logic to be a kind of underlying metaphysical pattern that helps to
integrate the natural and human sciences. Wilber (1995a) locates this
pattern in what he takes to be the most general metaphysical concept,
the concept of the *holon*. A holon is simultaneously both a whole (in
relation to the parts that are "lower"), and a part (of a greater whole that
is "higher"). Every thing, every phenomenon, is part of a hierarchially
organized "Great Chain of Being" made up of holons.

Although Wilber sometimes speaks of the process of "involution" (the
movement of Spirit from the highest to the lowest levels of reality and
development), and of the human movement of a "descending" spirituality that would move from realization of the One to the embrace of the
many, his focus in his many works is mostly on evolution and what he
calls "ascent." He has articulated this basic model of ascent in the
context of theories of individual human development, including
transpersonal (or spiritual) development (Wilber 1980; Wilber, Engler,
and Brown 1986), and human social evolution (Wilber 1983a, 1995a).
These themes are grounded in the more basic contexts of physical and
biological evolution (an evolution which in turn presupposes, for Wilber,
the involution of Spirit).

Individual Development

Wilber's theory of individual development is, like the theories of
Freud, Erikson, Piaget, and Kohlberg, a stage model. He often speaks of
nine or ten stages, the first five or so of which have close similarities to
Piaget's stages. To be somewhat simplistic, we might say that Wilber
accepts Piaget's model of cognitive development up to the rational competences associated with "formal operations," yet posits an additional
five stages. This includes both "prepersonal" stages, connected with
Piaget's sensory-motor cognition and the lack of emergence of a sense of
self and other (roughly age 0 to 2), and "personal" stages, connected
initially with pre-operational, magical thinking, and moving through to
the development of a rational, integrated self. Based both on contemporary psychological research on "adult development" and "dialectical
thinking," and the notion of a higher mode of integrative and dialectical
reason found especially in the Greek and German philosophical traditions, Wilber speaks of a stage of "vision-logic," involving the ability to
intuit directly complex patterns. He links this stage with the integration
of aspects often separated (or even repressed or dissociated) in earlier
modes of rationality, that is, with the integration of mind with body and
emotion or, on a cultural level, of culture with nature. Wilber sometimes

calls this stage that of the "centaur," half-horse and half-human, integrating human and animal, mind and body.

There follow four basic transpersonal (or "spiritual"), transrational stages. (Wilber is very clear that these stages are not "irrational" or "non-rational" or "a-rational." Rather, the rational competences are, Wilber argues, transcended but also preserved, and thus understood in different ways in the transpersonal stages.) What Wilber calls the *psychic* level he sometimes identifies with advanced forms of "nature mysticism" and shamanism, in which the "soul" emerges beyond the individual empirical ego and there are the first glimpses of the pure "witness." In his recent writings (1995a), Wilber sees the writings of Emerson as representative of this stage. There is an initial undercutting of the subject-object split, and there are sometimes experiences of direct identity with what was previously "other," with both human and non-human beings, as well as with what Emerson calls the "Over-Soul," or with nature as a whole or "Gaia."

At the *subtle* level, there is the emergence in consciousness of "archetypal" forms beyond the normal senses, such as the Platonic Forms, the power animals of the shaman, gods and goddesses, deities, the primal forms of inner light and sound as in some forms of Hindu yoga, and sacred beings and forms. At the summit of the subtle, there may well be union with these forms. Wilber sees the life and writings of Teresa of Avila on the union of soul with God in Christian mysticism as exemplary for this stage.

At the *causal* level, there is the emergence of a pure formless awareness, an awareness without object, that is also understood as the source of all manifestation. Wilber sees this level as encompassing the Buddha's nirvana, the Jewish Kabbalist's *ayin* or "nothingness," the pure witness of Hinduism, the identity of Godhead beyond the union of soul and God in Christian mysticism. Wilber finds Eckhart's writings to be particularly illustrative of this stage. Lastly, Wilber speaks of the *nondual* or *ultimate*, which is not so much a "stage" as it is the "ground" of all phenomena, unmanifest formless awareness, characterized by the lack of distinction of manifest form. This is the Buddhist unity of nirvana and samsara, or the Hindu *sahaj* ("unbroken" and "spontaneous") *samadhi*. Ramana Maharshi is Wilber's exemplar of such nondual mysticism.

With such a schema of development, which Wilber divides into prepersonal, personal, and transpersonal stages (or preegoic, egoic, and transegoic), he believes that he can address some fundamental yet unresolved contemporary questions, particularly concerning the relation between transpersonal development and other phases of development.

In an important essay on the *pre/trans fallacy* (Wilber 1990b, originally published in 1980), he claims that there is often a confusion between
prepersonal stages and transpersonal stages, for the reason that they
seem to share certain characteristics (e.g., they are not primarily
rational). In some of his most passionate (and controversial) writing
(1990b, 1995a), he criticizes many contemporary writers, including
Jungians, some deep ecologists and ecofeminists, and a number of contemporary advocates of learning from premodern cultures. He argues
that such writers are essentially counseling regression to prepersonal
states because of their inability to differentiate truly transpersonal
stages from prepersonal stages in which there seems to be a kind of
"merging" or "union." They urge us to drop or suspend rationality and
enter into this supposed merging with nature, or to return to the spontaneity and immediacy of bodily and emotional life characteristic of the
child, or to follow magical or mythical thinking (and believe that we are
beyond rationality).

Wilber argues that it is a mistake to theorize that there is some kind
of mystical transcendence of ego in these prepersonal stages, since no
stable ego yet arisen. He also criticizes Freudians and many rationalists
as well for a different version of the fallacy, for conflating truly transpersonal stages with prepersonal stages, for thinking that authentic
transpersonal expressions are no different than prerational mythical or
magical stages, as in Freud's view that mystical experiences represent a
kind of return to the "oceanic consciousness" of the infant.

Wilber uses his model of the developmental spectrum also to attempt
to resolve the question of how to make sense of the vast variety of
approaches to psychotherapy (and spirituality), each of them apparently
being claimed to be *the* way to resolve psychological suffering and difficulties (Wilber, Engler, and Brown 1986). He does this by linking each
developmental stage with specific pathologies or developmental difficulties, suggesting that different responses (some more psychological, some
more spiritual) are necessary for each kind of problem. The different
schools of therapy and contemplation can be distinguished according to
what kinds of problems and what levels of development they address.

Cultural and Social Evolution

Wilber also has developed accounts (1983a, 1995a), likewise at times
controversial, of how this schema helps make sense of human cultural
and social evolution. As in the work of Hegel, Gebser (1985, see also
Feuerstein 1987), and Habermas (e.g., 1979, 1984), Wilber claims that
general cultural forms can be interpreted as parallel to particular stages
of individual development. Following Gebser's and Habermas' work in

particular, he identifies the specific stages of the evolution of cultural worldviews (Wilber 1995a, 164ff.). Following the cultural stages that correspond to the child's sensory-motor stage, come the *magical* (or "magical-animistic") worldview, parallel to the pre-operational thinking of the child, in which there is, in brief, a lack of firm distinction between minds and bodies; mental intentions are thought to alter "magically" the "alive" physical world, as in voodoo or magical rituals. The next stage, the *mythical* worldview, is associated with concrete operational thinking, partial objectification of the natural world, and rulers who are supposedly connected with the gods and goddesses.

The *rational* worldview, corresponding with Piaget's formal operations and the ability to abstract, only begins to come fully into being with modernity. It is centered in the idea of a universalizing reason as the basis of knowledge and action and in a series of differentiations between church and state, theology and scientific knowledge, dogmatic religion and the inner life of the autonomous person. As we saw earlier in discussing Habermas' account of the rationalization of worldviews, this series of differentiations is required in order to make possible a rationality no longer under the sway of a dominating myth or theology and able to govern more and more of life—to make possible a science, a politics, and an inner life that are autonomous in relation to the former religious and metaphysical worldview.

Next, a further *centauric* worldview based on "vision-logic" would lead to a pluralistic, "worldcentric" approach, in which opposite views and differences no longer become the basis for polarized conflict (and war); the visionary dialectical thinking of this stage suggests a true planetary culture of "world citizens," a true "new world order," no longer, however, organized by nation states and the dominance of the most powerful states. And beyond "centauric" cultures lies the possibility of worldviews and ways of life organized by the modes of knowing and being of the transpersonal stages.

It is no doubt evident from this brief overview of Wilber's theory that the expectation that human culture as a whole will somehow soon move toward a "new age" of spirituality, with resultant cultural and political manifestations, is, to say the least, premature. Rather, Wilber argues, we have indeed, at the present point in history, scarcely moved, in terms of collective culture, into a stage corresponding to the initial personal stage of rationality. He, like Habermas, believes that the major challenge today is to consolidate further the rational mode identified with critical intelligence and an autonomous self. This especially involves the overcoming of what Wilber calls the "mythic-rational" cultural forms associated with using rationality to prop up the mythic dogmatisms of the world religions, or of contemporary secular ideologies (whether Marxist, nationalist, or capitalist).

Wilber does distinguish, however, between what he calls the "average" mode of consciousness of a given culture and the most "advanced" modes of consciousness (e.g., 1983a, 241ff.). There are always persons in a given culture at individual developmental stages beyond (sometimes far beyond) the individual stage that corresponds to the collective stage of the culture as a whole. For example, he believes that persons and traditions in prerational cultures often had developed to transrational, transpersonal stages, even though their cultures were at lower stages. But their insights could only be expressed within the mode of thinking of the times, e.g., in more limited magical and mythical ways. So, for instance, he argues that some shamans have evolved to "psychic" levels, and that many of the great mystics had evolved yet further, even while living in prerational cultures.

Ways of Knowing

Wilber's "full spectrum" model of consciousness also gives him a framework with which to approach epistemological questions, questions of the nature of knowledge, in an innovative way. In the first two essays in *Eye to Eye* (1990a, originally published in their present form in 1983), and later in *Sex, Ecology, Spirituality* (1995a) and *The Eye of Spirit* (1997a, 80-95), he argues for broadening our concept of "science" so as to make sense of the ways of knowing connected with transpersonal stages of development. He believes that there is a logic to such "contemplative" knowing akin to the basic logic of all modes of "science." A "scientist" of any kind, whether in the natural or contemplative sciences, essentially follows three basic guidelines: (1) he or she follows methods which are supposed to access the "data"; (2) there is observation or apprehension of the data of a given domain; and (3) findings are checked out or corroborated with other scientists in the community.

Yet it is nonetheless important to be aware of the variety of types of knowledge. Wilber outlines the distinctions between: (1) the empirical sciences, paradigmatically the natural sciences such as physics and biology; (2) the interpretive (or more purely "intellectual" or symbolic) sciences, such as philosophical argument, hermeneutics, phenomenology, and other "human sciences"; and (3) the contemplative sciences associated especially with many of the world's great spiritual traditions. Wilber points out the danger of "category errors" in using one mode to attempt to explore a domain best investigated by another mode, for instance, by using empirical science to interpret Shakespeare's *Hamlet* or to decide on spiritual claims, or giving philosophical arguments in order to evaluate the deepest contemplative insights.

The Contemporary Importance of Wilber's Work

It may be apparent at this point why Wilber's ambitious work has aroused both great enthusiasm and also considerable controversy. In many ways, he has almost single-handedly articulated a number of pioneering interpretations of how spiritual insights and disciplines might be taken seriously in a thoroughly contemporary way. At a time of confusion about the relationship of modern Western psychologies (and psychotherapies) to what we might call traditional spiritual psychologies, he has produced a rather intricate integrative model of these psychologies, claiming to identify with some precision the value and limits of the varieties of both modes of psychology. At a time of confusion about the status of spiritual insights, about whether such insights can be justified in a contemporary manner as any kind of knowledge at all or, on the other hand, whether they are somehow even closely related to the insights of recent physics, Wilber has systematically clarified such questions through elaborating the rudiments of an integrative epistemology. With such a model, he has attempted to distinguish clearly between the different ways of knowing, domains of knowledge, and their associated types of truth claims (Wilber 1995a, 1995c). He has done so while claiming to be arguing on the basis of accessible data and currently accepted general theories, drawn from the main contemporary fields of inquiry and scholarship, rather than aloofly developing metaphysical arguments or finding refuge solely in ancient traditions.

At a time when others in transpersonal studies have rarely given much attention to contemporary philosophical, historical, and cultural work, Wilber has done so, especially in his recent work, framing his theories from a variety of historical perspectives. He has engaged much of the contemporary philosophical and historical work on modernity and postmodernity within his own detailed accounts of the modern world, at a time when few of his transpersonal and spiritually-minded colleagues have even begun to absorb such work. At a time of personal, social, and intellectual fragmentation and specialization, Wilber has unabashedly developed an all-encompassing framework, in which he both integrates the insights and notes the limits of the main theoretical work and practical tendencies of our time, working self-consciously in the tradition of the great idealist German philosophers Hegel and Schelling and the contemporary philosopher and social theorist Habermas. And at a time when intellectual work and spirituality are commonly presented as polar opposites, Wilber has brought together committed intellectual inquiry with explorations of some of the depths of a spiritual life (1982a, 1991, 1995b).

Wilber has also given considerable attention recently to some of the neglected areas and imbalances of earlier transpersonal writings and practices, including his own, and to some of the historical distortions of religious and spiritual traditions. He has pointed out (1993,1995a), for example, how the world religions have all taken shape and evolved within cultures in which there is a devaluation of body, nature, and women. Correspondingly, there has commonly been an overvaluation of transcendence and "ascent" (to the "One"), as opposed to immanence and "descent" (to the "many" of the phenomenal world). While his earlier works do show an emphasis on transcendence and ascent, in his more recent works, he has begun to articulate a model of spirituality integrating ascent and descent and has argued for the contemporary importance and healing power of such a model. Within such a framework, he has attempted to work through a great deal of the literature on gender and ecology, with the intention of balancing concern with the pathologies of one-sided ascent with concern about the problems of a kind of one-sided (or even regressive) descent. Similarly, although his earlier works emphasized primarily the "inner" dimension of psychological and spiritual transformation, more recently he has stressed the limits of interpreting spirituality in an exclusively "inner" way.[3] Partly through his recent development of the "four quadrant" model, Wilber has argued for the fundamental interrelatedness of inner and "outer" (cultural and institutional) spiritual transformation and expression (1995a, 494ff.; 1996a, 312ff.). The two essays of Part I of this book, Roger Walsh's "Developmental and Evolutionary Synthesis in the Recent Writings of Ken Wilber" (chapter 2), and Michael Murphy's "On Evolution and Transformative Practice: In Appreciation of Ken Wilber" (chapter 3), help us to understand and explore Wilber's recent innovations in terms of transpersonal theory and practice.

CRITICAL QUESTIONS ABOUT WILBER'S WORK: BASIC ISSUES IN CONTEMPORARY TRANSPERSONAL THEORY AND PRACTICE

Despite the many insights, the great theoretical energy, and the excitement of much of his work, Wilber's writings have sometimes been controversial. The premise of this book is that these controversies, along with a number of questions raised about Wilber's work, can be connected, once the hot air has risen and dissipated, with fundamental theoretical and practical issues of the transpersonal movement. Admittedly, however, such controversy is found mostly among transpersonal and spiritual writers and practitioners. Among mainstream scholars of psychology, philosophy, religious studies, and anthropology,

Wilber's work (and that of most of the main writers in transpersonal studies) is little known or studied, although this may change. A recent panel dedicated to examining his work at the American Academy of Religion in 1995 marks the first large-scale public discussion of Wilber's work among scholars of religion, outside of transpersonal conferences. A weekend conference on "Ken Wilber and the Future of Transpersonal Inquiry" held in San Francisco in 1997 attracted overflow crowds. Hopefully, we can anticipate a series of discussions on the viability and contributions of transpersonal approaches (and Wilber's work in particular) in relation to more mainstream concerns in various fields.

Among most transpersonally minded writers, however, such as those taking part in the dialogue in this book, there is commonly considerable appreciation for Wilber's work, an honoring of his contributions, and a recognition of the new perspectives and directions his work has opened up. Nonetheless, some who are sympathetic to Wilber's intentions, insights, and achievements, and to transpersonal perspectives and practices generally, have questioned his claims.[4] Much of the discussion in this book follows these questions, while also exploring Wilber's innovations and insights. In this sense, our conversation is more like an ongoing "in-house" discussion among friends; the differences tend to be stressed somewhat more than the considerable commonalities. I would like to mention five areas of questions in particular which are addressed by the participants in this dialogue.

1. Questions of Interpretation

One set of questions concerns Wilber's interpretations of the fields, texts, and authors he considers and integrates in his writings. For example, some have questioned his interpretations of Aristotle, Plotinus, Emerson, and Jung, among others, especially in *Sex, Ecology, Spirituality* (e.g., diZerega 1997, diZerega and Smoley 1995, Frew 1995, Wittine 1995). Others have found significant problems (as well as important insights) in Wilber's depictions of such areas as physics, systems theory, deep ecology, ecofeminism, and feminism in general (for example, see the contributions of Zimmerman and Wright in this book, as well as diZerega 1996 and Weber 1982).[5] While these questions of interpretation are certainly important, the extent to which they compromise Wilber's core claims is less clear and is discussed by some of the contributors. In many cases, Wilber might well make adjustments to his interpretations of particular authors and fields while preserving the general thrust of his theories or, in other cases, simply acknowledge differences in interpretation.

2. Alternative Paradigms of Transpersonal Theory

A second set of questions go deeper and have to do particularly with whether Wilber's stage model of individual development makes sense of important data in the field. Might other transpersonal paradigms, such as those of Stanislav Grof and Michael Washburn, generally framed in terms of individual experience and development, make better sense of such data? These questions have similarities to questions raised about the stage models of Piaget and (especially) Kohlberg (Flanagan 1991). Essays on these issues are grouped in Part II.

For example, some wonder whether Wilber's theories of individual psychological and spiritual development do justice to the data basic to his theories, including developmental and clinical data, reports of transpersonal experiences, and observations from contemporary spiritual practice. Michael Washburn, in "The Pre/Trans Fallacy Reconsidered" (chapter 4), and Sean Kelly, in "Revisioning the Mandala of Consciousness: A Critical Appraisal of Wilber's Holarchical Paradigm" (chapter 6), suggest that careful consideration of such data leads to questioning the extent to which the basic "developmental logic" (and the idea of "holarchical integration") identified by Wilber really holds for the stage model. Washburn refers in particular to the developmental splits of mind/body and the related split of culture/nature, both of which are apparently only healed at the "centaur" stage, persisting without apparent integration over several stages. Kelly notes the spiritual experiences of children and so-called "primitives," and believes that such data can be better explained by conceiving of the transpersonal as an always available depth dimension of the psyche, rather than as reflecting advanced developmental stages.

Stanislav Grof, in "Ken Wilber's Spectrum Psychology: Observations from Clinical Consciousness Research" (chapter 5), argues that Wilber has not given adequate consideration to the phenomena of prenatal existence and biological birth and death, especially as they play a significant role in understanding psychopathology, regression, and development into transpersonal domains. Donald Rothberg, in "How Straight is the Spiritual Path?" (chapter 7), reports on conversations with Buddhist meditation teachers Joseph Goldstein, Jack Kornfield, and Michele McDonald-Smith. Their observations over the last twenty years of the experiences of thousands of primarily Western meditation students point to some of the complexities of and challenges for a stage model, particularly concerning the relationship between psychological and transpersonal development. They question, for example, whether the completion of one's "personal" psychological "work" is necessary before there can be sustained and stabilized transpersonal or spiritual development, as one would expect from Wilber's theory. On the basis of their teaching experience, they also question whether there are any typical general sequences of development and suggest the usefulness of metaphors other than that of *stages*, such as those of the *spiral* (which Washburn also uses) and the *mandala* (also suggested by Kelly).

3. Transpersonal Theory and the "Other": Nature, Women, Indigenous Traditions, and Relationships

A third set of questions related to Wilber's work, presented in Part III of this book, has to do with recasting our contemporary conception of spirituality, and hence of transpersonal studies, in response to three problem areas: (1) the historical devaluation of body, nature, women, and indigenous peoples in the world's religious and spiritual traditions; (2) the commonly related one-sided emphasis on ascent and transcendence; and (3) current Western tendencies to emphasize an excessively individualistic and "subjective" interpretation of spirituality. As we have seen, Wilber, in his recent work, has himself pointed out such problems. He writes (1993, 263):

> The entire pantheon of the Great [spiritual] Traditions will, in the coming years, have to be scrutinized thoroughly and "scrubbed clean" of the universal alienation of the three "Others"—nature, body, woman—but in a way that does not throw out the baby with the bathwater.

The discussions in this area build in part on Wilber's ideas and sort out some of the associated theoretical and practical issues which concern both long-standing spiritual traditions and contemporary transpersonal studies. Arguably the transpersonal field has tended to manifest these problem areas, although it also has a significant role, as most of the authors of this section suggest, in helping to address these problems.[6] The discussion also rests in part on some of the issues raised by Washburn and Kelly, among others, concerning the adequacy of the stage model of individual development.

Michael Zimmerman, in "A Transpersonal Diagnosis of the Ecological Crisis" (chapter 8), analyzes Wilber's account of the roots of the current ecological crisis and the role that religious models of "ascent" have played in generating this crisis. Yet Wilber also holds that the recent scientific and spiritual one-sided emphasis on "descent"—including what Wilber takes to be a regressive return to "primitive" cultures—is equally a part of the problem. What is needed, Wilber argues, is a transpersonally-grounded balance of ascent and descent.

While finding Wilber's general sketch helpful, Zimmerman argues that ecofeminists, deep ecologists, and contemporary nature mystics are questionably accused by Wilber of regression, and that these thinkers have much to contribute to contemporary ecological healing and spirituality. Similar views have been articulated in more depth by diZerega (1996), who has challenged the adequacy of Wilber's interpretations of deep ecology and nature mysticism.

While Peggy Wright applauds the idea of a mature spirituality conceived of as an integration of ascending and descending paths in her "Gender Issues in Ken Wilber's Transpersonal Theory" (chapter 9), she also looks at some of the difficulties of Wilber's account, as well as his insights, specifically with an eye on gender issues and transpersonal theory. She argues against some aspects of Wilber's interpretations of ancient matrifocal and Goddess-oriented cultures, seeing current interest in such cultures as more indicative of necessary "healing journeys" than of regression. She also raises questions about the anthropological material that Wilber uses to support his account of the social evolution of "masculine" and "feminine" domains.

Jürgen Kremer writes in depth on Wilber's treatment of anthropological and archeological data in "The Shadow of Evolutionary Thinking" (chapter 10), with a particular focus on his theory of cultural and social evolution (Wilber 1983a). Kremer continues in new ways a discussion opened up initially by Winkelman (1990, 1993), who has raised questions about Wilber's ability to integrate some of the basic data of anthropology.[7] As we noted, Wilber believes that he can, as it were, "rank" different religious experiences, sages, and cultural worldviews, finding some expressions to be signs of further development than others. Shamans, we are told, are generally less developed than the mystics associated with the world religions, and the "nondual" mystics are more developed than those who (merely) find union with God. Furthermore, certain cultures, such as indigenous cultures, are taken to be clearly less developed than modern ones, in terms of core cognitive, moral, and spiritual values.

For Kremer and others, these evaluations suggest an uneasy resemblance with some of the earlier ideologies of progress and past claims of the supposedly advanced character of modern Western societies—ideologies that at their worst supported several centuries of racism, imperialism, and war. Kremer questions what he takes to be Wilber's understanding of indigenous cultures as "pre-rational," pointing to considerable data suggesting rational competences. He also argues for the vital importance of examining the "shadow" of theories of cultural and social evolution—our tendencies to project onto those whom we don't understand and to deny the realities of genocide and the exploitation of indigenous peoples.

Jeanne Achterberg and Donald Rothberg, in "Relationship as Spiritual Practice" (chapter 11), take as a point of departure Wilber's analysis (based on his model of "four quadrants") of a spirituality that integrates not only ascent and descent, but also "inner" and "outer" transformation. They look particularly at what can be called "relational" models of spirituality, such as those found in intimate relationships, groups, communities, and societies. According to many contemporary writers, including Wilber, insofar as relational modes of thought, morality, and spirituality are emphasized—as they are by women and indigenous peoples, and in much current ecological thinking—these models help to reintegrate the "other" in all the aspects mentioned above. Relational models and the re-membering of the other as suggested by Wilber, Zimmerman, Wright, Kremer, Achterberg, Rothberg, and others will likely transform transpersonal theories and practices in significant ways.

4. Regression

The most charged set of issues generated by Wilber's writings concerns "regression." Readers of *Sex, Ecology, Spirituality* know that many of Wilber's most passionate and sometimes barbed comments occur in his critiques of those he deems advocates of cultural and individual regression. The targets include ecofeminists; deep ecologists (labeled "ecomasculinists"); ecopsychologists; "eco-romantics" and "retro-romantics"; students of ancient matrifocal cultures; enthusiasts of tribal cultures; critics of modernity; champions of the body, senses, and/or the unconscious (who would, according to Wilber, return to the "prepersonal" and call it wisdom); and others who ride what Wilber calls the "Regress Express." While admitting the place and value of "regression in the service of the ego" (1980, 151ff.; 1995a, 105, 664),Wilber cautions continually against any regression that abandons the framework of past "achievements" and the current level of development.[8]

Discussions of regression weave through Wilber's recent work and through many of the chapters of this book, although it is not always clear whether there is a commonly held definition of *regression*, or how suitable it is to understand certain experiences and behaviors primarily through developmental categories. Washburn and Grof, for example, give more importance than Wilber to the place of regression in psychological and spiritual development and seem less concerned with individual and cultural dangers. Kornfield speaks of the importance of his own "descent," and McDonald-Smith gives a moving account of her own seemingly regressive experiences.

Zimmerman, while sympathetic to many of Wilber's cautions about regression, suggests that ecofeminists and deep ecologists cannot so easily be painted as regressive. Wright argues for the value of "healing journeys" to ancient matrifocal and indigenous cultures and urges patience with the "messiness" of the process. Nonetheless, she seems to agree with Wilber in calling for the integration of what is learned in these journeys with contemporary modern and postmodern approaches. Whatever the outcome of these discussions, it seems evident that Wilber's views about regression have pushed transpersonal theorists to clarify its nature as well as its relationship to both individual development and social evolution.

5. How Do We Inquire Spiritually?

The tone of Wilber's (1995a) criticism of authors he deems regressive, which sometimes seems sarcastic, divisive, and ridiculing, suggests a further set of questions about the nature of transpersonal inquiry, scholarship, and practice. In particular, are combative rhetorical styles appropriate to transpersonal inquiry? More broadly, we can ask how to work collaboratively and cooperatively, in a transpersonal spirit, with significant differences of views. Contributors commenting on these issues include Michael Zimmerman (at the end of chapter 8), Robert McDermott, in "The Need for Philosophical and Spiritual Dialogue: Reflections on Ken Wilber's *Sex, Ecology, Spirituality*" (chapter 12), and Kaisa Puhakka, in "Contemplating Everything: Wilber's Evolutionary Theory in Dialectical Perspective" (chapter 13). (See also Robert Fisher [1997]). McDermott's and Puhakka's chapters are found in Part IV.

The larger question arising from these issues is: What does it mean to inquire theoretically or intellectually from a "transpersonal" or "spiritual" perspective? In particular, how might major differences and criticisms be expressed and explored?

Many transpersonal writers answer these questions in part by critiquing current academic practice. They lament the disconnection of intellect from emotions, personal experience, values, and social contexts, and the tendency toward polarized and apparently ego-driven "debates," in which opponents neither listen to nor recognize much value in each other's views. In academic contexts, "arguments" between those with different views sometimes seem more like "wars," as is evident from many of the metaphors commonly associated with argumentation (Lakoff and Johnson 1980, 4ff.).

But what are the alternative models and metaphors, and what in particular can transpersonal thinkers contribute to new models of dialogue and intellectual work? Should certain types of expressions be avoided in the name of cooperation, compassion, and the recognition of the importance of differences for the movement toward wisdom? Can intellectual inquiry be a kind of spiritual practice, as it certainly has been in different ways in the history of spiritual traditions (Rothberg 1994, Wilber 1995b)? What are appropriate contemporary forms of such practice (Kremer 1992a, 1992b; Macy and Rothberg 1994; Rothberg 1994)?

Wilber's work gives both some theoretical resources for understanding how to respond to these questions and evidence of some of the complexities and difficulties of practicing transpersonal scholarship. His account of the "advanced" rational mode of "vision-logic" suggests some reasons why the traditional academic model of rational discourse as the respectful exchange of reasons in search of the truth is so imperfectly realized. Puhakka's chapter (chapter 13) explores "vision-logic" in considerable depth. In this mode, rationality is integrated with body experience and emotions, forming a highly integrated personality in which thinking takes on both dialectical and intuitive qualities. The perspective of vision-logic is pluralistic yet not overly relativistic, making possible a sense of unity-in-difference in which many perspectives can be seen as offering contributions to a common discourse. Without this sense, however, rationality may remain disconnected from emotion and experience, driven by the individualistic needs of the separate self and less able to learn from and with the "other."

Wilber believes that his own stance in his writing is a transpersonally inspired use of vision-logic (1995a, 185). Yet it is not very clear what this actually means in terms of everyday intellectual practice, or how he would respond to some of the specific questions about such practice posed above.

In developing this book, the editors invited the writers to think of their contributions as an opportunity to explore not only the *content* but also the *process* of transpersonal inquiry and the nature of such an integrated, dialectical mode of vision-logic. Observing the process might lead us first of all to acknowledge the sometimes strong emotions and complex experiences linked with the issues discussed in this book, issues that are often presented as if such emotions and experiences did not exist. Editing the material for this book and discussing Wilber's work with colleagues has provided ample evidence of the winds blowing around the apparent calm of the printed page. Many of the themes treated by Wilber, particularly those connected with the question of regression, seem highly charged emotionally and "politically." We observed with some surprise what seemed at times to be the formation of groups of rather polarized "friends" and "enemies" of Wilber, catalyzed by their reactions and responses to Wilber's work.

Truly "transpersonal" inquiry, however, may thus not only require participants to examine the validity of reasons and evidence in relation to particular claims and theories. It may also obligate them to explore "internally," interpersonally, and socially the practical and experiential background of ideas, perhaps as a kind of contemplative practice. Instead of declaring war when presented with the differing views of a colleague, they might take the difference as the starting point for inquiry. What can I learn from this person or this perspective? What in my own understanding is unexplored or undeveloped and may be elicited by this person and his or her views and experiences? What different modes of inquiry and exchange are necessary to complement conventional rational dialogue (Heron 1996; Kremer 1992a, 1992b; Rothberg 1994)? How might transpersonal inquiry integrate the insights and practices of other attempts to give attention in inquiry to emotions, the body, and practical and social contexts (e.g., Freire 1970; hooks and West 1991; Jaggar 1989; Johnson 1994)?

This stance may give rise to new metaphors and new practices. Instead of defending territory and attacking enemies to win arguments, as in the old act of war, perhaps a meeting may be more like a dance, in which participants move through their partners' territories, recognizing mutual learning and enjoyment as well as the difficulties of new steps and new ways of moving. They may, as Puhakka suggests, balance the purpose and seriousness of intellectual inquiries with play, appreciating and perhaps even playing seriously with the creative tension between the two.

Seen in this way, we can readily acknowledge that though many of the contributors to this book explore differences with Wilber's claims and theories, their chapters are implicitly, and usually explicitly, a tribute to the person who made this dance, this purposeful play, this conversation, possible. We thank Ken Wilber for his work that has yielded many insights and made possible the insights of others.

Acknowledgments

The author would like to thank Mary Anne Cutaia, Tom Greening, Sean Kelly, Bonnie Morrissey, Roger Walsh, and Michael Zimmerman for their helpful comments on earlier versions of this chapter.

Notes

1. I am reminded of Nietzsche's statement (1962, 23, originally published in 1873) that every philosophical system represents one fundamental mistake to greater minds, and merely a sum of errors and truths to lesser minds.

2. It should be noted that there are a number of critics of such claims of the perennial philosophy among contemporary scholars of religion, many of whom question whether the idea of a common mystical core to various traditions is borne out by scholarly study. There have been several collections of essays dedicated to this issue; see, in particular, Katz (1978, 1983) and Forman (1990).

3. Typically, transpersonal studies focus on individual transpersonal experiences, often conceived of as "inner" experiences; the cited definition of "transpersonal experiences" by Walsh and Vaughan, for example, is their initial and basic definition of the transpersonal as such. Such an emphasis reflects both the origins of the transpersonal movement, particularly in humanistic psychology, and a tendency toward an individualistic and psychological interpretation of spirituality in terms of relatively "inner" and "private" experiences.

I have argued elsewhere (Rothberg 1993) that this latter interpretation also reflects the characteristically modern appropriation (and marginalization) of spirituality, in which spirituality is increasingly removed from the public domains of knowledge and action, and restricted to the private and subjective domain. In this context, the "experiential" emphasis in transpersonal studies and practices, while helpful initially for a variety of reasons (particularly in opening up new domains of experience and recovering the "inner" dimension of spirituality and religion), needs to be complemented by emphases on the meaning of spirituality in the interpersonal, social, political, and ecological domains. Such an approach, which is linked to what I have identified, in describing the transpersonal movement, as a third and most recent development to integrate the transpersonal in everyday life and mainstream institutions, will lead, I believe, to significant shifts in the very conception of the transpersonal—shifts facilitated in a clear way by Wilber's four quadrant model. It may lead as well to reflections on the appropriateness of the term "transpersonal," which seems oriented to the individual and the personal in ways that other terms (such as "spiritual," which is admittedly also problematic in other ways) is not. For an excellent discussion of the limits of an "experiential" emphasis in transpersonal studies and practices, see Ferrer (1997). See also the discussion of relational models of spirituality by Achterberg and Rothberg in this volume.

4. Wilber's work has also been criticized by some writers, such as Rollo May (1986, 1989) and Kirk Schneider (1987) from the somewhat "external" perspective of humanistic psychology. However, these criticisms have been made against most other transpersonalists as well. See also Wilber's (1989a, 1989b) responses.

5. Wilber has responded to some of these critiques. He responds to some of the points concerning Frew's critique of Wilber's treatment of Plotinus, although without mentioning the actual critique, in Wilber (1997a). A response to Capra's critique of Wilber's views on physics can be found in Wilber (1982a).

6. It seems a legitimate question to ask why most of the main writers in transpersonal studies are white males of European ancestry presently in North America, and what this means. A cursory glance at recent anthologies in the transpersonal field certainly might lead to raising the question. Walsh and Vaughan's (1993) collection contains 46 entries with 3 authored by women, 39 by men (2 apparently by Asians—Aurobindo and the Dalai Lama), and 4 co-authored by a woman and man. *The Textbook of Transpersonal Psychiatry and Psychology* (Scotton, Chinen, and Battista 1996) has 40 entries, including 2 by women, 36 by men, and 2 co-authored by a woman and man. Boorstein's (1996) anthology on transpersonal psychotherapy has 28 entries, with 1

authored by a woman, 25 by men, and 2 co-authored by a woman and man. Of course, it is difficult to know ethnic backgrounds on the basis of names, but it seems to be the case that there are very few among these contributors not having primarily or entirely European ancestry.

The point of these remarks is not somehow to de-value these works, which all arguably make significant contributions. The editors may well have made major efforts to increase the diversity of voices; for example, the editors of this volume had originally hoped for more gender balance among the authors than we presently have, but unfortunately three women who had initially agreed to submit essays were later not able to do so. Furthermore, many of the authors in the transpersonal field have immersed themselves deeply in practices and philosophies of cultures—particularly Asian and indigenous—other than those of their origins. They have developed perspectives that certainly often seem diverse and even "other" in relation to the dominant academic approaches and to the modern world in general.

In this context, it is also important to remember that the figures given above are rather typical of what we find in general anthologies in the fields of academic philosophy, religion, and psychology, suggesting the systemic nature of the problem across many fields. Hence, the more basic question concerns how to make sense of this phenomenon in general and specifically in relation to transpersonal studies. It is to ask about the extent to which the relative lack of voices of the "other" is linked to the devaluation of nature, women, and indigenous peoples in a way which influences significantly the very content of the transpersonal field. Another way to phrase the question is to ask whether transpersonal studies as it has developed, although aspiring to give a *general* and *universal* treatment of spiritual experiences and development as such, has, by not attending enough to the "other" and to its own cultural conditioning, given a more *particular* interpretation of spirituality. Such a more particular interpretation might well not be so attractive to those who remain "others." Yet I also want to suggest that although there may have been particular reasons for the ways that the transpersonal field has evolved up to the present, we now hopefully have more choices about the future directions of the field, and the possibility of responding to the exclusion or marginalization of the various "others."

7. Wilber (1995a, especially 526-28, 573-76) has responded with considerable depth and sharpness to Winkelman's critique, particularly to his advocacy of "cultural relativism."

8. Of course, there is some irony to these discussions, as many contemporary rationalists criticize any appeal to ancient religious traditions (and thus implicitly the work of Wilber and other transpersonalists) as irrational and regressive. Habermas, for example, writes (1984, 182): "From the viewpoint of a modern understanding of the world, one could certainly criticize the religious world views that give a definite meaning to ascetic exercises, to mystical illumination, to yoga, and the like as irrational."

References

Boorstein, S., ed. 1996. *Transpersonal psychotherapy*. 2nd ed. Albany: State University of New York Press.

diZerega, G. 1996. Ken Wilber's critique of deep ecology and nature religion. *The Trumpeter* 13 (2): 52-71.

diZerega, G. 1997. Accuracy, honesty, spirituality: A response to Ken Wilber. Unpublished manuscript.

diZerega, G., and R. Smoley. 1995. Up the down staircase. *Gnosis* (Fall): 86-87.

Ferrer, J. 1997. Transpersonal knowledge: An epistemic approach to transpersonality. Unpublished manuscript.

Feuerstein, G. 1987. *Structures of consciousness: The genius of Jean Gebser: An introduction and critique.* Lower Lake, Calif.: Integral Publishing.

Findlay, J. [1967] 1970. The logic of mysticism. In *Ascent to the absolute*, by J. Findlay. New York: Humanities Press.

Fisher, R. 1997. A guide to Wilberland: Some common misunderstandings of the critics of Ken Wilber and his work on transpersonal theory prior to 1995. *Journal of Humanistic Psychology* 37 (4): 30-73.

Flanagan, O. 1991. *The science of the mind.* 2nd ed. Cambridge: MIT Press.

Forman, R. ed. 1990. *The problem of pure consciousness: Mysticism and philosophy.* New York: Oxford University Press.

Freire, P. 1970. *Pedagogy of the oppressed.* New York: Herder & Herder.

Frew, D. 1995. The whole and the parts: Ken Wilber's treatment of Plotinus in *Sex, ecology, spirituality.* Internet: alexandria@world.std.com.

Gebser, J. [1953] 1985. *The ever-present origin.* Translated by N. Barstad with A. Mickunas. Athens: Ohio University Press.

Habermas, J. [1976] 1979. *Communication and the evolution of society.* Translated by T. McCarthy. Boston: Beacon Press.

———. [1981] 1984. *The theory of communicative action, vol. 1: Reason and the rationalization of society.* Translated by T. McCarthy. Boston: Beacon Press.

Head, S. 1996. The new, ruthless economy. *New York Review of Books* 43 (4): 47-52.

Heron, J. 1996. Spiritual inquiry: A critique of Ken Wilber. *Collaborative Inquiry* (18): 2-10.

hooks, b., and C. West. 1991. *Breaking bread: Insurgent black intellectual life.* Boston: South End Press.

Huxley, A. 1945. *The perennial philosophy.* New York: Harper & Row.

Jaggar, A. 1989. Love and knowledge: Emotion in feminist epistemology. In *Gender/body/knowledge: Feminist reconstructions of being and knowing*, edited by A. Jaggar and S. Bordo. New Brunswick, N.J.: Rutgers University Press.

Johnson, D. 1994. Sensitive inquiry. *ReVision* 17 (Fall): 34-41.

Katz, S., ed. 1978. *Mysticism and philosophical analysis.* New York: Oxford University Press.

———, ed. 1983. *Mysticism and religious traditions.* New York: Oxford University Press.

Kremer, J. 1992a. The dark night of the scholar: Reflections on culture and ways of knowing. *ReVision* 14 (Spring): 169-78.

———. 1992b. Whither dark night of the scholar? Further reflections on culture and ways of knowing. *ReVision* 15 (Summer): 4-12.

Lakoff, G., and M. Johnson. 1980. *Metaphors we live by.* Chicago: University of Chicago Press.

Macy, J., and D. Rothberg. 1994. Asking to awaken. *ReVision* 17 (Fall): 25-33.

May, R. 1986. Transpersonal psychology. *APA Monitor* 17 (5): 2.

———. 1989. Answers to Ken Wilber and John Rowan. *Journal of Humanistic Psychology* 29 (Spring): 244-48.

Nasr, S. 1981. *Knowledge and the sacred.* New York: Crossroad.

Nietzsche, F. [1873] 1962. *Philosophy in the tragic age of the Greeks.* Translated by M. Cowan. Chicago: Henry Regnery Company.

Rothberg, D. 1993. The crisis of modernity and the emergence of socially engaged spirituality. *ReVision* 15 (Winter): 105-14.

_____. 1994. Spiritual inquiry. *ReVision* 17 (Fall): 2-12.

Schneider, K. 1987. The deified self: A "centaur" response to Wilber and the transpersonal movement. *Journal of Humanistic Psychology* 27 (Spring): 196-216.

Schuon, F. 1984. *The transcendent unity of religions*. Rev. ed. Wheaton, Ill.: Quest Books.

Scotton, B., A. Chinen, and J. Battista, eds. 1996. *Textbook of transpersonal psychiatry and psychology*. New York: Basic Books.

Smith, H. 1976. *Forgotten truth: The primordial tradition*. New York: Harper & Row.

Walsh, R., and F. Vaughan. 1993. Introduction. In *Paths beyond ego: The transpersonal vision*, edited by R. Walsh and F. Vaughan. Los Angeles: Tarcher/Perigree.

Weber, R. 1982. The tao of physics revisited: A conversation with Fritjof Capra. In *The holographic paradigm and other paradoxes: Exploring the leading edge of science*, edited by K. Wilber. Boulder: Shambhala.

Wilber, K. 1977. *The spectrum of consciousness*. Wheaton, Ill.: Quest Books.

_____. 1980. *The Atman project: A transpersonal view of human development*. Wheaton, Ill.: Quest Books.

_____. [1979] 1981. *No boundary: Eastern and Western approaches to personal growth*. Boulder: Shambhala.

_____. 1982a. Odyssey: A personal inquiry into humanistic and transpersonal psychology. *Journal of Humanistic Psychology* 22 (Winter): 57-90.

_____. [1981] 1983a. *Up from Eden: A transpersonal view of human evolution*. Boston: Shambhala.

_____. 1983b. *A sociable god*. New York: McGraw-Hill.

_____. 1988. On being a support person. *Journal of Transpersonal Psychology* 20 (2): 141-59.

_____. 1989a. Two humanistic psychologies?: A response. *Journal of Humanistic Psychology* 29 (Spring): 230-43.

_____. 1989b. God is so damn boring: A response to Kirk Schneider. *Journal of Humanistic Psychology* 29 (Fall): 457-69.

_____. 1990a. *Eye to eye: The quest for the new paradigm*. Rev. ed. Boston: Shambhala.

_____. [1980] 1990b. The pre/trans fallacy. In *Eye to eye: The quest for the new paradigm*, by K. Wilber. Rev. ed. Boston: Shambhala.

_____. 1991. *Grace and grit: Spirituality and healing in the life and death of Treya Killam Wilber*. Boston: Shambhala.

_____. 1993. Paths beyond ego in the coming decades. In *Paths beyond ego: The transpersonal vision*, edited by R. Walsh and F. Vaughan. Los Angeles: Tarcher/Perigree.

_____. 1995a. *Sex, ecology, spirituality: The spirit of evolution*. Boston: Shambhala.

_____. 1995b. Mind and the heart of emptiness: Reflections on intellect and the spiritual path. *The Quest* 8 (4): 16-22.

_____. 1995c. An informal overview of transpersonal studies. *Journal of Transpersonal Psychology* 27 (2): 107-29.

_____. 1996a. *A brief history of everything*. Boston: Shambhala.

_____. 1996b. A more integral approach: A response to the *ReVision* authors. *ReVision* 19 (Fall): 10-34.

_____. 1997a. *The eye of spirit: An integral vision for a world gone slightly mad*. Boston: Shambhala.

_____. 1997b. An integral theory of consciousness. *Journal of Consciousness Studies* 4 (1): 71-92.

_____. 1998. *The marriage of sense and soul: Integrating science and religion.* New York: Random House.

Wilber, K., ed. 1982b. *The holographic paradigm and other paradoxes: Exploring the leading edge of science.* Boulder: Shambhala.

_____, ed. 1984. *Quantum questions: Mystical writings of the world's great physicists.* Boston: Shambhala.

Wilber, K., J. Engler, and D. Brown. 1986. *Transformations of consciousness: Conventional and contemplative perspectives on development.* Boston: Shambhala.

Winkelman, M. 1990. The evolution of consciousness: An essay review of *Up from Eden.* *Anthropology of Consciousness* 1 (3/4): 24-31.

_____. 1993. The evolution of consciousness? Transpersonal theories in light of cultural relativism. *Anthropology of Consciousness* 4 (3): 3-9.

Wittine, B. 1995. [Review of K. Wilber, *Sex, ecology, spirituality: The spirit of evolution.*] *Journal of Transpersonal Psychology* 27 (2): 237-43.

Part One

The
Spirit of
Evolution

2

Roger Walsh

It would have been hard to predict from observing Roger Walsh's early career as a young Australian M.D. and Ph.D. that he would become one of the leading researchers of meditation, altered states of consciousness, and the new field of transpersonal psychology. Walsh had achieved academic success at universities and medical schools in Australia. He had also been an Australian university champion in diving and trampolining, at one time holding the world record in high diving (set by diving over one hundred feet from a bridge!) and working as an acrobat in the Wirth-Coles circus. His promising early research on the brain was published in numerous scientific papers and eventually two books, and he organized several scientific symposia.

In 1972, Walsh came to California as a postdoctoral fellow in psychiatry at Stanford. At first he was a hard-core neuroscientist, but his initial denial of the value of "subjective" modes of inquiry and experience did not last long. The year-and-a-half he spent working with the well-known existential psychotherapist James Bugenthal radically changed his worldview and beliefs, as he later discussed in his autobiographical article, "Journey beyond Belief." He began to explore meditation, engaging in a ten-day vipassana or "insight" meditation retreat, which consisted of eighteen hours a day of silent sitting and walking meditation. In 1977, he undertook his first three-month retreat with Joseph Goldstein, Jack Kornfield, Sharon Salzberg, and others at the Insight Meditation Society in Massachusetts and has returned there for at least part of this annual retreat virtually every year since.

*Presently, Walsh is Professor of Psychiatry, Philosophy, and Anthropology in the Department of Psychiatry and Human Behavior at the University of California, Irvine, where he has been based since 1978. His research and writing has closely followed his initial inquiries, and he has been able to work out a remarkable balance of teaching, writing, and experiential investigation. He has become one of the main writers on meditation research, publishing very widely and coediting a series of anthologies on transpersonal psychology (*Beyond Ego, *published in 1980, recently revised as* Paths beyond Ego *in 1993), psychological and spiritual well-being, and meditation. He has frequently collaborated with his wife, Frances Vaughan, also a well-known writer and theorist in transpersonal psychology. His interest in applying the transpersonal approaches to the global crisis led to the well-received* Staying Alive: The Psychology of Human Survival *in 1984.*

In recent years, Walsh has explored shamanism theoretically and experientially, publishing The Spirit of Shamanism *in 1990, with a particular interest in comparing shamanic states with altered states of consciousness found in other traditions. He has also sought bridges between transpersonal approaches and mainstream psychology, philosophy, and religious studies, publishing in some of the more prestigious journals in these fields.*

Walsh's integration in his own life of rigorous research with committed spiritual practice has offered a particularly powerful model of an engaged scholar-practitioner, and he has been able to develop and express the virtues of both to a high degree. Walsh supported Ken Wilber in the early stages of his work, and they soon became close friends. As readers of Wilber's Grace and Grit *know, Wilber lived for a year at his and Frances Vaughan's home, during which time they introduced him to Treya. For a number of years, Walsh has found Wilber's writings especially useful for his own research, and has at times acted as an interpreter (and occasional critic) of Wilber's work.*

Walsh's contribution to this book is an overview of Sex, Ecology, Spirituality: The Spirit of Evolution *and* A Brief History of Everything. *Walsh's detailed discussion aims to give readers a clear sense of the main themes of these works: hierarchies, holarchies, and heterarchies; the physiophere, biosphere, and noosphere; Wilber's "four quadrants" and the integrated approach to studying "interiors" and "exteriors" in both their individual and collective forms; the relationship between physical, consciousness, and human social evolution; the nature of spiritual development and the "ascending" and "descending" modes of spiritual expression; and the impact of modernity and the "flatland" worldview. Wilber himself considers Walsh's chapter to be one of the best introductions to his recent writings.*

Further Readings

Shapiro, D., and Walsh, R., eds. 1984. *Meditation: Classic and contemporary perspectives.* New York: Aldine.

Walsh, R. 1977. Initial meditative experiences: Part 1. *Journal of Transpersonal Psychology* 9: 151-92.

_____. 1978. Initial meditative experiences: Part 2. *Journal of Transpersonal Psychology* 10: 1-28.

_____. 1981. *Towards an ecology of the brain.* Jamaica, N.Y.: Spectrum Press.

_____. 1984a. Journey beyond belief. *Journal of Humanistic Psychology* 24 (2): 30-65.

_____. 1984b. *Staying alive: The psychology of human survival.* Boulder: Shambhala.

_____. 1990. *The spirit of shamanism.* Los Angeles: Tarcher.

_____. 1992. Can Western philosophers understand Asian philosophies? The challenge and opportunities of states-of-consciousness research. In *Revisioning philosophy*, edited by J. Ogilvy. Albany: State University of New York Press.

_____. 1997. The psychological health of shamans: A reevaluation. *Journal of the American Academy of Religion* 65 (1): 101-24.

Walsh, R., and Shapiro, D., eds. 1983. *Beyond health and normality: Explorations of exceptional psychological well-being.* New York: Von Nostrand Reinhold.

Walsh, R., and Vaughan, F. 1994. The worldview of Ken Wilber. *Journal of Humanistic Psychology* 34 (2): 6-21.

Walsh, R., and Vaughan, F., eds. 1993. *Paths beyond ego: The transpersonal vision*. Los
    Angeles: Tarcher/Perigree.

Developmental and Evolutionary Synthesis in the Recent Writings of Ken Wilber

 SCIENTIFIC DISCIPLINES HAVE BEEN SUFFERING FROM AN embarrassment of riches. As data accumulate and disciplines fragment into subdisciplines, the search for some comprehensive synthesis seems both more appealing and more hopeless. Take psychology for example. From its humble beginnings at the end of the nineteenth century it has now exploded into a cacophony of competing schools and therapies. The cries and hand-wringing over the need for synthesis have grown increasingly distraught. Consequently, it is not surprising that the appearance of the book *The Spectrum of Consciousness*, which seemed to offer just such a synthesis—even though written by a young unknown author, Ken Wilber (1977), who was not even formally trained as a psychologist—was greeted with such excitement. Indeed, in some ways *Spectrum* did more than had been hoped for because it offered a synthesis of not only Western psychologies but Eastern ones as well.

Other equally encompassing books soon followed. In *The Atman Project*, Wilber (1980) integrated diverse developmental theories, again of both East and West, into a unified view that traced development from infancy into normal adulthood and then beyond into the postconventional stages "beyond normality" described by diverse contemplative disciplines. In *Up from Eden* (1981), he used his developmental model as a framework to attempt to map the evolution of human cognition and consciousness. Other works on sociology, religion, philosophy, and physics soon followed so that by 1987 he had created an interdisciplinary collection of rare scope and integrative power (Wilber 1981, 1983, 1984, 1991; Wilber, Engler, and Brown 1986; Anthony, Ecker, and Wilber 1987).[1]

Then followed a painful silence of more than five years. These were hardly uneventful years for Wilber. Ten days after their marriage, his wife Treya discovered a breast cancer and the next five years were devoted to helping her manage the disease and eventually to die. A further two years were devoted to mourning and to writing a moving book, *Grace and Grit* (1991), chronicling her life and death. In 1995, Wilber burst out with another major work, by far his largest to date, and what he describes as his first "mature work."

Sex, Ecology, Spirituality: The Spirit of Evolution (1995) is a massive, eight-hundred-page work which is volume I of a planned three-volume series. For those daunted by the size (and weight) of this volume, Wilber also offers a briefer (a mere three hundred pages), simpler version, *A Brief History of Everything* (1996), written in dialogue form.

The aim of these two books is to trace evolution—physical, biological, and human—and to set it within the context of the perennial philosophy: the common core of wisdom at the heart of the great religious traditions. Human evolution—of brain and mind, society and culture—is traced from early hominids to today and related to phenomena such as the evolution of gender relationships, human relationship to the earth, technology, philosophy, religion, and more.

The scope of the work is extraordinary. Only a handful of thinkers, such as Aurobindo in the East and Hegel in the West, have assembled such vast evolutionary visions. Yet Wilber's view is unique in not only providing a far-reaching vision but also in grounding that vision in contemporary research in fields such as cosmology, biology, anthropology, sociology, psychology, philosophy, and ecology.

Its vast scope and scholarship come at a certain cost. To say the least, *Sex, Ecology, Spirituality* is daunting to mere mortals. In addition, its scope makes it difficult to grasp and retain the whole gestalt or vision. In a three-month-long, interdisciplinary graduate seminar that I led at the University of California, all of us found that the book's scope, together with the sheer richness and profusion of ideas, made it hard to grasp the whole vision in a single reading.

The reason is not that the book is obtuse or badly written. On the contrary, considering the profusion and novelty of the ideas, the writing is remarkably smooth and lucid. Rather, the problem is that the sheer number of novel ideas means that those early in the book tend to be pushed out of memory. While the simpler *Brief History* is less problematic, the number of ideas it contains is still impressive.

The major purpose of this article is, therefore, to offer an overview that may give a sense of the whole gestalt and thereby provide a framework allowing easier and more retentive reading. Consequently, this is more of an overview than a detailed critical review. The books cover so many topics that probably no one person could hope to give informed critiques on all of them, and doing so would demand another book. I suspect that these books will be the topic of specialized critiques by disciplinary experts for several decades. What follows, then, is the central thread, shorn of numerous intriguing byways, arguments, and in the case of *Sex, Ecology, Spirituality*, 240 pages of detailed footnotes, many of them mini-essays on topics ranging from cosmology to postmodernism.

OUR FRACTURED WORLD VIEW

Wilber begins by drawing attention to our ecological crises. Ecological movements usually assume that these crises reflect a disastrously fractured world view; a worldview often damned as dualistic, mechanistic, atomistic, anthropocentric, patriarchal, and pathologically hierarchical; a world view that fragments humans from nature, mind from body, and spirit from everything. Consequently, movements such as deep ecology and ecofeminism advocate a new world view that is said to be more holistic, integrative, and relational.

Wilber explores the nineteenth-century scientific origins of this fractured world view when the "two arrows of time" were first recognized. Paradoxically, it was discovered that according to the second law of thermodynamics, the physical universe seemed to be running down toward increasing entropy whereas the discovery of evolution showed that life appeared to be moving toward greater complexity and differentiation (negentropy). The physiosphere and the biosphere, the physical sciences and biological sciences, therefore, seemed irrevocably divorced, and although there were a variety of theoretical attempts at integration, none was wholly satisfactory.

Only in the late twentieth century did science finally offer a firm basis for reunification when it was discovered that matter has a potential for producing greater order and complexity. For example, as the Nobel laureate chemist Ilya Prigogine discovered, certain biochemical systems called "dissipative structures" can grow in chemical complexity, in apparent defiance of entropy and the second law of thermodynamics. This apparent defiance is thought to provide a possible basis for the origin of life.

From this reunification, in part, were born the various system sciences of complexity such as general systems theory, cybernetics, nonequilibrium thermodynamic systems theory, chaos theory, and evolutionary systems theory. Some of these, such as evolutionary systems theory, specifically claim that similar patterns of process and evolution can be identified across the physical, biological, and noetic spheres. The key point is that there is now significant scientific evidence for a self-organizing, self-transcending process in matter, life, and mind.

Before he can proceed with developing his theory, Wilber needs to rehabilitate the concept of hierarchy, a concept central to his theory and that of many other evolutionary researchers. Hierarchy has become something of a dirty word in some circles, and some critics claim that all hierarchy necessitates ranking or dominating that oppresses, marginalizes, or destroys. It is not uncommon to hear the cry that we need to do away with all hierarchies. However, as Wilber points out, this cry con-flates different types of hierarchies—for example, value hierarchies and ontological hierarchies, pathological and healthy—and is an example of what philosophers call a "performative contradiction" since the prefer-ence for nonhierarchies over hierarchies is itself a hierarchical value judgment. Indeed, we cannot dispense with hierarchies; they are inher-ent in nature and qualitative distinctions are an inevitable part of human experience.

Moreover, systems sciences argue that hierarchy is essential for inte-gration, wholeness, and systems functioning. Understood in this systems context, hierarchy is simply a ranking of phenomena according to their holistic capacity. As such, it does not necessarily entail value hierarchies, and domination and oppression can be seen as pathological expressions rather than inherent components of hierarchy. For another excellent dis-cussion of contemporary criticisms of hierarchies and possible responses, see Donald Rothberg (1986).

Having rehabilitated the concept of hierarchy, or *holarchy*, as he prefers to call it, Wilber next turns to the common principles and processes that hold for systems and phenomena across the three great realms; physical, biological, and mental. For Wilber, the fundamental category is the *holon*, a term that implies that every entity and phe-nomenon in the universe is neither merely a whole nor a part, but both simultaneously.

Using the concepts of hierarchy and holon, Wilber is able to clarify the nature of various hierarchies and their misuse. For example, most popular general systems theories of ecology and ecofeminism are based on some version of a holarchy of being, a kind of "web of life." Humans are usually inserted into this web as one strand in the biosphere or Gaia. At first glance this move seems very neat, organic, and egalitarian. Humans are now intimately linked to, and on a more or less equal foot-ing with, all other forms of life.

However, in what is perhaps the most intellectually challenging part of the book, Wilber demonstrates that things are not quite this simple. Hierarchically ordered structures and *emergents* (properties or capaci-ties that emerge de novo at certain levels of hierarchy) cannot be inter-preted simply in terms of, nor considered as parts of, lower order phe-nomena. For example, when atoms of hydrogen and oxygen combine, the result is a molecule of water with novel emergent properties such as wet-ness. These emergent properties are largely unpredictable from the properties of its constituent atoms and cannot be described in terms of atoms. Likewise, the water molecule is not contained in its atoms (the water molecule and the properties of order of its constituent atoms are not part of atoms).

So too, life, or the biosphere, is not simply contained in, reducible to, or explicable simply in terms of, the physiosphere (the realm of pure matter). The biosphere is of a different ontological order, and life has properties and capacities that seem to defy description simply in terms of the movements of molecules. Likewise, the noosphere (the realm of sentient life) is not simply *in* the biosphere. That is, the noosphere is not an ontological component of the larger whole called biosphere but is an emergent. Rather, parts of the physiosphere and biosphere are actually components of sentient life and ontologically the noosphere thus cannot be reduced to, or considered merely as, a strand of the biosphere. Thus, contrary to popular assumptions (based primarily on relative size), aspects of the biosphere constitute *part* (the physical and biological levels but not the mental level) of the human. Humans are therefore compound individuals composed of all three levels and cannot be regarded simply as strands of the biosphere, which comprises only the physical and biological levels.

This is a difficult but important argument that can only be sketched briefly here. The key is to shift from thinking spatially (e.g., the biosphere fits into the larger space of the physiosphere) to thinking ontologically (aspects of the physiosphere constitute a component or part of the ontologically richer biosphere). This perspective appears to resolve a number of puzzles that have plagued ecological thinking, such as how one can simultaneously accord greater value to some forms of life, including humans, than to others while simultaneously honoring all life. Wilber argues at length that this perspective is not antiecological, as it might appear at first glance. Rather, he insists that it naturally results in an enhanced concern for life and the environment which are now recognized as parts of one's own compound individuality.

INTERIORITY

The schemes and hierarchies considered so far all deal exclusively with exteriors since general systems theories try to be empirically based. Hence, they almost entirely overlook interiority or subjectivity. In addition, since systems theories are empirical, the general principles they derive from all types of systems do indeed hold across the range of systems, including physical, biological, and psychological, as all of these have physical components. However, the price of this inclusiveness is that they necessarily cover only the lowest-common-denominator properties. Higher order biological and noetic systems, while following lower order physical principles, also follow additional principles, and no physical laws can account for the likes of art, language, and love. Thus systems theories are essentially theories of surfaces or exteriors. To understand interiors—subjectivity, experience, and consciousness—requires another approach, namely empathy, introspection, and interpretation. In short, systems theories have given us a very valuable but very partial view of systems and evolution. This in itself is not bad. However, major troubles ensue when systems scientists claim, as all too many of them do, to be mapping, or to be at least capable of mapping, *all* domains of reality.

THE FOUR QUADRANTS

Wilber wants to expand this view. He argues that comprehensive approaches need to include not only objective studies of the external behavior of individual holons, but also studies of social or group holons and, in addition, the interior or subjectivity of both individuals and groups. He therefore introduces what he calls the *four quadrants model*, with individual and social holons in the upper and lower halves, respectively, and exterior and interior in the right and left halves, respectively (figure 1).

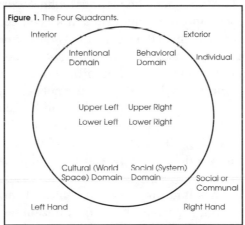

Figure 1. The Four Quadrants.

Interior   Exterior

Intentional   Behavioral   Individual
Domain   Domain

Upper Left   Upper Right
Lower Left   Lower Right

Cultural (World   Social (System)
Space) Domain   Domain   Social or
Communal

Left Hand   Right Hand

Right-hand disciplines or paths study neutral surfaces or observable behavior. Traditionally, they use empirical, objective epistemologies and objective "it" language, make propositional truth claims, and employ the validity criterion of truth (the match between map and territory). In the right-hand quadrants there are two camps: the atomists in the upper right quadrant, who study individuals, and the wholists in the lower right quadrant, who study larger systems.

The left-hand approach or path studies interiors that cannot be seen empirically (except indirectly, where some of their components may be embedded in material expressions such as art). Rather, this interiority requires interpretation of meaning in "I" and "we" language that is dialogical, experiential, and subjective (or intersubjective). Research here necessarily involves dialogue as opposed to the monological (one-way) experimental observation of exteriors of the right-hand path. For the upper left-hand quadrant of individuals, the validity criterion here is not truth but, following the work of German social philosopher Jurgen Habermas, sincerity. In the lower left-hand social-cultural quadrant, the question is one of cultural fit, and the validity criterion is not truth or sincerity but appropriateness, justness, intersubjective mesh, and/or mutual understanding.

Wilber argues that both left- and right-hand approaches are valuable and essential for balance and completeness because each holon has these four dimensions. When, as has all too often been the case, the right-hand approach is used exclusively, the result is ignorance, polarity, and reductionism, which are all the worse because their incompleteness usually goes unrecognized. All four quadrants are then reduced to the two right-hand quadrants, a process that Wilber calls *subtle reductionism*. Some theorists—for example, the Epicureans and atomists—go even further by attempting to explain all phenomena and higher order structures purely in terms of upper right-hand quadrant atomic/molecular components. This atomic reductionism Wilber calls *gross reductionism*.

Reductionism can seem reasonable since all holons do in fact have both left- and right-hand quadrants and empirical data can be so obvious. However, no quadrant is wholly reducible to another, and both gross and subtle reductionism can be destructive. This can be insidious in the case of some systems theorists, for example, because these people believe that they are truly embracing all reality in a holistic manner and seem quite unaware of just how much, and how much of value, is often missing from their world view.

At this stage Wilber has laid the conceptual groundwork for tracing development and evolution, especially human evolution, across all four quadrants. This he proceeds to do.

HUMAN EVOLUTION

Wilber uses the maps devised by cognitive developmental psychologists such as Jean Piaget to trace the psychological development of individuals. This individual development he ties to social and cultural evolution from early hominids up to present society. Wilber argues that through history there has been an evolution of both individual cognitive and cultural unfolding. Each evolutionary and historical epoch has been associated with a specific stage of individual cognitive development together with correlative, socially shared world views and moralities.

The general idea is that cultural evolution and individual development go hand in hand. Societies tend to foster individual development up to their normal level and hinder development beyond it, and there is a relatively close correlation between an individual's expectable psychological development and a culture's "developmental center of gravity." For example, drawing on both his own earlier work and the research of Jurgen Habermas, Wilber correlates a magical-animistic world view with an average individual cognitive development at Piaget's preoperational level, a mythological world view with concrete operational, and a rational world view with individual development centered around Piaget's highest or formal operational stage. This is of course a controversial claim, and in extensive footnotes Wilber attempts to counter potential criticisms. These criticisms come from cultural relativists (who claim that we cannot make valid cross-cultural evaluative comparisons because to do so means privileging one culture's value system over another's) and critics of certain forms of the "ontogeny recapitulates phylogeny" thesis (which claims that individual development follows or recapitulates species evolution) (Winkelman 1990, 1993).

Wilber pays particular attention to the evolution of gender relations and the human relationship to the environment at each historical stage. Drawing on a significant body of feminist research, he particularly points out that contrary to popular assumptions, the historical inequality of women cannot be attributed solely to male domination and oppression. Rather, it is also attributable in part to biological factors such as differential strength, to economic-productive factors such as types of tools and modes of food acquisition, and to developmental stages and world views in which equality was not a salient feature or moral imperative. This allows him to view the emergence of liberation movements as a partial reflection of the emergence of rationality and to interpret the previous gender inequalities as a function of more than merely the male malevolence and female timidity implied by some feminists.

It also allows him to draw some chilling conclusions about the possible nonegalitarian and gender divisive effects of new information technologies that are currently so male dominated. I had simply assumed that women's liberation was a largely irreversible evolutionary dynamic. Wilber, however, points to the power of a culture's technoeconomic base in determining its social hierarchy and argues that there is no guarantee that future technologies, such as computers and the Internet, will necessarily foster equality, a concern which seems to have been largely overlooked by feminists.

TRANSPERSONAL DEVELOPMENT

The formal operational stage of individual cognitive development and the rational world view are the highest individual and cultural levels that are widely recognized by conventional mainstream science. However, Wilber goes on to point to evidence for the existence of higher stages and potentials latent in each of us. The first of these he calls *vision-logic*, a kind of network logic able to envision multiple relationships among individual concepts simultaneously. Of course Wilber is not alone here. Several developmental researchers—such as Bruner, Flavell, Arieti, and Gebser—have suggested a similar stage. Wilber is unique, however, in recognizing a similar stage in the developmental maps offered by contemplatives such as Plotinus and the great Indian philosopher-sage Aurobindo.

Beyond vision-logic, for Wilber, lie four further major stages which he calls *psychic, subtle, causal, and nondual*. These are transpersonal stages inasmuch as the self sense now begins to expand beyond the personal—what Alan Watts so picturesquely called "the skin encapsulated ego"—to encompass aspects, or even the whole, of humankind, life, the internal and external universe, and consciousness itself.

Before describing these stages in detail, Wilber handles common objections that have been raised about the value and validity of transpersonal experiences. For example, it has been claimed that since transpersonal states are private and interior they cannot be publicly validated and therefore cannot be researched. However, Wilber points out that this is no more true for transpersonal research than for any and all nonempirical endeavors, ranging from mathematics, literature, and linguistics to psychoanalysis and historical interpretation. No one has seen, nor will they ever empirically see, the square root of minus one, but that does not stop it from being a valuable, in fact invaluable, tool for mathematics.

For Wilber, then, transpersonal experiences are simply the higher developmental stages of the upper left-hand quadrant. These involve interior experiences known by direct acquaintance that can be objectively described but only adequately comprehended by a community of people at the same developmental depth, capable of interpreting at that same depth. At any developmental stage, higher stages and their worlds are effectively invisible or at least partly incomprehensible. This is effectively a restatement—now couched in developmental terms—of the principle of *adequatio*, which states that we only see or appreciate those aspects of reality to which we are adequate. As Aldous Huxley (1945, viii) summarized the problem in *The Perennial Philosophy*, "knowledge is a function of being. When there is a change in the being of the knower, there is a corresponding change in the nature and amount of knowing." Talmudic wisdom puts it succinctly: "We do not see things as they are but as we are."

For Wilber, validity claims for transpersonal experiences, states, and stages are in essence no different from those in other realms. In any realm, testing knowledge claims involves three steps: injunction, observation, and confirmation. One is first given an injunction by those familiar with the phenomenon as to how to create the conditions in which to observe it; one then observes, and then tests one's observation against the observations of adequately developed and trained individuals. Contemplative paths designed to induce transpersonal experiences and stages possess all these three strands of valid knowledge accumulation and therefore are open to the falsifiability criteria of all genuine knowledge. That is, they set out the injunctions to practice this discipline; then you can carefully observe your own experience, and finally test your observations against those of people at similar or more advanced stages.

Having handled these objections, Wilber then goes on to describe the psychic, subtle, causal, and nondual stages. These he associates with four types of mysticism: nature, deity, formless, and nondual and suggests as exemplars of each of these Emerson, St. Teresa, Meister Eckhart, and Ramana Maharshi.

Psychic seems an unfortunate choice of terms, being loaded with so much semantic baggage. However, as Wilber uses it, it has nothing to do with ESP or other psi phenomena. Rather, it refers to an initial transpersonal stage at which experience is still largely somatically based, such as in the experiences of *kundalini* energy or of the divinity of nature. By the time the subtle levels have emerged, experience is more interior and concerned with subtle experiences of light and sound (*shabd* and *nad* yoga) or archetypal imagery, for example, the shaman's power animals, the Hindu *Ishta Deva*, the Christian contemplative's sacred figures. At the causal level all form and experiences drop away leaving only pure consciousness, such as the Buddhist's *nirodhasamapatti*, the Vedantist's *nirvikalpa samadhi*, the Gnostic's abyss. Finally, at the nondual culmination, phenomena reappear but are immediately and spontaneously recognized as projections, expressions, or manifestations of consciousness and as none other than consciousness. This is the Hindu's *sahaj-samadhi* and the Mahayana Buddhist's "form is emptiness."

Needless to say, these advanced contemplative experiences can be very hard for most of us to conceive. To my mind the best metaphor for *sahaj-samadhi* is lucid dreaming, dreaming in which we know that we are dreaming. Such lucidity has been described by yogis for millennia, denied by psychologists for decades, but now is well validated by labora-

tory studies. Here what initially appeared to be an objective, solid, independent world impinging on a physical body on which one's life depends
is recognized as a subjective, dependent projection of mind. And with
that recognition the dreamer becomes lucid, the apparent victim of experience becomes it creator, and the suffering and anxiety that seemed so
overwhelming are recognized as illusory. Such is said to be the mind-boggling central recognition of both lucid dreaming and awakening to the
nondual.

Thus far Wilber has traced evolution from early hominids to postmodernism, and individual development from infancy to the nondual,
and has correlated these with the developmental/evolutionary profiles of
a host of related phenomena such as world views, morality, identity, gender relations, and ecological relations, among others. Clearly it seems
time to finish the book and have a beer. Not so! For Wilber, this is only
Part One of the book and only half the picture: namely, the ascending
half or "the path of ascent." In Part Two he traces another movement,
"the path of descent." And it is the divorce of these two that Wilber
claims to be one of the most fundamental of all Western dualisms.

ASCENT AND DESCENT

For Wilber, the two Western exemplars of philosophers-sages who
have integrated the paths of ascent and descent are Plato and Plotinus.
Plato, for example, maps out a path of ascent toward "the Good" in *The
Republic* and *The Symposium*. From this perspective, the Platonic Good
is a direct mystical experience of the causal realm—beyond qualities and
manifestations, and therefore transrational and transverbal—beside
which the physical world is merely a cave of shadows. This is a classical
description, perhaps the classical Western description, of ascent to the
causal level. And this ascent and escape from the world became the
archetypal Western goal.

Many critics assume that Plato was only an "ascender." However, a
more careful reading reveals that Plato maps out both the paths of
ascent and of descent. Having ascended to the Good he then reverses
course. The world is now seen as an expression or an embodiment of the
transcendent, and indeed at its consummation "a visible, sensible God."
The Self-sufficing perfection of the Good is also a Self-projecting, Self-
emptying fecundity. The Good is therefore not only the summit and goal
of life but also the source and ground of the world, with which it is co-
essential. And the source is made "more complete" by manifestation.
Plato therefore integrates ascent and descent in the classic nondual
stance found in both East and West which Wilber summarizes as

Flee the many, find the One
Embrace the Many as the One

In the East, disentangling oneself from the world and realizing the One is equated with wisdom. Subsequently, descending and returning to embrace the Many is equated with compassion, and the integration of ascent and descent is called the union of wisdom and compassion.

From this nondual perspective, creation, the world, and the flesh are not evil or degraded. However, becoming entranced by them, that is, becoming entrapped in *maya*, illusion—what psychologist Charles Tart calls the consensus trance—and thereby losing awareness of the transcendental domains and our unity with them is disastrous. Once lost, the challenge is to regain this awareness through a discipline of "recollection" that opens "the eye of the soul" (Plato), "the eye of the heart" (Sufism), or "the eye of Tao" (Taoism). The goal is an illusion-shattering wisdom that recognizes our true transcendental nature and that is variously known as Hinduism's *jnana*, Buddhism's *prajna*, Islam's *ma'rifah*, and sometimes as Christian gnosis.

The Platonic integration of ascent and descent was continued by Plotinus, in whom, according to St. Augustine, "Plato lived again." He created a vast synthetic vision drawing on diverse traditions and grounded in his own mystical experience. His was the first comprehensive version of the Great Chain of Being, a view that sees the cosmos as a vast gradated hierarchy of existence extending from the physical through various subtle mental realms to the realm of pure consciousness or spirit.

As Wilber makes clear, what is crucial is that the systems of Plato and Plotinus, and similar Eastern philosopher-sages such as Aurobindo, are not primarily philosophies or metaphysics. Rather, they are descriptions of direct, replicable, phenomenological apprehensions arising in people who have developed to requisite stages. All too often, however, they have been interpreted as "mere metaphysics."

For Plato, Plotinus, and Aurobindo, during developmental ascent each stage subsumes or envelops lower stages. In so doing, development retraces in reverse order the stages of involution or manifestation by which the Great Chain of Being was said to be created. In the words of Heraclitus, "The way up is the way down, and the way down is the way up."

For Plato, the process of ascent is driven by *eros*, the drive to find greater and greater unions. Complementarily, for Plotinus, at each stage of ascent the lower has to be embraced so that *eros* is balanced with *agape* (love and concern for the lower). This vision of a multidimensional *kosmos*, as the Greeks originally called it, interwoven by ascending and descending currents of love, would be a central theme of all subsequent neo-Platonic schools and would exert a profound influence on thought up to and beyond the Enlightenment.

But according to Wilber, both *eros* and *agape* can go astray when they are not integrated in the individual, ideally by direct experience of the causal One. Then *eros* can degenerate into *phobos*: aversion to, alienation from, and repression of lower levels of the Great Chain of Being and especially the world, the body, and sensuality.

Likewise *agape*—the pull to descent and embrace of the lower levels of the Great Chain—when divorced from and unbalanced by *eros*, can become *thanatos*. This is the flight from or denial of the higher levels and is manifested as developmental arrest, regression, and denial. One example of this might be what the psychologist Abraham Maslow called the *Jonah complex*: fear of our potential and greatness.

Wilber suggests that the great Sigmund Freud represents a paradigmatic example of this divorce of eros and agape. Freud himself finally postulated two drives—*eros* and *thanatos*—and suggested that the aim of eros is "to establish unity." For Freud, much human misery results from the battle or conflict between the powers of ascent and descent. But Freud did not carry ascent to its transpersonal conclusion in union with the One. In fact, he denigrated and pathologized such attempts as neurotic immaturities, thus confusing transpersonal progression with prepersonal regression, a confusion that Wilber calls the *pre/trans fallacy*. Hence, Freud gave us a truncated vision of human possibilities, and his prognosis for humankind was eternal conflict.

This misunderstanding or even pathologizing of development beyond conventional levels to transpersonal stages is tragically typical of the West. In much of the East, causal and nondual realization were recognized and acknowledged as the summit of psychological-spiritual development. Sages such as Nagarjuna and Shankara elaborated these realizations into highly sophisticated philosophies of Madhyamika Buddhism and Advaita Vedanta, respectively, which coexisted and harmonized with mythological interpretations. Individuals could thus draw inspiration from either philosophy or mythology or both according to their interests, capacities, and development. In the West, however, mythic level Christianity became institutionalized and dominant as "The Church," which declared its own mythic level interpretations alone as true and higher transrational interpretations as blasphemous.

This is a specific example of the general principle that stages higher than one's own tend to be misunderstood, pathologized, and viewed as threatening. Mythic Christianity, therefore, tended to condemn the higher stage expressions of rationalism (science and its demands for empiricism and evidence); psychic nature mysticism (because this made God seem too this-worldly); subtle level mysticism (which brought God and soul too close); and causal identity with the divine (which was enough to make one end up on a funeral pyre).

Of course Jesus himself had met a similar fate for his own causal realization that "The Father and I are one." But Jesus' own causal realization was interpreted by conventional theology not as a natural developmental potential available to us all, but rather as proof of his utterly unique nature and of divine intercession by God. Jesus himself was thus ontologically divorced from the rest of humanity as *the* Son of God—not only human but God and man—and the church would spend hundreds of years, split into dozens of sects, and snuff out thousands of lives arguing over his nature and his precise mix of God and man.

But no matter what formula finally won the day, Wilber points out that the net effect on spiritual development and evolution in the West was catastrophic. The possibility of causal realization for the rest of us was dismissed, liberation in this world was denied, and the whole realm of mysticism became ambivalent and at times downright embarrassing for the church. Of course the church was not alone in this embarrassment.

Wilber focuses on Christianity, but similar confusion and ambivalence toward mysticism seem characteristic of other traditions that fix final authority in a historical text and are therefore embarrassed by breakthroughs of new mystical insights. Thus, Judaism has largely downplayed its mystical dimensions for centuries, and there has long been tension between conventional Islam and its mystical wing of Sufism.

Fortunately, there are now growing efforts to revitalize contemplative practices and wisdom in each of these traditions. Unfortunately, this revitalization comes at the end of a millennium in which the possibility of awakening was effectively blocked in the West, and to this day mysticism remains widely misunderstood in Western culture.

Of course, the drive to transcendence could not be completely overwhelmed. Periodically there arose spectacular individuals—St. Augustine, Eckhart, Dame Julian, St. Teresa, the Rhineland mystics, and more—in whom transcendence triumphed over institutional barriers and who thereby faced themselves and the church with the difficult and dangerous task of reconciling conventional mythology with transconventional realization.

One of the earliest of these spiritual geniuses was St. Augustine, who was an inheritor of the neo-Platonic tradition. For Augustine, self and God could be known through introspection. All could be doubted except one's immediate awareness, or soul as Augustine identified it, and this awareness is similar to Plato's "Spectator" and Plotinus's "ever-present wakefulness." Augustine found that in his immediate awareness there was no subject/object split and primal awareness was not separate from God; rather God was the ground of that awareness. This awareness was the source of Augustine's famous exclamation that "He who knows himself knows God," a claim repeated two centuries later by Mohammed. As Wilber points out, this realization is very similar to that of several Eastern traditions, and hence he describes it as a Western form of Vedanta, the great Indian tradition whose central realization was that "Atman (individual consciousness) and Brahman (universal consciousness or God) are one."

The daunting problem for Augustine, as for subsequent causal realizers, was how to accommodate his realization to the body of literal-concrete myths he had inherited and to which, as a good church man, he held allegiance. Of course the general problem was not new and represented the recurring dialectic of philosopher-sage versus mythology, a dialectic which extended back to ancient Greece. In Greece, the sages had either dismissed myth, which could prove lethal as Socrates discovered, or attempted to reinterpret it rationally as did Plato.

This problem and its attempted solution for Christianity were exemplified in the life of Origen, who lived in the third century and who has been described as the church's greatest theologian. Origen's solution was the allegorical method by which myth could be both negated and preserved. Thus for Origen, myth—which in this case meant much of the Old Testament—was to be interpreted on three levels: literally as historical fact; ethically for behavioral guidelines; and allegorically for mystical, spiritual, or transpersonal interpretations. This effectively allowed rational and transrational use of myth. Unfortunately, this reinterpretation did not sit well with the conventional church, as Origen discovered to his dismay, and myth largely reigned supreme until the rise of modernity.

MODERNITY

For Wilber, modernity is marked by two major trends that represent the good news and the bad news of this period. The good news of modernity is the supersession of myths by rationality and the demand for empirical evidence. The bad news is that ascent was conflated with the mythic and the cry of "No more myths!" became effectively, "No more ascent!"

With the denial of the possibility of developmental ascent, attention turned downward to the world; instead of an infinite above, there was now a horizontal, infinite ahead. The universe was no longer seen as a great multidimensional holarchy of being. Rather, it became an ontological "flatland" or great interlocking order to be investigated by empirical (right-hand) approaches only. This overlooking of left-hand internal quadrants and reducing of phenomena to their right-hand external dimensions alone constitutes what Wilber calls subtle reductionism. With the left-hand quadrants gone, so too are the grounding and validity of subjective phenomena such as values, meaning, and purpose. The result is a barren, meaningless flatland that has also been described as a "dedivinized," disqualified, or disenchanted world.

With empirical approaches and dimensions dominant, quality was now measured in terms of quantitative fit with the system or with "God's will." Substitute "Gaia" for "God's will" and one has the "new paradigm" of many contemporary ecophilosophers.

This worldview presented philosophers with a problem, the so-called central problem of modernity, namely, the nature of human subjectivity and its relation to the world. The rational ego might say it was merely a strand in the great web of life, but that reduced the subjective to the empirical, the left- to the right-hand quadrants. Now the question of the good life was whether to seek either autonomous agency of the rational ego generating its own morals and aspirations separate from the brute drives of nature or, on the other hand, to seek communion with the natural world by connecting and communing with nature, including its vital, sensual, and sexual elements. This tension Wilber refers to as the conflict between the *ego camp* and the *eco camp*.

Immanuel Kant is the exemplar of the ego camp. For him, the rational ego, the moral subject, is free only to the degree it disengages from the pulls of egocentric desire and of lower social forces and is effectively autonomous. Thus arose the subjective part of the Enlightenment paradigm, the so-called self-defining subject, the autonomous ego, disengaged self, philosophy of the subject, or self-sufficient subjectivity.

The problem with the cruder forms of the ego camp was overemphasis on the right-hand, empirical representation of knowledge that focuses on surfaces, ignores interiority, and avoids dimensions of meaning, value, and purpose. Thus, there emerged around the eighteenth century attempts to study and know the subject in objective "it" language terms. For the philosophers Habermas and Foucault, these objectifying "sciences of man" are pseudosciences that do not just study the objective dimensions of humankind but reduce humans to only these dimensions.

The eco camp, on the other hand, felt, quite reasonably, that this representational reflection paradigm of knowledge left the subject split from an alien, monochromatic world. The eco camp therefore argued for a return to nature so that the "living sources" of human existence could be recontacted and renewed. Consequently, the appropriate mode of knowing was held to be powerful feeling rather than disinterested thought, and the best means of expression and enhancing participation with nature were felt to be poetry and art.

The problem for the eco camp was just how to insert humans back into the stream of life without losing the benefits of reason. This proved particularly problematic since these thinkers tended to confuse differentiation and dissociation. Thus, the developmental and evolutionary differentiation of the prerational fusion of self and world was seen not as a necessary developmental differentiation phase allowing subsequent higher order integration, but rather as a pathological process (dissociation) leading to paradise lost.

Eco camp thinkers believed that something had gone terribly wrong historically. They therefore saw culture primarily as a distortion and eulogized earlier times and lifestyles. Medieval ages and classical Greece were early objects of veneration, but the same general principle of historical wistfulness continues to the present day. Today's ecofeminists tend to eulogize horticultural societies whereas what Wilber calls "eco-masculinists" may reach further back to the prehorticultural Eden of hunting-gathering tribal cultures.

Yet an unblinking look discloses an embarrassing number of facts that suggest that these times and tribes may have been considerably less than paradisiacal. Consider only that the inability to devastate the environment does not necessarily imply profound ecological wisdom, that slavery was taken for granted, and that the average life span was probably around thirty years, and the power of the rose-colored glasses through which these societies have been viewed seems quite impressive.

As with all things, both ego and eco projects eventually faltered under the weight of their own limitations (what Hegel called "contradictions" and Schelling described as "checking forces"). The rational ego camp sought freedom from egocentric motives, natural impulses, and conventional social domination. However, in doing so it often alienated, repressed, and dissociated other goods, including transpersonal experiences and the prepersonal domain of "elan vital," body, and sensuality.

The eco camp, on the other hand, sought freedom from excessive objectivity, autonomy, and instrumentality. However, it ended up overvaluing emotional, irrational impulses and effectively saw nature as the source of sentiment rather than as the embodiment of Spirit as had Plato and Plotinus.

The ego-eco conflict was most clearly expressed philosophically in the contrasting views of Fichte and Spinoza. Fichte eloquently described the pure ego or infinite subject, a description similar in many ways to that of the Atman of Vedanta. From this view, autonomy, freedom, and Spirit were to be found in the absolute subject.

The eco camp, conversely, drew on somewhat dubious interpretations of Spinoza. Spirit was seen as the total objective system of the world into which ego was inserted. This too was an attempt to introduce Spirit but now found by radicalizing eco. An enormous amount of thought and effort went into the attempted integration of absolute subject and absolute object, of Fichte and Spinoza. It was a major intellectual project around the beginning of the nineteenth century and, for Wilber, the solution was provided by Schelling.

THE SPIRIT OF EVOLUTION

Schelling began by reacting to the Enlightenment notion that rationality alone is the acme of ascent. For him, the Enlightenment had differentiated mind and nature but had largely forgotten the transcendental ground of both. The scientific reflection paradigm of mind mirroring nature cleaved nature as object from reflecting self and subject, which also made humans objects to themselves.

For Schelling, this dissociation could not be healed by regression to childhood or to the immediacy of feeling but only by progression beyond reason to discover both mind and nature as different movements of one spirit manifesting in successive stages of evolutionary unfolding. As Hegel would put it, Spirit is not one apart from Many, but the very process of the One expressing itself in successive unfoldings as and through the Many.

Thus, for Schelling and Hegel, the absolute is both the alpha and the omega of development, both source and summit, and is present in the evolutionary process as both *telos* and *eros*. Nature is now seen as "slumbering spirit" and all life as manifestation of Divine Life. With the emergence of mind, Spirit becomes self-conscious. Thus for Schelling, nature is objective Spirit, mind is subjective Spirit. These two can be seen as totally unrelated, as the ego and eco camps had tended to see them, but these two "apparent absolutes" are synthesized in the third great movement of Spirit which is the trancendence of both and the radical union as "one absoluteness." This is the identity of subject and object, Spirit knowing itself as Spirit, and a glimpse of the nondual.

Thus, for both Schelling and Hegel, Spirit goes through three major phases. It first effluxes or manifests as objective, evolving nature. It then awakens to itself in subjective mind, and finally recovers its original identity in nondual awareness in which subject and object, mind and nature are unified. Similar evolutionary stages—prepersonal, personal, and transpersonal—can be found in the East, most notably in Aurobindo's ideas.

It was Schelling who first conceived the very influential concept of alienation. For him, this meant Spirit losing itself in manifestation. This loss was the central source of human suffering, and the overcoming of this was the purpose of evolution.

German idealism barely outlived its founders. Shortly after their deaths it was dismissed on logical and philosophical grounds as mere metaphysics. However, Wilber suggests that its failure may lie more in practical than in purely philosophical causes. These idealists seem to have managed genuine glimpses of the nondual and some of its manifestations and implications. However, there is an enormous difference between obtaining spontaneous glimpses and securing sustained vision or even obtaining significant glimpses at will. Many contemplative traditions speak of two distinct tasks: first of obtaining an initial, transient breakthrough glimpse—a "peek" experience—and second of being able to reproduce this glimpse at will and even stabilize it as an enduring vision. The challenge is to make a spontaneous experience a voluntary experience, to extend a peak experience into a plateau experience, or as the religious scholar Huston Smith put it so eloquently, "to transform flashes of illumination into abiding light."

This transformation requires a rigorous, authentic contemplative discipline and the idealists had none. Consequently, they were unable to offer a means by which other explorers could reproduce their insights, which were thus largely unfalsifiable and dismissed as "mere metaphysics." By contrast, Asian idealists such as Shankara and the Yogachara Buddhists offered both an art of transcendence by which practitioners could glimpse and then stabilize an experience of the nondual, as well as idealistic philosophies that have endured over centuries to articulate the insights that emerge.

Darwinian theory also exerted a chilling effect on the vision of evolution. Natural selection allowed science to deny any sort of *eros* or transcendent/ emergent drive in nature. More recently this denial has been called into question because it is now apparent that although Darwinian natural selection can account for microevolution, it has a much more difficult time accounting for macroevolution: the great evolutionary leaps and breakthroughs such as the production of functional wings.

In addition, the mind-boggling investigations of the big bang are now pushing knowledge back to the absolute temporal limit dictated by Planck's constant, which is the first 10^{-43} of a second. These findings indicate that the laws of physics were operative from the earliest conceivable instant. Materialistic explanations have a very hard time accounting for this, so the big bang theory has changed many reflective people into philosophical idealists. In light of all this, it is therefore not surprising that Wilber regards the creation of an adequate idealism as one of the essential challenges for the contemporary West.

The net result of these cosmological and evolutionary discoveries is that many philosophers of science now acknowledge some sort of self-transcendent drive in evolution. One of the major effects of Darwinian theory was thus not that it discovered a mechanism of macroevolution—it did not—but rather that for so long it obscured the recognition that an authentic evolutionary theory must acknowledge some self-transcendent drive akin to *eros* in the cosmos.

Wilber suggests that this self-transcendent drive is beginning to move increasing numbers of people beyond the conventional developmental level of rationality into transrational, transpersonal stages.[2] He argues that the evolution of this process can be facilitated or hindered by the degree of sensitivity with which these intuitions of transpersonal stages are unpacked. All interiority and subjectivity must be interpreted, and the quality of this interpretation is vitally important to the birth of successive depths of that interiority. The types of error to which this unpacking and interpretation are prone can be categorized according to which of the four quadrants they emphasize or overemphasize.

Many people intuit higher stage experiences in purely upper left-hand quadrant (individual, subjective) terms only. This interpretation focuses on subjective phenomena such as the "higher self," "pure awareness," etc., omitting the "we" and "it" (the right- and lower left-hand) quadrants, namely the social, cultural, and objective manifestations. This effectively omits from consideration appropriate types of community activity and service demanded by higher stages and the appropriate techno-economic infrastructures necessary for supporting them.

A particularly unfortunate result can be the assumption that higher stage realizations free one from concern with the world. By contrast, deeper insights and understanding make it clear that higher development necessarily entails embracing and serving the world, which is no longer seen as separate from one's Self. The challenge, therefore, is not just to contact the higher self but to see it embraced in culture, embodied in nature, and embedded in social institutions.

On the other hand, others interpret their higher stage intuitions primarily in "it" terms, describing spirit as the sum total of all phenomena or the great web. This right-hand interpretation results in a descended flatland world view that tends to ignore the left-hand quadrants of the "I" and "we" dimensions. Consequently, while advocates of this view urge the embrace of all life, they usually do not understand the degree of inner transformation essential for this embrace, let alone the transformations required for union with the Good and the recognition of the world as "a living sensible God." An unfortunate result is a descended world view that confuses Spirit with the sum total of shadows in the cave.

Thus, for Ken Wilber, further individual development, cultural integration, ecological preservation, and recognition of our true nature require appreciation of the possibility of development to transpersonal stages, a practice to realize them, and the use of all four quadrants to express them. Only by such a comprehensive vision, he says, can the spirit of evolution reach its fulfillment in us and through us. Though it will doubtless be amended and refined, Wilber's vision seems to be a major contribution to this process of evolution.

Notes

1. For a collection of Wilber's articles, see Walsh and Vaughan (1993). For a review of his writings, see Walsh and Vaughan (1994).

2. For a summary of the major intellectual challenges of our time, see Wilber's article, "Paths Beyond Ego in the Coming Decades" (Walsh and Vaughan 1993).

References

Anthony, D., B. Ecker, and K. Wilber, eds. 1986. *Spiritual choices*. New York: Paragon House.

Huxley, A. 1945. *The perennial philosophy*. New York: Harper & Row.

Rothberg, D. 1986. Philosophical foundations of transpersonal psychology: An introduction to some basic issues. *Journal of Transpersonal Psychology* 18:1–34.

Walsh, R., and F. Vaughan. 1994. The worldview of Ken Wilber. *Journal of Humanistic Psychology* 34 (2): 6–21.

Walsh, R., and F. Vaughan, eds. 1993. *Paths beyond ego: The transpersonal vision*. Los Angeles: Tarcher/Perigree.

Wilber, K. 1977. *The spectrum of consciousness*. Wheaton, Ill.: Quest Books.

———. 1980. *The Atman project*. Wheaton, Ill.: Quest Books.

———. 1981. *Up from Eden: A transpersonal view of human evolution*. New York: Doubleday.

———. 1983. *A sociable god*. New York: McGraw-Hill.

———. 1990. *Eye to eye: The quest for the new paradigm*. 2nd ed. Boston: Shambhala.

———. 1991. *Grace and grit*. Boston: Shambhala.

———. 1995. *Sex, ecology, spirituality: The spirit of evolution*. Boston: Shambhala.

———. 1996. *A brief history of everything*. Boston: Shambhala.

Wilber, K., ed. 1984. *Quantum questions: Mystical writings of the world's great physicists*. Boston: Shambhala.

Wilber, K., J. Engler, and D. Brown, eds. 1986. *Transformations of consciousness: Conventional and contemplative perspectives on development*. Boston: Shambhala.

Winkelman, M. 1990. The evolution of consciousness: An essay review of *Up from Eden* (Wilber 1981). *Anthropology of Consciousness* 1 (3/4): 24–31.

———. 1993. The evolution of consciousness? Transpersonal theories in light of cultural relativism. *Anthropology of Consciousness* 4 (3): 3–9.

3

Michael Murphy

Michael Murphy has been a practical visionary at the heart of America's exploration of human consciousness and potential. Born in Salinas, California, he attended Stanford University during the 1950s and was drawn to the study of philosophy. After graduation and two years in the army, he lived for over a year at the Sri Aurobindo Ashram in Pondicherry, India. After returning to the U.S., he and Richard Price founded the Esalen Institute near Big Sur, California, in 1962, on land owned by Murphy's family, formerly the home of the native tribe known as the Esselen.

Several hundred feet up the cliffs from the Pacific Ocean, amidst natural hot springs, Esalen soon became the world's most famous "growth center," where teachers, thinkers, and seekers have held forth in a dazzling and at times bewildering array of workshops in humanistic and transpersonal psychology and psychotherapy, bodywork, movement disciplines, and spiritual philosophy, among other offerings. Still going strong, Esalen offers about 450 seminars to some 10,000 people a year and sponsors a wide variety of innovative national and international programs.

Although Murphy remains chairman of the board of Esalen, he has for many years pursued his own projects. He has written four novels and several visionary nonfiction works. His first novel, Golf in the Kingdom, *told the story of the mystical Scottish golfer Shivas Irons. It may soon be made into a movie by Warner Brothers. Murphy has just finished a sequel,* The Kingdom of Shivas Irons. *His interest in extraordinary sports experiences led him to develop an extensive archive of studies of exceptional functioning, which is now housed in the Stanford University Medical School. He published an anthology of such experiences—*In the Zone, *with Rhea White—and has consulted with the San Francisco 49ers football team.*

A related interest in the body-centered dimension of spiritual transformation led to a second novel, Jacob Atabet, *a delightful speculative exploration, and the recent massive nonfiction study,* The Future of the Body. *In the latter, Murphy presents evidence of extraordinary body experiences in the context of evolutionary theory and an "integral" model of transformation as it occurs on many levels: physical, emotional, intellectual, volitional, and spiritual.*

   Murphy has also tried to bring his findings more directly into the mainstream. He helped found the Esalen Institute "Re-Visioning Philosophy" program (1987-1989), which brought together innovative contemporary philosophers seeking to reclaim the link between philosophy and the practical pursuit of wisdom. With martial artist George Leonard, he has written The Life We Are Given, *which suggests contemporary "transformative practices" that integrate in their curriculum the various dimensions of human growth, including philosophical, psychological, and spiritual study, body disciplines, emotional growth, contemplative practice, and community activity.*

   Given his interest in evolution and transformation, it is not surprising that Murphy finds considerable affinities with Ken Wilber. In the following chapter, he suggests that Wilber's work represents a "new canon" of philosophy and religious thinking. This new canon is based on the view that the divine (or Spirit) is transcendent, yet also evolves and is present or "immanent" in time and history. Murphy believes that this view will increasingly capture the imagination of a culture that is hungry for Spirit, yet also needs Spirit to be married to contemporary science and transformative practices. He finds Wilber's work, particularly Sex, Ecology, Spirituality, *to be a powerful guide for our collective cultural direction as well as to our individual transformations.*

Further Readings

Anderson, W. 1983. *The upstart spring: Esalen and the American awakening.* Reading, Mass.: Addison-Wesley

Leonard, G., and M. Murphy, 1995. *The life we are given.* New York: Tarcher Putnam.

Murphy, M. 1972. *Golf in the kingdom.* New York: Delta.

_____. 1977. *Jacob Atabet: A speculative fiction.* Millbrae, Calif.: Celestial Arts.

_____. 1982. *An end to ordinary history.* Los Angeles: Tarcher.

_____. 1992a. The evolution of embodied consciousness. In *Revisioning philosophy*, edited by J. Ogilvy. Albany: State University of New York Press.

_____. 1992b. *The future of the body: Explorations into the further evolution of human nature.* Los Angeles: Tarcher.

_____. (In press). *The kingdom of Shivas Irons.* New York: Broadway Books.

Murphy, M., and S. Donovan. 1997. *The physical and psychological effects of meditation.* Rev. ed. Sausalito, Calif.: Institute of Noetic Sciences.

Murphy, M., and R. White. 1995. *In the zone: Transcendent experience in sports.* New York: Penguin Books.

Schwartz, T. 1995. Nurturing the human potential: Michael Murphy and the founding of Esalen. In *What really matters: Searching for wisdom in America*, by T. Schwartz. New York: Bantam Books.

On Evolution and Transformative Practice:
In Appreciation of Ken Wilber

 IN THE EARLY EIGHTEENTH CENTURY, ISAAC NEWTON, THE MOST famous scientist of his day, supported the claim of Bishop Usher that from the Book of Genesis it could be calculated that the world began in 4004 B.C. Newton wasn't alone among prominent thinkers and scientists in believing that the Earth was no more than a few thousand years old.

But within decades, this foreshortened perspective started to change. Geology, paleontology, astronomy, and other fields began to show that the Earth and the universe had histories that stretched back for millions of years. This recognition of our world's great age, which by 1800 had been accepted by scientists and philosophers as diverse as Lamarck and Immanuel Kant, comprises one of history's swiftest and most fundamental alterations of worldview among intellectual elites.

At the same time, there was increasing belief in social advance. The growth of science and technology, the advent of democracy, and the burgeoning prosperity of Western Europe, were prompting many thinkers to celebrate the idea of progress (e.g., Bury 1932). And this belief, that humankind was capable of further development, was reinforced by the discovery of evolution.[1] After Darwin's publication of *The Origin of Species* in 1859, more and more people came to see that the world had developed for eons and might continue to develop for many more.

With the dawning of this evolutionary worldview, many thinkers began to ask: What is the relation of our ancient and evolving world to God? What is humankind's role in the world's advance? If the world is moving toward a higher condition, can human nature itself and human institutions progress? To what extent can consciousness and the body evolve? What are the means of their development?

In the early 1800s, a compelling response to these questions began to emerge among such philosophers as Hegel and Schelling, which, briefly, can be stated like this: While remaining transcendent to all created things, the divine spirit involved itself in the birth of the material world. The process that followed, the uneven, often meandering, but inexorable emergence of higher organization from matter to life to humankind, is then the unfolding of hidden divinity. Evolution follows involution. What was implicit is gradually made explicit, as the spirit within all things progressively manifests itself. In the words of the Indian philosopher Sri Aurobindo, "apparent nature is secret God."

The historian Arthur Lovejoy (1936, 242) called this shift of world-view "the temporalization of the Great Chain of Being," by which the manifest world with all its hierarchies was conceived "not as the inventory but as the program of nature." We might also call it "evolutionary emanationism" or "evolutionary panentheism." (Pan*en*theism, in distinction to pantheism, is the doctrine that the divine is both immanent in and transcendent to the universe). This "temporalization" of the Great Chain, or evolutionary panentheism, has been developed in different ways by the German philosophers Fichte, Hegel, and Schelling; by Henry James, Sr., the father of William and Henry James; by the French philosopher Bergson; by the Jesuit theologian Teilhard de Chardin; and by twentieth century thinkers such as Jean Gebser, Alfred North Whitehead, Charles Hartshorne, and Sri Aurobindo. Here I would like to propose that the evolutionary worldview represented by these philosophers and theologians comprises a canon of sorts, a body of insight and proposals that will increasingly capture the world's imagination. It has great implications for philosophy, psychology, and religion. Ken Wilber is its latest major philosopher.

The set of ideas implicit to this canon is extremely fertile. For example:

• It helps us understand our yearnings for God. If the entire universe presses to manifest its latent divinity, then we share that impetus, which is evident in our desire for the self-surpassing love, self-existent delight, knowledge by identity, and other apparent attributes of the Transcendent we experience in our highest moments.

• It helps explain humankind's inextinguishable creativity. If all the world is a play or unfolding of divinity, creativity must be accessible to us all.

• The best things in life often seem to be given rather than earned, spontaneously revealed rather than produced by laborious effort (though religious, artistic, moral, or other practices set the stage for many of them). This sense of grace in human affairs, which is shared by people in every land, is understandable if life's highest goods were involved in the world from the start, waiting for the right conditions to manifest.

• It gives us a compelling reason for the resonance between human volition, imagery, cognition, emotion, and the flesh through which psychosomatic transformations appear to be mediated. If all our parts arise from a common source, they must be profoundly connected. Our cells, feelings, and thoughts resonate with each other because they are parts of the same omnipresent reality. Body responds to mind, and mind to body, because they arise from the same ever-present origin.

• It gives us a theoretical basis for understanding why such human attributes as perception, cognition, volition, and love can rise to extraordinary levels. If we are secretly allied with the source and impetus of this evolving universe, we must to some degree share its all-encompassing powers of transformation. We are capable of radical development, and can realize metanormal capacities, because that is our predisposition.

• For all the reasons just noted, evolutionary panentheism helps us understand the effectiveness of practices that embrace the whole person, that is, of integral practices.

But much more than this falls out of the idea that the divine is implicit in the evolving universe. Each of the thinkers noted above has helped to unpack this fundamental principle, bringing his own experience and insights to the process. Hegel showed that we can extend it to the unfoldment of ethics, metaphysics, religious beliefs, politics, and various human institutions, and elaborated the idea that successive forms of consciousness transcend and integrate (aufheben) the ones that precede it. Henri Bergson placed mystical experience at human evolution's cutting edge, giving mystics more centrality for the world's advance than his predecessors had done. Drawing on historical and anthropological discoveries not available to Hegel and Schelling, Gebser extended the identification of human developmental stages back into the stone age. And Sri Aurobindo, the greatest practicing contemplative among the thinkers just noted, developed an elaborate psychology of the higher life, a rich phenomenology of metarational consciousness, and the idea that the transformation of all our parts, including the body, is central to the world's further development. Each of these thinkers added something new to all this, partly from their special gifts, but also in part because they could draw upon discoveries not available to their forerunners. Like all of them, Wilber has added to the canon of evolutionary panentheism. To be more specific:

• More than anyone else, he has shown ways to integrate the methods and findings of dynamic psychiatry, developmental psychology, cognitive psychology, personality theory, and transpersonal psychology within an evolutionary worldview. Transpersonal psychology didn't exist when Gebser wrote, and Aurobindo didn't have much acquaintance with Freudian and post-Freudian insights into the stages and psychopathologies of human development. No primary exponent of the involution-evolution perspective has contextualized as many discoveries of contemporary psychology as Ken Wilber (see, for example, Wilber's contributions to Wilber, Engler, and Brown 1986).

• He has also done more than his predecessors to relate theories of moral, cognitive, and social development, as well as general systems theory, to the further reaches of consciousness and evolutionary panentheism generally.

• In his "four quadrants" approach, he has elaborated the kind of epistemology we need to comprehend adequately social and personal development in both their objectively and subjectively known aspects. No one else has brought into coherent purview philosophers, contemplatives, and scientists as diverse as Freud, Piaget, Aurobindo, Plotinus, the Buddha, Nagarjuna, B. F. Skinner, John Locke, Thomas Kuhn, Hegel, Teilhard, Max Weber, Talcott Parsons, Comte, and Marx! In doing this, he has called into question, or refuted, many excessive claims to ultimacy of insight or method made by thinkers of various persuasions. The reach of his work is, to say the least, extraordinary.

• He has extended the insight of Aurobindo and others that human advance requires both an integral understanding of human nature and disciplines that embrace the different levels and dimensions of human nature in both its individual and social aspects (Wilber 1997).

WILBER AND INTEGRAL TRANSFORMATIVE PRACTICE

My appreciation of Wilber's work has grown as I've studied extraordinary human functioning and worked with George Leonard to develop what he and I call "Integral Transformative Practices" (ITP), that is, long-term practices which aim to produce positive changes in a person or group through the systematic and simultaneous cultivation of the physical, vital, affective, cognitive, volitional, and transpersonal dimensions of human functioning. In our ITP programs, we emphasize the balanced development of one's various attributes, including their metanormal expressions, while grounding all of our practices in the development of that essential awareness which in many Buddhist traditions is called "mindfulness." Appreciating the magic and necessity of community for long-term personal growth, we encourage the building of creative groups to support these disciplines. (For a fuller description of ITP see Leonard and Murphy 1995, chapter 2.)

For all of this, Wilber's work has been wonderfully helpful. His demonstrations that our further advance requires both personal and social transformation realized through disciplines that embrace all aspects of human life, his elaboration of the dangers inherent in one-sided beliefs and practices, and his dramatization of the differing emphases on "ascent" or "descent" in various worldviews, as well as other components of his philosophy, provide strong support for our vision of integral transformation. Again and again, we have found his theories to be deeply practical.

Long-term transformative practices, like all serious callings, are strengthened by, and often require, a sustainable supporting philosophy. In dedicating ourselves to disciplines that will last for many years or the rest of our lives, we need to know why we must avoid certain pitfalls, give up particular habits, learn new skills, cultivate unfamiliar virtues, and develop various attributes. We need to know how the different parts of our practices fit together, how they support each other, and why we need them all. My work with Leonard, as well as my experience at the Esalen Institute since 1962, has emphatically taught me that few can endure the resistance from self and others, the doubts, frustrations, and inevitable ups and downs of long-term discipline without a good set of reasons for doing so. In our classes on integral transformative practice, Leonard and I have recommended Wilber's *Sex, Ecology, Spirituality, A Brief History of Everything,* and *The Eye of Spirit,* along with Aurobindo's *The Life Divine* and other works that support our theory and disciplines. We have done so because these books help orient our practice, add excitement and vigor to the quest, and provide essential components of our guiding philosophy. For us, Wilber's philosophical work helps to ground and stabilize practice. It has helped counter criticisms that our many-sided approach attempts too much, or that by its inclusiveness neglects this or that more important cause.

But we have not depended on the works of Aurobindo, Wilber, and other philosophers as if they are written in stone. Ultimately, they are subject to revision. In *The Life We Are Given* (Leonard and Murphy 1995, 169) we wrote:

> The need for a basis in theory becomes clear when the practitioners of an integral discipline have to make course corrections. The principles that guide our work have enabled us to assess the effectiveness of our programs and the progress of class members. They have helped us improve certain exercises and invent better ways to make our program effective. There is an analogy here with science in that our theory of integral transformation has been tested by the experience of class members, while, at the same time, members' experience has been guided by theory. Both our theory and our practice have developed from their mutual give and take.

Because we take theory to be provisional, and its propositions to be falsifiable, we find Wilber to be a reliable comrade. As much as any speculative thinker I know, he reminds his readers not only of philosophy's limitations but of past changes in his own thought, from what he describes as "Wilber I" to "Wilber II" to "Wilber III" to "Wilber IV" (Wilber 1997, chapters 1, 6, 7). He sets a remarkable example in this regard, one that I wish more theorists of human development and higher consciousness would follow. Delineating levels and pathologies of metanormal experience, for example, must, as Wilber reminds us, be a tentative exercise given our limited acquaintance with them;[2] and our understanding of human nature in its so-called normal functioning is limited as well. Though Wilber sometimes exercises an effervescent polemic (which I usually find to be wonderfully entertaining), he frequently revises points or emphases to be found in his earlier writings. This is especially evident in his most recent books. Having been inspired first to my own work by Sri Aurobindo, who constantly revised his poetry, yoga, and philosophy in the light of his developing experience (Heehs 1981), I find Wilber's essential pragmatism to be congenial, admirable, and eminently sensible.

And it is also liberating. His philosophy gives us enormous room to move, in both thought and transformative practice. The freedom that Wilber gives himself to explore different conceptual and spiritual domains is exhilarating to me. For a lot of us, it is contagious.

Notes

1. It is important here to distinguish between the *fact* and the *theory* of evolution. The publication of Darwin's *The Origin of Species* helped establish evolution as a fact, and at the same time put forth the theory of natural selection, which is part of a still-incomplete theory of evolution's mechanisms.

2. Even Sri Aurobindo, a deeply realized yogi, kept changing his schema of metarational mind, adding "overmind," for example, as a level between "intuitive mind" and "supermind" after writing his first version of *The Life Divine*. Compare *The Life Divine* as it appeared in Aurobindo's journal *Arya* with its subsequent (1939-40) edition, which can be found in Aurobindo's *Collected Works*.

References

Bury, J. 1932. *The idea of progress*. New York: Dover.

Heehs, P. 1981. *Sri Aurobindo*. London: Oxford.

Leonard, G., and M. Murphy. 1995. *The life we are given*. New York: Tarcher Putnam.

Lovejoy, A. 1936. *The great chain of being*. New York: Harper & Row.

Wilber, K. 1997. *The eye of spirit: An integral vision for a world gone slightly mad*. Boston: Shambhala.

Wilber, K., J. Engler, and D. Brown. 1986. *Transformations of consciousness: Conventional and contemplative perspectives on development*. Boston: Shambhala.

Part Two

Alternative
Paradigms of
Transpersonal
Theory

4

Michael Washburn

Along with Wilber and Stanislav Grof, Michael Washburn is among the few contemporary theorists to have proposed a comprehensive transpersonal paradigm. A professor in the Department of Philosophy at Indiana University, South Bend since 1970, Washburn grew up in Southern California and attended the University of California at Riverside as an undergraduate. He married Pamela Warren in the early 1960s; they have three daughters and three grandchildren. He went on to do graduate studies in philosophy at the University of California at San Diego, receiving his Ph.D. in 1970 under the supervision of Herbert Marcuse, the renowned German philosopher and critical theorist. Washburn's interest in transpersonal studies dates from the late 1960s when, in the spirit of the counter-culture, he was drawn to yoga and Eastern meditation, which he practiced for ten years.

The spiritual search begun in those early years of the transpersonal movement gradually became an intellectual search as well. Washburn began publishing papers on transpersonal theory in 1977, specializing in the philosophy of psychology and the psychology of religion. In addition to authoring his own articles and two books, since 1991 he has edited a series of books in the philosophy of psychology for the State University of New York Press, many of them important new contributions to transpersonal psychology.

Although Washburn has received considerable attention as a critic of Wilber—his first book, The Ego and the Dynamic Ground, *was largely framed as an alternative to Wilber's paradigm—his work is in fact an attempt to place transpersonal theory within the psychoanalytic tradition. This tradition includes not only the depth psychologies of Freud and Jung, but also contemporary developments, such as ego psychology and relational psychoanalysis. Washburn has given primary consideration to the link between transpersonal theory and psychoanalysis. He asks, for example: How does early childhood development toward a well-functioning ego create obstacles to eventual ego transcendence? How can gender differences in early childhood help us understand gender differences in later spiritual awakening and transformation? To what extent is spiritual awakening a re-awakening of energies and psychic potentials already present in the soul? What patterns of relationship characterize spiritual maturity?*

In the chapter that follows, Washburn begins by honoring Wilber's contributions to transpersonal psychology and the seminal influence of his work on Washburn's own development as a theorist. He traces the emergence of Wilber's mature position and its constellation around the idea of the pre/trans fallacy. In his critique of Wilber's paradigm, Washburn draws particular attention to Wilber's depiction of the transition from the body ego to the mental ego—which is always accompanied by a certain degree of repression or dissociation—and the transition from the mental ego to the integrated body-mind of what Wilber calls the "centaur." To Washburn, these transitions seem to violate Wilber's claim that development follows a hierarchical pattern and suggest, instead, that development proceeds in a spiral.

Washburn also challenges Wilber's assumption that the prepersonal stage of infancy and the transpersonal stage of spiritual maturity are expressions of two different sets of basic psychic structures. Washburn agrees with Wilber that prepersonal and transpersonal stages are profoundly different and that caution is needed to avoid reducing trans to pre or promoting pre to trans. But Washburn challenges Wilber's assumption that the only way to explain the differences between prepersonal and transpersonal stages is to posit two corresponding levels of basic psychic structures. According to Washburn, this assumption is unparsimonious and rests on the fallacy of inferring a structural conclusion from a developmental premise. A more elegant—and, Washburn believes, empirically justified—view of human development is that many non-egoic "potentials" have both pre and trans expressions. In other words, as Washburn suggests in the following chapter, although the infant's consciousness and spiritual wholeness are by no means the same, they may nevertheless both be expressions of an ultimate common ground, which Washburn calls the Dynamic Ground.

A more elegant—and, Washburn believes, empirically justified—view of human development is that many non-egoic "potentials" have both pre and trans expressions. In other words, as Washburn suggests in the following chapter, although the infant's consciousness and spiritual wholeness are by no means the same, they may nevertheless both be expressions of an ultimate common ground, which Washburn calls the Dynamic Ground.

Further Readings

Washburn, M. 1978. Observations relevant to a unified theory of meditation. *Journal of Transpersonal Psychology* 10 (1): 45-65.

_____. 1987. Human wholeness in light of five types of psychic duality. *Zygon* 22 (1): 67-85.

_____. 1990. Two patterns of transcendence. *Journal of Humanistic Psychology* 30 (3): 84-112.

_____. 1994. *Transpersonal psychology in psychoanalytic perspective*. Albany: State University of New York Press.

_____. 1995. *The ego and the dynamic ground: A transpersonal theory of human development*. 2nd ed. Albany: State University of New York Press.

_____. 1996. On finding one's way by losing it. In *Sacred sorrows: Understanding depression in body, mind, and spirit*, edited by J. Nelson and A. Nelson. Los Angeles: Tarcher/Perigree.

The Pre/Trans Fallacy Reconsidered

 ALTHOUGH THIS CHAPTER IS CRITICAL OF KEN WILBER'S THOUGHT, it is also a tribute to Wilber.[1] For like almost everyone else devoted to transpersonal theory, I am greatly indebted to Wilber. His work—along with that of Stanislav Grof—clearly led the way during the 1970s and 1980s. Wilber's genius at synthesizing ideas and his particular integration of spirituality and psychology, breathtaking in scope, elevated transpersonal theory to a much higher level. Wilber, along with Grof and Jung, was a primary influence on me when I was first struggling to clarify my own thinking on transpersonal issues. My first book, *The Ego and the Dynamic Ground,* although critical of Wilber, was very much a product of Wilber's influence, as is evident on almost every page. That book, now out in a second edition (1995), was conceived as a critical response to Wilber's structural-hierarchical perspective. It was written with Wilber in mind as both a formidable intellectual adversary and a towering intellectual role model. Wilber has played a vitally important role in my intellectual development, and I want to begin this chapter—especially because it is a critical chapter—by expressing my appreciation for the immense contribution he has made to transpersonal theory and to my own understanding of transpersonal ideas.

Wilber's work, especially *The Spectrum of Consciousness* (1977), *The Atman Project* (1980a), and *Up from Eden* (1981), came upon the transpersonal scene in dramatic fashion. These books were stunning intellectual achievements. They integrated a wide range of sources from comparative religion and contemporary psychology within a transpersonal framework of great power. I was extremely impressed with these books and with Wilber's thought as a whole. I eagerly awaited each new work from Wilber's pen to see where he would go next. Wilber's work in the late 1970s and early 1980s had such a great impact on transpersonal psychology that it virtually defined the field. And it still does for many of Wilber's followers.

I was so impressed with Wilber's theoretical synthesis that I assimilated it whole. I not only pored over his writings but also followed his lead by trying to learn some of the many sources from which he drew. I had been trained in Western philosophy and was only superficially acquainted with Eastern philosophy and contemporary psychology. Wilber opened my eyes to the cross-cultural and multidisciplinary riches available—and, indeed, indispensable—to anyone interested in transpersonal theory. As Wilber told Roger Walsh and Frances Vaughan

(1994), he does his homework. Indeed he does! And as a result almost everyone in transpersonal psychology owes a significant part of her or his education to him. In the late 1970s and early 1980s, Wilber integrated sources that earlier would have been thought to be completely unrelated—for example, sources from Eastern spirituality (primarily Vedanta and Buddhism) and from Western psychology (primarily structurally oriented developmental stage theory). And in *Sex, Ecology, Spirituality* (1995), Wilber has integrated a good deal of Western philosophy (primarily in its idealistic variations) and evolutionary theory into his system of thought.

In my opinion, Wilber's two most important works are *The Atman Project* (1980a) and "The Pre/Trans Fallacy" (1980b). These two works at any rate are the writings in which Wilber's mature position was first presented. All of Wilber's subsequent writings have applied or extended, but not significantly departed from, the general position set forth in these works. Also, incidentally, *The Atman Project* and "The Pre/Trans Fallacy" are the works by Wilber which had the greatest influence on my own thinking. Accordingly, in what follows I shall be giving these two works a good deal of attention, without, however, ignoring Wilber's other writings, in particular *Up From Eden* (1981), *Eye to Eye* (1990a), and *Sex, Ecology, Spirituality* (1995).

The Atman Project (1980a) put the spectrum psychology introduced in *The Spectrum of Consciousness* (1977) into a new form that for the first time clearly set Wilber's perspective apart from other transpersonal perspectives. As Wilber notes in the preface to *The Atman Project* (1980a), he had only recently understood the importance of the pre/trans distinction, that is, the distinction between preegoic (lower, primitive, or infantile) states on the one hand and transegoic (higher, psychic, or spiritual) states on the other.[2] The pre/trans distinction, he realized, is crucial to transpersonal psychology because preegoic and transegoic states, although widely different, appear similar from the point of view of the ego and, therefore, are frequently mistaken for each other. Lower states are mistaken for higher states or higher states are mistaken for lower states, and in either case regrettable consequences ensue for both theory and practice. Awakening to the importance of the pre/trans distinction, Wilber set about rethinking the ideas of *The Atman Project* (1980a), parts of which had appeared in preliminary form as articles in *ReVision*. He sought to clarify his own thinking on just how preegoic and transegoic states differ and how they are related, if at all.

In reworking *The Atman Project* (1980a), Wilber arrived at a way of explaining the difference between preegoic and transegoic states that laid the foundation for all of his subsequent work. *The Atman Project* is the first work in which Wilber presented the view that preegoic and transegoic states are expressions of two different, lower and higher sets of psychic structures and, therefore, that developmental movement toward transegoic levels of experience is a purely ascending movement aiming at higher structures. The psyche, in this new view, is a hierarchy of preegoic, egoic, and transegoic structural levels, and human development is a level-by-level climb up this hierarchy.

This structural-hierarchical conception of the psyche and linear-ascending conception of development brought Wilber into disagreement with the Jungians. For Wilber could no longer accept the Jungian view that preegoic and transegoic states have a common basis and, therefore, that transpersonal development follows a course leading back to psychic resources active early in life on the way to a higher, transegoic integration of the ego with those resources. Wilber, having earlier been in substantial agreement with this view, now clearly disagreed. He now believed that preegoic and transegoic states, rather than having a common basis, are expressions of different sets of psychic structures. And he now believed that transpersonal development, rather than retracing old ground on the way to higher ground, is a straight ascent to higher levels of structural articulation and (top-down) inclusive wholeness.[3]

The publication of "The Pre/Trans Fallacy" in 1980 brought Wilber's new view and his disagreement with the Jungians into sharp focus. Wilber graciously sent me a prepublication copy of the paper. In reading the manuscript, I knew that Wilber had written a landmark piece for transpersonal theory. "The Pre/Trans Fallacy" (1980b) poses what is perhaps the most important theoretical question for transpersonal psychology, and Wilber answers this question in a way that gives decisive formulation to his own position (already set forth initially in *The Atman Project* [1980a]). The question—which I shall call *the pre/trans question*—is, as I understand it, this: Do apparent similarities between preegoic and transegoic states imply that these states are expressions of the same or similar psychic structures? Basing his response on the structural-hierarchical conception of the psyche set forth in *The Atman Project* (1980a), Wilber answered this question with an emphatic no. He held that any similarities between preegoic and transegoic states are merely superficial and misleading and that, in fact, the psychic structures expressed in preegoic and transegoic states differ from each other in the widest possible way. Preegoic and transegoic structures are more different from each other than either is from egoic structures. Preegoic and transegoic states are not expressions of the same or similar structures; they are, rather, expressions of distinct and widely dissimilar sets of structures. This position, first adopted in *The Atman Project* (1980a) and then vigorously advanced in "The Pre/Trans Fallacy" (1980b), is perhaps Wilber's single most important theoretical commitment, which he continues staunchly to defend (see *Sex, Ecology, Spirituality* [1995], 205–8).

In insisting that preegoic and transegoic states are expressions of dissimilar sets of psychic structures, Wilber allows that these states appear similar to the ego and, therefore, that the structures corresponding to these states can be grouped together in pairs. For example, in "The Pre/Trans Fallacy" (1980b) Wilber matches the following preegoic and transegoic structures: (1) the primary matrix of infancy (narcissistic oceanic fusion) and higher spiritual wholeness, (2) the polymorphous somatic experience of the body-ego and the higher mind-body unity of the centaur (Wilber's term for existential mind-body integration),[4] (3) illusory magic (imaginal thinking subject to primary-process condensations and displacements) and genuine psychic ability, and (4) prerational mythic thinking and suprarational archetypes (Platonic ideal patterns).[5]

In matching these preegoic and transegoic structures, Wilber's intention is not to suggest that they have any real affinity. His point, rather, is to *contrast* these structures, to match them so that their wide differences can be clearly seen. For, he believes, failure to appreciate these differences leads inevitably to one or the other of two basic pre/trans errors or "fallacies"—namely, either to a misconceiving of the trans as the pre (reductionism) or to a misconceiving of the pre as the trans (elevationism). That is, failure to distinguish properly between corresponding pre and trans structures leads inevitably either to a cynical reduction of the transegoic to the preegoic (which Wilber abbreviates *ptf-1*) or to a naive elevation of the preegoic to the transegoic (which Wilber abbreviates *ptf-2*).

Describing these errors in "The Pre/Trans Fallacy" (1980b), Wilber says:

> In *Up from Eden* I therefore examined eight or so major structures of consciousness in order to discover how they may have been subjected (in the context of both historical development and present-day theories) to either ptf-1 or ptf-2. . . .
>
> My conclusions were that, almost without exception, some lower structure, such as magic, has been and still is confused with some similar-appearing higher structure, such as psychic, and then either the former is elevated to the latter, or the latter reduced to the former. In other words, the pre/trans fallacy. (1990a, 253–54)

Freudians, for example, tend to reduce spiritual wholeness to narcissistic oceanic fusion and transegoic archetypes to the primitive imag-

inal symbols of the primary process. They commit ptf-1. Jungians,
Wilber believes, do just the opposite. They, for example, tend to elevate
the primary matrix to the transpersonal Self and merely archaic or
infantile imaginal symbols to transegoic archetypes. They commit ptf-2.
According to Wilber, one must acknowledge that pre and trans are two
different levels of psychic structures, or else one will inevitably succumb
to either ptf-1 or ptf-2. He insists that there is no middle ground.

In my opinion, there *is* middle ground. One does not need to double
the number of nonegoic psychic levels to avoid a pre/trans error. Such a
doubling is unnecessary and unparsimonious. It is entirely possible that
many nonegoic structures—or, to use a term I prefer, nonegoic *potentials*[6]—have both pre and trans developmental expressions. It is entirely
possible that nonegoic potentials such as dynamism, the body, instinctuality, feeling, and the creative imagination express themselves early in
life in pre ways and then express themselves later in life—that is, after
the ego is mature and has been reconnected with nonegoic potentials—
in trans ways. For example, although the primary matrix and spiritual
wholeness are by no means the same, they may nonetheless be expressions of a common ultimate ground, what I have called the *Dynamic
Ground*. The primary matrix can be understood as preegoic fusion with
this Ground, spiritual wholeness as a higher reunion of the ego with this
Ground. Also, for example, although preegoic magico-mythical symbols
and transegoic archetypes are by no means the same, they also may have
a common source: the creative, autosymbolic imagination. Preegoic symbols can be understood as spontaneous productions of the autosymbolic
process forged in response to the prerational, preoperational body-ego,
higher transegoic archetypes as spontaneous productions of the
autosymbolic process forged in response to the mature ego (once it has
embarked upon the path of transcendence). I have mapped these and
other pre and trans expressions of nonegoic potentials in *The Ego and
the Dynamic Ground* (1995) and *Transpersonal Psychology in
Psychoanalytic Perspective* (1994).

The point here is that Wilber's conception of the psyche is unparsimonious. Rather than positing an ego in relation to nonegoic potentials
(many if not most of which can express themselves in both pre and trans
ways), Wilber posits three distinct levels of psychic structures: preegoic,
egoic, and transegoic. This positing of an extra psychic level is a consequence of Wilber's unfortunate answer to the pre/trans question. The
similarities between many pre and trans states need not be completely
misleading, as Wilber maintains. These similarities may indicate—and I
believe they do—that pre and trans states draw on many of the same
psychic potentials. Wilber is correct in holding that pre and trans should

be carefully distinguished both as psychic states and as developmental stages. Pre and trans *are* widely different as states and stages: preegoic states and stages are developmentally inferior to egoic states and stages, and transegoic states and stages are developmentally superior to egoic states and stages. In recognizing this important difference between pre and trans states and stages, however, it is not necessary to conclude that there is a corresponding difference between pre and trans *structures* (i.e., basic structures or psychic potentials). The fact that pre and trans differ developmentally and phenomenologically does not entail that they are dissimilar structurally, that is, in their underlying psychic sources. To infer structural dissimilarity from developmental-phenomenological difference, as Wilber does, is itself a type of pre/trans fallacy, as I shall explain later. Wilber's answer to the pre/trans question, then, is not the only logically viable one and is itself the product of a faulty inference.[7] There is no need to posit different levels of pre and trans structures in order to distinguish properly between pre and trans as states and stages. Wilber's answer to the pre/trans question, I believe, forced him to proliferate psychic levels and structures beyond need.

In committing himself to the view that pre and trans are different sets of psychic structures, Wilber at the same time committed himself to the view that, for the ego, movement toward the pre and movement toward the trans are movements unfolding in completely opposite directions. For Wilber, any movement by the ego in the direction of the pre (or what *was* pre[8]) is a purely descending movement, and any movement by the ego in the direction of the trans is a purely ascending movement. Accordingly, for Wilber, any return to psychic resources articulated during preegoic stages is necessarily a movement *away* from ego transcendence. The path of transcendence does not retrace old ground; it moves exclusively to new and higher ground. It proceeds straight from egoic structures to higher and previously unarticulated transegoic structures. Wilber, then, rules out the possibility of a *spiraling* path of transcendence, a path that bends back toward origins on the way to a higher integration with lost psychic potentials. In distinguishing between pre and trans not only as states and stages but also as structures, Wilber rules out the possibility that a return to what *was* pre is a return to what *could be* trans.

In rejecting the idea that movement toward the trans follows a spiraling course, Wilber is forced to interpret any process that is said to follow such a course as a merely regressive descent to origins, as a simple U-turn to what is structurally and, therefore, *only* pre.[9] This is how Wilber interprets the Jungian theory of individuation in "The Pre/Trans Fallacy" (1980b). According to Wilber, the Jungian theory of individuation is dangerously mistaken, for in stipulating that the ego must return to its collective origins in the deep psyche this theory points away from higher trans structures and toward similar-appearing but nonetheless exclusively lower pre structures. That is, it points away from transcendence and toward mere regression. In charging Jung with ptf-2, with misconceiving the pre as the trans, Wilber also charges Jung with misconceiving regression as transcendence. He says:

> In my opinion, Jung errs consistently to the opposite side [to the side opposite Freud and ptf-1]. He correctly and very explicitly recognizes the transpersonal or numinous dimension, but he often fuses or confuses it with prepersonal structures. . . . Thus not only does Jung occasionally end up glorifying certain infantile mythic forms of thought, he also frequently gives a regressive treatment to Spirit. (1990a, 225)

Wilber notes that Jung avoids many regressive difficulties because he (properly) stresses the importance of a strong ego. Jungian individuation, Wilber observes (1990a, 228–29), is not as regressive as the paths of self-change promoted by many human potential therapies, which not only glorify the pre but encourage the abandonment of the "rigid" and "repressive" ego as well. Jungian individuation, however, is still regressive according to Wilber, for, he believes, despite presupposing a strong ego, it turns the ego away from the trans and toward what is merely pre and, therefore, sets the ego on a merely descending, regressive course.

But this, I suggest, is a serious *mis*interpretation of Jung. For although it is true that Jungian individuation involves a descent—namely, a descending return of the ego to the nonegoic potentials of the deep psyche—this descent is not a merely regressive U-turn to origins. It is, rather, the first phase of a return-then-ascend, reroot-then-regenerate spiral. It is a retracing of ground that, in submitting the ego to the transformative power of the deep unconscious, leads ultimately to a higher ego-unconscious, whole-psyche integration (the alchemical *coniunctio*, the sacred marriage or *hieros gamos,* the *coincidentia oppositorum*). Jung's theory of individuation is, accordingly, a spiral theory. Wilber, however, having ruled out the possibility of a spiral to transcendence, interprets Jung's account of the ego's return to the collective unconscious as a simple U-turn of regression.

Working my way through "The Pre/Trans Fallacy" (1980b), I realized that I disagreed with Wilber's answer to the pre/trans question and that, in general perspective, I sided with Jung. Wilber's challenge to Jung thus helped me clarify my own thinking. Specifically, it led me to the idea of *regression in the service of transcendence*, which is a kind of regression that, by no means a merely regressive about-face, is the downward loop of a developmental spiral that reconnects the ego with its nonegoic sources on the way to a higher integration with those sources. The idea of such a regression is essentially Jungian (the night sea journey of individuation) and, therefore, is not new.[10] My awakening to this idea, however, occurred as I was in the midst of my own night sea journey and was struggling to find a response to "The Pre/Trans Fallacy" (1980b). Wilber's "Pre/Trans Fallacy," which gives expression to his turn *away* from Jung, was the intellectual stimulus that led me to turn *toward* Jung.

After working through "The Pre/ Trans Fallacy" (1980b), I reread *The Atman Project* (1980a) and saw that, from a spiral perspective, Wilber's structural-hierarchical theory of development can be called into question at two main developmental junctures: (1) the transition from preegoic stages to the egoic or, more precisely, mental-egoic stage; and (2) the transition from the *mental-egoic* stage to the "centauric" stage of higher mind-body integration and dialectical-holistic cognition (which Wilber calls *vision-logic*). These two transitions are the developmental turning points at which the spiral model of development and Wilber's structural-hierarchical model are most emphatically at odds.

According to Wilber, all normal developmental transitions are movements of ascent to higher levels of inclusive wholeness in the sense that new and higher structures are articulated without losing touch with previously articulated structures.[11] In normal development, consciousness *differentiates* itself from the structural level being transcended without *dissociating* itself from that level. Transcended levels are not repressed and lost; rather, they are assimilated and reorganized within the higher level to which consciousness ascends. Wilber acknowledges that repression and dissociation can occur during developmental stage transitions, but he holds that this is pathological, not the pattern of normal development. Wilber makes these points about normal development in almost all of his works.

In Wilber's structural-hierarchical theory, the transitions from preegoic stages to the mental-egoic stage and from the mental-egoic stage to the centauric stage should, assuming normal development, be movements of straight ascent to higher levels of inclusive wholeness. In a spiral view, in contrast, the two transitions in question are points of disconnection and reintegrating return, respectively. They are points at which the ego loses touch with many of the potentials of the deep psyche (transition from preegoic stages to the mental-egoic stage) and then begins a reintegrating, transcending return to those potentials (transition from the mental-egoic stage to the centauric stage). With this in mind, I looked closely at Wilber's descriptions of the two transitions in question to see how well they conform to his linear-ascending model of development.

What I found is that these transitions are problematic for Wilber in that his treatment of them—despite his efforts to make them fit the linear-ascending scheme—reveals the disconnection and higher reintegration hypothesized by the spiral view. For instance, in discussing the unconscious in *The Atman Project* (1980a) and *Eye to Eye* (1990a), Wilber acknowledges that the psychic potentials that Freud assigned to the id and that Jung assigned to the collective unconscious are indeed unconscious and unavailable to the mental ego. Here is what he says:

> Such is the archaic-unconscious, which is simply the most primitive and least developed structures of the ground-unconscious—the pleroma (physical matter), the uroboros (alimentary drives), the typhon (emotional-sexual energies), and various primitive mental-phantasmic forms. They are initially unconscious but unrepressed. . . . Self-reflexive awareness is out of the question with these structures, so they always retain a heavy mood of unconsciousness. (1980a, 107–8)

> At any rate, following both Freud and Jung, we can say in general that the somatic side of the archaic-unconscious is the id (instinctual, limbic, typhonic, pranic); the psychic side is the phylogenetic phantasy heritage. On the whole, the archaic-unconscious is not the product of personal experience; it is initially unconscious but not repressed; it contains the earliest and most primitive structures to unfold from the ground-unconscious, and, even when unfolded, they tend toward subconsciousness. They are largely preverbal and most are subhuman. (1990a, 108)

As these passages make clear, Wilber believes that the somatic, dynamic, and creative potentials of Freudian and Jungian depth psychology are not only inherently preegoic in nature but also inherently unconscious. These potentials, he says, are so primitive in character that they inherently "tend toward subconsciousness." They belong by their very nature to the "archaic-unconscious."

The potentials of the archaic-unconscious are inherently unconscious, according to Wilber, because they are prereflexive and preverbal; they cannot be brought into reflective focus or expressed through verbal-conceptual categories. The mental ego, it seems, can neither reflect upon nor translate these potentials and, therefore, is unable to experience them within the boundaries of consciousness. The mental ego, accordingly, is out of conscious contact with much of somatic life, instinctuality, body-based energy, and the creative process that forges the images of the primary process (Freud) and the mytho-archetypal imagination (Jung).[12] The mental ego, Wilber acknowledges, does not integrate these psychic potentials, as would happen in normal structural-hierarchical stage transition. The mental ego is unable to thematize or cognitively process these potentials—and, as Wilber says in *Up from Eden* (1981), is prone actively to dissociate itself from them as well (more on this in a moment).

Whether Wilber is correct in these views about the ego and the archaic-unconscious is not at issue here. The point here is simply that these views depart from Wilber's account of normal developmental stage transition. Despite holding that normal development includes rather than excludes lower levels, Wilber acknowledges that the somatic, dynamic, and creative potentials of the deep psyche are not assimilated and reorganized within the higher level of mental-egoic consciousness. To accommodate the Freudian and Jungian conceptions of the unconscious, then, it seems that Wilber is forced to allow an exception to his conception of developmental stage transition.

If Wilber's discussion of the transition from preegoic stages to the mental-egoic stage reflects the disconnection implied by the spiral view, his discussion of the transition from the mental-egoic stage to the centauric stage, I believe, reflects the higher integration implied by the spiral view. Even though Wilber explicitly rejects the idea that we need to return to the pre (or what *was* pre) in ascending to the trans, his description of the centaur indicates an awareness on his part that a retrieval and higher integration of previously articulated psychic potentials occurs in the transition from the mental-egoic stage to the centauric stage.

Wilber describes the centaur as a higher unity in which consciousness is able to incorporate all earlier, lower levels into a fully integrated totality. He says:

> Now as consciousness begins to transcend the verbal ego-mind, it can integrate the ego-mind with all the lower levels. That is, because consciousness is no longer identified with any of these elements to the exclusion of any others, all of them can be integrated: the body and mind can be brought into a higher-order holistic integration. . . . This integrated self, wherein mind and body are harmoniously one, we call the "centaur." (1990a, 90)

> Precisely because awareness has *differentiated* from (or disidentified from, or transcended) an *exclusive* identification with body, persona, ego, and mind, it can now [in the movement to the centauric level] *integrate* them in a unified fashion, in a new and higher holon with each of them

as junior partners. Physiosphere [the level of material exis-
tence], biosphere [the level of life and life processes], noosphere [the level of mind and thought]—exclusively identified with none of them, therefore capable of integrating
each of them. (1995, 262) (Wilber's italics)

These passages raise the following question: If normal development
includes rather than excludes lower levels *at each stage transition*, why
do we need to wait until the centauric stage to integrate all lower levels?
In normal development, according to Wilber, each psychic level attained
is already an integrated totality including all previous levels; each stage
transition to a new level simply integrates a lesser totality within a
greater totality. If human development follows a normal course, then,
transition from the physiosphere to the biosphere should integrate the
physiosphere within the greater totality of the biosphere, and transition
from the biosphere to the noosphere (the level of the mental ego) should
integrate the physiosphere-biosphere totality within the even greater
totality of the noosphere, and so forth. Nothing would be lost along the
way; there should be no need to wait until after the noospheric or mental-egoic stage to integrate lower levels.

But Wilber says that there *is* such a need. To be consistent, then, he
should acknowledge that human development prior to the centauric level
departs from the pattern of normal development by alienating rather
than integrating transcended structures. We have seen how, in effect, he
acknowledges such alienation in his account of the archaic-unconscious,
which, he says, consists of preegoic structures that are inherently
unavailable to consciousness. He also acknowledges alienation of previously transcended structures more directly in other discussions. For
example, in "The Pre/Trans Fallacy" (1990a, 233–37), Wilber observes
that, since Freud, European society has come to recognize that a pathological split exists between the mind and the body (including sex,
instinct, emotion) and that this split needs to be healed. Wilber states
that this pathological split reflects a miscarriage of development at some
point, but he does not explore the matter further. His point in "The
Pre/Trans Fallacy" is not to explain the derivation of the mind-body split;
it is, rather, to warn against Reichian and neo-Reichian (and even
Rogerian) attempts to mend the split, which attempts, he contends, are
susceptible to pre/trans confusions and to a merely regressive capitula-
tion of mental, civilized life.

Wilber returns to the subject of the mind-body split in *Up from Eden*
(1981, 191–200, 262–65), where he argues that the emergence of the
mental ego carries with it an inherent tendency toward dissociation from
"typhonic realms" (the body, instinct, emotion, nature). The mental ego

suffers from this tendency, he says, because self-awareness, which emerges with the mental ego, is at the same time an awareness of finitude and death, which the mental ego tries to deny by defining itself as pure disembodied thought. According to the discussion in *Up from Eden* (1981), the mental ego's tendency to dissociate itself from typhonic life has been especially pronounced in the West, where it has led to what Wilber, following L. L. Whyte (1950), calls the "European dissociation."

Wilber again takes up the subject of the mind-body split in *Sex, Ecology, Spirituality*, where he suggests that the mind-body split—and the split between consciousness and biophysical life more generally— emerges concomitantly with language:

> For if it is indeed with language that the child can differentiate mind and body, differentiate the noosphere and the biosphere, that *differentiation* (as always) can go too far and result in *dissociation*. The mind does not just transcend and include the body, it represses the body, represses its sensuality, represses its sexuality, represses its rich roots in the biosphere. Repression, in the Freudian (and Jungian) sense, comes into existence only with the "language barrier," with a "no!" carried to extremes. (1995, 222) (Wilber's italics)

According to Wilber, then, both the fear of death and the language barrier render us susceptible to repressing the psychic potentials belonging to the biosphere.

And the inertia of history also plays an important role. In *Sex, Ecology, Spirituality* (1995), Wilber says that the split between the mind and the biosphere has been implicit in the West at least since Plato, that the pathology lurking in this split has been acutely evident since the Enlightenment, and that the mending of this split is the primary task of the postmodern world.

Wilber, then, allows that we suffer from a split between egoic structures and typhonic-biospheric potentials first articulated during preegoic stages. Moreover, he allows that this split is a condition to which we are inherently predisposed, that it has roots going back over two thousand years, and that it has now reached crisis proportions. These acknowledgments suggest that, for Wilber, the mind-body split is deeply enough rooted and sufficiently widespread to count as a statistically prevailing "fact" of the human developmental process.

But is this really Wilber's view? To my knowledge, Wilber never explicitly states that the mind-body split is statistically the rule rather than the exception. If this is his view, though, he should say so. And he should say as well that, because the mind-body split is the rule, human development does not follow the ascending-*inclusive* pattern which he stipulates as the norm. If the mind-body split is a deviation from the ascending-inclusive norm and if, as a rule, human development falls prey to the mind-body split, then it follows that human development itself is a deviation from the ascending-inclusive norm. If the mind-body split is statistically the rule, then it follows that human development is not an example of normal development as Wilber conceives it.

But what if Wilber's view is that, despite being deep-seated and widespread, the mind-body, noospheric-biospheric split is *not* statistically the rule, that it is, rather, a pathology that afflicts only a minority of human beings? Wilber says things which suggest that this might be his view. As we saw in *Up from Eden* (1981), Wilber, following L. L. Whyte, calls the mind-body split the "European dissociation," implying that it does not apply to non-European or non-Western people. And in *Sex, Ecology, Spirituality* (1995) his discussion of the mind-body split focuses exclusively on the Western tradition. Perhaps, then, Wilber believes that most people in the non-Western world do not fall prey to the mind-body split, that they undergo development entirely according to the ascending-inclusive pattern.

Once again, however, if this is Wilber's view, he should say so. And he should say as well, then, that the centauric stage—understood as a stage that integrates previously articulated levels—does not apply to non-Western people.[13] If non-Western people do not succumb to the mind-body split, then they do not need to achieve centauric mind-body integration. If non-Western people avoid the mind-body split, then they remain integrated *as mental egos* and, therefore, do not need to achieve a reintegration with the body, and with typhonic-biospheric life generally, in order to transcend the mental ego.

However, if Wilber does not say that the mind-body split is statistically the rule, neither, to my knowledge, does he say that it is statistically the exception. He seems to straddle these positions without committing himself to either. In acknowledging that the mind-body split is a type of pathology, he leaves it unclear whether it is a pathology that afflicts humankind generally or a pathology that afflicts Europeans exclusively. In allowing that the mind-body split is a deviation from the ascending-inclusive norm, he leaves it unclear whether it is also an exception to the statistical norm.

Wilber needs to clarify his position on this point. Such clarification, however, would create difficulties, for, as we have seen, both available alternatives require concessions that Wilber would rather not make. If, in clarifying his position, Wilber were to say that the mind-body split is statistically the rule, then he would have to concede that human development is not an example of normal development as he conceives it. And if, on the other hand, he were to say that the mind-body split is statistically the exception, then he would have to concede that centauric integration is statistically the exception as well and, therefore, that centauric integration is not a true developmental stage.

The upshot of these considerations is that Wilber *does* acknowledge both a disconnection from psychic potentials active during preegoic stages and a corresponding need to reconnect with those potentials if and when development moves beyond the stage of the mental ego. He strains the consistency of his theory in accepting these points, but he does recognize both points.

This established, the following question arises: How does Wilber conceive the process of reconnection and higher integration? Does he anticipate a return to the pre (or to what *was* pre) on the way to ascending to the trans, as projected by the spiral perspective? Although Wilber acknowledges the therapeutic value of regression in the service of the ego,[14] he most definitely does not believe that a return to the pre (or what *was* pre) is needed in order to ascend to the trans. As we have seen, he believes that movement toward the pre (or what *was* pre) and movement toward the trans proceed in opposite directions without coinciding at any point. The former movement unfolds in an exclusively descending direction toward lower psychic structures; the latter movement unfolds in an exclusively ascending direction toward higher psychic structures. Wilber rejects the possibility that return to the pre (or to what *was* pre) is part of movement toward the trans. Any such return, he says in "The Pre/Trans Fallacy" (1980b), would be a mere U-turn to origins forfeiting the gains of previous development. Or, as he puts it in *Sex, Ecology, Spirituality* (1995), any such return would be a one-way trip on the "regress express" of "retro-Romanticism."

Having thus ruled out the possibility of a descending-then-ascending spiral, Wilber has no choice but to find a *non-descending* route to the higher integration of the centaur. Having rejected the idea that we need to return to psychic potentials that we have left behind if the split in our nature is to be mended, Wilber is left with no alternative but to hypothesize that we are somehow reconnected with these potentials without having to return to them. This is the position he takes in *Sex, Ecology, Spirituality*, where he says that the split in our nature will be mended for us by an Absolute Spirit. He says:

> Does not the Good of Spirit, its Eros [i.e., its telic "pull"], release both Nature and Mind from the torments we have inflicted on them in vain attempts to make them each the

source of infinite value? Does not the Goodness of Spirit, its
Agape [i.e., its outflowing emanation and grace], embrace
both Mind and Nature in a loving caress that heals the self-
inflicted wounds? Does not the refluxing movement of God
and the effluxing movement of the Goddess embrace the
entire Circle of Ascent and Descent? Can we not round out
the original insights and see that Spirit always manifests
in all four quadrants [i.e., the subjective, cultural, func-
tional-social, and material dimensions of existence] equally? Is not Spirit here and now in all its radiant glory, eter-
nally present as every I and every We and every It? Will not
our more adequate interpretations of Spirit facilitate
Spirit's rescue of us? (1995, 522)

Rather than allowing a spiraling path to higher integration, Wilber
believes that we will be rescued from above by an Absolute Spirit. We do
not need to descend in order to ascend because there is an Absolute
Spirit, a Supernatural Savior, to do this for us. Absolute Spirit will
descend upon us with healing grace and draw us up to a higher, integrated transcendence. Absolute Spirit will somehow reconnect consciousness (mind, ego, culture, reason, operational cognition) with
nature (body, body-based energy, instinct, sexual-emotional affect,
mytho-archetypal imagination) in a higher harmonious unity.

Moreover, Absolute Spirit will accomplish this reconnection despite
the fact that, according to Wilber, the body, body-based energy, instinct,
sexual-emotional affect, and mytho-archetypal imagination belong to the
archaic-unconscious and, therefore, are inherently unconscious. If we
remember, Wilber believes that these psychic potentials, even when
unrepressed, are prereflexive and preverbal and, therefore, that they
inherently "tend toward subconsciousness." As Keith Thompson (1995)
observes, then, the mind-body integration of the centaur is for Wilber not
only a *supernatural* integration but also a *miraculous* integration. It is a
supernatural integration because it is accomplished from on high by an
Absolute Spirit, and it is a miraculous integration because it is incomprehensible in terms of Wilber's own conception of the unconscious.

In sum, although Wilber maintains that normal stage transitions
incorporate rather than alienate previous levels and, therefore, ascend to
higher levels without needing to return to earlier levels, he nonetheless
acknowledges both (1) that basic somatic, energic, instinctual, affective,
and imaginal potentials are excluded from the mental ego's consciousness, and (2) that developmental movement beyond the mental ego
requires a mending of a split between consciousness and precisely these
potentials. These two admissions, together with the supernatural-mirac-

ulous account of how the split in the human psyche is to be mended, are serious anomalies that call into question Wilber's structural-hierarchical, linear-ascending perspective as applied to human development.

Turning now to concluding observations, let me repeat that Wilber was once a Jungian. It was only in writing *The Atman Project* (1980a) that he posed the pre/trans question and answered it in a way that committed him to an anti-Jungian, exclusively structural-hierarchical, linear-ascending perspective. Moreover, in formulating the notion of the pre/trans fallacy, Wilber argued that his answer to the pre/trans question is the only logically viable one. He tried to prove that any attempt to bring pre and trans together is to fall prey to either ptf-1 or ptf-2. But Wilber, I believe, is wrong on this crucial point. As I have argued, it is possible that pre and trans states are lower and higher developmental expressions of the same nonegoic potentials. This might not be true in all instances, but it is at least possible in some instances (no logical error is committed in thinking so). Wilber made an invaluable contribution to transpersonal theory in pointing out that pre and trans states, despite similarities, are widely different and should not be confused with each other, either by way of reduction of the trans to the pre or elevation of the pre to the trans. It is a serious mistake to conflate pre and trans states. It is a fallacy to infer structural identity from phenomenological similarity. But inferring structural identity from phenomenological similarity is only one kind of pre/trans fallacy. There is another kind—inferring structural dissimilarity from phenomenological difference. It is equally a fallacy to argue that pre and trans states, in differing in phenomenologically crucial ways, must for that reason be expressions of two different and widely dissimilar sets of psychic structures, the many phenomenological similarities between pre and trans states notwithstanding. Wilber, it seems, commits just this fallacy—which, following his abbreviation scheme, can be called *ptf-3*.

Wilber, in awakening to the many subtle and insidious forms of ptf-1 and ptf-2, understandably wanted to modify his own thinking to avoid these errors, and so he revised *The Atman Project* (1980a) as he was preparing it for publication. But Wilber, I suggest, went too far; he substituted one extreme for another. Not wanting to collapse similarity into structural identity, he made the mistake of stretching difference into structural dissimilarity. He fallaciously inferred a structural conclusion from a developmental premise. He fallaciously inferred dissimilar pre and trans psychic structures from differing pre and trans developmental states. He committed ptf-3.

Pre/trans fallacies, as Wilber has shown, have serious practical consequences. In misconceiving the trans as the pre, ptf-1 runs the risk of repressing or otherwise forfeiting the trans; and in misconceiving the pre as the trans, ptf-2 runs the risk of regressing—in a merely descending, U-turn way—to the pre. What about ptf-3? What are its practical consequences? The answer, I believe, is that ptf-3 may have the same consequences as ptf-1. Notice that I am saying that ptf-3 *may* have the same consequences as ptf-1, not that it does so *as a matter of fact*. For if the conclusion of ptf-3 is true—namely, that pre and trans states are expressions of two different sets of psychic structures—then ptf-3, although still a fallacy, does not incur the risk of forfeiting the trans. In this case the trans would lie entirely "above" the ego and not at all "below" it, such that movement to the trans would properly be a purely ascending movement, a movement to higher ground that does not need to retrace old ground. If, on the other hand, the conclusion of ptf-3 is false (as I believe it is), then ptf-3 does incur the risk of forfeiting the trans. For if, contrary to the conclusion of ptf-3, pre and trans are (in at least some instances) developmental expressions of the same psychic potentials, then it follows that a refusal to yield to what *was* pre is at the same time a closing of oneself to what *could be* trans. In this case, one *does* need to retrace old ground, and refusing to do so has the consequence of forfeiting the possibility of attaining higher ground.

In *Sex, Ecology, Spirituality* (1995), Wilber distinguishes between two types of false transcenders: (regressive) Descenders and (repressive) Ascenders.[15] Descenders are those who, having fallen prey to ptf-2, yield to regression in the false belief that, in doing so, they are achieving transcendence. Ascenders, in contrast, are antiworldly spiritualists (e.g., Gnostics) who believe that to rise to the trans one must distance oneself from everything pre (or everything that *was* pre): nature, body, instinct, desire. Wilber, of course, believes that Jung is a Descender. In "The Pre/Trans Fallacy" (1980b), as we have seen, he charges Jung with ptf-2 and, therefore, with misconceiving transcendence in merely descending, regressive terms. I have already explained why I believe these charges against Jung are unwarranted.

Ironically, Wilber may himself be an Ascender. Again, I use a weak *may* rather than a strong *is* because Wilber might be right in holding that psychic potentials active during preegoic stages are exclusively pre and, therefore, that we should resist any temptation to yield to such potentials in aspiring to the trans. If, however, as I have argued, pre and trans are (in at least some instances) lower and higher developmental expressions of the same psychic potentials, then it follows that to resist what *was* pre in aspiring to the trans is in effect to do exactly what Ascenders do: it is to reach for the trans while denying the very bases of transegoic experience. It is to attempt to get to heaven by refusing to stand on the ground.

Notes

1. Sean Kelly and Donald Rothberg read earlier versions of this paper and guided me through the revision process. They gave me excellent advice on matters of both substance and style. They also suggested the title. I greatly appreciate their help.

2. Following Wilber, I shall frequently shorten *preegoic* and *transegoic* to *pre* and *trans*, respectively.

3. Wilber's conception of development is not completely linear. He (1990c) holds that each developmental ascent to a higher rung of the psychic ladder involves a death-then-rebirth loop or mini-spiral: movement to a higher rung begins with a disidentifying differentiation from the structures of the rung being transcended (death) and then proceeds to a reappropriating integration and reorganization of those structures within the higher structures of the rung being attained (rebirth). Wilber's conception of development, then, is not a "flat" linear conception. The overall course of development, however, remains linear and ascending. For although there is a loop or mini-spiral at each stage transition, there is no return to structures of previously transcended levels on the way to higher levels.

4. The centauric stage is not a transegoic stage. Wilber places it right at the boundary between egoic stages and transegoic stages. Nevertheless, the centauric stage lies beyond the stage of the mental ego, and for that reason Wilber is able to match it as a higher form of mind-body unity with the lower mind-body unity of the body-ego.

5. In "Structure, Stage, and Self" (1990b), Wilber distinguishes between basic structures and transitional or replacement structures. Basic structures are *constitutional* structures which, as such, belong to the psyche inherently and permanently, whether in a potential-enfolded or actual-unfolded way. Transition or replacement structures, in contrast, are *developmental* structures which, as such, are merely stage specific. Transition structures are "the way the world is experienced" through the basic structures of a psychic level and, therefore, unlike the basic structures of that level, are not preserved when development proceeds to a higher psychic level. Applying this distinction, it seems that most of the matching structures listed here would be considered basic structures by Wilber. Preegoic magic and mythic thinking are exceptions. In "Structure, Stage, and Self" Wilber explains that magic and mythic thinking are merely stage-specific world views, the way the world looks when there are symbolic images but no concepts proper (magic) and when there are conceptual representations but no ability to perform formal operations (mythic thinking). Although magic and mythic thinking are transition structures, the cognitive abilities on which they are based—namely, the ability to form symbolic images (magic) and preoperational and early concrete operational cognition (mythic thinking)—are, according to Wilber, basic structures.

6. Wilber uses the word *structure*—or, more precisely, the expression *basic structure* (see note 5)—to refer to all native psychic resources, whether egoic or nonegoic, whether somatic, dynamic, instinctual, affective, imaginal, volitional, conceptual-operational, supersensory, or spiritual. Since my thinking is grounded in the psychoanalytic, depth-psychological tradition, I prefer a basic terminological distinction between *ego functions* and *nonegoic potentials*. Ego functions are the operations by which the ego unifies, organizes, and exercises control over experience. Principal ego functions are synthesis, reality testing, self-reflection, impulse control, and ego-active thinking (e.g., sensorimotor and operational cognition). In contrast to these ego functions, non-

egoic potentials are dynamic, spontaneously active resources lying beyond the ego's immediate domain and range of control. Principal nonegoic potentials are dynamism (libido, psychic energy, spiritual power), somatosensory sensitivity, conation, feeling, and creative, autosymbolic imagination. All of these nonegoic potentials are semi-independent in relation to the ego. The ego never gains the same kind of control over them that it exercises over its own functions.

7. Fallacious inferences do not always lead to false conclusions. Accordingly, in saying that Wilber's answer to the pre/trans question is the product of a faulty inference, I am not saying that it is false *for that reason*. I do believe that his answer to the pre/trans question is false, but not because it is a product of a pre/trans fallacy. It is false, I believe, because it unnecessarily doubles the number of nonegoic psychic levels and, as we shall see, because it fails to provide an adequate account of the mind-body relationship.

8. The parenthetical qualification "(or what *was* pre)" is necessary to indicate that psychic potentials first articulated during preegoic stages may not, as Wilber believes, be inherently or constitutionally preegoic. It leaves open the possibility that such potentials may, later in life, be the bases of transegoic states and stages. I shall continue to use the expression "pre (or what *was* pre)" and similar constructions—for example, "what *was* pre *could be* trans"—to make sure that this possibility, which is easily obscured, is kept in mind.

9. The term *U-turn* is borrowed from Wilber (1982).

10. As Jung realized, the notion of a deep restorative regression is a timeless archetype portrayed not only in images of being swallowed and then disgorged by a beast dwelling in oceanic depths (the night sea journey [see Frobenius (1904)]) but also in such images as those of the hero's journey into the underworld, the alchemical reduction of base metal (the ego) to prime matter and transubstantiation into gold, and the dismemberment and rememberment, death and rebirth of shamans, saviors, and gods.

11. More precisely, new and higher structures are articulated without losing touch with previously articulated *basic* structures. See note 5 for Wilber's distinction between basic structures (which are preserved in stage transition) and transitional or replacement structures (which are not preserved).

12. The term *mytho-archetypal* is used here and later to refer to the Jungian archetypal imagination *as interpreted by Wilber*. I disagree with Wilber's interpretation of Jungian archetypes as exclusively archaic (magical and mythical), preegoic images. This disagreement aside, however, my purpose here is simply to avoid terminological confusion by fixing the term *mytho-archetypal* in the manner indicated.

13. Wilber usually describes the centauric stage as a stage not only of higher mind-body integration but also of *vision-logic*, that is, of holistic, dialectical thought. Unlike mind-body integration, which is a union of structures that have already been articulated, vision-logic is a new, previously unarticulated structure. Accordingly, if, for consistency's sake, Wilber were to drop centauric integration from the developmental agenda, he would not, in doing so, have to drop vision-logic.

14. Speaking of regression in the service of the ego, Wilber says: "In these instances [when stage transition represses and alienates rather than integrates previously articulated levels], as Freud demonstrated, therapy involves in some sense, a reintegration of the dissociated aspects, a re-membering of components previously dismembered" (1990a, 233). Also, in *Sex, Ecology, Spirituality*, after saying that the noosphere (or mental

ego) can repress and alienate the biosphere, he says that the cure for this is regression in the service of the ego: "Thus the cure: regression in service of a higher reintegration—a regression that allows evolution to move forward more harmoniously by healing and wholing a previously alienated holon" (1995, 105).

15. The parenthetical qualifications are inserted because descent and ascent can be understood in an exclusively structural (rather than developmental) way. For Wilber, one can descend nonregressively to any psychic level that has already been developmentally transcended (provided that the level was transcended in a nonrepressive, inclusive manner). Following such a descent, one can ascend back to the psychic level from which the descent began. This kind of descent and ascent is simply a shifting back and forth between structural levels already achieved. It has nothing to do with developmental regress or progress and, therefore, nothing to do with strategies for transcendence.

References

Frobenius, L. 1904. *Das Zeitalter des Sonnengotes (The age of the sun god)*. Berlin: G. Reimer.

Thompson, K. 1995. On the threshold of global consciousness. [Review of K. Wilber, *Sex, ecology, spirituality: The spirit of evolution*.] *San Francisco Chronicle*, 9 July.

Walsh, R., and F. Vaughan. 1994. The worldview of Ken Wilber. *Journal of Humanistic Psychology* 34 (2): 6-21.

Washburn, M. 1994. *Transpersonal psychology in psychoanalytic perspective*. Albany: State University of New York Press.

———. 1995. *The ego and the dynamic ground*. Rev. ed. Albany: State University of New York Press. (First edition published in 1988.)

Whyte, L. 1950. *The next development in man*. New York: New American Library.

Wilber, K. 1977. *The spectrum of consciousness*. Wheaton, Ill.: Quest Books.

———. 1980a. *The Atman project*. Wheaton, Ill.: Quest Books.

———. 1980b. The pre/trans fallacy. *ReVision* 3 (Fall): 51-72. Reprinted in Wilber (1990a).

———. 1981. *Up from Eden*. Garden City, N.Y.: Anchor Press/Doubleday.

———. 1982. Odyssey: A personal inquiry into humanistic and transpersonal psychology. *Journal of Humanistic Psychology* 22 (1): 57-90.

———. 1990a. *Eye to eye: The quest for the new paradigm*. Rev. ed. Boston: Shambhala. (First edition published in 1983.)

——— 1990b. Structure, stage, and self. In Wilber (1990a). [Originally published in different form in 1981 under the title Ontogenetic development: Two fundamental patterns. *Journal of Transpersonal Psychology* 13 (1): 33-58.]

———. 1990c. Two patterns of transcendence: A reply to Washburn. *Journal of Humanistic Psychology* 30 (3): 113-36.

———. 1995. *Sex, ecology, spirituality: The spirit of evolution*. Boston: Shambhala.

5

Stanislav Grof

Perhaps no one has given a richer map of the varieties of states of consciousness than Stanislav Grof. A psychiatrist with over forty years of experience of research into nonordinary states of consciousness, Grof is one of the founders and chief theoreticians of transpersonal psychology.

He was born in Prague, Czechoslovakia, where he also received his scientific training, earning an M.D. from the Charles University School of Medicine and a Ph.D. in medicine from the Czechoslovakian Academy of Sciences. His early research on the clinical uses of psychoactive drugs was conducted at the Psychiatric Research Institute in Prague, where he was principal investigator of a program exploring the therapeutic potential of LSD and other psychedelics.

Grof began his research as a classical Freudian, with the hope that psychedelic substances might serve to accelerate the psychoanalytic process. The unparalleled richness and intensity of the experiences which surfaced during the LSD sessions, however, soon convinced him of the theoretical shortcomings of Freud's model of the psyche and of the materialistic and mechanistic worldview which it reflects. The new map of the psyche developed by Grof, which emerged out of these investigations, has come to include three distinct domains: 1) the (Freudian) personal or biographical unconscious; 2) the transpersonal unconscious (which includes Jung's more restricted notion of the archetypal or collective unconscious); and 3) the perinatal unconscious which, centering around the transformative potential of the experiences of biological and symbolic birth and death, seems to mediate between the personal and the transpersonal.

In 1967, Grof was invited to be Clinical and Research Fellow at Johns Hopkins University in Baltimore. After completion of this two-year fellowship, he remained in the United States and continued his investigations as Chief of Psychiatric Research at the Maryland Psychiatric Research Center and as Assistant Professor of Psychiatry at the Henry Phipps Clinic at Johns Hopkins. In 1973, he became Scholar-in-Residence at the Esalen Institute in Big Sur, California, where he lived until 1987. During his years at Esalen, he devoted himself to writing books and articles, giving lectures and seminars and, with his wife Christina, developing "Holotropic Breathwork," an innovative experiential therapy which combines deep, accelerated breathing with music, focused bodywork, mandala drawing, and group sharing, within a safe, supportive, and sacred environment. Grof is also the founding president of the International Transpersonal

Association (ITA), for which he has organized large international conferences during the last two decades in the United States, India, Australia, Czechoslovakia, and Brazil.

At present, Grof is a professor at the California Institute of Integral Studies (CIIS) in San Francisco, in the Philosophy, Cosmology, and Consciousness Program. He continues to write and conduct training seminars for professionals in Holotropic Breathwork and transpersonal psychology ("Grof Transpersonal Training"). Grof's work thus offers a practical, therapeutic approach, honed over many years, which complements and offers the possibility of testing the implications of his theoretical work. He is perhaps unique in the field of transpersonal psychology in connecting practice and theory which are both so highly developed.

Grof's contribution to this book is an extension of his earlier response to Wilber's work (see Grof's Beyond the Brain, *pp. 132-37). To begin, he draws attention to what he considers a peculiar blind spot in Wilber's otherwise detailed and comprehensive theory, namely Wilber's lack of recognition of the significance of pre- and perinatal experiences for the theory and practice of psychology, psychiatry, and psychotherapy. In Grof's view, Wilber fails to understand that the perinatal domain is of a completely different logical type than subsequent developmental stages. Grof stresses that the perinatal is not limited to the fetal stage, but rather encompasses patterns of psychospiritual transformation which run through the entire spectrum of human development. Grof also believes that Wilber trivializes the importance of biological death and of life-threatening situations—beginning with birth itself—by assimilating them to the "release" which must accompany each movement up the spectrum of consciousness.*

Grof goes on to argue that, without a sufficient appreciation of the significance of birth and death, Wilber's theory is incapable of making sense of essential features of psychopathology, such as the linkage of sexuality and aggression, which Grof associates with traumatic residues of the birth process. Finally, Grof takes issue with what he takes to be Wilber's overly linear interpretation of regression as involved exclusively with a return to "prepersonal" structures. Grof's own extensive experience with nonordinary states of consciousness, as well as existing accounts from the world's spiritual traditions, suggest that regression to the perinatal domain often constitutes the experiential prerequisite for access to the transpersonal. In contrast to Wilber's strict adherence to the idea of the pre/trans fallacy, Grof proposes a more complex model of the psyche in which the personal and the transpersonal, the biological and the spiritual, coexist in a state of interpenetration.

Further Readings

Grof, C., and S. Grof. 1990. *The stormy search for the self.* Los Angeles: Tarcher.

Grof, S. 1975. *Realms of the human unconscious: Observations from LSD research.* New York: Viking Press.

_____. 1980. *LSD psychotherapy.* Pomona, Calif.: Hunter House.

_____. 1985. *Beyond the brain: Birth, death, and transcendence in psychotherapy.* Albany: State University of New York Press.

_____. 1988. *The adventure of self-discovery: Dimensions of consciousness and new perspectives in psychotherapy and inner exploration*. Albany: State University of New York Press.

Grof, S., and C. Grof, 1980. *Beyond death: The gates of consciousness*. London: Thames & Hudson.

Grof, S., and J. Halifax. 1977. *The human encounter with death*. New York: E.P. Dutton.

Grof, S., and H. Bennett. 1992. *The holotropic mind*. San Francisco: HarperCollins.

Ken Wilber's Spectrum Psychology:
Observations from Clinical
Consciousness Research

WHEN ADDRESSING THE WORK OF A THEORETICIAN WHOSE pioneering work reaches the scope and quality achieved by Ken Wilber, even a critical essay has to begin with compliments and words of appreciation. In a series of books beginning with his *Spectrum of Consciousness* (Wilber 1977), Ken has produced an extraordinary work of highly creative synthesis of data drawn from a vast variety of areas and disciplines, ranging from psychology, anthropology, sociology, mythology, and comparative religion, through linguistics, philosophy, and history, to cosmology, quantum-relativistic physics, biology, evolutionary theory, and systems theory. His knowledge of the literature is truly encyclopedic, his analytical mind systematic and incisive, and the clarity of his logic remarkable. The impressive scope, comprehensive nature, and intellectual rigor of Ken's work have helped to make it a widely acclaimed and highly influential theory of transpersonal psychology.

However, for a theory of such importance, it is not sufficient to integrate material from many different ancient and modern sources into a system that shows inner logical cohesion. While logical consistency certainly is a valuable prerequisite, a viable theory has to have an additional property that is equally, if not more, important. It is generally accepted among scientists that a system of propositions is an acceptable theory if, and only if, its conclusions are in agreement with observable facts (Frank 1957). Since speculations concerning consciousness, the human psyche, and spiritual experiences represent the cornerstone of Ken's conceptual framework, it is essential to test their theoretical adequacy and practical relevance against clinical data. Ken himself does not have any clinical experience, and the primary sources of his data have been his extensive reading and the experiences from his personal spiritual practice. For this reason, evaluating his ideas in the light of actual experiences and observations from transpersonal therapy and from modern consciousness research seems particularly important and necessary.

My own background and approach have been almost polar opposites to Ken's and might thus serve as a useful complement to his theoretical work. For almost four decades, my primary interest has been clinical work exploring the healing and heuristic potential of nonordinary states of consciousness (NOSC). Whatever theoretical writing I have done over the years has been based primarily on the reports of the people I have worked with. An additional important source of information and inspiration has been my own experiences of nonordinary states induced by psychedelics and various nondrug means. The choice of professional literature I have studied has been strongly determined by observations from my clinical work and the need to put them into a larger conceptual framework.

The observations and data on which this paper is based come from two major sources: approximately two decades of clinical psychedelic research with LSD and other psychoactive substances, and another twenty years of work with holotropic breathwork, a powerful nondrug therapeutic method that I have developed jointly with my wife, Christina. It combines faster breathing, evocative music, and a specific form of energetic release work. The subjects in the psychedelic research projects were psychiatric patients with various emotional and psychosomatic disorders, alcoholics, drug addicts, terminal cancer patients, and "normal" volunteers—mental health professionals, scientists, artists, clergy, and students. The breathwork sessions have been conducted in the context of a long-term training program of professionals and of experiential workshops with a broad cross-section of the general population. In addition to material from psychedelic and holotropic breathwork sessions, I am also drawing in this paper on my observations from work with individuals undergoing spontaneous mystical experiences and episodes of psychospiritual crises ("spiritual emergencies") (Grof and Grof 1990).

Over the years, Ken Wilber and I have exchanged some ideas, which involved both compliments and critical comments about our respective theories. During this time, the thinking of both of us has undergone certain changes and developments, as can be expected in an area as rich and complex as mapping the human psyche and exploring the dimensions of consciousness. I first addressed the similarities and differences between Ken's spectrum psychology and my own observations and theoretical constructs more than a decade ago. In my book *Beyond the Brain: Birth, Death, and Transcendence in Psychotherapy* (Grof 1985), I dedicated a special section to Ken's spectrum psychology, in which I briefly described where my own findings agreed and disagreed with Ken's theories.

In my critical comments, I addressed what I saw as logical inconsistencies in Ken's conceptual system (omission of the pre- and perinatal period and misrepresentation of the problem of death) and the lack of correspondence between his conjectures and the facts of clinical observation (concerning the dynamics of spiritual development, the nature of psychopathology, and the strategy of psychotherapy). In what follows, I will elaborate on the comments I made at the time and focus on a few additional areas. I will also reflect on Ken's extensive written reply to my criticism that has appeared in the notes to his recent book *Sex, Ecology, Spirituality: The Spirit of Evolution* (Wilber 1995).

OMISSION OF THE PRE- AND PERINATAL DOMAIN IN SPECTRUM PSYCHOLOGY

My main reservation about Ken's comprehensive and detailed theoretical system concerns what I perceive as his surprising conceptual blind spot in relation to the role and significance of prenatal existence and biological birth for the theory and practice of psychiatry, psychology, and psychotherapy. The discovery of the psychological and psychospiritual importance of these two periods of human development is one of the most important contributions of experiential psychotherapy and modern consciousness research to psychology. The observations in this area have been so impressive and consistent that they have inspired the development of pre- and perinatal psychology, including regular international meetings and a rapidly growing body of literature. These observations have been so convincing that they have profoundly influenced the actual birthing practices and postnatal care of many open-minded obstetricians and pediatricians. In view of these facts, I found it very surprising that Ken, with his meticulous and comprehensive approach, has completely ignored the vast amount of data from both modern and ancient sources suggesting the paramount psychological significance of prenatal experiences and of the trauma of birth, as well as their relationship to spirituality. This bias is evident in his writings focusing on cosmology, human evolution, developmental psychology, psychopathology, and psychotherapy.

Ken's description of the evolution of consciousness of an individual begins with the pleromatic stage (the undifferentiated consciousness of the newborn) and continues through the uroboric, typhonic, verbal-membership, and mental-egoic levels to the centauric stage. He refers to this progression, from the newborn infant to the adult with fully integrated functioning of the ego, persona, shadow, and body, as the *outward arc*. According to Ken, at the evolutionary stage of centaur begins the truly spiritual development, or the *inward arc*, that takes the individual to the lower and higher regions of the subtle and causal realms and finally to the boundless radiance of Formless Consciousness and the ultimate unity with the Absolute (Wilber 1980).

In his account of cosmogenesis or consciousness involution, Ken closely follows the highly culture-specific archetypal map from the Tibetan *Book of the Dead, Bardo Thodol* (Evans-Wentz 1960), rather than creating a more general and universal description that would be applicable in any cultural and historical context. His account of cosmogenesis thus begins with the ultimate consciousness, the immaculate and luminous Dharmakaya, proceeds through the specific visions of the Tibetan bardo realms, and ends—like the *Bardo Thodol*—with the moment of conception when the individual who has missed all chances for spiritual liberation is facing another incarnation. This is perfectly logical and understandable for the Tibetan text, which describes the experiences in the intermediate state between death and the next incarnation. However, it results in a major logical gap in Ken's system that allegedly portrays the entire cosmic cycle of involution and evolution of consciousness.

By ending the process of the involution of consciousness at the moment of conception and beginning the account of consciousness evolution with the undifferentiated pleromatic experience of the newborn, Ken leaves out the entire embryonic development between conception and the moment of birth. I find this to be an astonishing omission for a system that is otherwise worked out with meticulous attention to detail and has received much acclaim for its logical cohesion and clarity of thinking. Even if the fetus had no conscious awareness during these periods and the pre- and perinatal events were not recorded in the brain (a position taken, increasingly implausibly, by academic psychiatry), this omission would leave a strange gap in Ken's cosmic cycle. After all, we are talking here about a period of nine months of embryonic life during which the fetus undergoes a complex process of development from the fertilized ovum to a fully formed and differentiated organism. This is then followed by many hours or even a few days of a potentially life-threatening process of biological birth in which the fetus experiences a radical transformation from an aquatic organism to an air-breathing one.

However, there exists important clinical and experimental evidence indicating that the fetus might be conscious during these nine months, that pre- and perinatal events play a critical role in the individual's psychological history, and that the memories of these early experiences are available for conscious recall and reliving. The memory of birth represents an important reservoir of difficult emotions and physical sensations that can contribute later in life to the development of various forms of emotional and psychosomatic disorders. Reliving and integrating pre-

and perinatal traumas can have very beneficial effects; it can result in healing and profound psychospiritual transformation. Therapists working with powerful forms of experiential psychotherapies, such as primal therapy, psychedelic work, rebirthing, and holotropic breathwork, or with individuals in psychospiritual crises, see these phenomena daily in their practices. Reliving of such events often is photographically accurate and occurs even in people who have no intellectual knowledge about their birth. The fact that it is often possible to verify various details of these experiences leaves little doubt that they represent authentic memories (Grof 1987).

In addition, episodes of this kind are often accompanied by various specific physical manifestations that can be noticed by an external observer. The postures and movements of the body, arms, and legs, as well as the rotations, flections, and deflections of the head, can accurately recreate the mechanics of a particular type of delivery, even in people without elementary obstetric knowledge. Many details of such experiences can be confirmed if good birth records or reliable personal witnesses are available. In his recent book, Ken calls this evidence "controversial" (Wilber 1994, 585), but the practitioners of experiential therapies would certainly disagree.

The fact that the psychological importance of prenatal and perinatal events has not been accepted by mainstream psychiatry reflects the rigidity of deeply ingrained beliefs rather than the ambiguity of clinical observations. The most important of these is the conviction that the brain of the newborn is not capable of registering the traumatic impact of birth because the neurons in its cortex are not fully myelinized. This is not a well-substantiated scientific fact, but a very problematic assumption that is in conflict not only with observations from experiential therapy, but also with rich experimental data concerning prenatal sensitivity of the fetus and its capacity to learn (Chamberlain 1988; Tomatis 1991). In any case, it is hard to imagine that hours of dramatic and often life-threatening experiences during biological birth would be psychologically less important than the immediately following pleromatic experiences of the newborn that receive much of Ken's attention and have an important role in his scheme. We will return to this problem later in the section discussing Ken's ideas about psychopathology.

In addition to leaving out the entire pre- and perinatal periods from his cosmic cycle of the involution and evolution of consciousness and ignoring the extensive evidence from modern experiential psychotherapies indicating the great psychological significance of these periods, Ken also fails to acknowledge the pioneering work of Otto Rank (1929), who emphasized the paramount importance of the intrauterine experience and of the trauma of birth. Rank is the only major figure in the history of depth psychology whom Ken treats in this way. Without any explanation, he neither incorporates Rank's work concerning the birth trauma into his scheme of spectrum psychology, nor subjects it to critical analysis.

In addition to ignoring all the clinical and experimental data concerning the prenatal and perinatal periods, Ken shows the same selective bias in regard to spiritual sources. Since he draws so exclusively on Tibetan sources in the discussion of cosmogenesis, it is particularly striking that he does not pay any attention to Tibetan texts that discuss in detail the challenges of prenatal development and birth (Sgam.po.pa 1971, 63–66). In Vajrayana, the intrauterine state is actually described as one of the six intermediate states or bardos (Evans-Wentz 1960, 102). And the Buddha himself made specific references to the trauma of birth as a major source of human suffering.

Ken responded to my critical comments concerning his omission of the pre- and perinatal period in the copious notes to his *Sex, Ecology, Spirituality: The Spirit of Evolution* (Wilber 1995, 585–88, 741–63). We have had some exchange about this issue over the years, but this was the first time that he formulated his reaction in written form. He expresses his amazement about the difficulties that various people perceived in the task of "integration of the Grof and Wilber models." According to him, such integration is actually a relatively simple matter. He points out that it was actually this lack of perceived difficulty, together with complications in his personal life, that prevented him from making the necessary adjustments in his theory at least ten years earlier.

Opening the discussion on this subject, Ken makes a vague reference to a "large body of theory and (controversial) evidence for the intrauterine state and the birth process (and birth trauma)" [Ken's parentheses]. And then, "having simply allowed that some of this evidence could indeed be genuine," he creates for this entire domain a new category in his developmental scheme, fulcrum 0 (F-0) preceding the fulcrum of the pleromatic stage (F-1) and the six subsequent ones (Wilber 1995, 585–88). At this point, I will not argue with Ken whether the evidence for the psychological importance of the birth trauma deserves to be considered controversial. I have addressed this problem earlier and will return to it in another context. Instead, I will briefly describe and discuss his proposal. He suggests that the new fulcrum shows the same general features as any other fulcrum, namely:

1. An initial state of undifferentiation or indissociation (in this case the prenatal state)

2. A period of intense and often difficult differentiation (the birth process/trauma itself)

3. A period of postdifferentiation and (post-uterine) consolidation and integration, in preparation for the next round of dif-
ferentiation/integration (F-1)

The extensive and complex experiential patterns associated with the consecutive stages of biological birth that I call *basic perinatal matrices* (BPMs) would thus simply become three subphases of fulcrum 0, with BPM II and BPM III both subsumed into a single subphase (subphase 2). BPM I would thus be subphase 1 of F-0, reflecting the oceanic indissociation experience of the fetus, both in its undisturbed and disturbed aspects. BPM II would be the beginning of subphase 2, or the differentiation process, that involves "cosmic engulfment" and "no-exit" hellish pressure. BPM III would be the later stage of subphase 2, with the beginning of the expulsion from the womb,"volcanic" ecstasy, sadomasochistic pleasure/pain, experience of dismemberment, etc. And, finally, BPM IV would be subphase 3, the postpartum neonatal state, during which the child must integrate its new sense of separation from the mother. At the same time, this is the beginning of the pleromatic F-1, during which the infant with its new self-sense still cannot distinguish its own self-boundaries from those of the physical world around it.

As much as I appreciate Ken's acknowledgment of the existence of the perinatal level of the unconscious and its inclusion in his developmental scheme, I feel that the ad hoc addition of another fulcrum (F-O) and the fusion of two perinatal matrices into one of its subphases do not do justice to the importance of this domain. Although it might render an impressive graphic scheme that pleases the eye and satisfies the need for logical order, it fails to grasp the real parameters of the perinatal experience. The easy solution that Ken offers is in fundamental conflict with the facts of observation. First of all, the second and third matrix are related to two phases of birth that are in many respects radically different from each other, both physiologically and experientially. For this reason, lumping them together into one subphase of F-0 makes little sense.

In addition, the urgency and extreme intensity of birth experiences and their association with a serious threat to body integrity and to survival of the organism put them into a completely different category than the stages of postnatal development. A radical transition, from an aquatic form of life whose needs are being continually satisfied by placental circulation to the extreme emotional and physical stress of the birth struggle and then to a radically new existence as an air-breathing organism, is an event of paramount significance that reaches all the way to the cellular level. Even a relatively normal birth without complications is certainly a process of an entirely different order than learning to speak or developing an ego. This is clearly evident from the amount of time it

takes in experiential therapy to bring the perinatal material into consciousness and integrate it. And a difficult birth and poor postnatal circumstances can constitute a profound trauma that colors the entire life
history of the individual.

Much of what has been said above is related primarily to prenatal
and perinatal events occurring in the context of the early psychobiological evolution of the individual. It seems that much of Ken's initial hesi-
tation to include these stages in his scheme was based on his uncertainty whether the events from this time are consciously experienced by the
fetus and/or recorded in the memory banks. However, this is only one
aspect of the problem. Perinatal matrices are not defined as stages of the
psychobiological evolution of the fetus, but as experiential patterns that
occur in self-exploration of adults involving NOSC. They are thus primarily related to psychospiritual evolution and only secondarily serve as
indirect evidence for the importance of the early psychobiological events.
In other words, they are much more than simple records of the original
fetal experience. Besides containing distinct fetal elements, they also
function as an important interface with the archetypal and historical
domains of the collective unconscious and with species consciousness.
For this reason, they cannot be simply reduced to a fetal fulcrum. I will
return to this point later in this article.

THE PSYCHOLOGICAL IMPORTANCE
OF BIOLOGICAL DEATH

Another major difference between my own observations and Ken's
model involves the psychological importance of biological death, both in
connection with the perinatal level and independently from it. In his
early writings, Sigmund Freud expressed the opinion that the problem
of death is irrelevant for psychology, since our unconscious does not know
linear time and thus does not recognize and acknowledge our mortality
and impermanence. However, later clinical observations related to the
phenomena that seemed to challenge his concept of the "pleasure principle" led him to the conclusion that it is impossible to have a viable psychological system without including the phenomenon of death as an
essential element (Freud 1955).

This realization represented an important turning point in Freud's
theoretical speculations. To account for psychopathological disorders
that seemed to defy the "pleasure principle" (such as sadomasochism,
automutilation, and violent suicide), he formulated in the last two
decades of his life a psychology that was significantly different from his
early writings. In his final version of psychoanalysis, he described the
psyche as a system reflecting the conflict between two opposing forces,

the sexual instinct, Libido or Eros, and the death instinct, Destrudo or Thanatos (Freud 1964).

According to a statistical survey conducted by Brun (1953), 94 percent of psychoanalysts refused to follow Freud in this final stage of his thinking. The observations from NOSC clearly show that Freud was essentially correct in his assessment of the importance of death for psychology, even though they do not specifically support his understanding of Thanatos. These new findings show that what Freud refers to as Thanatos is not a biological instinct, but a psychological force reflecting the individual's encounters with life-threatening events from postnatal biography and, particularly, from the perinatal period. These connections make the element of biological death essential for the understanding of the disorders that defy Freud's "pleasure principle" and a variety of other psychological phenomena (Grof 1985).

In addition, the psychological representation of death has deeper sources in the archetypal domain of the collective unconscious in the form of eschatological deities and motifs and also plays an important role in karmic experiences. Freud saw Thanatos as a biological instinct and did not recognize the deep psychological connection between death and the trauma of birth. He also refused to accept Jung's concept of the collective unconscious and its archetypal dynamics. And, as a materialist, he wanted to anchor psychology deeply in biology and was not ready to give serious attention to the karmic dimension of the psyche. However, in his general awareness of the psychological importance of death and in his (unfortunately superficial and fleeting) recognition of the possible significance of birth, Freud was far ahead of his followers, whose writings Ken uses as his main sources.

Ken does not simply ignore Freud's later writings as do the majority of Freud's followers. He actually keeps the term *Thanatos*, but changes the meaning of this concept in a way that dilutes and trivializes Freud's insights. For Freud, Thanatos was a brutal force that operates throughout our life and finally reduces us back to the inorganic state. For Ken, Thanatos is a relatively meek evolutionary mechanism associated with the transformation of consciousness from one level to the next. It is instrumental in the process of abandoning one developmental stage and moving to the next one (Wilber 1980). This involves generally a long and slow transition that is part of natural evolution, a kind of psychological equivalent of the first and second teething. The problems that might occur during these developmental transitions have a different degree of relevance than acute emergency situations that threaten the individual's survival or body integrity.

In an extensive critique of the way various theorists use the term *Thanatos* and of the resulting confusion (Wilber 1983), Ken emphasizes the importance of distinguishing between biological death and the "ego-death," or "Death" and "death." However, he himself entirely misses the psychological importance of the experiences associated with life-threatening events and makes no distinction between "dying" to a developmental level and *the experiences associated with biological death*. He equates dying with abandoning the exclusive identification with a particular structure of consciousness, which makes it possible to transcend that structure and move to the next level. This mechanism would thus apply to such extended and gradual processes as learning to speak and developing an ego.

The situation is further confounded by the fact that, in another context, Ken also sees Thanatos as the force that drives the involution of consciousness and thus cosmogenesis (Wilber 1980). In the outward and inward arc of consciousness evolution, Thanatos is, according to Ken, the principle that dissolves the structures associated with various forms and levels of what he calls *the Atman project*. It is the principle that is responsible for abandoning substitute selves and substitute gratifications and mediates the movement toward the Absolute. However, in the context of cosmogenesis, Ken equates Thanatos with the force that drives consciousness away from the reunion with the Dharmakaya and into incarnation. Here it thus allegedly prevents the only true gratification there is, which is the union with the Absolute, and drives consciousness in the direction of unsatisfactory substitute gratifications that characterize the Atman project.

The experiences of encounter with biological death receive no attention at all in Ken's spectrum psychology. This is in sharp contrast with clinical observations from deep experiential self-exploration and psychotherapy (primal therapy, rebirthing, holotropic breathwork, psychedelic therapy, and work with people in psychospiritual crises). In all these situations, memories of life-threatening events such as serious diseases, accidents, and operations in postnatal life, the process of biological birth, and crises of intrauterine life represent a category of special psychological significance. In NOSC, additional profound encounters with death occur in the context of transpersonal experiences, such as karmic and phylogenetic memories and archetypal sequences. This material clearly supports the view that it is essential to distinguish the process of transition from one developmental stage to another from the life-threatening events that endanger the very survival of the organism.

Learning to speak and thus "dying" to the typhonic stage of development or developing an ego and thus "dying" to the verbal-membership stage does not stand comparison with situations that threaten the survival or integrity of the organism, such as near drowning, a serious operation, a car accident, a difficult birth, or an imminent miscarriage. Equally powerful and compelling can be experiences of death in a previous incarnation, identification with an animal attacked and killed by a predator, or annihilation by a wrathful deity. Life-threatening experiences are of a different logical type and are in a metaposition in relation to the mechanisms involved in evolutionary processes on various developmental levels that Ken describes as Thanatos. They endanger the existence of the organism as a separate biological entity without regard to the level of its development. Thus, a critical survival threat can occur during embryonal existence, at any stage of the birth process, or at any postnatal age, without regard to the level of consciousness evolution.

In my 1985 critique of Ken's views, I expressed my opinion that any model of human nature that lacks a genuine appreciation of the paramount significance of birth and death is bound to be incomplete and unsatisfactory. The inclusion of the perinatal level of the unconscious and of the phenomenon of biological death and acknowledgment of their relevance would give Ken's model more logical consistency and greater pragmatic power. However, since he lacks genuine understanding of the perinatal dynamics and does not appreciate the psychological significance of the experience of death, his model cannot account for important clinical data, and his description of the therapeutic implications of his model will remain the least useful and convincing part of his work for clinicians dealing with the practical problems associated with various emotional and psychosomatic disorders.

THE SPECTRUM OF PSYCHOPATHOLOGY

Ken's interpretation of psychopathology is another area which is in fundamental disagreement with the observations from experiential therapies, psychedelic research, and work with individuals in psychospiritual crises. This is related to the fact that he uses as his sources schools of depth psychology (particularly classical psychoanalysis and ego psychology) whose members use verbal methods of psychotherapy, are conceptually limited to biographical models of the psyche, and do not have even an elementary understanding of the perinatal and transpersonal domains. Modern revisions of classical psychoanalysis that Ken heavily relies on have refined the understanding of postnatal dynamics and object relationships, but share Freud's narrow biographical focus.

Ken basically uncritically accepts the dynamic classifications of emotional and psychosomatic disorders developed by the pioneers of classical psychoanalysis beginning with Sigmund Freud and Karl Abraham

(Fenichel 1945) and later modified and refined by representatives of ego psychology, such as Otto Kernberg, Margaret Mahler, and Heinz Kohut (Blanck and Blanck 1974). The common denominator for the theories of all these authors is that they do not see biological birth—whether it has a normal or pathological course—as an event that has psychological relevance. They thus accept the perspective of academic psychiatrists who do not consider birth to be a psychotraumatic experience and fail to see that it has any implications for psychopathology, unless it causes irreversible damage to the brain cells. As I have suggested earlier, there is a general belief in official academic circles that the newborn child lacks consciousness and that the neonatal cortex is incapable of registering the birth process and storing the information about it because it is not fully myelinized.

Ken has essentially accepted this position and incorporated it into the main body of his work. At the time when he did most of his theoretical writing about psychology and psychopathology, his theoretical speculations about psychological development and its vicissitudes had their starting point in the pleromatic stage of the newborn. Even today, he does not have an adequate understanding of the perinatal dynamics, their deep connection with the transpersonal realm, and their role in psychopathology, as well as spiritual development. For this reason, he has not been able to notice this deficit in his sources. And although he has a deep and extensive knowledge of the transpersonal realms, he sees them as being essentially irrelevant for the development of the common forms of psychopathology.

Ken's conclusions are in sharp conflict with the experience of the practitioners of various experiential approaches, such as rebirthing, psychedelic therapy, and holotropic breathwork, who witness dramatic reliving of the birth process daily in their work. However, one does not have to have such first-hand clinical experience to be able to see the logical inconsistency in current academic thinking concerning the psychological impact of birth. The representatives of all the schools of dynamic psychotherapy attribute a critical psychological role to the early mother-child relation and to the subtleties of nursing. A good example is Harry Stack Sullivan, who claims that the nursing infant is able to distinguish between the "good nipple" (the breast of a loving mother that gives milk), the "evil nipple" (the breast of a rejecting or nervous mother that gives milk), and the "wrong nipple" (a thumb or big toe that does not give milk at all). He sees such experiences as instrumental in the future development of emotional and personality disorders (Sullivan 1955).

And yet the same dynamic psychologists who attribute to the infant such sensitivity and discrimination deny that it can be in any way influenced by the experience of biological birth. We are asked to believe that it is possible for the infant not to experience and/or register in memory many hours or even several days of a highly taxing and life-threatening situation and then immediately after birth become a "connoisseur of female nipples" capable of differentiating nuances in the experience of nursing. This is hardly an example of rigorous logical thinking or a well-grounded scientific conclusion. It is much more likely a result of psychological repression and denial of this extremely painful and frightening event, rationalized by the use of scientific language.

The justification of this position by references to incomplete myelinization of the cerebral cortex of the neonate can hardly be taken seriously in view of the fact that the capacity of memory exists in many lower organisms that do not have a cerebral cortex at all, including unicellular life forms that possess primitive "protoplasmatic memory." The image of the newborn as an unconscious being who is incapable of registering and remembering the process of biological birth is also in sharp conflict with extensive research data showing extraordinary sensitivity of the fetus already during intrauterine life (Verny 1987). Ken, who is usually extremely astute, sharp, and discriminating, does not notice these extraordinary discrepancies and takes all the psychodynamic schools at their face value.

According to psychoanalysis and ego psychology, psychogenic disorders can be adequately understood in terms of postnatal biographical events and related psychodynamic processes. Different psychopathological syndromes are explained as resulting from problems in specific stages of postnatal libidinal development and from the difficulties in the evolution of the ego and of the object relationships. Psychoses thus allegedly have their origin in early infancy while neurotic or psychosomatic disorders are anchored in later childhood. Accepting this way of thinking, Ken sees psychoses (autistic psychoses, symbiotic infantile psychoses, most adult schizophrenia, and depressive psychoses) as results of regression to early developmental stages of postnatal development, and thus as fully prepersonal and prerational disturbances. He then associates various psychoneuroses with later fulcrums of postnatal development. By contrast, difficulties of spiritual development are for him transpersonal and postrational disorders.

As I have already indicated, in the recent modification of his model Ken makes some concessions to perinatal dynamics by creating for it a new fulcrum (F-0) and briefly outlining his ideas about the implications of this revision for psychopathology (Wilber 1995, 585–86). According to him, the new fulcrum (F-0) would participate in the development of psychopathology in a way similar to all the other fulcrums. Developmental malformations of its specific subphases (disruption at the dissociation, differentiation, or integration subphase) would result in specific pathologies.

A fixation at the fusion/indissociation subphase might thus predispose a person to "somatic mystical" fusion with the world; a disruption at the differentiation subphase might create a predisposition to the "hellish no exit" vital shock, intense sadomasochistic activity, and involutional depression; and fixation at the integration stage might lead to delusional messianic complexes. Similarly, the formations and malformations at this F-0 would "incline (but not cause)" subsequent development to tilt in the same direction. Thus a profound "no exit" malformation of the differentiation subphase might, for example, create a strong disposition to depression, withdrawal, and inhibitions. Ken offers here a comparison with the formation of a pearl, where a grain of sand influences the shape of subsequent layers.

However, even with this modification, Ken does not begin to account in his theory for actual clinical observations. In experiential psychotherapies using NOSC, people working on various forms of depression, psychoneuroses, and psychosomatic disorders typically discover that these disorders have a multilevel dynamic structure. In addition to their connections with traumatic events in infancy and childhood, as expected by traditional academic thinking, these disorders have important roots in the perinatal domain and also beyond that in the transpersonal realm (Grof 1985). Therapeutic work on psychoneuroses and psychosomatic disorders, guided not by the therapist but by the spontaneous healing mechanisms activated by NOSC, will thus typically take the clients beyond postnatal biography to the perinatal and transpersonal domains.

Under these circumstances, the therapeutic process does not follow a linear trajectory. If it is not restricted by the straitjacket of the therapist's professional convictions, it will freely move between the biographical, perinatal, and transpersonal levels, often even within the same session. For this reason, effective work with emotional and psychosomatic disorders requires a therapist who uses a framework that is open to all the bands of the spectrum. The idea of breaking the therapeutic process into stages during which he or she is seen by different therapists, each of whom is a specialist in fulcrum-specific treatment modality, is thus highly unrealistic. In addition, since both the perinatal and transpersonal experiences have the quality that C. G. Jung called "numinosity," it is impossible to draw a clear line between therapy and spiritual evolution. With an open approach, the process that initially began as "therapy" will often automatically change into a spiritual and philosophical quest.

The integral link between psychopathology and the perinatal, as well as transpersonal, domains is even more obvious in psychotic conditions.

While in psychoneuroses and psychosomatic disorders the perinatal and transpersonal roots are not immediately obvious and have to be discovered in experiential therapy, in psychoses they often represent a manifest aspect of their phenomenology. Without this recognition, the phenomenology of psychotic experiences and their relationship to mystical states will continue to present a serious challenge for Ken's conceptual system. In discussing the relationship between schizophrenia and mysticism in his book *The Atman Project* (Wilber 1980, 152), he describes his position as being "somewhere between" the approach of traditional psychiatry, for which both schizophrenia and mysticism are purely pathological, and the attitude taken by researchers like R. D. Laing and Norman O. Brown, who see both as examples of ultrahealth.

Ken accepts the position of Anton Boisen, R. D. Laing, Julian Silverman, and others who observed that, under favorable circumstances, the psychotic episode can actually result in healing and become a growth experience: by regression in the service of the ego, the psychotic patient returns to

> A deep structure (bodyself or otherwise) that was "traumatized" during its construction in infancy or childhood . . . and then, as it were, re-builds the personality, ground up, from that point. . . . After re-contacting or "re-living" that deep complex or deep structure disturbance, then the upper layers of consciousness spontaneously reshuffle or rebuild themselves around the newly refurbished deep structure. (Wilber 1980, 157)

According to Ken, this process of regressive healing and transformation remains restricted to the fulcra of postnatal biography. However, the psychotic process is not limited to material from infancy and childhood. It also frequently includes the theme of death and rebirth and the specific symbolism characteristic of perinatal matrices. Should we believe that for some mysterious reasons the process of this reparative regression has to stop short of the split caused by the trauma of biological birth, Ken's new fulcrum 0? It certainly does not stop there in deep experiential work using NOSC. There this regression proceeds to the perinatal level where the process often connects to the transpersonal domain.

John Perry's observations from many years of clinical work with psychotic patients clearly demonstrate that similar mechanisms operate also in the psychotic process. They show that the reparative regression and restructuring of personality typically includes the motif of death and rebirth as an essential element and reaches deep into the archetypal level to the Self or the "central archetype" (Perry 1953, 1974). John

Perry's pioneering work that C. G. Jung welcomed as "a messenger of a time when the psyche of the mental patient will receive the interest that it deserves" (Jung's foreword to John Perry's book *The Self in Psychotic Process* [1953]) has unfortunately not been mentioned in Ken's discussion of schizophrenia and mysticism.

This brings us to the problem of the participation of transpersonal elements in the experiences of psychotic patients. While emphasizing that a sharp distinction between pre- and trans- is all-important for this matter, Ken admits that the disruption of the egoic syntax opens the individual not only to "mythic thinking and magical references," but somehow also to "invasion" of material from transegoic realms that can lead to valid spiritual revelations. He suggests that the disruption of the editing and filtering functions of egoic translation leaves the individual open and unprotected from both the lower and the higher levels of consciousness. As the egoic translations begin to fail and the self is drawn into preegoic realms, it "is also open to invasion (castration) from the transegoic realms" [Ken's parentheses]. He emphasizes that he personally does not see any other way to account for the phenomenology of the schizophrenic break than to assume that a dual process is set in motion: the individual begins to regress to the lower levels of consciousness while, at the same time, he is invaded by the higher (Wilber 1980, 152).

This peculiar mixture of regressive phenomena and transpersonal elements in psychotic (and mystical) experiences cannot be easily accounted for without understanding that the perinatal realm of the psyche is not just a repository of memories of biological birth, but also a natural experiential interface with the transpersonal domain. Without this realization, the fact that genuine spiritual insights can sometimes be channeled through psychotic personalities and experiences will have to remain for Ken's system "a mystery"—a fact that he himself admits. Similarly unexplained in his theory remains the observation that "true mystics occasionally reactivate regressive complexes on their way to mature unity states." In spite of the fact that Ken acknowledges frequent mysterious invasion of transpersonal insights in psychotic patients, mysticism remains for him miles apart from psychosis. It represents for him a purely transegoic progression, whereas psychosis is primarily characterized by a regression to early infancy in the service of the ego.

The lack of recognition of the perinatal and transpersonal elements in the dynamics of unusual experiences leads Ken to simplistic interpretations that sometimes border on the bizarre and absurd. A salient example is his approach to the experiences of ritual satanic cult abuse, a complex and baffling phenomenon that in the last decades has reached epidemic proportions in the United States. Ken attributes them to the emergence of distorted childhood memories and gives as an illustration the infant's observation of his or her mother carving the Thanksgiving turkey (Wilber 1994, 303). Serious researchers of the UFO phenomena and of alien abduction experiences would also be surprised to find out that Ken believes that a similar misinterpretation of childhood memories could adequately account for the rich spectrum of fascinating and puzzling observations in their field. I feel that personal experience of working with clients suffering from problems of this kind would give Ken more respect for the extraordinary nature of these phenomena and the depth of the issues involved.

Ken actually uses his understanding of psychoses as F-1 pathologies as a theoretical justification for pharmacological and physiological treatments as primary therapeutic interventions in these disorders:

> Most forms of severe or process psychoses do not respond well (or at all) to psychoanalytic therapy, psychotherapy, analytic psychology, family therapy, etc.—despite repeated and pioneering efforts in this area. These disturbances seem to occur on such primitive level of organization (sensori-perceptual and physiological) that only intervention at an equally primitive level is effective—namely, pharmacological or physiological (which does not rule out psychotherapy as an adjunct treatment). (Wilber, Engler, and Brown 1986, 127)

Ken does not mention here the possibility of successful psychotherapeutic work with many people who by traditional psychiatry are or would be diagnosed as psychotic. While the earlier psychotherapeutic interventions based on the psychoanalytic model were severely limited by the therapists' tendency to interpret all psychotic phenomena in terms of postnatal development, strategies using larger cartographies of the psyche and supporting the experiences of the clients, rather than discouraging or suppressing them, are actually very promising (Perry 1974; Grof and Grof 1990).

The manifest content of many psychoses, as well as the material emerging during experiential work with them, shows a preponderance of perinatal and transpersonal themes, such as experiences of diabolical torture, eternal damnation, hell and no exit, identification with Jesus Christ, sequences of death and rebirth or destruction and re-creation of the world, satanic and demonic elements, messianic ideas, encounters with archetypal beings, or past incarnation experiences. These are in no way occasional mysterious "infusions" or "transfusions" of archetypal material, but essential and integral parts of the psychotic process.

This is evident in the already-mentioned work of John Perry, who conducted systematic psychotherapy with people undergoing acute psychotic episodes untruncated by tranquilizing medication. He was able to show that the major themes and motifs emerging in their experiences were identical with those that played an important role in royal dramas performed in New Year's festivals of a large number of ancient cultures at a particular period of their history, the "archaic era of incarnated myth" (Perry 1974). Perry's work clearly reveals the important role that archetypal dynamics play in such episodes and shows their meaningful connection to the evolution of consciousness. The essential role of archetypal elements and the collective unconscious in many psychotic episodes has also been demonstrated by many other Jungians and by Jung himself.

A comprehensive approach to functional psychoses, mysticism, and their mutual interrelations requires a vastly expanded cartography of the psyche that includes the perinatal and the transpersonal domains. As the work with NOSC clearly shows, the current academic understanding of psychoses and their relationship to mysticism is superficial and needs a radical revision. However, Ken's conceptual framework in its present form does not offer a viable alternative. With his linear understanding of the pre/trans fallacy, he sees psychotic states as essentially regressive and mystical states as progressive.

This is in clear conflict with clinical observations that show a much more complex and intimate relationship between many psychotic episodes and mystical states. David Lukoff (1985) speaks in this regard about at least four possible combinations: mystical states, mystical states with psychotic features, psychotic states with mystical features, and psychotic states. In my experience, the problem of the mystical versus the psychotic is often a problem of coping with and integrating perinatal and transpersonal experiences.

The success of this integration seems to depend more on the history and personality structure of the individual than on the nature of the experiences themselves. In one place, Ken himself interprets schizophrenic break with religious content as a result of influx of material from the subtle level meeting the "false self" of an individual whose personality structure was developmentally compromised (Wilber 1980, 157). Traumatic experiences of the early stages of postnatal development that in various psychodynamic schools are seen as the causes and sources of psychotic phenomena can certainly play an important role as factors interfering with the ability to cope with perinatal and transpersonal experiences, as well as the capacity for successful integration and adequate grounding of such experiences. However, early childhood traumas cannot possibly create the often rich and intricate content of psychotic experiences, which is clearly transbiographical in nature. To account for it, we have to consider such concepts as the transpersonal domain of the psyche, the archetypal and historical realms of Jung's collective unconscious, the Universal Mind (*anima mundi*), or cosmic consciousness.

This has its parallel in the differences in the capacity of various people to integrate such experiences in psychedelic sessions. The administration of psychedelic substances can account for the emergence of unconscious material from the depth of the psyche, but not for the specific content of the resulting experiences. The complex and intricate experiential sequences in psychedelic sessions cannot be explained simply as toxic artifacts of the interaction between the psychedelic substances and the neurophysiological processes in the brain.

However, while the content of the experiences by far transcends the biography of the individual, biographical factors can play a very important role in the final outcome of this process. Depending on the history of the individual and on the set and setting of the session, these experiences can lead to personality disintegration and long-term psychopathology, or to powerful spiritual opening and personality transformation. Such observations show that postnatal events are not the causes and sources of psychotic experiences, but important contributing factors.

My observations of persons in nonordinary states suggest that prenatal, natal, and early postnatal experiences encountered in regressive work have a distinctly numinous quality and freely merge with the elements from the archetypal and mystical realms. The memories of intrauterine life are not just episodes of primitive failure to perceive differences, as Ken suggests (Wilber 1995, 587), but are associated with profound mystical insights that reveal fundamental unity behind the world of separation. Similarly, the "no exit" stage of birth typically coincides with archetypal images of hell, the struggle in the birth canal is often accompanied by identification with archetypal figures representing death and rebirth, and the moment of birth and reunion with mother can take the form of divine epiphany, of an encounter with the Great Mother Goddess, or of mystical marriage. The presence of transpersonal elements on this level seems to be an integral part of this process, rather then a mysterious "infusion" of material from a remote part of the developmental spectrum.

When this understanding is applied to clinical work, the distinction between mystical states with an evolutionary potential and various psychotic states with mystical features does not depend exclusively on the nature and content of the experiences themselves and their association with radically different fulcrums of consciousness evolution. It is also important to take into consideration the overall context, the person's experiential style, and his or her ability to integrate the experiences into everyday life. In addition, the belief system of the surrounding culture and of the professionals treating the individuals involved should not be underestimated as factors that play a paramount role in shaping the nature of this process and its outcome. The therapeutic implications of this approach to mysticism and psychosis have been discussed in detail in publications specifically focused on the problem of spontaneous psychospiritual crises or "spiritual emergencies" (Grof and Grof 1989, 1990).

BACK- AND FRONT-DOOR ENTRY INTO THE TRANSPERSONAL

In his last book, Ken also addresses the problem of our disagreement concerning the "chronological order of the unconscious disclosures." He points out that in my theoretical system the dividing line between the personal and transpersonal appears to be on the level of the perinatal matrices, whereas in his map it is at the level of the centaur. This naturally constitutes a problem, since on his linear spectrum, these two domains are far apart. Ken's explanation for this discrepancy is that the observations on which my cartography is based come from regressive work. This process takes individuals from ordinary ego to Freudian childhood traumas and from there to the birth trauma and the intrauterine state. Ken suggests that at this point, "they may cease identifying with the physical body-mind altogether and thus fall into transpersonal, supra-individual states" (Wilber 1995, 587).

He emphasizes that his own map is based primarily on "broad-scale growth and development patterns" and thus runs in the other direction; however, he points out that it covers essentially the same general territory. It reflects the order in which "these domains enter awareness as a stable adaptation and not as a temporary experience." According to Ken, the work with NOSC forces its way to the transpersonal domain through the "back door," whereas he describes spiritual evolution that leads there through the "front door" and is conducive to stable developmental patterns.

The importance of distinguishing between temporary experiences and permanent structures was emphasized a long time ago by William James (1961) and again by Ralph Metzner (1980) who discussed the difference between transcendence and transformation. While I certainly agree that it is important to distinguish between transient experiences involving various levels of consciousness, on the one hand, and reaching a certain evolutionary level as a stable personality structure, on the other, I have certain reservations concerning Ken's position and his formulations.

Ken's description of the mechanism through which the regressive process reaches the transpersonal domain via the perinatal process (through the "back door") is far from plausible or satisfactory. As I will show later on, the transpersonal realms that open up when an individual regresses to the prenatal state involve much more than a simple loss of connection with the physical body-mind. Such experiential identification with the fetus appears to be a genuine mystical state of a very specific kind that is often accompanied with rich archetypal imagery and profound insights of cosmic relevance. Episodes of undisturbed intrauterine existence can open up into culture-specific archetypal images of paradises or celestial realms, experiential identification with aquatic animals, or complex astronomical vistas. Experiences of intrauterine disturbances coincide with encounters with insidious demons and authentic identification with aquatic life forms in polluted waters.

Moreover, Ken's argument about entering the transpersonal, supraindividual space by ceasing to identify with the physical body-mind is further weakened by the fact that the encounter with rich archetypal imagery is not limited to the prenatal state, but occurs in connection with all the perinatal matrices, including those that deeply and painfully engage the body. The no-exit stage of birth (BPM II) is often associated with images of hell and archetypal figures representing eternal damnation, such as Sisyphus or Tantalus, as well as identification with victims of various eras drawn from the collective unconscious, and with corresponding past-life experiences. Typical experiential concomitants of the struggle through the birth canal are archetypal images of deities representing death and rebirth and scenes of revolutions appearing as collective or past-life memories. Similarly, the reliving of birth is accompanied by culture-specific images of the Great Mother Goddess and scenes of divine epiphany or sacred marriage (Grof 1985, 1987; Grof and Bennett 1992). These observations suggest an intimate and organic a priori association between the perinatal and transpersonal levels.

I would like to mention in this context the work of Christopher Bache (1996), professor of religion and philosophy at the State University in Youngstown, Ohio, who has very creatively further elaborated and clarified the concept of perinatal dynamics and made an important contribution to the understanding of the relationship between the personal and transpersonal dimensions of this domain. Having analyzed many accounts of nonordinary experiences with perinatal features, he concludes that the perinatal matrices, as I have described them, reflect an operational mode of consciousness in which the personal and transpersonal blend, sharing organizational patterns and structures.

By identifying with intense experiences of the fetus, the individual connects by resonance to the larger field of species consciousness that can be described in terms of Sheldrake's morphogenetic fields, of C. G. Jung's collective unconscious, or of the over-soul. This involves experiences of wars, revolutions, and atrocities, as well as triumphs of humanity associated with emotions of unimaginable intensity. It is thus conceivable—and subjects frequently report this as their insights—that by experiencing the agonies and ecstasies on a collective scale that represent an integral part of the perinatal process, the individual heals not just himself or herself, but contributes to the healing of humankind itself in the sense of the Buddhist archetype of the Bodhisattva or the Christian archetype of Christ.

There are other important observations that support the notion that the perinatal domain represents an important interface with the spiritual domain. Perinatal experiences are a strange amalgam of three aspects of human life—birth, sex, and death—all three of which are known to be potential gateways to transcendence. Birth and death represent the beginning and the end of individual life and are thus natural frontiers with the transpersonal domain not only in experiential work, but also in everyday life. Delivering women and people in near-death situations often have profound transcendental experiences. Meditation with dying individuals and personal confrontation with death in cemeteries and burning grounds have been used in certain forms of spiritual practice as powerful catalysts of mystical opening. The transindividual nature of sex is evident from its critical role in species preservation and its potential as a gateway into the spiritual realm is best illustrated by the practice of maithuna, ritual sexual union used in left-handed Tantra (*Vamamarga*) (Mookerjee and Khanna 1977).

We can now return to the problem of entering the spiritual domain through the "back door" and the "front door." Many prominent figures in the spiritual history of humanity whom Ken uses as examples for his developmental stages, including shamans, saints, sages, and founders of the great religions such as the Buddha, Jesus, Mohammed, Ramakrishna, St. Anthony, St. Teresa, St. John of the Cross, and others, all experienced powerful visionary states that initiated and catalyzed their spiritual development. These experiences typically involved perinatal sequences that were strikingly similar to those that can be regularly observed in psychedelic and holotropic sessions. Christopher Bache has clearly demonstrated this in his studies of St. John of the Cross (1991) and St. Teresa of Avila (1985). The reports from powerful experiential sessions often read like passages from the Vedas, Upanishads, the Pali canon, the ancient books of the dead, the texts of Christian mystics, and other spiritual scriptures.

The above examples show that spiritual opening typically involves powerful NOSC, often with prominent perinatal features. These, of course, might or might not be followed by a good integration and stabilization on a new developmental level. It is certainly possible to have powerful mystical experiences that do not result in spiritual evolution. On the other hand, it is also questionable how much spiritual development can occur without powerful experiences of NOSC. Ken emphasizes that he is writing in his work about "broad-scale growth and development patterns," about a process through which "these domains enter awareness as a stable adaptation and not as a temporary experience" (1995).

However, he does not describe the mechanism that would be involved in such an evolution and transformation. If there is one, it would certainly not apply to most of the prominent figures he uses as examples. It is not clear what Ken's entry into the spiritual realm through the "front door" would actually look like. If it is something resembling William James's "educational variety" of spiritual development, where one would gradually open to the mystical dimension over a long period of time, in the way in which one learns to speak or develops an ego, it does not seem to be the mechanism driving the spiritual evolution of humanity. As the above examples illustrate, the spiritual opening of most famous mystics involved dramatic episodes of NOSC.

During my work with psychedelics and holotropic breathwork, I have been aware of the difference between mystical experiences and consciousness evolution. I have written in different places about the personality changes following spiritual experiences and paid great attention to the circumstances that are conducive to permanent beneficial changes and factors that facilitate good integration. I have not yet attempted to offer a comprehensive theoretical framework dealing with the problems of consciousness evolution that would summarize my observations over the years. However, these observations leave no doubt in my mind that under good circumstances powerful "regressive" experiences can be harnessed in such a way that they actually result in permanent changes of the developmental structure.

At the core of our controversy is a disagreement concerning the nature of "regressive" experiences and the role that they play in spiritual opening. Ken criticizes the position of the people that he calls "peak theorists" who believe that the entire spectrum of consciousness is always available, fully formed but submerged. According to him, transpersonal experience might involve the "reentering" or "reexperiencing" of a prepersonal occasion, such as pleromatic indissociation, perinatal patterns, archaic images, phylogenetic heritage, or animal/plant identification. However, this for Ken does not mean that the transpersonal elements reside in these archaic structures. It is transpersonal awareness that is instrumental in this process, not the archaic structures themselves. In his opinion, not a single prepersonal structure can in and of itself generate intrinsic transpersonal awareness. It can become the object of transpersonal awareness, and thus be "reentered" and "reworked." It can then become a type of vehicle that is used, but never its source. Ken insists that in these cases the concept of the pre/trans fallacy, however occasionally paradoxical, thus remains firmly in place.

The critical issue here is that "regressive" experiences, not only perinatal and prenatal, but also ancestral, racial, karmic, phylogenetic, and even those that reach farther back into the history of the cosmos often seem to form an integral part of spiritual opening. Whether we interpret this fact as the transpersonal awareness re-entering these archaic structures, as Ken prefers to describe it, or as manifestation of transpersonal potential inherent within them seems less relevant. Since, according to perennial philosophy and Ken's own system, all of creation and the entire evolution in nature and in the cosmos is, in the last analysis, created by involution of Absolute Consciousness, I do not see any need to treat these elements as *inherently different* from the spiritual realm. The fact that superior creative intelligence guides the creative process and manifests on all its levels certainly leaves such a possibility open.

In any case, Ken severely misunderstands the nature of perinatal experiences if he sees them as nothing but a replay of the actual experience of the fetus. His main objection is that regression to the pre- and perinatal state cannot convey any revelations about existence, because "the fetus in the womb is not aware of the whole world of intersubjective morals, art, logic, poetry, history, and economics" (Wilber 1995, 755). I do not see, however, how this makes any difference, since in discussing perinatal experiences, we are not talking about the fetus, but about an adult who is reliving the experiences of the fetus. This regression is experienced by an individual with differentiated personality and intellectual faculties that include and integrate the development through all the postnatal fulcrums. This vast amount of information is not lost during the regressive experience and forms an integral part of it. It certainly is conceivable that the NOSC facilitates an entirely new creative integration of all structures with the transpersonal domain, thus facilitating the unfolding of still new structures. Similar mechanisms have played an important role not only in religious revelations, but also in many scientific discoveries and artistic inspirations (Harman 1984).

Besides including the intellectual and emotional repertoire of the adult individual, regressive experiences also mediate direct extrasensory access not only to what Ken calls "intersubjective space" but also to information about various aspects of space-time and about the archetypal realms of the collective unconscious. I have made over the years numerous observations in this regard and reported them with many illustrative case histories (Grof 1985, 1987; Grof and Bennett 1992). In addition, the processes involved are characterized by multiple holographic enfolding and unfolding of space and time and escape any efforts of the intellect to arrange and categorize them into a neat linear system. Ken clearly does not understand the nature and complexity of the experiences involved, as can be illustrated by the example of the oak and acorn that he uses to criticize Richard Tarnas's application of the dynamics of perinatal matrices to the intellectual development of Western civilization (Wilber 1995, 755).

To ridicule the idea that regression to the womb could convey genuine mystical insights, Ken uses the image of an oak and the acorn from which it came. He argues that the regression to the fetal state cannot any more mediate a true mystical union with the world than an oak can unify its leaves and branches or become one with the forest by identifying with the original acorn. According to him, the "original union," whether conceived as the actual womb or as the prehistorical *participation mystique* of primitive cultures is not a union, but an undifferentiation.

This certainly is a logical conclusion we would be inclined to draw on the basis of external observation of these conditions when they occur in the context of linear individual and historical development. However, our only source of information about the subjective aspect of the original situations comes from regressive work. For this reason, all we will ever be able to say about them apart from what we learn from experiential work, will be educated fantasies and guesses, no matter how plausible they might appear to our logical mind. Yet we have ample knowledge about the regressive return to these situations and we know that it is not a simple replay or unearthing of the memories of the original state as understood by materialistic science. The experiences involved represent extremely complex, multidimensional, and even paradoxical phenomena that transcend attempts to fit them neatly into linear schemes. Neither Richard Tarnas nor myself have ever thought, said, or written that the perinatal experiences are nothing but a mechanical replay of the original birth situation, yet this is exactly the way Ken consistently misinterprets these experiences.

To more adequately portray the nature of perinatal experiences and the insights that they mediate, the oak of Ken's simile would have to regress to the original acorn and, while experiencing its oak/acorn identity, become simultaneously aware of its entire (acorn and oak) environmental context involving the cosmos, nature, the sun, the air, the soil,

and the rain. This would also be associated with a sense of its imbed-
dedness in the forest and its descent from a line of preceding oak trees
and acorns, as well as its entire development from the acorn to its present form. And an important aspect of such an experience would be its
connection with the archetypes of Mother Nature or Mother Earth and
with the creative divine energy that underlies all of the above forms.

If the nature of regressive experiences in NOSC is correctly understood, it does not seem surprising that they represent an important
mechanism of spiritual opening and of spiritual evolution. Besides ample
evidence from modern consciousness research, this notion can be supported by many examples from the spiritual history of humanity. The
experience of psychospiritual death and rebirth, or "second birth," that is
closely associated with the conscious reliving of biological birth, is an
essential component in the ritual and spiritual life of many cultures. It
plays an important role not only in shamanism, aboriginal rites of passage, and the ancient mysteries of death and rebirth, but also in
Christianity (as indicated by the conversation between Jesus and
Nicodemus about the importance of second birth, "birth from water and
spirit"), Hinduism (becoming a *dvija* or twice-born), and other great religions. Some spiritual texts also indicate that—in spite of the obvious differences—there are certain significant similarities between the mystical
state and the child's perception of the world ("you have to become like
children to enter the kingdom of God").

There are other important aspects of spiritual development for which
regression to earlier stages of evolution is absolutely essential. The most
important of these are the concepts of reincarnation and karma, ideas
that seem to be surprisingly neglected in Ken's discussions of spirituality in spite of their paramount cultural significance. The concept of reincarnation and karma represents a cornerstone of Hinduism, Buddhism,
Jainism, Sikhism, Zoroastrianism, and Taoism, as well as many other
human groups throughout history. Since such beliefs are based on experiences of events in other historical periods, they involve as a necessary
prerequisite temporal regression of consciousness to earlier stages of
human evolution.

Conscious re-experiencing of episodes from human history and from
the evolution of the species, of the earth, or of the entire universe has
been an important part of many mystical experiences resulting in spiritual opening and growth. The psychospiritual alchemical process has
been described as *opus contra naturam*, working against nature, since
it involves the discovery of the spiritual dimensions of existence by
retracing not only one's own psychological history, but the entire history of creation and bringing its various stages to full conscious aware-

ness (Fabricius 1976). Retracing the ancestral lineage and returning to the origins is an important part of the rites of passage of many aboriginal tribes. These observations suggest that spiritual evolution typically does not follow a direct linear trajectory from the centaur to the subtle and causal levels, but involves a combined regressive and progressive movement of consciousness with good subsequent integration of the experiences involved.

Deep experiential regression can lead to full conscious manifestation of the spiritual dimension of various stages of evolution, a dimension that was implicit and latent in them, but not consciously experienced at the time of the original unfolding of the evolutionary process in linear time. In this way, what was lost in involution, or cosmogenesis, is regained in regressive revisiting of its previous stages. A new creative synthesis of the historical and transcendental is then integrated into the present. Thus, the distinction between pre- and trans- has a paradoxical nature; they are neither identical, nor are they completely different from each other. The spiritual opening often follows a spiral trajectory during which consciousness enfolds into itself reaching back into the past and then again unfolds into the new present. Michael Washburn argues, correctly I believe, along similar lines in his book *The Ego and the Dynamic Ground* (1988) when he emphasizes the "spiral concept of ego transcendence" versus Ken's "ladder concept of ego transcendence." (See Washburn's article in this book.)

The problem of entry into the spiritual realm through the "back door" or the "front door" is closely related to the question of whether children can have transpersonal experiences and whether true spirituality can exist in cultures that are at what Ken refers to as the "magical" or "mythical" stages of development. If reaching the centauric level were a necessary prerequisite for entry into the spiritual realm on the individual and collective level, transpersonal experiences should not be possible in children. The ritual and religious life of shamanic cultures and ancient civilizations at the mythical stage of development would then be interpreted as prepersonal activity that lacks a genuine spiritual dimension.

However, actual observations have shown that transpersonal experiences, both spontaneous and evoked, are fairly common in children. Ian Stevenson's meticulous study of spontaneous past-life experiences in children, involving more than three thousand cases, is just the most salient example (Stevenson 1966, 1984, 1987). I have myself observed several clearly transpersonal experiences, including sequences of psychospiritual death and rebirth, in ten- and twelve-year-olds who have participated in sessions of holotropic breathwork. Shamanic literature, as well as the personal experiences of many anthropologists with shamans, leaves little doubt that they regularly have spiritual experiences not only of the subtle realms, but also of the causal realms. For many shamans, the entry into the spiritual domain is mediated by the "shamanic illness," a spontaneous visionary episode with distinct perinatal and transpersonal features. It would also be difficult to deny that the Eleusinian mysteries of death and rebirth, conducted in ancient Greece regularly for a period of almost two thousand years, as well as other mystery religions in the Mediterranean area, were authentic spiritual activities (Wasson, Hofmann, and Ruck 1978).

Although Ken himself admits the possibility of transpersonal experiences in children and shamans, he again considers them, like the transpersonal experiences of psychotics, as "invasions" alien to the corresponding fulcrums of his developmental scheme rather than natural and regular occurrences. As Roger Walsh pointed out in his study of shamanism, according to Ken's scheme, the shamans who have consistently subtle experiences would have to be short-cutting two major developmental stages, one of them actually being the rational one (Walsh 1990).

Concluding this brief discussion of the differences between Ken Wilber's spectrum psychology and my own work, I would like to emphasize that forty years of research into NOSC have convinced me of the limitations and relativity of all models and theoretical constructs. As Thomas Kuhn showed in his groundbreaking work *The Structure of Scientific Revolutions* (1970), the entire history of Western science could easily be written as a history of human errors rather than major triumphs. None of the theories considered definitive at any given time has survived later discoveries, except the most recent ones that have not yet been challenged. Reality is clearly much more complex than any of the theories that we make about it.

Whatever transpersonal psychologists have discovered and described during the first quarter of a century of the existence of this discipline will necessarily be complemented, revised, and modified. The future will show how the upcoming generations of professionals will view the issues explored in this article in the light of their own experiences and findings. They will very likely scrutinize the statements on both sides and change or adjust them to accommodate new observations and theories. I therefore feel very strongly that instead of engaging in the battle of models as if they were or ever could be definitive and all-inclusive, it is wise to do the best we can to improve them and bring them into consonance, but leave the field wide open for surprises and new discoveries.

References

Bache, C. 1985. A reappraisal of Teresa of Avila's supposed hysteria. *Journal of Religion and Health* 24:21–30.

———. 1991. Mysticism and psychedelics: The case of the dark night. *Journal of Religion and Health* 30:215–36.

———. 1996. Expanding Grof's concept of the perinatal. *Journal of Near-Death Studies* 15(2): 115-39.

Blanck, G., and R. Blanck. 1974. *Ego psychology: Theory and practice*. New York: Columbia University Press.

Brun, A. 1953. Ueber Freuds Hypothese vom Todestrieb. (On Freud's hypothesis of the death instinct.) *Psyche* 17:81.

Chamberlain, D. 1988. *Babies remember birth*. Los Angeles: Tarcher.

Evans-Wentz, W. 1960. *The Tibetan book of the dead*. New York: Oxford University Press.

Fabricius, J. 1976. *Alchemy: The medieval alchemists and their royal art*. Copenhagen: Rosenkilde and Bagger.

Fenichel, O. 1945. *The psychoanalytic theory of neurosis*. New York: W. W. Norton.

Frank, P. 1957. *Philosophy of science: The link between science and philosophy*. Westport, Conn.: Greenwood Press.

Freud, S. 1955. *Beyond the pleasure principle. The standard edition of the complete works of Sigmund Freud*, vol. 18., edited by J. Strachey. London: Hogarth Press and the Institute of Psychoanalysis.

Freud, S. 1964. *An outline of psychoanalysis. The standard edition of the complete works of Sigmund Freud*, vol. 23., edited by J. Strachey. London: Hogarth Press and the Institute of Psychoanalysis.

Grof, C., and S. Grof. 1990. *The stormy search for the self*. Los Angeles: Tarcher.

Grof, S. 1985. *Beyond the brain: Birth, death, and transcendence in psychology*. Albany: State University of New York Press.

———. 1988. *The adventure of self-discovery*. Albany: State University of New York Press.

Grof, S., and H. Bennett. 1992. *The holotropic mind*. San Francisco: HarperCollins.

Grof, S., and C. Grof, eds. 1989. *Spiritual emergency*. Los Angeles: Tarcher.

Harman, W. 1984. *Higher creativity: Liberating the unconscious for breakthrough insights*. Los Angeles: Tarcher.

James, W. 1961. *The varieties of religious experience*. New York: Collier.

Kuhn, T. 1970. *The structure of scientific revolutions*. Rev. ed. Chicago: University of Chicago Press.

Lukoff, D. 1985. The diagnosis of mystical experiences with psychotic features. *Journal of Transpersonal Psychology* 17:155.

Metzner, R. 1980. Ten classical metaphors of self-transformation. *Journal of Transpersonal Psychology* 12: 47–62.

Mookerjee, A., and M. Khanna. 1977. *The tantric way*. London: Thames and Hudson.

Perry, J. 1953. *The self in psychotic process*. Dallas, Tex.: Spring Publications.

———. 1974. *The far side of madness*. Englewood Cliffs, N.J.: Prentice-Hall.

Rank, O. 1929. *The trauma of birth*. New York: Harcourt Brace.

Sgam.po.pa. 1971. *The jewel ornament of liberation*. Berkeley: Shambhala.

Stevenson, I. 1966. *Twenty cases suggestive of reincarnation*. Charlottesville: University of Virginia Press.

————. 1984. *Unlearned languages*. Charlottesville: University of Virginia Press.

————. 1987. *Children who remember previous lives*. Charlottesville: University of Virginia Press.

Sullivan, H. 1955. *The interpersonal theory of psychiatry*. London: Tavistock Publications.

Tomatis, A. 1991. *The conscious ear*. Barrytown, N.Y.: Station Hill Press.

Verny, T. 1987. *Pre- and peri-natal psychology*. New York: Human Sciences Press.

Walsh, R. 1990. *The spirit of shamanism*. Los Angeles: Tarcher.

Washburn, M. 1988. *The ego and the dynamic ground*. Albany, N.Y.: State University of New York Press.

Wasson, G., A. Hofmann, and C. Ruck. 1978. *The road to Eleusis: Unveiling the secret of the mysteries*. New York: Harcourt Brace Jovanovich.

Wilber, K. 1977. *The spectrum of consciousness*. Wheaton, Ill.: Quest Books.

————. 1980. *The Atman project: A transpersonal view of human development*. Wheaton, Ill.: Quest Books.

————. 1983. *Eye to eye: The quest for the new paradigm*. Garden City, N.Y.: Anchor Press/Doubleday.

————. 1994. Guide to sex, ecology, spirituality. Unpublished manuscript.

————. 1995. *Sex, ecology, spirituality: The spirit of evolution*. Boston: Shambhala.

Wilber, K., J. Engler, and D. Brown. 1986. *Transformations of consciousness: Conventional and contemplative perspectives on development*. Boston: Shambhala.

Photograph of Stanislav Grof by Michael Jang.

6

Sean M. Kelly

Sean Michael Kelly is most at home in the interface between religion, philosophy, psychology, and science. He is particularly interested in the possibility of a "New Paradigm" of wholeness in which facts and values, nature and spirit, the profane and the sacred are recognized as complementary expressions of a fundamentally unitary reality. Kelly's work as a teacher and writer is devoted to the exploration and articulation of the varied forms of such a paradigm.

Kelly was born in 1957 in the Ottawa Valley to Irish- and French-Canadian parents. His childhood fascination with the Apollo mission and the wonders of the cosmos were followed in his teens by a period of intense, if unstructured, exploration of inner space in the spirit of the waning counter-culture. He studied English literature (focusing on Blake and Coleridge) and religion as an undergraduate at Carleton University; Gnosticism and Jungian psychology for his M.A.; then went on to the University of Ottawa for his Ph.D. in Religious Studies, specializing in Hegel and transpersonal theory.

Kelly began teaching as a graduate student, during which time he also served as Program Director for the C. G. Jung Society of Ottawa. In 1986-87, he received a grant from the French government to work in Paris with the leading French thinker, Edgar Morin. It was at this time that Kelly had the first of several meetings with physicist and philosopher David Bohm, who, along with Jung, Hegel, and Morin, has had the most profound influence on his thinking. His book, Individuation and the Absolute: Hegel, Jung, and the Path toward Wholeness, *sought to characterize this way of thinking as "complex holism." By using the qualifier "complex," Kelly seeks to avoid a facile holism which involves the totalitarian subordination of parts to a given whole—what Wilber has described as "subtle reductionism." For Kelly, a more adequate (or complex) holism recognizes "that such terms as nature and spirit, the finite and the infinite, the universal and the particular, and the individual and the collectivity, are dialectically related or mutually implicative."*

During his years as a professor at the University of Windsor, Carleton University, the University of Ottawa, and most recently at the California Institute of Integral Studies, Kelly has sought to communicate to his students his passion for the thinkers, traditions, and movements which seem most to embody this spirit of wholeness to which he is drawn. He has developed a particular interest in the relation of contemporary transpersonal theory and New Paradigm Thought to their historical antecedents, from the Romantics and Hegel to Frederick Myers (one of the founders of the British Society for Psychical Research), William James, and Carl Jung. With respect to the New Paradigm, Kelly has been working to introduce the ideas of Edgar Morin—who has written extensively on the nature of paradigms and the principles of complex thinking— to the larger English-speaking world. His translation, with Roger Lapointe, of Morin's Homeland Earth: A Manifesto for the New Millennium *is forthcoming from Hampton Press.*

Alongside these theoretical preoccupations, Kelly has studied, taught, and trained intensively in the Chinese Internal Arts (T'ai Chi, Pa Kua, and Hsing I) as comprehensive disciplines which seek the practical integration of body, mind, and spirit. From 1992 to 1997, he also practiced as a transpersonally oriented counselor.

Kelly's contribution to this book represents a significant shift in his relation to Wilber's thought. While in his previous writing and teaching he shared his excitement at having found Wilber to be a powerful contemporary voice in the tradition of Hegel and Jung, he now brings to light what appear to be problems in Wilber's theoretical formulations. In particular, he draws attention to how, in Wilber's own account, several of the stages of consciousness evolution do not conform to the principle of "holarchical integration" as Wilber defines it. (Wilber maintains that each more advanced stage "includes" as well as transcends the structures of earlier stages and that structures and stages cannot be bypassed.) In Kelly's view, only at the stage of the "centaur," with its relative integration of body and mind and its use of "vision-logic"—a synthesis of the body ego's more symbolic with the mental ego's more conceptual way of knowing—does a truly integrative holarchical consciousness emerge.

Kelly also points out that the transpersonal structures as described by Wilber (psychic, subtle, and causal) are of a distinctly different logical type than the prepersonal and personal structures. Kelly proposes that the transpersonal states of consciousness might be conceived of more fruitfully as expressions of the subtle, already present, depth dimension of the personal—along the lines of Bohm's notion of the "implicate order"— rather than as involving the emergence of new transpersonal structures. To do so, however, requires a radical revisioning of Wilber's root metaphor of the Great Chain of Being and of his corresponding formulation of the principle of holarchical integration.

As an alternative, Kelly argues that all of Wilber's structures can be generated from the relation between two axes—one running from the personal to the transpersonal, the other running from the symbolic (related to the body ego) to the conceptual (related to the mental ego)—which together generate a new mandala of consciousness embodying the principle of complex holism.

Further Readings

Bohm, D., and S. Kelly. 1990. Dialogue on science, society, and the generative order. *Zygon* 25 (4): 449-67.

Bohm, D., S. Kelly, and E. Morin. 1996. Order, disorder, and the absolute: An experiment in dialogue. *World futures* 46: 223-37.

Kelly, S. 1988. Hegel and Morin: The science of wisdom and the wisdom of the new science. *The Owl of Minerva: The Biannual Journal of the Hegel Society of America* 20 (1): 51-67.

_____. 1991. The prodigal soul: Religious studies and the advent of transpersonal psychology. In *Religious studies: Issues, prospects and proposals*, edited by K. Klostermaier and L. Hurtado. Atlanta: Scholars Press.

_____. 1993a. *Individuation and the absolute: Hegel, Jung, and the path toward wholeness*. New York: Paulist Press.

_____. 1993b. A trip through Lower Town: Reflections on a case of double synchronicity. *Journal of Analytical Psychology* 38 (2): 191-98.

_____. 1993c. The great mother/goddess and the psychogenesis of patriarchy. *The Journal of Dharma* 28 (2): 114-24.

Revisioning the Mandala of Consciousness:

A Critical Appraisal of Wilber's Holarchical Paradigm

 KEN WILBER HAS BEEN DESCRIBED AS THE EINSTEIN OF consciousness research and the Aquinas of transpersonal psychology. Like Einstein, he has proposed a few fundamental principles which, if valid, allow for a recasting and integration of mainstream psychological theories within an overarching paradigm. Like Aquinas in his *Summa*, Wilber seeks, with this paradigm, to reconcile contemporary psychological orthodoxy with the wisdom of the ancients in the form of the so-called perennial philosophy. A central doctrine of this wisdom, and one of the first principles of Wilber's paradigm, is that of the "Great Chain of Being," the view that reality "is composed of several *different* but *continuous* dimensions . . . grades or levels, reaching from the lowest and most dense and least conscious to the highest and most subtle and most conscious" (Wilber 1993a, 214). The most commonly used terms to describe the major "links" in the chain are Body, Mind, and Spirit. As an evolutionary or developmental sequence, these three terms correspond to the movement "from nature to humanity to divinity, from subconscious to self-conscious to super-conscious, [and] from prepersonal to personal to transpersonal" (Wilber 1983c, 204; see also Wilber 1995, 489). Each dimension or level is said to transcend yet include (in the manner of Hegel's *Aufhebung*) the ones that emerge before it. The sequence, in other words, constitutes a nested hierarchy, or "holarchy," as Wilber has

recently described it, where each successive level represents "an increase in wholeness and integrative capacity" (Wilber 1993a, 215).

The number of disparate theoretical approaches Wilber manages to integrate within his holarchical paradigm is truly stunning. (For instance, over seven hundred authors are listed in the references to *Sex, Ecology, Spirituality*.) In an age of hyperspecialization and hypercompartmentalization, where both inter- and transdisciplinary communication has become as difficult as it is necessary, one must applaud Wilber's exceptionally synthetic vision. In what follows, however, I wish to explore a few highly problematical claims made by Wilber, consideration of which throws into question both the purportedly holarchical nature of his paradigm and his appropriation of the notion of the Great Chain of Being. This exploration will allow for a revisioning of the mandala of consciousness (here I allude to the suggestive title of one of Wilber's seminal essays: "A Mandalic Map of Consciousness" [1983b]) in provisionally holarchical, but no less holistic, terms.

PERSONAL AND TRANSPERSONAL AS PARALLEL DOMAINS

To begin with, according to the principle of holarchical integration, "the more holistic [i.e., inclusive, and therefore "higher" in the chain] patterns appear *later* . . . because they have to await the emergence of the parts they will then integrate or unify. . . ." (Wilber 1995, 20). It is because of his strict adherence to this principle that Wilber claims, in *Up from Eden*, that "one does not and can not reach the transpersonal without first firmly establishing the personal" (1983a, 323). He makes this claim in even stronger terms in *The Atman Project*: "It is ridiculous to speak of realizing the transpersonal until the personal has been formed" (1980, 90). "The pace of this climb [from the prepersonal through the personal to the transpersonal]," he has written most recently, "can be accelerated, but the fundamental stages cannot be bypassed (nobody can form concepts without having images, and so on)" (1995, 627).

The problem with this claim, and the principle of holarchical integration upon which it is founded, is that Wilber himself implicitly contradicts both of them in other parts of his work. In *Up from Eden*, for instance, he traces "two strands of evolution: the evolution of the *average* mode of consciousness [which for a good part of its evolution is prepersonal] and the evolution of the *most advanced* [transpersonal] mode of consciousness" (1983a, 319), both of which transpire *concurrently*. Summarizing his findings, he writes:

> We saw that, in general, when the average mode of consciousness reached the typhonic level [2], the advanced

mode of consciousness—in a few highly evolved individuals
or shamans—reached level 5, or the Nirmanakaya. When
the average mode reached the mythic-membership stage
[3], the advanced mode—in a few saints—reached level 6,
or the Sambhogakaya. And when the average mode
reached the mental-egoic level [4], the advanced mode—in
a few sages—reached level 7/8, or the Dharmakaya.
(1983a)

The typhonic level is associated with the "magical" world view (with
its preponderance of primary process thinking and lingering participation mystique) of the "prepersonal" body-ego around which it is organized. The Nirmanakaya is alternately described by Wilber as the "psychic" (or "astral-psychic") or "low subtle" realm, and includes such things
as "out-of-body experiences, certain occult knowledge, the auras, true
magic, 'astral travel,' . . . [and] what we would call 'psi' phenomena: ESP,
precognition, clairvoyance, psychokinesis, and so on" (Wilber 1980, 67).
It is here that "consciousness *starts* to go transpersonal" (1980, 66).

According to *Up from Eden*, the magical-typhonic phase of consciousness (as the highest nontranspersonal phase yet to emerge) lasted
until around 12,000 B.C.E. In calling this phase prepersonal, however,
does this not imply that before 12,000 B.C.E. individuals of the species
Homo sapiens were not yet "persons," or worse still (given Wilber's correlation of personal with "humanity"—see 1983c, 204), were not yet fully
human? If so, the same would have to be said for the many aboriginal
cultures encountered by modern, mental-egoic, "rational," cultures capable of formal-operational thinking. Given Wilber's adoption of the principle of ontogenetic recapitulation (see 1983a, 25 and 218; and 1995, 149ff.
and 208f.), this would hold as well for the very young (or mentally challenged, for that matter) who fail to manifest fully differentiated operational thinking. To avoid drawing such conclusions, it would perhaps be
more appropriate to grant that consciousness is always "personal," at
least insofar as it takes the form (however rudimentary) of the separate
self-sense. Otherwise, it is difficult to make sense of the transpersonal
epiphanies of individuals in archaic societies or those of the very young.[1]
For how could they experience the transcendence of that which had not yet
emerged? While one can, following Piaget, legitimately point to a pre*operational* stage of consciousness, I suspect that the body-ego of typhonic consciousness appears pre*personal* only from the point of view of a self-system
that is itself unconsciously identified with the mental-egoic structure.

Apart from throwing into question the whole notion of the prepersonal, the fact that "the first true psychics [i.e., individuals at the first

transpersonal stage] . . . emerge[d] in the magic period" [a so-called prepersonal collective stage] (Wilber 1995, 322) also renders highly problematical the general principle of *linear continuity* (levels/stages cannot be bypassed) implied in the metaphor of the Great Chain of Being. For if it is possible for typhonic individuals to experience a transpersonal epiphany or "influx" (i.e., the psychic or low subtle realm) prior to the emergence of the mental ego, then it clearly makes no sense to conceive of the transpersonal as following the mental-egoic (Wilber's "personal" consciousness) in the same manner that the mental-egoic follows the membership and typhonic. Again, to do so would require an explanation of how it is possible for a supposedly holarchically "higher" structure— in this case the psychic—to transcend as it includes a "lower" structure— in this case the mental-egoic—that had not yet emerged. Wilber himself recognizes that "at any of its stages of stable growth and development, the self has access to temporary experiences ('influxes' or 'infusions' or 'transfusions') from the transpersonal domains (1995, 743). However, while he has no doubt that "infants and young children can have an infusion of transpersonal states (usually subtle), . . . this is an infusion into an intersubjective space that is fundamentally *preconventional* and *egocentric*, not *postconventional* and *compassionate*" (1995, 757). But if all levels of the Great Chain manifest the same principles of holarchical integration, why is it possible for *transpersonal* influxes to occur at virtually any "lower" level of organization (even if they don't attain to enduring traits), whereas it is impossible for someone at, say, cognitive stage 2 (preop) to experience, again however fleetingly, an influx from cognitive stage 4 (formop)? Clearly, the transpersonal "levels" as a whole are of a completely different order than the ones that "precede" them.

Instead of saying that the "highest" an individual at the typhonic stage can reach is the psychic, one could perhaps render more coherent and fruitful Wilber's important insight into the correlation between the two realms by reconceptualizing the psychic as the ground, depth dimension, or "implicate order" (to borrow Bohm's seminal concept—see Bohm 1982) of typhonic consciousness or the body-ego itself. Thus, experiences of "ecstatic body trance, of actual psychic opening, and so on" (80), which Wilber sees as typical of the psychic realm, could be seen as experiences of the body-ego insofar as it enfolds subtle energies and information about the general environment to which, in its ordinary or "explicate" mode, the body-ego does not have access.

By the same token, the high subtle realm (Sambhogakaya) could be seen as the implicate order of "mythic-membership" consciousness, and the "causal" (Dharmakaya above) as the implicate order of the mental-egoic. According to Wilber, "the key feature of the membership structure is language" (1995, 91) which, through the generation of "proto-concepts, verbal abstraction, and elementary class formation" (1980, 23), allows consciousness "to picture things and events which are not *immediately* present to the body senses" (1983b, 88). Correlatively, the high subtle realm is said to be "the seat of actual archetypes, of Platonic forms, of subtle sounds and audible illuminations . . . , of transcendent insight and absorption" (Wilber 1984, 29). In *The Atman Project*, Wilber describes this realm as the locus of "symbolic visions" and "higher presences, guides, angelic beings, ishtadevas, and dhyani-buddhas"—all of which, he clearly states, "are simply high archetypal [or implicate] forms of one's own being . . ." [in this case, the verbal mind or mythic structure] (1980, 68).

Although mythic-membership consciousness is already "mental" (because symbolic), as a developmental stage, it is not yet, or in itself, fully "rational," in the sense of being capable of formal operational thinking. (To what extent Wilber considers it to be personal is an open question.) It is, in a sense, a transitional or hybrid structure/stage, still dominated by the "magical" (preoperational) thinking of the body-ego, but already manifesting the ability to abstract which is the proper element of the mental ego. The mental ego, according to Wilber, is "the first structure that can not only think about the world but think about thinking; hence, it is the first structure that is clearly self-reflexive and introspective. . . . It is also the first structure capable of hypothetico-deductive or propositional reasoning ('if a, then b'), which allows it to apprehend higher or purely noetic *relationships*" (1984, 20).

Mirroring the capacity for unalloyed abstraction and reflexivity of the mental ego, and as its implicate order or "esoteric core," the causal realm is initially characterizable as that of "final-God," as "the ground or essence of all . . . archetypal . . . manifestations . . . [where simultaneously] one's own Self is . . . shown to be that final-God" (Wilber 1980, 71). As the absolute identity which is Other to all particular (and universal) forms, however, this final-God (the "low" causal) passes into "total and utter transcendence and release into Formless Consciousness" or "Consciousness as Such" (the "high" causal) (Wilber 1980, 72). However, while Wilber may *say* (or write) that the causal transcends the thought categories of the mental ego, his description of causal consciousness (as "causal") invokes the *category* of causality (along with that of oneness or unity—"One without a second") which, in its "high" causal variant, is "void" of any external relations, or relations pure and simple. This vacuum of relations is the result of the mental ego's abstraction not only from the manifold of sense (typhonic consciousness) but from the totality of mental categories for which this "One" in fact stands.[2]

To summarize, what we have so far are two *parallel* domains of consciousness—the personal/explicate (Wilber's magical-typhonic, mythic-membership, and mental-egoic structures) and the transpersonal/implicate (the psychic, subtle, and causal).[3] While one is perfectly free to picture the transpersonal as being "higher" than the personal, we have seen the problems with conceiving of the former as following the latter in a continuous or linearly holarchical fashion (in the manner of the root metaphor of the Great Chain of Being). Apart from the transpersonal standing to the personal as the implicate to the explicate, the subtle to the manifest, or the esoteric to the exoteric, I would draw attention to the developmental movement, within each domain, from the aesthetic to the abstract, or in specifically cognitive terms, from the symbolic to the conceptual (magical/mythical and psychic/subtle to mental and causal) (see figure 1).

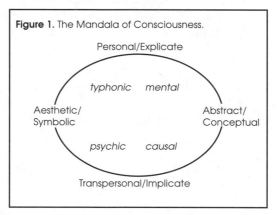

Figure 1. The Mandala of Consciousness.

Personal/Explicate

typhonic   mental

Aesthetic/   Abstract/
Symbolic   Conceptual

psychic   causal

Transpersonal/Implicate

THE CENTAUR AND VISION-LOGIC

We have already seen how the transpersonal domains can be conceived as running parallel to the development of the personal. Although it would appear that, developmentally (both individually and collectively), the mental ego follows the body-ego as conceptual consciousness (formal operational thinking) follows upon symbolic consciousness (preoperational thinking), Wilber's claim that the two egos and modes of consciousness are hierarchically/holarchically related is again highly problematic. While it is true that concepts "contain" symbols, they do so for the most part unconsciously. Concepts are, to a certain extent at least, *abstracted* from symbols, which therefore "contain" the former implicitly. It is only insofar as consciousness identifies with its conceptual articulation that symbols—or rather, the names (or signs) of the symbols—are "contained" in the concept. By the same token, and in more general terms, while the mental ego "includes" the body as a representational or

conceptual component of its self-construct and can (within limits) operate on the body, both consciously and unconsciously, the body nevertheless maintains a certain autonomy relative to the mental ego (as evidenced in organically based psychoses or in chemically induced alterations of consciousness, to take the most obvious examples). The mental
ego itself, for that matter, is not necessarily a fully integrated structure,
as Wilber himself recognizes:

> Very few individuals survive childhood with an ego intact
> in consciousness, or even largely intact, for "after the
> super-ego is established, it decides which drives or needs
> will be permitted and which suppressed." That is to say,
> under the influence of the super-ego, and dependent upon
> the whole history of the prior developmental levels of the
> self, certain concepts-affects are split off, or alienated
> (May), remain undifferentiated or forgotten (Jung), are
> projected (Perls), repressed (Freud), or selectively screened
> out of awareness (Sullivan). (1980, 33)

In other words, progress along the "outward arc," though involving
greater differentiation, complexity, and operational autonomy, also
involves a series of self-limiting contractions and splittings. (This
process is fundamental to the argument of *The Spectrum of
Consciousness* and *No Boundary*, and is implicit, though muted, in
Wilber's later writings.) This process culminates in the "normal" mental-
egoic state of relative dissociation between the structures of the body-
ego, the persona, and the shadow. The development of consciousness
leading from "the simple and primitive fusion-unity of the pleroma"
(Wilber 1983b, 91) to the mental ego, therefore, is not necessarily equivalent to a continuous evolution toward greater unity and wholeness.

Given the correlation or parallelism that I have suggested exists
between the personal and the transpersonal, the same can be said for the
"development" or "evolution" from the psychic/subtle to the causal. The
causal epiphany would be seen as "superior" to the psychic/ subtle only
from the logocentric perspective of the mental ego (with its greater degree
of contraction and dissociation). This perspective is prone to a version of
the "fallacy of misplaced concreteness," as Whitehead might put it, whereby the conceptual is given priority over the symbolic, the abstract over the
aesthetic. From the magico- or mythocentric perspective of the body-ego,
by contrast, the psychic/subtle epiphany would be experienced as superi-
or, or at the very least, as equally "whole." Wilber himself seems to recognize this when he grants that "the merely unmanifest Spirit (causal) is in
a type of *tension* or 'envy' with manifestation. . . ." (1995, 325–26) (my

emphasis). In other words, the causal, as causal, does not "include" or integrate all prior levels—it is in "tension" with them.

Apart from perhaps the body-ego, the only personal structure that manifestly fulfills Wilber's criteria for holarchical integration is that of the "centaur," which "represents the stage where mind and body, after being clearly differentiated, are brought into a higher-order integration" (1983a, 319; see also Wilber 1995, 186ff. and 258ff.). Wilber characterizes the stage of the centaur as the midpoint of the Great Chain—at once the culmination of the personal and the threshold to the transpersonal. As I have suggested, however, each phase of personal development is potentially open to the transpersonal in and as the implicate order of the personal itself. Because the centaur is the first true holon following the emergence of the body-ego, its transpersonal correlate is also the only structure/phase/realm (such words begin to fail us here, as we shall see momentarily) to truly include, as it transcends, all other structures/phases/realms. Wilber calls this realm the Svabhavikakaya, which he recognizes (though only once in a footnote to *Up from Eden*) as "the esoteric reach of the centaur" (1983a, 320).

The Svabhavikakaya is elsewhere characterized by the terms "Ultimate," "Absolute," "Spirit," and more recently as the "Nondual"— the Holon of holons, in effect, or simply the Whole. Consciousness of the Whole is equivalent to

> the radically perfect integration of all prior levels—gross, subtle, and causal, which, now of themselves so, continue to arise moment to moment in an iridescent play of mutual interpenetration. This is the final differentiation of Consciousness from all forms in Consciousness, whereupon Consciousness as Such is released in Perfect Transcendence, which is not a transcendence from the world but a final transcendence as the World. Consciousness henceforth *operates*, not on the world, but only as the entire World Process, integrating and interpenetrating all levels, realms, and planes, high or low, sacred or profane. (Wilber 1983b, 99) (italics in original)

Rather than simply manifesting the implicate order of the centaur, therefore, consciousness of the Whole reveals the "mutual interpenetration," as Wilber describes it, of all levels of implication and explication which constitute the Whole. (Bohm's evocative notion of the holomovement comes to mind here—see Bohm 1982, 150ff.)

The abstract, formal-operational thinking of the mental ego is not able, by itself, to grasp the true nature of this Whole. To do so requires the mobilization of what Wilber calls "vision-logic" or "mandalic reason," which he explicitly links with the stage of the centaur (see Wilber 1995, 186ff.). Mandalic reason is "the mind's attempt to put into mental symbols that which is finally trans-mental, and the result is always eventually paradoxical" (Wilber 1984, 113). Like Hegel's notion of "speculative reason" or Jung's "transcendent function" (see Kelly 1993a, 105ff.), vision-logic is the mode of cognition which comes into play when "the mind attempts to reason about spirit [or the Whole]" (Wilber 1983e, 175). I see such cognition as the product of the circuitous or recursive dialectic of the aesthetic/symbolic ("vision") and the abstract/conceptual ("logic") modes of grasping the Whole, a dialectic that mirrors the holarchical nature of the centaur.

Despite my criticisms of Wilber's recasting of the root metaphor of the Great Chain of Being, the lineaments of this dialectic are clearly visible throughout his work, from his initial spectrum analogy to his most recent and more mandalic proposal of the "Four Quadrants" of the Kosmos (see the inside cover to Wilber 1995). In tension with this dialectic, however, is Wilber's claim (1983e and 1984) that there exists a pure "gnosis" (Spirit knowing itself as Spirit) which is superior to vision-logic or mandalic reason. But again, such knowing is in fact indistinguishable from the same process of abstraction on the part of the mental ego associated with the causal insight into the "Void." Such knowing is "superior" or "higher" only from the point of view of a mental ego identified with its own process of abstraction which it thereby mistakes for the Whole. Without further qualification, this kind of knowing, as Hegel once characterized Schelling's insufficiently articulated notion of the Absolute, is equivalent to "the night in which all cows are black" (Hegel 1981, paragraph 16). While Wilber himself is anything but benighted, neither is he content—and for this we must be thankful—to abide in that silence which alone might mirror the knowing of which he sometimes speaks.

CONCLUSION

This critique of Wilber's holarchical paradigm does not, as Wilber aptly phrases it, demand "getting rid of holarchy per se, but [of] arresting (and integrating) arrogant holons" (1993a, 217)—or would-be holons in this case. It does, as we have seen, reveal fundamental problems with the root metaphor of the Great Chain of Being (especially when the latter is conceived in a literalistic or hypostatic fashion). At the same time, however, it clears the way for a revisioning of the mandala of consciousness in a manner that is more consistent with the principle of complex holism[4] which the mandala itself embodies (on the principle of complex holism, see Kelly 1988, 1992, 1993a).

"The work of the coming decade," Wilber has recently written, "is to find a way to unite and honor both . . . currents—the Finite and the Infinite [or the personal and the transpersonal], the Manifest and the Unmanifest [or the explicate and the implicate] . . . without reducing one to the other or privileging one over the other" (1993b, 264). As one of the first comprehensive and systematic attempts at articulating a "psychology of fundamental wholeness" (1980, 101), Wilber's holarchical paradigm has already achieved a great deal in this respect. An essential task for transpersonal theory will be to set Wilber's paradigm in dialogue with those of Grof (1985) and Washburn (1988), currently the two most substantial alternatives to Wilber's paradigm (for some preliminary essays in this direction, see Kelly 1991, 1993b).[5] In any such dialogue, and along the path toward wholeness to which transpersonalists aspire, Wilber's will surely remain a resonant and creative voice.

Acknowledgments

I would like to thank Donald Rothberg and Michael Washburn for their helpful comments on an earlier draft of this paper.

Notes

1. See in this connection the story of the Hopi girl, Natalie, aged eight (and thus, by Wilber's reckoning, not yet at the stage of formal operational thinking), who seems consistently to inhabit a transpersonal worldspace (in Coles 1990, 148ff.). See also Jan Ehrenwald's article on the telepathic elements (which in Wilber's model are evidence of the first, "psychic" level of the transpersonal) involved in "mother-child symbiosis" (1971). Finally, see Jenny Wade's summary of evidence for a "transcendent source of consciousness" active before, during, and shortly after birth (1996).

2. This, in essence, is the same critique that Hegel leveled against Kant's doctrine of the unknowable *noumenon* or "thing-in-itself," and that I have applied to Jung's correlative pronouncements as to the unknowability of the archetype "in-itself." (See Kelly 1993a, 22–26).

3. I have just been made aware of a book by Allen Combs (1996) in which he proposes that Wilber's transpersonal bands in the spectrum of consciousness be considered as *states* rather than as *structures* (the latter being reserved for the prepersonal and personal bands only). He too draws attention to the fact that these states are potentially available to consciousness at any point in its personal development and thus are clearly of a different order than the holarchical structures that, in Wilber's developmental schema, they are supposed to follow.

4. I have argued for a holism that is "complex" so as to avoid not only the more familiar kind of reduction of wholes to their constituent elements or parts, but also the more "subtle," as Wilber puts its (1995), reduction of the parts to a given whole. The principle of complex holism, as I have written elsewhere, received its foundational articulation in Hegel's concept of the Absolute. This principle recognizes that such terms as nature and spirit, the finite and the infinite, the universal and the particular, the individual and the collectivity, are dialectically related or mutually implicative. Any posi-

tion which maintains the absolute priority of either term is necessarily abstract and, therefore, ultimately false. The only concepts not subject to the same constraints are those of the Whole or the Absolute which, though normally contrasted with the notions of the parts and the relative, explicitly include these, their apparent opposites, in their very concepts (1993a, 2).

5. My proposal for a revised mandala of consciousness is consistent with Washburn's "dynamic-dialectical" paradigm to the extent that his "ego" and "Dynamic Ground" correspond more or less to my personal/ explicit and transpersonal/implicate dimensions, respectively. Intersecting this vertical axis, however, is the horizontal one of the body-ego and mental ego, through either of which the non-egoic potentials of the Dynamic Ground can, as we have seen, manifest themselves.

Unlike Washburn (and Wilber), Grof does not highlight the distinction between body-ego and mental ego. Nor does he speak of the prepersonal as such. ("Pre," in fact, does not seem to figure as a category in his paradigm at all.) While he recognizes, and appears to condone, Wilber's hierarchical arrangement of transpersonal experiences, the most critical distinction in his paradigm is that between the "hylotropic" and "holotropic" modes of consciousness, which again correspond to my categories of personal/explicate and transpersonal/implicate, respectively.

References

Bohm, D. 1982. *Wholeness and the implicate order.* London: Routledge and Kegan Paul.

Combs, A. 1996. *The radiance of being: Complexity, chaos, and the evolution of consciousness.* New York: Paragon House.

Ehrenwald, J. 1971. Mother-child symbiosis: The cradle of E.S.P. *The Psychoanalytic Review* 58 (3).

Grof, S. 1985. *Beyond the brain: birth, death, and transcendence in psychotherapy.* Albany: State University of New York Press.

Hegel, G. [1807] 1981. *The phenomenology of spirit.* Translated by A. V. Miller. Oxford: Oxford University Press.

Kelly, S. 1988. Hegel and Morin: The science of wisdom and the wisdom of the new science. *The Owl of Minerva* 20 (1): 51–67.

———. 1991. The prodigal soul: Religious studies and the advent of transpersonal psychology. In *Religious studies: Issues, prospects, and proposals,* edited by L. Hurtado and K. Klostermaier. Atlanta: Scholars Press.

———. 1992. Beyond materialism and idealism. *Idealistic Studies* 22 (1): 28–38.

———. 1993a. *Individuation and the absolute: Hegel, Jung, and the path toward wholeness.* New York: Paulist Press.

———. 1993b. The great mother/goddess and the psychogenesis of patriarchy. *The Journal of Dharma* 28 (2): 114–24.

Wade, J. 1996. *Changes of mind: A holonomic theory of the evolution of consciousness.* Albany: State University of New York Press.

Washburn, M. 1988. *The ego and the dynamic ground: A transpersonal theory of human development.* Albany: State University of New York Press.

Wilber, K. 1980. *The Atman Project.* Wheaton, Ill.: Quest Books.

———. 1983a. *Up from Eden.* Boston: Shambhala.

———. 1983b. A mandalic map of consciousness. In *Eye to eye,* by K. Wilber. Garden City, N.Y.: Anchor Press.

―――. 1983c. The pre/trans fallacy. In *Eye to eye*, by K. Wilber. Garden City, N.Y.: Anchor Press.

―――. 1983d. Structure, stage, and self. In *Eye to eye*, by K. Wilber. Garden City, N.Y.: Anchor Press.

―――. 1983e. Reflections on the New Age paradigm. In *Eye to eye*, by K. Wilber. Garden City, N.Y.: Anchor Press.

―――. 1984. *A sociable god*. Boulder: Shambhala.

―――. 1993a. The great chain of being. In *Paths beyond ego: The transpersonal vision*, edited by R. Walsh and F. Vaughan. Los Angeles: Tarcher/Perigree.

―――. 1993b. Paths beyond ego in the coming decades. In *Paths beyond ego: The transpersonal vision*, edited by R. Walsh and F. Vaughan. Los Angeles: Tarcher/Perigree.

―――. 1995. *Sex, ecology, spirituality: The spirit of evolution*. Boston: Shambhala.

7

Donald Rothberg

Donald Rothberg's work is centered in helping to explore appropriate forms for contemporary spiritual life and practice. He has particularly focused on two areas: (1) the meaning of a "socially engaged" spirituality in which spiritual life unfolds in the midst of interpersonal, social, political, and ecological relationships; and (2) how to bring spiritual dimensions into mainstream education and theories of knowledge.

Rothberg was born in 1950 in Washington, D. C., the grandson of immigrants from what is now Lithuania and Moldovo, and grew up in Maryland. He was encouraged by his parents to balance academic achievement with development in other areas. Although he eventually gave up his childhood wish to become a professional baseball player, he did swim competitively for many years. Living for a year in Cambridge, England in 1964-1965 with his family, he became much more aware of cultural and political issues. A summer in 1966 at the "Encampment for Citizenship" in New York City brought him in contact with many young Civil Rights, Black Power, and anti-war activists.

By the late 1960s, Rothberg had moved away from what had seemed like a likely career as a scientist; he had earlier spent two summers in research in molecular biology at the National Institutes of Health in Bethesda, Maryland, where his father was a biochemist. He entered Yale University in 1968 and studied politics, social theory, philosophy, psychology, and film.

After graduation from Yale and a year living in the mountains of Western Massachusetts and Virginia, Rothberg began graduate work in philosophy, studying at Heidelberg University in Germany and Boston University, with Dieter Henrich, John Findlay, Thomas McCarthy, and Alasdair MacIntyre. Shortly thereafter, he started Buddhist contemplative practice, having met Joseph Goldstein and Jack Kornfield at the Naropa Institute in Boulder, where he spent two summers. He soon was deeply drawn into intensive meditation retreats at the Insight Meditation Society in Masschusetts and, over a four-year period, averaged some hundred days a year on retreat. Though these retreats and daily practice were in many ways profoundly transfomative, he continued his graduate work, intending to complete his Ph.D., then go to Asia for more intensive practice.

Instead of going to Asia, Rothberg completed his doctorate and moved to rural Ohio to teach philosophy, partly to engage more socially and balance his more intro-

verted study and meditation, partly to follow a vision of an integrated spirituality "in the world." Over the next seven years, he taught philosophy (and meditation on the side) at Bowling Green State University in Ohio, the University of Kentucky, and Kenyon College in Ohio. In 1989, he was offered a position at the Saybrook Institute in San Francisco, where he has taught since 1990, working largely with mid-career professionals in the human sciences and psychology and with a number of transpersonally-inclined colleagues.

Rothberg began publishing his essays in 1986, initially bringing his background in philosophy, psychology, social theory, and comparative religion to bear on understanding transpersonal studies, controversies about interpreting mysticism, and the relation of critical social theory and spirituality. He became more active in the transpersonal field, serving as Associate Director of the Esalen Institute "Re-visioning Philosophy" program (1987-1989), and as an Executive Editor of the journal ReVision *(since 1991). He has edited and contributed to six special theme issues, including* Toward a Socially Engaged Spirituality *(Winter 1993),* Spiritual Inquiry *(Fall 1994), and* Responding to Violence *(Fall 1997).*

Since being in California, he has also become more active in exploring and reflecting on socially engaged spirituality. For many years he has served on the board of the Buddhist Peace Fellowship (BPF) and has helped to organize several summer institutes and many workshops in socially engaged Buddhism. He has also led a number of small groups and written widely in the area. Starting in 1995, he has been one of the main mentors and organizers for BPF's BASE (Buddhist Alliance for Social Engagement), developing training programs for those involved in social service or social action.

In "How Straight Is the Spiritual Path?", Rothberg gives an analysis of critical questions about the nature of spiritual development, with particular reference to Wilber's ideas and in the context of the conversations with Joseph Goldstein, Jack Kornfield, and Michele McDonald-Smith which follow.

Further Readings

Femi, I., and D. Rothberg. 1997. Unlearning oppression: Healing racism, healing violence. *ReVision* 20 (Fall): 18-24.

Macy, J., and D. Rothberg. 1994. Asking to awaken. *ReVision* 17 (Fall): 25-33.

Rothberg, D. 1986a. Philosophical foundations of transpersonal psychology: An introduction to some basic issues. *Journal of Transpersonal Psychology* 18: 1-34.

_____. 1986b. Rationality and religion in Habermas' recent work: Some remarks on the relation between critical theory and the phenomenology of religion. *Philosophy and Social Criticism* 11: 221-43.

_____. 1990. Contemporary epistemology and the study of mysticism. In *The problem of pure consciousness: Mysticism and philosophy*, edited by R. Forman. New York: Oxford University Press.

_____. 1992. Buddhist responses to violence and war: Resources for a socially engaged spirituality. *Journal of Humanistic Psychology* 32 (Fall): 41-75.

_____. 1993. The crisis of modernity and the emergence of socially engaged spirituality. *ReVision* 15 (Winter): 105-14.

_____. 1994. Spiritual inquiry. *ReVision* 17 (Fall): 2-12.

_____. 1996. What is to be done? Small groups and engaged Buddhist practice. *Turning Wheel: Journal of the Buddhist Peace Fellowship* (Winter): 43-45.

_____. 1998. The challenges of socially engaged Buddhism. In *Buddhisms in America*, edited by C. Prebish and K. Tanaka. Berkeley: University of California Press.

Sivaraksa, S., Santikaro Bhikkhu, and D. Rothberg. 1997. Structural violence and spirituality: Socially engaged Buddhist perspectives. *ReVision* 20 (Fall): 38-42.

Photograph of Donald Rothberg by G. Paul Bishop, Jr.

How Straight Is the Spiritual Path?
Conversations with
Three Buddhist Teachers

 HOW DOES SPIRITUAL OR TRANSPERSONAL DEVELOPMENT OCCUR? Do we find the same kinds of sequences of development among contemporary Westerners as those sometimes outlined in ancient spiritual texts? How and to what extent are the individual complexities and idiosyncrasies of each person's life related to general sequences of development? What are the different dimensions of spiritual development (e.g., involving mode of cognition, the emotions, the body, the sense of self, morality, interpersonal and social relations, etc.), and how are these different dimensions related to each other? How is a developmental emphasis balanced with a "nondual" (or nondevelopmental) spiritual emphasis? Further, what metaphors or models make sense of spiritual development? How does a person ascend or descend, climb a ladder, move across different stages, follow a path (straight or crooked), ride waves, spiral, cycle around, unfold, emerge, evolve, or become whole or balanced or integrated? To what extent is the notion of "development" itself a kind of metaphor? How can the use of such metaphors and models help or hinder spiritual practice?

I explore these questions by introducing and then presenting conversations on spiritual development conducted in November and December, 1995, with three well-known contemporary Western Buddhist teachers: Joseph Goldstein, Jack Kornfield, and Michele McDonald-Smith. Each has worked with many thousands of people over the last fifteen to twenty years, particularly through guiding intensive retreats in the practice of "insight" (*vipassana*) meditation, an approach drawn from the Theravada Buddhist tradition predominant in south and southeast Asian countries such as Sri Lanka, Thailand, Burma, and Cambodia. In this form of meditation, the focus is generally on cultivating a moment-to-moment direct, nonjudgmental attention to what is taken to be the primary content of experience, first in formal meditation and then increasingly in everyday life (Goldstein and Kornfield 1987; Kornfield 1977). However, while the views and observations of these teachers certainly reflect the particular perspectives and practices of this tradition, I believe that their teaching experiences are also of general interest and likely parallel many of the experiences of contemporary Western teachers and practitioners from other traditions and approaches.[1]

My interest in presenting these conversations is to help connect some of the more theoretical discussions of spiritual development to examination of ongoing contemporary Western spiritual practice, particularly in the context of Ken Wilber's work. In doing so, I also hope to suggest some of the patterns of a massive "data base" that might be further researched. Before turning to these conversations, however, I would like to clarify Wilber's general model of individual development and the types of claims that he makes about development in relation to some of the points made by Goldstein, Kornfield, and McDonald-Smith. I would also like to raise (although not resolve) a number of questions about Wilber's model. (However, some readers may wish to start with the conversations themselves, and then return to this more theoretical discussion.)

KEN WILBER'S STAGE MODEL OF INDIVIDUAL DEVELOPMENT IN THE CONTEXT OF THE CONVERSATIONS

Wilber's resolutions of many of the issues concerning individual spiritual development have been articulated through a *stage model*. Like the developmental psychologists Piaget and Kohlberg, and like the social theorist Habermas, Wilber suggests that development is best conceived as ordered according to a sequence of structured wholes (or stages) that occur in succession. For Wilber, these stages comprise, as it were, the journey from birth to final enlightenment (1980, 1986, 1995, and 1996, 137–48). Three prepersonal stages are followed by three personal and three transpersonal stages, although Wilber often stresses the somewhat arbitrary character of the distinctions between stages.

Yet what kind of a stage model has Wilber presented? What are Wilber's basic assumptions and claims about stages and development in general, and transpersonal development in particular? How do the observations of these three spiritual teachers support and/or lead to questions about his theory?

It may be helpful first to identify the general claims associated with Piaget's theory of *cognitive* development, which has provided a kind of prototype for stage theorists, and then examine how Wilber's theory does and does not follow this model. Piaget proposed a sequence of four stages: the sensory-motor stage in which the child comes to experience his or her body and the things of the world in a sensory manner (zero to two years), the preoperational stage of learning to use words and mental images to represent experiences (roughly two to seven years), the concrete operational stage of manipulating such initial representations in various ways (seven to eleven years), and the formal operational stage of representing these representations abstractly (eleven years and beyond).

Piaget made four general claims about these stages which, if valid, together establish the basis for a theory of great scope, explanatory power, and wide applicability. First, he believed that these stages are not culturally specific, but rather *cross-cultural* and *universal*. The entire sequence is found in all cultures. Furthermore, all normal individuals go through this sequence and reach the endpoint; the sequence is rooted in the process of biological maturation. Second, each stage is a *logically coherent, relatively stable, structured whole* (rather than being, say, an arbitrarily marked-off segment of a continuous spectrum or a set of disconnected fragments). Each structure is identified by specifying particular ways of categorizing and schematizing the world. Third, Piaget also claimed that each person moves through the stages in the same *invariant sequence*. There is *no skipping* of stages and *no regression* (barring physiological damage). Lastly, there is a basic kind of *developmental logic* at the heart of this sequence. Each stage is more *differentiated, inclusive, and hierarchically integrative* than its predecessor. Earlier competences are integrated in later stages; dissociation from or loss of these competences is not normal. In this sense, each succeeding stage gives a *more adequate understanding of reality*.

Wilber retains many of the core claims of such a stage model, but, like Kohlberg in his theory of moral development, modifies some of the claims and drops others. In essence, he differentiates between several different kinds of developmental structures, some of which (the "basic structures") occur in Piaget-like stages, others of which (the "transitional structures" and the "self-system") do not (1986; 1990a; and 1996, 138–48).[2] He also distinguishes these three components of consciousness further from transient "states" of consciousness (in press).

The *basic structures* are essentially *cognitive* structures (rather than moral or emotional or self-structures) and include Piaget's stages but also four further stages. There is the integrative, advanced rational stage of "vision-logic," involving intuitive insight into complex patterns and dialectical reasoning. This stage is similar to the "postformal" or "contextual" or "dialectical" stage of thinking suggested by many developmental psychologists (Richards and Commons 1990). Then, there are three transpersonal stages: the "psychic" (marked by the emergence of the "soul" and the first glimpses of the pure "witness"), the "subtle" (marked by the emergence of archetypes like the Platonic forms), and the "causal" (marked by the emergence of pure formless awareness). The "ultimate" stage (integrating form and formless) is the ground for these and all other structures (Wilber 1995, 279–316).

Wilber also speaks of *transitional* structures, such as the stages of moral development. Transitional structures do not integrate the concepts and ways of understanding of earlier transitional structures but rather replace them totally. For example, Wilber thinks (contrary to Kohlberg [1981, 168–73], by the way) that moral stages, as conceived by Kohlberg or Gilligan, are best understood as merely transitional. For example, stage 6 in Kohlberg's model, in which one acts according to universal ethical principles, does not somehow "integrate" the categories and achievements of the egocentric stage 1 or those of the conformist stage 3, in which what is "good" is doing what others expect of one. Rather, Wilber believes that one moral stage simply *substitutes* for the earlier stage, rather than building on it in the usual mode of differentiation and integration.[3] Wilber also identifies what he believes are other transitional structures: the world views linked with particular cognitive structures (e.g., what he speaks of as magical, mythical, or rationalist world views) or the various emerging self-identities (the persona; the ego; the "centaur" linked with vision-logic and the integration of mind, body, and emotion; or the soul).

For Wilber, the *self-system* (or *self*) mediates between the basic and transitional structures (1986, 78–80). The self is the locus of several kinds of operations: identification (by which identity and self-other distinctions are formed, inwardly and outwardly), organization (the attempt to give unity or coherence to experience), will, defense, "metabolism" ("digesting" and assimilating past experiences), and "navigation" (moving in particular developmental directions). Wilber believes that when the self identifies with a basic structure, transitional structures are generated or supported (i.e., the self tends to support particular world views or self-identities available in a given culture). When the self moves to a new and "higher" basic structure or stage, the self first fuses with a new structure, then differentiates from that structure, and finally fuses with a further structure while integrating the core competences of the earlier structure.

To add somewhat more complexity to the picture, Wilber also maintains, following many theorists, that it is best to speak of several somewhat independent modes or *lines of development*: cognition, affect, morality, sense of self, and interpersonal relationships, among others (1990b, 118ff.). In other words, development doesn't somehow proceed in some simple way through a series of a few comprehensive stages which unify all aspects of growth. For example, a person may employ advanced cognitive abilities while expressing a very low stage of morality, as we know all too well. Furthermore, the self can be, Wilber claims, "all over the place" (in press) even if there is general movement toward "higher" or "deeper" structures. There can be temporary movement to different stages (in regression or "spiraling") and often a lack of stability and unity among the different aspects of development. The developmental lines may in fact be in tension with each other at times. Furthermore, some lines do not typically show evidence, Wilber believes, of coherent stages; Wilber notes that according to Kohlberg's research, a person is typically in two or three moral stages at a given time. Lastly, some of the developmental lines may be constructed in different ways according to gender, as Gilligan's work (1982) suggests in terms of morality, although Gilligan's approach still follows, Wilber believes (in press), the general sense of a stage model.

With this background in Wilber's developmental theory, we are in a position to compare the claims of the theory, particularly insofar as they concern "spiritual" or transpersonal development, with the claims of a prototypical Piagetian stage model for (1) universality; (2) coherent, structured stages; (3) an invariant sequence of stages; and (4) an underlying developmental logic in which new stages represent further differentiation and hierarchical integration of earlier stages. We might then more easily assess to what extent the observations of Goldstein, Kornfield, and McDonald-Smith corroborate Wilber's claims and/or raise questions.

(1) *The universality of stages.* Wilber claims that the "basic structures" of vision-logic and the transpersonal stages are *cross-cultural and universal.* But he does not make this claim in the same way that Piaget did. All individuals in all cultures do not somehow go through all stages, at least within the context of a given lifetime. (Wilber typically does not discuss the idea of rebirth or reincarnation, although it does enter into Goldstein's reflections in my conversation with him.) Like Kohlberg, Wilber thinks that the more advanced structures only emerge for a relatively few persons, at least at this point in human history. Yet he holds that his stages are, nonetheless, universal. He claims that the basic transpersonal structures can be reconstructed from the study of developmental accounts and maps drawn from a number of different philosophical and spiritual traditions. He takes his own work as an example of such reconstruction and points also to the work of his coauthor Brown (Wilber, Engler, and Brown 1986) and advocates of the "perennial philosophy" (e.g., Schuon 1984; Smith 1976). Similarly, there is the claim that development through transitional structures broadly follows a universal progression. For instance, moral stages move from preconven-

tional to conventional to postconventional. Of course, claims about universality raise many complex, controversial, and unsettled issues that I do not have room to investigate here, although these issues mostly do not come up in the conversations with the spiritual teachers. For example, both Piaget's and Kohlberg's theories have been criticized on the basis of cross-cultural research (e.g., Dasen 1977; Shweder, Mahapatra, and Miller 1987), as has Wilber's stage model (see essay 10 by Kremer in this volume, and Winkelman 1990).

(2) *The coherence of stages.* Wilber believes that the basic transpersonal structures also meet Piaget's criterion of being logically coherent, structured wholes. Even though he acknowledges the somewhat arbitrary quality of his characterization of the three transpersonal stages in the light of many models of spiritual development outlining many more stages, he does claim that these structures are somehow "functionally dominant" and "not entirely arbitrary" (1986, 74). Each of them, furthermore, can be represented in terms of discrete modes of knowing. The "psychic" stage seems to involve the initial differentiation of the "witness" (awareness no longer identified with earlier stages of cognition and self) and the integration of rational structures as subsystems. There also seems to be a diminishing of the separation between knower and known. At the "subtle" stage, there is knowing through (and ultimately unity with) the cognitive structures identified by Wilber as "archetypal," a transcendence and integration of the ordinary process and content of knowing and the earlier psychic structures. Finally, with the "causal" stage, "knowing" moves beyond any subject-object differentiation and content whatsoever, to pure formless awareness. Logically, the claim that these basic transpersonal structures are coherent wholes or "broad patterns of stable adaptation" (Wilber 1995, 742) seems at least plausible, although considerable further work clarifying these structures conceptually, phenomenologically, and comparatively seems necessary.

The situation becomes more complicated when we consider the transitional structures and the self-system.[4] Wilber believes that the transitional structures may not necessarily show us structured wholes. As I mentioned, Kohlberg's empirical research on moral development has indicated that individuals commonly operate in two or more stages, even though he has asserted that one stage is primary. This clearly raises the question of the extent to which the coherence and wholeness of moral structures occurs "operationally," in experience, or (merely) more theoretically through conceptual constructs or "ideal types." Flanagan (1992, 188), for example, has suggested that the normal moral experience of contemporary Westerners may be a kind of stable amalgam of rather disparate moral approaches: Judeo-Christian, Kantian, utilitarian, and

individualistic. Other transitional "structures" may also show only limited coherence; Piaget himself believed that human personality is not
organized according to the same structural principles as cognition, but is
made up of complex and often contradictory processes (Noam 1990, 375).

Similar questions about coherence arise when we examine development *as a whole*. Wilber does not claim that the different developmental
"lines" or modes are necessarily coherently unified. Cognitive development may be in some ways rather independent from moral or ego or emotional development. There might be a high level of development cognitively, a medium level interpersonally or morally, and a low level emotionally. These disparities of development seem especially conditioned by
general cultural values and styles. For example, modern Western educational models generally give priority to cognitive development over other
types of intelligence and development (Gardner 1983). Further, cognition
and morality are commonly understood as relatively disembodied and
dispassionate, as in the abstract thought identified with Piaget's end-
stage of formal operations or Kohlberg's stage 6 of moral thinking based
on "universal ethical principles." Many critics have linked these models
with issues related to gender, class, and ethnicity (e.g., Jaggar 1989;
Keller 1985; Scheman 1993).

McDonald-Smith notes such disparities and calls for transpersonal
approaches reflecting a more balanced development of these different
modes. She observes a major current shift of attention in the spiritual
practice of many of her students to bodily experience, emotions, and relationships. Goldstein and Kornfield also each question an overemphasis
on formal meditation and argue for the importance of spiritual approaches which integrate different lines of development, including those of emotional and bodily awareness and interpersonal relationships. Kornfield
points out some of the problems in spiritual communities that result
from a lack of attention to interpersonal development. In many ways,
these reflections parallel recent discussions by Wilber (1995), identifying
the problems of models of spiritual development that convey a one-sided
focus on "ascent" and transcendence; a devaluation of body, emotion,
women, and nature; and an exclusive emphasis on the "interior" aspects
of spirituality.

However, recognizing somewhat independent and unevenly connected lines of development does raise a number of questions and complexities. To what extent does the self, following the emergence of transpersonal structures, not only perhaps employ an amalgam of moral strategies and self-senses but also analogously a multiplicity of sometimes
uncoordinated cognitive structures, not necessarily organized by the
most "advanced" structure? To what extent is the situation in relation to

modes of cognition more like the apparently fragmented situation in moral development, particularly when we consider transpersonal modes of cognition? Wilber has recognized some aspects of these issues and apparently does not accept a strict Piagetian model in which one stage must be *completed* before another stage begins. Rather, he follows some developmental theorists in claiming that the basic structures only *emerge* in an invariant order and then, as it were, "branch out," continuing to develop or mature through the person's lifetime (Wilber 1990a, 284–86). A given structure apparently need not be fully developed before another more advanced structure emerges. Wilber seems to believe that there can be significant further development of several different *basic* structures simultaneously. Only the sequence of the emergence of structures is claimed to be invariant; development itself is only sequential in this limited sense. Unfortunately, there is very little discussion in Wilber's work on this important point.

In the light of these considerations, it may not be possible to claim that the basic transpersonal structures can meet the Piagetian criterion of being structured wholes. Further, we can ask about the extent of incoherence and fragmentation possible between different lines of development and how this can be understood. We can also ask whether transpersonal development is best understood by centering on *cognitive* structures or needs to be given a more "integrative" reading, identifying the apparently many modes of development.

Although Wilber has recently (1995) focused on some of the complexities, problems, and pathologies with the general "ascent" model of development, his usual presentation of the stages of development seems to suggest considerable coherence among the different lines of development.[5] In an earlier work (1986, 81), for instance, he generalizes about development as a whole in this way:

> Once identified with the new and higher basic structure, a
> new and phase-specific self-stage swings into existence: a
> new self-sense, with new self-needs, new moral sensibili-
> ties, new object relations, new forms of life, new forms of
> death, new forms of "food" to be metabolized, and so forth
> . . . . Once on the new and higher level, the self then seeks
> to consolidate, fortify, and preserve *that* level, until it is
> once again strong enough to die to that level, *transcend*
> that level (release or negate it), and so ascend to the next
> developmental rung.

We might easily assume from a reading of this passage, for example, that stabilized transpersonal development of the basic structures only occurs following the attainment of the integrated ego that Wilber calls "centauric" (i.e., integrating the human and the animal, the mind and the body). Yet something like this latter claim is questioned by all three of the spiritual teachers, who each note that certain types of transpersonal development (as opposed to transient experiences of transpersonal "states") can coexist without such development of the "self," that is, that different lines of development are often not very coordinated. Both Kornfield and McDonald-Smith's often moving accounts of their own personal development provide support for questioning the claim. Indeed, McDonald-Smith suggests that the mature integration of cognition, bodily awareness, and emotion, supposedly accomplished in the last of the "personal" self structures, is very rarely accomplished, even among those with seemingly high levels of transpersonal development in some dimensions. This observation might be seen in the light of the finding that as few as 1 to 2 percent of adults reach Loevinger's "autonomous" level in which intellect and affect are relatively integrated (Alexander, Druker, and Langer 1990, 305–06).

(3) *The invariant sequence of stages.* As we have seen, Wilber holds that the basic structures emerge or unfold in an *invariant sequence,* without skipping stages (1990a, 284–86; 1995, 623). He admits that there may be "peak" (or "peek") experiences of the transpersonal structures at any time, as is also very evident from the spiritual and psychological literature. There may furthermore be extensive "spiraling" back by the self between more and less advanced structures; the centrality of such spiraling is noted by all three teachers. Yet there cannot be stabilization of these transpersonal structures without first stabilizing to some extent what Wilber takes to be prior developmental structures. How much stabilization is necessary, however, seems unclear in light of Wilber's account of the "branching" nature of the development of each structure.

Similarly, Wilber distinguishes between a general regression in terms of basic structures and "regression in service of ego," that is, in service of the integrated self (1980, 151ff.; 1995, 105, 664). Following Piaget, Wilber believes that the first kind of regression is not really possible. The second kind of regression, however, can be vital in terms of accessing places of dissociation, trauma, or incompleteness. However, Wilber understands such regressive work in terms of the movement of the "self" to areas of incomplete or truncated development in the interests of reintegrating these areas and continuing development. He criticizes many "retro-Romantic" theorists whom he believes champion regression through their attacks on the modern and rational differentiations that have actually made possible further development (1995, e.g., 105).

McDonald-Smith's account of regression seems to provide an example of such "regression in service of ego." She claims that her regressive work was made possible through a grounding in transpersonal cognitive modes (particularly high levels of meditative "mindfulness" that made reexperiencing traumatic experiences possible with less "identification") and caring interpersonal and intrapsychic approaches.[6]

Yet a number of questions can still be asked about the claim to an invariant sequence, although I will only raise a few of the many possible questions here. For example, two of the other most prominent theorists in transpersonal psychology, Grof and Washburn (see their contributions in this issue), believe that regression plays a more central (rather than simply occasional) role in development and that successful regressive work may not always be so securely based in more advanced structures. Furthermore, some interpreters of moral development believe that regression of the first kind sometimes seems to occur (Flanagan 1991, 159–60). Another question about invariance can be raised concerning exactly how and why the transpersonal stages require the emergence and stabilization of the two "rational" stages. This question particularly comes up in examining the texts or accounts of the apparently transpersonal experiences of persons in cultures in which the two rational stages do not seem very evident. Additional discussion of this issue by Wilber and others would help make sense of this apparent gap. A further question concerns how advocates of stage models can make sense of the types of sequences reported by Kornfield, McDonald-Smith, and many others, of a sustained and stabilized transpersonal development followed by "downward" movement to attend to emotions, the body, and relationships.

Some of the questions discussed earlier about whether the basic structures are indeed structured wholes are also linked to questions about sequence. If the self can be developing in several stages (including cognitive stages) at once, it becomes unclear exactly how a supposedly more advanced structure emerges in relation to the preceding structure. As we have seen, Wilber's claim about invariance concerns only the sequence of the initial emergence of structures; later structures supposedly only emerge once earlier structures have emerged. This in turn raises the question, central in much of the literature on development, as to the extent to which basic structures emerge with a significant degree of coherence, or are gradually "uncovered," or "mature," or require a kind of "construction." Piaget's model presumes a more constructivist position, but we might ask whether it sometimes makes more sense to speak of "uncovering" what seem to be innate structures. How, for example, can we think of transpersonal archetypes or pure awareness being "constructed"?

(4) *The "logic" of development.* Wilber also make claims for a core *developmental logic* underlying his stage theory, although again these claims seem modified in comparison to the stronger claims of Piaget. More "advanced" structures supposedly "include" or "integrate" earlier structures, contain newly differentiated aspects as well, yet logically presume the competences associated with earlier structures. Earlier competences are not normally repressed or dissociated. The intelligences associated with later structures thus supposedly are more adequate, since the former competences are retained, yet further competences are added.

However, as I earlier suggested, Wilber gives up the claim to a developmental logic for many of the transitional structures, such as the structures of moral development. Relaxing the strictures of a developmental logic also helps Wilber to make more sense of the notion of the (transitional) stage of the "centaur" and the "integrated ego."

This stage is understood as involving an integration of mind, body, and emotion, yet the question has been raised (for example, by Washburn and Kelly in chapters 4 and 6 in this volume) as to whether such a stage conforms to the underlying developmental logic, and why the initial differentiation of rational structures seemingly presumes a *normal* dissociation rather than integration of bodily and emotional competences. Only with "vision-logic" and the self-sense of the "centaur" is there integration. Is this a culturally rooted developmental oddity linked with gender issues and the several thousand years of cultural devaluation of body and emotion in dominant Western cultural models, or does this pattern reflect the normal mode of development? While identifying this pattern with transitional rather than basic structures helps take off the logical pressure, it also raises questions about the extent to which Wilber's theory takes on an ad hoc quality.

However, questions can also be raised concerning the extent to which the emergence of basic structures as well follows a developmental logic.[7] A "later" *basic* structure is supposed to presume the competences of earlier structures (although we have seen that how this is the case is not very clear in terms of the relation between the rational and the transpersonal stages). Yet in the context of the "branching" nature of basic structures, it is also unclear *how much* development of earlier stages is necessary for transpersonal stages to emerge. The developmental logic can only be preserved if it is somehow assumed that there are "core" competences, as it were, for each structure that furnish the basis for more advanced structures, given that advanced structures do not necessarily presuppose the "completion" of earlier stages. Again, there seems a risk of the theory becoming excessively ad hoc.

For example, in what ways do transpersonal stages presuppose and "integrate" the rational stages and what is the evidence for this? How does the emergence of the transpersonal "witness" depend on the prior emergence of vision-logic? How do the rational cognitive structures become, as it were, "subsystems" in the more comprehensive systems of transpersonal cognition (Alexander, Druker, and Langer 1990)? How are earlier conflicts and problems at the rational levels resolved at later levels? Responding to these questions is particularly important in light of the earlier question about whether it makes sense to presume fully developed stages of rationality in accounts of transpersonal experiences originating in cultures not organized around such rationality or in children (Hunt 1995). It also is important in light of the widespread confusion concerning the relationship between rationality and spirituality.

Before turning to the conversations themselves, it is important to mention that the above discussions and questions, which are rather theoretical and technical at times, do have profound practical implications. This is evident in the conversations. How development is conceptualized may lead to valuing some lines of development over others or giving some kinds of development little or no attention, sometimes at the cost of considerable suffering. The question is also raised by Goldstein and Kornfield about the practical importance both of having clear models and of using such models wisely, understanding the theoretical and practical limits of any model as such. It is striking, in this regard, that all of the teachers apparently place less importance on the available Asian and contemporary Western developmental models than on a trust in—and somewhat of an awe regarding—the "organic" unfolding of the different parts of what Kornfield calls the mandala of awakening.

These reflections suggest the importance for transpersonal approaches of dynamic relationships of both theory and evidence, and theory and practice. One of the ways that the ambitious developmental models of Piaget, Kohlberg, Gilligan, and Habermas are particularly rich, whatever their problems, is in their close connection with empirical work and, in the case of Habermas's model, practical (social and political) involvement. While Wilber's pioneering work perhaps necessarily has thus far taken on a high degree of generality, it seems crucial at this point not only to develop more clarity theoretically, but also to connect more fully and explicitly the theoretical accounts of transpersonal development with empirical and textual studies, as well as with contemporary therapeutic and spiritual practice.

In the context of these perspectives and questions, we can now turn to the reflections of these three spiritual teachers, whose everyday lives are centered on the observation and promotion of spiritual or transpersonal development. What sequences of development have they observed? What models and metaphors do they use? What are their views of stage models? How do they understand the interrelationship of the different lines of development?

Joseph Goldstein

One of the most beloved and respected contemporary meditation teachers, Joseph Goldstein has been one of the main links between Asian Buddhist contemplative traditions and rigorous spiritual practice in the West. With clarity, spaciousness, and humility, he has guided and inspired thousands of meditators over twenty-five years.

Goldstein was born in 1944 and raised in New York's Catskill Mountains, where his parents ran a summer resort. As a teenager, he experienced the deaths of his father, grandfather, and a cousin, and came to cultivate a philosophical understanding of life and death as a way of responding to these events.

He studied philosophy at Columbia University, but instead of going on to graduate studies, he entered the Peace Corps in 1965. Although his first choice was to go to Africa, he was assigned to Bangkok, Thailand. There he felt drawn to learn more about Buddhism. He visited Buddhist temples, sometimes with a copy of Spinoza's Ethics under his arm, and conversed with the monks, asking so many questions at first that other Westerners, upon hearing that he was coming, would steer clear of him. When he found out about meditation, he became very excited and interested. Although at first he used an alarm clock set at five minutes to make sure that he did not sit too long, soon he was practicing sitting and walking meditation for days on end.

After leaving the Peace Corps in 1967, Goldstein traveled to Bodh Gaya, India, the place of the Buddha's enlightenment. He began studying with the Bengali teacher Anagarika Munindra, a student of the famous Burmese teacher Mahasi Sayadaw ("Sayadaw" means teacher), and lived in the Burmese Vihara for a good part of the next seven years. His practice of insight (or vipassana) meditation was aimed at developing a nonjudgmental, direct and "bare" attention to whatever arises in experience. His persistence and discipline became somewhat legendary in India among Western practitioners.

In 1974, he was invited by Ram Dass, who had met him in Bodh Gaya, to teach at the newly formed Naropa Institute in Boulder, Colorado. There he met Jack Kornfield. Goldstein and Kornfield, along with Sharon Salzberg and others, began leading medi-

tation retreats. In 1976, they found and were able to buy an old Catholic monastery in Barre, Massachusetts, seventy miles west of Boston, which became the Insight Meditation Society (IMS) retreat center.

Since that time, Goldstein's life has been remarkably consistent. Each year, he co-leads the three-month retreat at IMS in the fall, leads other retreats around the world, and typically takes time for his own retreats, often of several months' duration. A number of books and audio tapes have developed from his talks. He now lives most of the year in a house built next to IMS as a gift from students and works with the Barre Center for Buddhist Studies, which he helped establish in 1989.

In addition to his studies with Sayadaw U Pandita, the successor to Mahasi Sayadaw, Goldstein has also studied the Tibetan Buddhist practice of Dzogchen, working with Tulku Urgyen Rinpoche and Nyoshul Khenpo Rinpoche, two renowned teachers. He also explored Jungian psychotherapy, working with James Hillman.

Goldstein's approach to spiritual life has gone through some shifts of emphasis, but has stayed centered on the cultivation of "non-attachment" or non-clinging—to one's views and judgments, comfort and desires, likes and dislikes, wonderful and difficult experiences. He emphasizes the simplicity yet difficulty of this most basic teaching of the Buddha. He has also cautioned against any "watering down" of this practice of liberation, and the dangers of some attempts to make spirituality appealing to Westerners by reinterpreting contemplative life through the forms of psychotherapy or relaxation techniques, for example.

Goldstein's vast experience in practice and teaching, including guiding and observing the spiritual development of thousands of persons during week-long or months-long retreats, certainly makes his reflections very pertinent in examining Wilber's accounts of stages and states of consciousness. Yet where Wilber develops numerous theories, Goldstein tends toward a kind of agnosticism. "Who knows?" is one of his favorite mantras. "Is the mind 'attached'?" is another. He is particularly interested in how we are attached to or cling to models or views of spiritual practice and suggests that models and views are "skillful means" to help liberate the mind. He evaluates models and views in terms of their usefulness for given people at given periods in their lives in a given culture, rather than as indicating how things "really are."

Yet Goldstein nonetheless finds that there is also a general movement in spiritual life from attention to what is "gross" or apparent, to what is more subtle, even if what is gross and subtle are relative to a given person. He prefers to look at the "degree of attachment" in an experience, rather than speaking of stages, or linking levels of development to the presence of transpersonal experiences. A less "advanced" person might be attached to "deep" spiritual experiences, while a more "advanced" person might be unattached to a wide range of relatively ordinary experiences.

Again and again, Goldstein returns to what he takes to be the simple but challenging practice of seeing whether one is free in a given moment. In the context of such a practice, we may sometimes realize better the vastness of the process of spiritual awakening, the extent to which our theorizing is or is not skillful, and how even our best models and views give only a tiny glimpse of this vastness.

Further Readings and Resources

Fields, R. 1992. *How the swans came to the lake: A narrative history of Buddhism in America*. 2nd ed. Boston: Shambhala.

Goldstein, J. [1976] 1987. *The experience of insight*. Boston: Shambhala.

_____. 1993. *Insight meditation: The practice of freedom*. Boston: Shambhala.

_____. 1994. *Transforming the mind, healing the world*. New York: Paulist Press.

_____. 1995. The flavors of anatta: Reflections from a Theravada perspective. *Inquiring Mind* 11 (2): 4.

_____. 1996. The mind of no clinging. *Inquiring Mind* 13 (1): 4, 7.

Goldstein, J., and J. Kornfield. 1987. *Seeking the heart of wisdom: The path of insight meditation*. Boston: Shambhala.

Inquiring Mind, a twice-yearly journal of the insight meditation community, is available at P.O. Box 9999, N. Berkeley Station, Berkeley, CA 94709.

Kornfield, J. 1989. Possibilities of the path: An interview with Joseph Goldstein. *Inquiring Mind* 6 (1): 1, 8-9, 12.

Nisker, W. 1984. Conversation with a spiritual friend: An interview with Joseph Goldstein. *Inquiring Mind* 1 (1): 1, 3-4.

Audio tapes of Joseph Goldstein's talks are available from Dhamma Seed Tape Library, Box 66, Wendell Depot, MA 01380, tel.: 413-772-1848. Information on retreats with Goldstein is available in *Inquiring Mind* (see above); and from the Insight Meditation Society, 1230 Pleasant Street, Barre, MA 01005, tel.: 508-355-4378.

Neither This Way Nor That Way:
Developmental Models as Skillful Means

Donald Rothberg: Are there any general developmental patterns related to spiritual practice that you've observed over the years in yourself, your students, and your peers? Are there any particular models or metaphors that make sense of spiritual development?

Joseph Goldstein: (Long pause.) My understanding of spiritual practice is increasingly predicated on a vision of how vast spiritual life is. It's so vast that it can contain every model. Or we might say that many different models can describe different aspects of the spiritual journey. So for me it's not a question of it being this way or that way; it's all of the ways. The bottom line seems to be the realization or the experience of the mind completely free of attachment to anything. Put simply, the rest is all skillful means. There is a vast array of skillful means, addressing different kinds of attachments. The attachments are innumerable and exist on all different levels.

DR: It sounds like there's no one "big picture" of the sequence of learning, how one kind of learning occurs first or necessarily follows another kind of learning.

JG: Well, there are some models that describe a general unfolding process, such as the models of the stages of insight in the Theravada tradition, or of the ten Oxherding pictures in Zen, or of the various stages of development in Tibetan *Lam Rim* or Mahamudra teachings. But I think that the process of liberating the mind from attachment is also an individual journey, influenced by all of our particular conditioning.

DR: Some contemporary authors also suggest a big picture, or at least some general patterns of spiritual development. For example, Jack Engler (1986) and others claim that there has to be a "self" established and a certain amount of what we might call "psychological" work done before real spiritual development occurs.

JG: I think that it's much more complex than that. Even in the context of a single lifetime, but certainly if one holds a vision of many lifetimes, there's no knowing the hidden unfolding of karma. One would have to have something like the Buddha-Mind really to know. For example, I could well imagine a person having some really neurotic habit, yet still being able to reach deep levels of understanding and realization without necessarily going through a therapeutic process. For others, the untying of psychological knots may first be necessary. The reality of our beings seems to me much more complex, rich, and in many ways unfathomable, than any simple view about how development is supposed to occur. However, it also seems true that a certain base line of mental health and balance is necessary for spiritual practice and that coming to that place of balance is itself part of the spiritual journey.

DR: How do you understand Buddhist developmental models? Are they at best "skillful means" that may be helpful for certain people in certain periods of their lives in certain cultures?

JG: Yes, but I would not minimize the importance of skillful means with the phrase "at best." I think that skillful means are everything. A given model is a skillful means for some and may not be one for others. If spiritual practice is at root about freeing the mind from attachment, then there are many tools, many ways, and many metaphors to help us do that.

Let me give you an example. The Burmese tradition of Mahasi Sayadaw is very much based on the synthesis of Abhidhamma and Sutta study. The Abhidhamma gives a very psychologically oriented model with elaborate analysis of states of mind and consciousness.

This has been very accessible to many Western students, because of the emphasis on the psychological as perhaps the basic way of understanding our own culture. But another approach, such as Zen, could be more poetic. Abhidhamma resonates with some people for whom it makes complete sense; they may find the poetic approach obscure and unnecessarily opaque. To others, the psychological model seems very dry and the poetic approach very appealing. So different skillful means, in this case different models or metaphors, are appropriate for different people.

DR: Do you think that these Buddhist models are understood as metaphorical in Asian Buddhist contexts, for example, in Burma?

JG: Probably not. (Laughter.) I have the feeling that often the model is taken more literally, as how it really is.

I've been thinking about models more the last couple of years, especially since becoming interested in some Tibetan practices. Having been immersed for a long time in the Theravada tradition, when I first engaged in Tibetan-style practice, I was thrown into an amazing dilemma of mind, trying to synthesize two very different metaphysical systems, both of which I resonated with a lot. I spent some months on a retreat really driving myself crazy, saying: "Well, if this one is right, then the other can't be right." I would ask myself, "Is this just Mara [the personification of forces antagonistic to enlightenment] trying to tempt me into 'wrong view'?" After quite a while, I finally realized that I would never figure out the issues through thinking about them. I would only really know—perhaps—when I was fully enlightened. This insight inspired me to further my practice. I also came to see all metaphysics as skillful means. With this understanding, everything changed; I could see these two somewhat different systems as not in conflict, but rather both as skillful means to help bring the mind to more openness and attention. I settled much more into the wonderful practice of developing the mind of no-craving, not putting this off as some goal in the future. In this context, any technique or method or system simply became a way of helping me with this practice.

DR: So then you could follow such a general practice, make use of Tibetan teachings, and not think that you were abandoning Theravada.

JG: Exactly. I realized: "Look, I'm practicing the mind of no-craving, no-clinging." I didn't think that anybody would argue with that. The Tibetans would agree; the Burmese would agree. It felt as if this expressed the essence of the free mind. This insight was reinforced when I reread the "housebuilder" passage from the Buddha: "Housebuilder, you have been seen. You will build no house again . . . . Realized is the unconditioned. Achieved is the end of craving." Of course, I had read this passage hundreds of times, but somehow being on retreat, it struck me in a fresh and different way. It seemed such a simple and profound expression of what the whole spiritual path is about. This helped me to cut through all the issues about the superstructures of system and belief. It helped make my practice very alive.

DR: You've worked with many thousands of people over the last twenty years or so. Do you see any general sequence to their development?

JG: I'm about to state what is very obvious. People work from the more apparent to the subtle. Initially in practice, there are some common experiences. For example, in doing sitting meditation, people typically learn the possibility of equanimity with pleasant and unpleasant feelings in the body, learning to rest in awareness without grasping for the pleasant or pushing away the unpleasant. People also learn to distinguish between being lost in a thought and being aware of a thought. These may not be particularly subtle insights, but they are nonetheless quite profound, going to the heart of the nature of the free mind. As practice continues, there may be learning to extend the same qualities of equanimity and nonidentification to the experience of previously hidden and more and more subtle aspects of our being. Various emotions may arise or be uncovered; students learn to distinguish between identification with emotions as "self" and letting the emotions go, seeing them as a succession of appearances. On a yet more subtle level, there can be insight into and letting go of the identification with consciousness and awareness, which forms a kind of overlay on awareness. Subtle attachments that are like "fixations," almost of an energetic nature, are also uncovered. These are not thoughts or emotions, and may be so subtle that we may for a long time not even realize that the mind is holding on to these fixations.

So I do see an evolution in practice occurring from the apparent to the subtle. The particular content of what arises for a given person is very individual, although, as you know, I see the content as less important than insight into the general process.

DR: Does what is obvious or what is subtle vary significantly between individuals? Might something that is subtle for one person be gross for another?

JG: I think so. This goes back to what I was saying at the beginning, that there's just no knowing all the infinite past histories of people. Some students have a very easy time noticing the nature of awareness and are at ease with formlessness. For others, these words only connote abstractions.

DR: For the first person, what is subtle might be very different than for the second person. The first person might be at ease with formlessness, but have a hard time getting a job.

JG: That could be. Actually, I don't normally use the word "advanced" in describing someone's spiritual practice. But if I did use it, I would relate it to the *degree of attachment* connected with a given experience. One person could be very attached to great formless awareness, and another person could be watching the breath and be deeply unattached. So for me the measure is the degree of attachment rather than the content of the experience. Again, it comes back to the nature of the free mind.

DR: Do you find people having what are traditionally taken as "deep" realizations or insights, which coexist with plenty of attachments on grosser levels?

JG: I think that *we* do. We have. (Laughter.)

DR: Yes. We speak for ourselves. (Laughter.)

JG: Sometimes there are unrealistic expectations about the effects of realization experiences. However, to the extent that there has been some realization of selflessness, even though attachments may still be quite in evidence, there's a certain degree of transparency to the attachments. This may be hard to see from the outside.

Again, however, I think that there is the general pattern that we move from gross to subtle, although there are some exceptions. People usually find it easier to begin bringing attention to obvious things. Generally, people first examine issues having to do with the body, aspects of their personalities, and everyday life, although sometimes the order is reversed and people have more subtle spiritual experiences first. Also, people don't necessarily completely resolve these initial issues. In many ways, the spiritual path spirals around, again and again, to many of the same initial areas. So, a person might withdraw for a period of time for meditation. He or she might develop some equanimity with respect to pain and pleasure, become more open to emotions, and come to some important insights. As the journey continues, the person would return with deeper levels of nonattachment and equanimity in relation to the body and emotions. The first time through doesn't necessarily resolve the deeper and more subtle levels of attachment.

DR: How do you understand and work with what appears to be "regression," in which a student will return to very early issues?

JG: The meditative process is one of opening to all different levels of our nature. As the mind becomes more still and concentrated, there's a space that's created in us for whatever is in us to come up. I usually think of apparently regressive phenomena in this context. We open generally to different levels of attachment, surfacing patterns that are deeply rooted at least in this life, and perhaps in past ones. Sometimes these experiences are very traumatic and may be at times overwhelming, especially in more "classic" regression, in which people seem like they are lost back in a previous world.

DR: My initial spiritual practice involved attending many retreats. Generally, they were wonderful, full of calm and insights, although of course there were also many difficult periods. But I only noticed many areas of my own attachments, to use that language, in other kinds of settings, outside of retreats: in intimate relationships, in work, in relating to the earth, in engaging in social and political processes. How do you understand the balance of learning in and out of retreats?

JG: Again, this is all so vast. Even a whole lifetime may not illuminate all the places of attachment. Furthermore, what people bring to any particular lifetime is so varied. So I don't have any particular model of what people should do or should not do; it's very individual. Some people may have been working, for example, on relationships for several lifetimes. (Laughter.) In this lifetime, they could be nuns or monks. Or somebody may have been a nun or a monk for several lifetimes and not dealt with relationship issues. From the outside, it's very hard to judge. That's why I'm a little leery of laying any particular trip on somebody, about what he or she should or shouldn't be doing. It's much more a question of really listening carefully.

I also think that we don't necessarily need to put ourselves in every situation that might stimulate our attachments or conditioning. That would be endless; there would be no way to be in every possible situation. If that were the only way to become free, it wouldn't work. I think that we need generally to integrate working with things that come up, either in our life in the world or in meditation practice, and penetrating with insight into the empty nature of it all.

That might be done with a broad range of experiences. But it could also be done with a very narrow range of experiences. If the depth of the realization is sufficient, then that wisdom will automatically be brought to bear on every situation in which we find ourselves.

DR: How can we make sense of the important observation that there often seem to be deep insights, while, at the same time, fundamental "personal" work has not been completed? This observation was a main focus, for example, at the recent Western Buddhist Teachers' meeting in May 1995 in California. Some teachers had experienced, early on in their spiritual practices, sustained periods of deep insights, but then realized that much of the rest of their lives was a mess and that they needed to work on the mess. This often meant giving more attention to relationships and to ethics.

JG: I have a lot to say about all these questions. First, I want to reiterate an earlier point. If there's some level of realization, it's easier to work with the more personal "stuff," because there's some insight into its emptiness.

Secondly, I do see somewhat of a tendency for people in the West to limit spiritual practice to the experience of meditation. But the Eightfold Path, which the Buddha laid out as the path to enlightenment, is a very integrated path. It's about our life in the world and how we relate to others, as well as being about meditation. We often don't take the nonmeditative aspects of the path, including Right Speech, Right Action, and Right Livelihood, as seriously as we should, as part of our spiritual practice. If we did take these aspects seriously, it might not be so much a question of going back and cleaning up this other stuff, because attending to this other stuff is largely included in the different aspects or steps of the Eightfold Path. My vision of the journey and the path is to give equal weight to each of these steps.

Thirdly, I want to point to the general expectation in our culture that we will get quick results from whatever we do. We often evaluate our path or the fruits of the path in what I think is a rather superficial way. Someone may do a few years of intensive practice and then come out and say, "I still have all this other personal 'stuff.' What didn't work with this spiritual practice?" There are some wonderful stories in the *Theragatha* and *Therigatha* [the enlightenment verses of early Buddhist monks and nuns, respectively]. I'm thinking especially of some of the songs of enlightenment of the nuns. It's typical to read the account of a nun saying something like: "I've been practicing for sixty years and didn't have one moment of a still mind. Then in a moment my mind opened and peace was attained." We need to make our assessments of what practice does and doesn't do in the context of a much longer time frame. This isn't to say that we shouldn't be asking how things are going, or in what directions, just that great constancy and perseverance is needed in this great journey of awakening.

Jack Kornfield

For thirty years, Jack Kornfield has been involved in presenting authentic Buddhist teachings and practice in accessible ways to Western audiences and exploring how Buddhism might develop in ways appropriate to the needs and potentials of Western culture. One of the main teachers to introduce Theravada Buddhism to the West, he has been a meditation teacher, psychotherapist, founder and builder of spiritual institutions, and prolific writer.

Graduating from Dartmouth College in 1967, having studied with the great scholar of Chinese traditions, Dr. Wing-Tsit Chan, and explored psychedelics and "hippie" life, Kornfield set off for Asia. He served two years in the Peace Corps in Thailand and then became a Buddhist monk for several years, particularly at Wat Ba Pong ("forest monastery of marsh and pong"—pong is a type of high grass), near the Thai-Lao border. The abbot of the monastery was Ajahn (an honorific meaning "Teacher") Chah (1918-1993), who himself had studied briefly with the great Thai-Lao yogi and teacher, Ajahn Mun (1870-1949). Each had spent years as wandering forest monks, walking through dense forests amidst tigers and elephants, usually alone, doing sitting and walking meditation. At the monastery, Kornfield followed the simple routines of a life dedicated to moment-to-moment awareness, ethical integrity, and the cultivation of life wisdom. He also studied with other teachers, including the famous Mahasi Sayadaw of Burma, who had helped to revitalize the practice of vipassana *meditation.*

After returning to the United States in 1972, he drove a cab, worked in a mental hospital, and completed a Ph.D. in Psychology at the Humanistic Psychology Institute (now the Saybrook Institute). After helping to found the Insight Meditation Society in 1976, he has worked with hundreds of students each year there and around the world.

In 1984, after many years as a wandering teacher, Kornfield's life shifted significantly. Within the next few years, he moved to the San Francisco Bay Area, married Liana Chenoweth, had a daughter, Caroline, rented a home, and helped found the Spirit

Rock Center in rural Marin County, north of San Francisco. The vision for Spirit Rock was significantly broader than that of IMS. The new center would offer both a retreat and a community center, and there would be a strong emphasis on the meaning of Buddhist spiritual teachings for daily life in the West, with retreats and workshops on such themes as family practice, intimate relationships, women's and men's issues, and social activism, as well as more conventional Buddhist trainings.

Since his move to California, Kornfield has been exceedingly active for a former monk who once spent an entire year mostly doing sitting meditation practice in a small cottage in the forest in Asia. In addition to leading retreats and workshops, Kornfield has worked as a psychotherapist, published a number of influential books, given Monday night talks at Spirit Rock Center to several hundred people each week, and helped to organize meetings of Western Buddhist teachers, both in Asia with the Dalai Lama and in the United States.

Kornfield's broad experience gives him a base from which he can usefully evaluate Wilber's theories. Starting with his doctoral thesis on the psychology of mindfulness meditation, he has long wrestled with the nature of spiritual and meditative development. His own life and observations raise a number of questions about Wilber's view of spiritual development: How can a stage model such as Wilber's make sense of Kornfield's personal story of "descent" from initial transpersonal realizations while a monk to a focus on emotions, relationships, and body experience? More broadly, to what extent do stage models help make sense of the development of the thousands of spiritual practitioners that Kornfield has observed?

Kornfield suggests that metaphors other than "stages" are sometimes more appropriate for understanding and expressing development. He also questions whether a general completion of one's "psychological" work is necessary before spiritual or transpersonal dimensions of one's being open up, as Wilber's work seems to suggest.

Further Readings and Resources

Fields, R. 1992. *How the swans came to the lake: A narrative history of Buddhism in America*. 2nd ed. Boston: Shambhala.

Goldstein, J. and Kornfield, J. 1987. *Seeking the heart of wisdom: The path of insight meditation*. Boston: Shambhala.

Inquiring Mind, a twice-yearly journal of the insight meditation community, is available at P.O. Box 9999, N. Berkeley Station: Berkeley, Calif. 94709.

Kornfield, J. 1977. Intensive insight meditation: A phenomenological study. *Journal of Transpersonal Psychology* 11 (1): 41-58.

_____. 1993a. *A path with heart: A guide through the perils and promises of spiritual life*. New York: Bantam Books.

_____. 1993b. *Teachings of the Buddha*. Boston: Shambhala.

_____. 1994. *Buddha's little instruction book*. New York: Bantam Books.

_____. 1995. *Living dharma*. Boston: Shambhala. [Originally published in 1977 as *Living Buddhist masters*. Santa Cruz, Calif.: Unity Press.]

Kornfield, J. and Breiter, P., eds. 1985. *A still forest pool: The insight meditation of Achaan Chah*. Wheaton, Ill.: Quest Books.

Kornfield, J. and Feldman, C., eds. 1996. *Soul food: Stories to nourish the spirit and the heart*. San Francisco: HarperSanFrancisco.

Schwartz, T. 1995. Seeking the heart of wisdom: Where Jack Kornfield and Joseph Goldstein parted ways. In *What really matters: Searching for wisdom in America,* by T. Schwartz. New York: Bantam Books.

Walsh, R., D. Goleman, J. Kornfield, C. Pensa, and D. Shapiro. 1978. Meditation: Aspects of research and practice. *Journal of Transpersonal Psychology* 10 (2): 113-33.

Audio tapes of Jack Kornfield's talks are available from Dhamma Seed Tape Library, Box 66, Wendell Depot, Mass. 01380, tel.: 413-772-1848. Information on retreats with Jack Kornfield is available in *Inquiring Mind* (see above), and from Spirit Rock Center, P.O. Box 909, Woodacre, Calif. 94973, tel.: 415-488-0164.

The Mandala of Awakening

 **Donald Rothberg:** At the beginning of *A Path with Heart* (Kornfield 1993), you spoke about your own personal development as being somewhat of a reversal of the common model of an "ascent." Following many years of spiritual insights and realizations, you found it appropriate to focus for many more years on the "heart," emotions, and relationships, and then, some years later, on your bodily experience. You wrote:

My own practice has been a journey downward, in contrast to the way we usually think of our spiritual experiences. Over these years I've found myself working my way *down* the chakras (the spiritual energy centers of the body) rather than up. My first ten years of systematic spiritual practice were primarily conducted through my mind. I studied, read, and then meditated and lived as a monk, always using the power of my mind to gain understanding. I developed concentration and *samadhi* (deep levels of mental absorption), and many kinds of insights came. I had visions, revelations, and a variety of deep awakenings. . . .

But alas, when I returned to the U.S. as a monk, all of that fell apart. . . . Although I had arrived back from the monastery clear, spacious, and high, in short order I had discovered . . . that my meditation had helped me very little with my human relationships. I was still emotionally immature, acting out the same painful patterns of blame and fear, acceptance and rejection that I had before my Buddhist training; only the horror now was that [as] I was beginning to see these patterns more clearly . . . I was forced to shift my whole practice down the chakras from the mind to the heart. I began a long and difficult process of reclaiming my emotions, of bringing awareness and understanding to my patterns of relationship, of learning how to feel my feelings, and what to do with the powerful forces of human connection. . . .

After ten years of focusing on emotional work and the development of the heart, I realized that I had neglected my body. Like my emotions, my body had been included in my early spiritual practice in only a superficial way. . . . I had to move further down the chakras. I learned that if I am to live a spiritual life, I must be able to embody it in every action: in the way I stand and walk, in the way I breathe, in the care with which I eat. . . . In beginning to reinhabit my body, I discovered new areas of fear and pain that kept me away from my true self, just as I had discovered new areas of fear and pain in opening my mind and opening my heart.

As my practice has proceeded down the chakras, it has become more intimate and more personal. It has required more honesty and care each step of the way. It has also become more integrated. . . . So that as I have been working my way down, the vision of my practice has expanded to include, not just my own body or heart, but all of life, the relationships we hold, and the environment that sustains us. (6–8)

Here, you use the image of a "descent." What other kinds of images or models help you to make sense of your observations of the patterns of psychological and spiritual development that you've noticed both in yourself and in your students and peers?

Jack Kornfield: The images or metaphors that seem to work best for me in understanding human development are the mandala and the spiral. Neither the mandala nor the spiral has a strongly hierarchical nature. If we imagine the mandala as an expression of human development, it's clear that one can have great openings to the transpersonal, only to close down a week or a month later and have to deal with the earliest infantile or traumatic childhood incidents. One might work with that material, only to discover that a whole other dimension of the mandala, for example, having to do with respect for one's own physical body, integration of the physical senses, and sexuality has not been touched. What development appears to require is a broad container that allows for all of these realms to arise, a deep technology to foster opening in these various dimensions, and then a willingness to respect the organic openings of beings. These openings seem to occur in a mandala-like way, much like the petals of a flower. From this perspective, one can begin to trust the particular types of opening that need to happen.

Development is also like a spiral. One may have a profound insight or a transcendent vision and then go through a period of what feels like regression, identification with a smaller sense of self, with what we sometimes call the "body of fear." However, in many cases reexperiencing this more limited sense of self with some of the understanding connected with the transcendental vision allows one to go more deeply into the painful material. Then, one may come back again to new modes of transpersonal experience. This sequence may happen again and again, in a kind of spiral. A person may return over and over to the particular themes that form that individual's life. Yet these themes are increasingly felt, seen, and known with more and more understanding, as well as with more irony and a sense of the metaphorical nature of the themes.

We have learned that one of our great mistakes of the earlier years of bringing Eastern spiritual maps and models to the West is what we could call the "linear mistake." This is the (mistaken) view that if one had an experience of *satori* in a Zen *sesshin*, or an experience of "stream entry" and nirvana through the progress of insight in *vipassana* meditation, then that would somehow automatically clean up one's physical, emotional, and psychological karmic house, so to speak.

We have learned over and over that there is no such thing as a "spiritual bypass" or "end run." Actually, enlightenment is more like the *beginning* of a journey. As one rests more and more in the center of one's being, as the sense of Buddha nature or sacred presence is remembered more deeply and becomes a ground of being that is increasingly accessible, then it becomes more and more apparent which aspects of the mandala are still causing suffering, are still incompletely developed. Then a wise teacher, with a wise system of practice, will listen for where the areas of entanglement are and direct the psychological and spiritual practice of a person into those areas of entanglement in order to free those dimensions of the person's being.

My teacher, the late Ajahn Chah, one of the greatest and most respected masters in southeast Asia, was enormously intuitive and perspicacious in that way. He would listen for what particular area of difficulty had arisen for a monk and then tailor a practice or situation for him to work with that area. For example, a monk who had become an excellent meditator might at some point start to deal with depression. Ajahn Chah would give that person a practice of community relations to create the relational bonding necessary to untangle the knot of depression. A monk who had a great deal of grief arising, perhaps after a period of delightful living in the monastery, because of the loss of a family member or some other loss, might well be assigned to attend all the monastic and community funerals for a year. This would really untangle the knot of identification around loss and grief for that monk. Another monk who was very social might be sent by Ajahn Chah to a cave monastery. He might assign a monk who was attached to silence to the greeting monastery in Bangkok.

However, this wasn't done according to some preordained map. Human inner development is perhaps more like the weather than like a train line. One responds to the immediate situation, to what kind of monsoon season arises, whether there's a great deal of rain or not. Sometimes Ajahn Chah would know, as I am learning, that even though a particular person might have very deep suffering and entanglement in a certain part of his or her life, the person would not be ready to tackle it yet. In that case, Ajahn Chah would provide a container of support, nurturance, steadiness, and the deepening of a spiritual perspective, that would eventually allow that person to enter the difficult area. We need, I think, to have an enormous respect for the defenses that we have used to survive, as well as for the possibility of opening. In that sense, the most skillful teachings may often be those which melt one open, rather than somehow pry open the door, which later only slams shut. From this perspective, the heart is melted open, like the flower that is nurtured to the point at which its petals open naturally. It's the ripening of the fruit on the tree so that the fruit drops of its own accord.

DR: You've spoken about Ajahn Chah in a way which more or less fits the metaphor of the mandala. There's a general sense of looking wherever in the mandala there is greed, hatred, and delusion, to use Buddhist language—that is, not having a fixed model of the sequence of unfolding. But there also are models in Buddhist traditions of what seems like more linear development.

JK: The Tibetans have such models. Zen has the Oxherding pictures and a sense of a progressive sequence in working with koans. Theravada Buddhism has the model of the seven purifications or the progress of insight. These models do give useful maps of the territory. It is also the case that development can follow such models, at least in a very broad sense; they can suggest very generally the direction of development.

However, our experience as Western teachers over several decades has been that, more often than not, people's practice does not follow these linear models. Of course, practice will occasionally follow such models. At certain levels of *samadhi* (or concentration), there's a progression of jhana states that will arise, one after another, quite beautifully mapped by the texts and some teachers. In a small percentage of people, the states of the "progress of insight" may arise. There is typically a dissolution of the identification with the physical and mental events of body and mind and an opening to the dimension of dissolution and death with its attendant imagery and fear. Finally, there is a resolution, usually with enormous equanimity. This process can also be found in shamanic journeying, in the sequences of death and rebirth in holotrophic breathing as developed by Stan and Christina Grof, and in many other practices. However, the actual unfolding is still very individual. Even the most sophisticated teachers may not be able to judge what exactly is happening with a given person's process.

For example, one Western monk was studying with U Pandita Sayadaw, a highly regarded contemporary Burmese Buddhist master. He was studying with U Pandita Sayadaw to be a teacher. He had mastered the Theravadin developmental maps and had himself had many of the experiences detailed in these maps. He was sitting in on interviews with meditation students doing long retreats with U Pandita Sayadaw, both in Burma and in the West. However, thinking that he was not understanding the maps well, he began to ask the simple question, "At what stage is this person?" After he asked that question, U Pandita Sayadaw's translator, himself a very experienced yogi and meditator, got into a dialogue and actually argued with U Pandita Sayadaw about the assessment of a particular person. The translator reported back to the Western monk that they had some disagreement about the assessment. These differences of opinion occurred a number of times in several monasteries connected with U Pandita Sayadaw. In fact, in one monastery based on promulgating more linear models, there have been passionate and often difficult debates among the monks about whether a given person has really attained various levels of opening. There have been strong disagreements and even factions growing easily and quickly, all because the monks couldn't really tell the supposed levels of people.

This example suggests to me the limits of working experientially with these models. The models may look beautiful when they're on the screen of a computer, or on the page of a book at a monastery, or in a psychology journal.

DR: Do you think that there has to be a significant degree of completion of the basic tasks of psychological growth before real spiritual development occurs?

JK: Jack Engler (1986) has expressed this most simply and, I think he would agree, most simplistically as: "You have to have a self before you can lose one." Of course, if one knows any of the major and admired transpersonal or spiritual figures, one finds they are human beings just like the rest of us, who have not at all finished their own psychological work and are quite honest about that. But although this slogan sounds good on paper, my actual experience is that the "psychological" and the "spiritual" are parallel dimensions, as it were.

My observation over several decades of the experiences of Western spiritual students and meditators is that the psychological and the spiritual are two dimensions of the one process of opening, allowing the spiritual light to come through our lives in both a transcendent and an immanent way. Often, in a person's experience, there will come a constellation of fear, inner attachment, and difficulty that on one level is related to personal history, to trauma in childhood or in this life; this constellation arises together with emotions, beliefs, and a bodily store of contraction, the "body of fear." As the person enters this complex or knot with awareness, interest, and compassion and opens to it, then it begins to dissolve, as it is seen, understood, and allowed. The constellation is naturally transformed in this process into spiritual energy or spiritual perspective.

The notion that the psychological and the spiritual somehow refer to separate domains is not at all, in my view, an accurate picture of how human development actually occurs. Increasingly, I can't myself even separate the two anymore. I simply see, as my own master Ajahn Chah taught me, that there is, to refer to the basic Buddhist principle, suffering and the end of suffering. Suffering comes in the form of grasping or identification with many layers of the body of fear and its concomitant stories and traumas. Such suffering can be released. To say that it's psychological or spiritual is to make an arbitrary division not actually found in the psyche. In fact, the beings whom I know who are the most spiritually mature among Western students in all the various traditions are those in whom there has been a maturing and development of emotional, psychological, personal, and historical, as well as universal, understanding. Such understanding has been tested for these persons again and again through the fire of relationships (thinking of relationships in the broadest sense): relationships to work, to community, to other individuals, and to their environments. In that sense, there's no sense of any separation between the psychological and spiritual.

I'd rather speak about the "universal" and the "personal." I believe that this distinction is more accurate. There are transcendant or universal understandings that we can have, and there are also personal dimensions of spiritual awakening. The two need to be integrated; this is what we've been talking about. Spiritual maturity, that is, a real freedom of heart and great compassion, requires freedom on both the universal and the personal levels.

DR: Can you make any generalizations about the developmental patterns that you've observed among students and peers?

JK: There are generalizations that I can make. The mandala itself reflects a general principle. Further, a teacher like my own teacher Ajahn Chah looked at perhaps a dozen different dimensions of a human being's life; these dimensions might correspond to Ken Wilber's basic structures or stages. For example, a person might be assessed following the Buddhist models of the Four Foundations of Mindfulness or the Eightfold Path of development. Can this person really live well in his or her body, for example, in terms of eating and exercise, honoring incarnation in a body as an aspect of awakening? Can this person deal well with all the various moods and emotions? If not, there might be training to help emotions to be held in compassionate understanding rather than being a source of bondage. Are the person's various relationships approached wisely? Is there Right Livelihood? Then, what are this person's thoughts, beliefs, and understandings about the nature of self and world?

These different areas are not arbitrarily selected at all; there's a very clear mandala of the different dimensions of our lives. Each of these dimensions radiates out from a center of compassion and freedom that is our true nature. Whenever a person is not free in respect to one of these dozen or so dimensions, then that part of his or her life smacks the person over the head. It gets right in the person's face. The person can say, "Well, that's not spiritual. I'm not going to deal with it." Or he or she can say, as Ajahn Chah taught, "Oh! Here is another place of suffering, identification, and grasping. Here's also a place of freedom, of the liberation of energy." Increasingly, one can enter any dimension of life with compassion and freedom.

I've come to trust *deeply* the psyche itself in its knowing how and when to open. The psyche knows for a given individual which dimension of the mandala needs to open and produces experiences in quite trustworthy ways, much as a rose knows how to open, petal by petal. Over and over again, with thousands of students, I've seen that unfolding work.

DR: In these kinds of openings do you see any particular patterns? Do certain dimensions of the mandala need to open up before others do? Or is the process completely individual?

JK: It's interesting. It's often quite individual. Some individuals' unfoldings may be quite opposite in sequence from that of others. One doesn't necessarily start with attention to the body or with early childhood experiences. One does not necessarily first develop a self and then lose that sense of self. And one can't necessarily know the nature of a particular person's sequence. Michele McDonald-Smith, for example, had some very deep and quite extraordinary meditative experiences for a number of years. Then, as a result of and following those experiences, there arose some years of profound personal work concerned with her history of abuse and trauma. Without working on and integrating this area, she couldn't have matured or even have lived very well. Her development was in the reverse order, if you will, from what is suggested in more linear theories. I could give a hundred other examples like that very easily.

DR: Is there any particular order in which "deeper" spiritual experiences appear?

JK: Not necessarily. However, as I said earlier, with the "progress of insight" in vipassana practice there are certain patterns that sometimes occur, but only a small percentage of students go through this sequence.

DR: Given this discussion and a sense of some of the limits of these theories, what do you think are the role and value of models of consciousness and development?

JK: I think that the models are very important in clarifying the maps and the territory of consciousness and development. I think that it's enormously helpful to have these maps of different possibilities of human experience from the ancient spiritual literature and from various kinds of modern spiritual and psychological literature. What's often missing, however, is a sense of how one actually travels through this territory; we've discussed some of the very basic principles. In some cases this sense of how one travels may be missing because the person who has created the map has not himself or herself completed a systematic journey through the territory. The map may be partly just a bunch of neat ideas. So, we need to talk more accurately about what helps one to know and work with, both as an individual and with another individual, these various dimensions of ourselves.

DR: One implication of what you were saying is that it would be a mark of wisdom for a person or a teacher really to honor exactly what was unfolding at a given moment. Yet, as we know, there often are strong preferences in "spiritual" settings to have "spiritual" unfoldings rather than other kinds of unfoldings.

JK: As if there was something that was not "spiritual."

DR: To what extent has this been a problem among your students and in your communities?

JK: It's common. People often try to impose a particular spiritual map onto their spiritual practices, whether meditation or chanting or doing some other practice. If one has a map of what is supposed to happen, and then an experience arises regarding one's relationship with one's father, or regarding how one eats, or regarding the person sitting on the next cushion at the meditation retreat, the person might well say, "That's not spiritual." One might suppress the experience, or be angry at oneself, or not want to work with it, rather than seeing the experience as reflecting a place of entanglement, whose untangling can lead to compassion and freedom. The big danger of using a map is the inclination to impose it unwisely on the natural opening of experience.

Photograph of Jack Kornfield by Glen McKay.

Michele McDonald-Smith

Michele McDonald-Smith is widely regarded as one of the most skilled guides for those wishing to combine emotional healing with traditional Buddhist meditation practice. For the past sixteen years, she has worked with thousands of meditators, at the annual three-month retreat at the Insight Meditation Society, as well as near her home in Hawaii and worldwide. She has focused on integrating intensive retreat practice, daily life practice, psychotherapy, and an ecologically-grounded spirituality.

McDonald-Smith's interests and sensitivities have come very directly from her attempts to find wholeness in her own life. She recalls very early in her life sitting on a chair looking out the living room window, and wondering, "How is it that I am living in this house, in this neighborhood, with these parents and sisters? What am I doing here?" Much of her childhood was spent exploring alone the nearby woods, ponds, and lake, and often finding there a sense of inner quiet and peace. Throughout her life, such contemplative immersion in nature has provided a primary spiritual practice. As a teenager, she watched her mother fall ill and eventually die; this prompted her to look for something that transcended life and death.

At college and in her early twenties, McDonald-Smith followed her love of the natural world, working for the Massachusetts Audubon Society, teaching environmental education in Massachusetts and Maine, and later homesteading in northern Maine. She also worked with people with learning disabilities and with the mentally ill. She began participating in Buddhist retreats in 1975 and soon found herself deeply drawn to meditation practice. She served on the staff and later on the board of directors of the Insight Meditation Society for several years, attending many one-week to three-month retreats. She has worked with a wide range of Western and Asian teachers, including Joseph Goldstein, Jack Kornfield, Sharon Salzberg, Christopher Titmuss, Christina Feldman, Dipama (of Calcutta), Mahasi Sayadaw (of Burma), Ajahn Chah (of Thailand), and Taungpulu Sayadaw (of Burma).

Because of the depth of her insight and practice, she was invited to become a teacher herself. She has taught the three-month retreat at IMS since 1982, as well as other retreats worldwide since 1984. She has also for many years taught an annual retreat for teenagers. In 1983, she moved to Honolulu, helping to found and guide Vipassana Hawaii and the Hawaii Insight Meditation Center with her husband Steven Smith. She has continued with many meditation retreats, particularly with the eminent

*Burmese teacher, Sayadaw U Pandita, has worked as a practitioner of sandplay thera-
py since 1985, and has helped to raise a daughter, Chandra. She has recently participated in exploring ecologically sustainable living in Hawaii.*

*Yet what might sound like a life of continually deepening spiritual insight, com-
mitment, service, and recognition has also been marked by many intense and difficult
experiences. As McDonald-Smith recounts in the following conversation, in the early
1980s, she began to experience a "downward" or "descending" movement quite unlike,
in many ways, the "upward" or "ascending" course of her earlier insights and breakthroughs. Finding little guidance from the illustrious teachers with whom she had
worked, she was initially left on her own to attempt to make sense of experiences of
agony and terror that invariably followed spiritual openings. Eventually working with
a therapist, McDonald-Smith came to understand her descent as a kind of necessary
regression, made possible by her spiritual base in mindfulness practice, to face the unresolved traumas of an abusive early childhood. Healing would come, but only after years
of hard work and considerable courage in facing the unknown.*

*This background gives McDonald-Smith important vantage points from which to
examine Wilber's work. She is particularly interested in how we "split off" from parts
of ourselves, whether because of personal trauma, cultural conditioning, or some other
reason. Indeed, she describes herself as having a good "nose" for discerning spiritual
teachers and teachings with unresolved "splits." She speaks of the unfortunate tendency for some people to regard themselves as highly developed spiritually, when in fact
they are attending only to particular experiences, such as profound breakthroughs,
while ignoring others. Consequently, they may "act out" under the influence of unac-
knowledged anger, fear, desire to control or dominate, or need for approval.*

*What does it mean, she asks, to develop an "integrated" spirituality, in which for-
merly "split-off" parts of the self are acknowledged, accessed, and gradually incorporated into conscious experience? She finds that, for many contemporary spiritual seekers, part of the answer is attending to their sense of disconnection from bodies and emotions. Yet the quest for healing and growth through the body and emotions may look
considerably "messier" than is promised in many of the maps of spiritual development.
It may involve what seems at times to be regression, and it may not always involve a
movement through the discrete "stages" identified by Wilber.*

*McDonald-Smith focuses on what she calls the "levels" (or aspects) of spiritual
development, making use of the Buddhist teaching about the* paramis, *the spiritual
"perfections" or virtues, such as wisdom, lovingkindness, generosity, patience, and
effort. Her emphasis is on integrating many kinds of development and particularly on
encouraging development of typically neglected aspects, such as the "feminine" and
relational dimensions of our lives. Such an integration, she concludes, is vital for a culture out of touch both with its pain and grief and with its body, our earth.*

Further Readings and Resources

McDonald, M. 1986. The ecology of the heart. *Karuna: A Journal of Buddhist Meditation* 3
    (Fall/Winter): 7-8.

_____. 1987. On equanimity. *Karuna: A Journal of Buddhist Meditation* 4 (Summer): 8-9.

McDonald-Smith, M. 1997. Of mud and broken windows: Teaching the wounded soul. In *Being bodies: Buddhist women on the paradox of embodiment*, edited by L. Friedman and S. Moon. Boston: Shambhala. [An earlier 1995 version of this essay is also found in *Blind Donkey: Journal of the Diamond Sangha* 15 (Winter): 12-15.]

McDonald-Smith, M., and S. Smith. 1992. Sharing the path: Steven and Michele McDonald-Smith talk about committed relationships and spiritual practice. *IMS* (Spring): 1, 5-6 (available from the Insight Meditation Society, 1230 Pleasant Street, Barre, Mass. 01005).

Audio tapes of many of Michele McDonald-Smith's talks are available from Dhamma Seed Tape Library, Box 66, Wendell Depot, Mass. 01380, tel.: 413-772-1848. Information on retreats with McDonald-Smith is available in *Inquiring Mind*, P.O. Box 9999, N. Berkeley Station, Berkeley, Calif. 94709; from the Insight Meditation Society, 1230 Pleasant Street, Barre, Mass. 01005, tel.: 508-355-4378; and from the Vipassana Hawaii and Hawaii Insight Meditation Center, P.O. Box 240547, Honolulu, Hi. 96824.

Bringing Awareness Back Home:
Toward an Integrative Spirituality

Donald Rothberg: There are many different models and metaphors of development. Some people speak of going "up"; others of going "down." Your own development has taken you to many of the very traditional Buddhist spiritual insights, but has also brought you outside of the main available models. You've had to work with regressive experiences and to integrate the tools of spiritual practice with therapeutic approaches. Can you describe some of your experiences?

Michele McDonald-Smith: In my first years of Buddhist practice, I touched so many places of freedom that it seemed that there was nowhere to go from there but "up"—to more and more transcendence, and an easier and easier life. The model seemed linear and direct. I didn't have any idea that I would experience many hell realms after that.

When I practiced longer retreats, I began to have an ever-deepening experience of freedom, a very positive sense of the loss of identification with a self. It was healthy and awakening, everything you've read about. Sometimes after that I would experience the opposite: It was like falling into a black hole. The self was disappearing, but it was agony. It was a kind of annihiliation, everything you don't read about. Over and over again in my practice, I would experience incredible freedom and openness, at times followed by this incredible black hole—a total closing down of my being. I didn't understand what was going on. I didn't think that anyone understood. At the time, I couldn't even describe it—the sense of going back and forth between such clarity and openness and such darkness. It was extraordinary. The more I had access to the deep places in meditation, the more I was accessing the darkness and the shutting down.

Eventually I started having preverbal memories of profound trauma from when I was two or three years old, and from birth, and also memories of deprivation and neglect. These were all memories I'd never had before. It was as if Pandora's box opened up.

I'd like to try to describe the initial years of working with that sense of annihilation. It was as if I was a beautiful glass window, and someone took a giant rock and threw it through the window. It was like being totally dissolved, totally annihilated. In the beginning I rarely had enough power of awareness to go through that experience mindfully. Gradually I learned to do it somewhat mindfully, but I would have to look at the experience from a distance. (I learned very young to leave my body and look at myself from a distance.) I'd look at this broken, damaged being and think, "Well, should I try to replace the window? Or should I try to glue all these pieces together?" I had no idea what to do. And I wasn't getting any clues from those around me; no one else seemed to know what to do either.

Now, after years of working with this in and out of retreats and getting some skillful therapy, I feel that I finally have a language for it. Gradually—and it's important to emphasize the gradualness—I started to have the strength to go through that experience of annihilation mindfully, with the awareness connected inside my body. But it's taken much more strength and equanimity than I could imagine.

I had to learn about regression. When my practice became concentrated, there would be a certain point at which I would regress to age two or three or birth and just be going through the trauma. I had never learned to bring my adult presence to that child part of me. That hurt part of myself was totally alone, and I wouldn't know what to do. So what accompanied the annihilation were layers of terror, rage, grief, hopelessness, and deprivation. When I started going through these layers, I felt betrayed by the linear spiritual model. I thought that because I had had these very deep experiences in meditation practice, I wouldn't ever have to go through anything like that. It wasn't in the model. That sense of betrayal was so much of my suffering: How could I experience that kind of hopelessness after such clear insights? It took me so long to understand that this was regression. I was just right back there at three years old. There was a tremendous split between the wise part of me and this damaged child.

I can say now that, of course, it's by reexperiencing those emotions with mindfulness, with lovingkindness, with compassion, that the pieces of the window get glued back together. Then there is no need to split off from the body or the emotions, because one is no longer afraid of them. The child feels safe because finally there is a compassionate adult present within oneself.

DR: So if you had to use a metaphor to describe your own general patterns of development, which one would you choose?

MM: I tend to see development as *cyclical*, in the framework of a multiplicity of diverse dimensions of growth. I think that we have the potential to work on all the levels all the time. We may focus on one dimension at a given time, drop it, and return to it later. I don't think that we somehow do spiritual work starting at age ten, and then at age twenty-five focus on the body, and at age thirty start with something else. That seems simplistic. In the very course of a twenty-four-hour day we often experience all the different levels. Each dimension is very, very rich, and some are accessible more easily at some times rather than at others. For example, for me embodiment has been very hard to access, while having transcendent spiritual experiences has been relatively easy. It's really different for each person, although we're very conditioned by our culture as well. Being "split off" from body and emotions is very common in the world.

Yet I feel lucky in some ways. Given that I had quite a lot of preverbal trauma to my body and emotions from early childhood (and even prior to birth), I feel very grateful that I had so many years of meditative training which provided me with a "container" for working later with my memories of these experiences. Without access to an awareness that I'd learned in meditation that is not identified with any particular content of experience and compassion, I probably couldn't have worked through these difficult areas. In a sense, the sequence of my learning was fortunate; I needed all that transcendence in order to be able to face some very difficult experiences. Most of us, or maybe all of us, in all cultures have some or many difficult, closed areas and for a long time don't have the strength to open to them. A spiritual base helps us to follow the path of opening to these areas.

Metaphors of "ascent" and "descent" seem to me sometimes to suggest that we have to leave our bodies "to ascend," or that we "come down" into our bodies. I don't think of giving attention to our bodies, or to earth and our emotions, as somehow "descending." (Laughter.) Rather, I think of this as a balanced expression of what it means to be human. But perhaps we use these words when we're split. Actually, my own experience has never been that I have to leave my body in meditation in order to have a transcendent experience. So I don't think of such experiences as going "up." When I do go up, I tend to be split. If I have a sense of leaving, it's often actually dissociation. (Laughter.) Actually, one of the greatest spiritual insights is that there's nowhere to go.

DR: You've worked with many thousands of meditation students since 1981. I'm interested in your observations about the nature and sequences of these students' development. You talked earlier about your sense of your own "cyclical" development. Others, as in some Buddhist traditions like that of Mahasi Sayadaw or in Western developmental psychology, speak of "stage models." There is a sequence or unfolding of learning, each stage built on and requiring the earlier stages. Ideally, it means that there isn't splitting; there isn't a loss of earlier competences or abilities.

MM: I don't generally observe people going through clear sequences of stages. Nor does my mind work easily with a stage model. When a person comes in for an interview with me, especially if it's an extended retreat and we have time together, I first try to look at the ways in which a person is able to be present. I want to nourish these abilities, developing and strengthening mindfulness and compassion. Then, I see where the person can't be present, can't be here. For all of us, there are reasons why we can't be present, connected with our defenses. My intention is to help bring awareness into any area where it's not present. A person might initially bring in childhood material, maybe a fear from when the person was three years old; I try to help bring attention to that. The next time, perhaps some days later, the person may be having the deepest kind of traditional spiritual insight about impermanence. Again, the work is to bring nonjudgmental awareness to whatever arises, moment by moment.

I believe that all of the stages are accessible all the time. Say a person starts meditating and has no openness to emotions. How the practice unfolds for that person will be very different than for someone experiencing a lot of emotionally charged content. However, the awareness brought to these two different contents is the same. In fact, the person in the midst of very difficult emotional material, if taught how to practice in a balanced way, often can access other levels. There can be work on different levels in a particular period of time, and this can help give "space" to the work on the more difficult level. A person may be without access to the body or emotions and be much "in the head" or even have transcendent experiences not integrated with bodily and emotional experience. I wouldn't try to push such a person into his or her body and emotions. I would try to strengthen awareness gradually where it does exist. If, for example, I had been pushed into my body and emotions too quickly, it would have been too much. My ability to concentrate saved my life, even if that ability wasn't initially integrated.

DR: So you're really talking about trusting the process, trusting the organism to find out what surfaces and develops next.

MM: To me, the whole job of a teacher is really to let the person unfold from the inside, not to direct development from the outside. To have a stage model might be to second-guess this inner unfolding. But people are full of surprises. Each person is unique. Some people might never in this lifetime access emotion. Another person might never access the traditional stages of enlightenment. Actually, I doubt it. My observation as a teacher has been that, if a person is given the space to unfold from the inside, all the levels develop.

DR: Have you noticed anything like stages?

MM: People don't usually come in off the street and go quickly through all the traditional stages as described by Mahasi Sayadaw. Experiencing these traditional stages of insight is based on spiritual ripeness and on the presence of the *paramis* [the "perfections," the virtues cultivated in spiritual practice, such as wisdom, lovingkindness, generosity, patience, and effort]. The development of the paramis is gradual over lifetimes. When there's ripeness, however, growth can be very sudden. One can go through all the traditional stages of insight in seconds if there is ripeness.

At the present time, there seems to be a growing appreciation of nurturing feminine values and an interest in finding the expression of liberation in the midst of life in the contemporary world. I certainly didn't have that model at first. Initially, after retreats, awareness wasn't very well integrated into my life; there were deep experiences but not so much ability to connect these experiences with the different dimensions of my life. But now I find that most people want this integration of spirituality with everyday life. They want liberation to be expressed in their relationships, in the healing of our culture, and in addressing oppressive political structures; in other words, they want liberation to happen on many levels of their lives. Spiritual practice is not separate from driving to work or changing the diapers. This to me is exciting. The appropriate metaphors may be more those of *balance* or *integration* than that of *ascent*. However, there's not necessarily a movement first into meditation practice and then into attention in daily life, because people's backgrounds are so different. Some people's spiritual practice may be developing greatly in their daily lives even if they don't do retreats.

DR: It has been helpful to me to notice that attention to some parts of my life require certain kinds of settings or relationships. In retreats, I didn't find a natural movement of awareness to all the dimensions of my inner life. For example, to bring fuller attention to my emotions basically required further depth in relationships. Of course, that wouldn't be the case for everyone. Other dimensions only surface in the context of communities, or social and ecological relationships. Personally, I've needed to complement a more individual model of spiritual practice with a more relational model.

MM: The "relational" and "connective" are culturally defined as "feminine." But I think that the main reason that it's difficult to access the relational dimension on retreats is because it's difficult to access that dimension, period. If our culture and all our institutions were based on relational models, it would be easier to access. Actually, what's ironic to me is how much a deep sense of connection comes out of the profound solitude and silence of a retreat setting, how the ability to connect is related to the ability to have intimacy with oneself. For me to be intimate with another requires great mindfulness. Otherwise, it's all projection! (Laughter.) It may be primarily or entirely thinking about what someone else is experiencing, rather than just being open and able to listen.

DR: This is where there is an intersection of mindfulness and the more personal or psychological work. For many people, it's easier to be mindful in solitude. But how can I be mindful when all my "stuff" gets activated?

MM: This is what I think is the new territory. It's exciting. So is that an "ascent" or a "descent"? I couldn't say that it's an ascent or a descent. I think that it's a movement toward healthy connection right here in the present moment that comes out of learning how to be mindful and that it's been missing in many ways from our practice. The predominant model is one of solitude. There's no teaching about how to be mindful or generally how to do spiritual work with your partner or children or parents. Of course, there is the emphasis on *sila* [ethics or morality] and the paramis. But what are the nuts and bolts of doing this, the actual practices to carry out with other people?

DR: I don't think that we have too much sense of how to practice with a partner, a group, a community, or an ecosystem. We really need explorations and models in these areas. How can we be mindful in relationships? In my experience, if we explore this kind of practice, whole new worlds open up. But I don't find much guidance in the traditional Buddhist practice except in general terms.

MM: Well, of course that traditional practice is brilliant. There is the basic foundation of *sila*, of nonharming within relationships. There's the foundation of mindfulness, the sense that each moment is complete. From the perspective of this practice, there's in a way no place for a sense of evolution. If each moment is complete, evolution actually only occurs in the moments that aren't complete, until each moment is complete!

We have to look at when and why we don't find moments of completion in relationships. I really appreciate when people have resistance to relationships, because I've seen how hard it is. I've seen how immense the reservoirs of fear and self-hatred are. There is so much personal work to do. I think that developing a compassionate relationship to the self may be what is hardest for people.

Anywhere that we haven't opened to an experience or an underlying emotion, there is no movement. We're stuck. People in meditation or therapy keep coming across these places where they're closed and identified with something and are not aware of this identification. We act out these patterns continually in the world of relationships, or the difficult area comes up endlessly in meditation, or we continually fantasize. In all these cases, something that is stuck is wanting to move. If we could actually experience the emotion related to the stuckness, it would come unstuck, live itself out, and disappear.

We hold these difficult areas chronically in our bodies, emotions, and minds. I think that our bodies particularly are sacrificial areas. Actually, I think of these areas as sacred sites. Parts of our bodies hold our difficulties, until we have the strength to experience them with mindfulness. Without mindfulness, the cycles only continue, because there's still identification.

DR: To the extent that we are split off from our bodies and emotions, our thoughts may be much less helpful to us than more direct experiences of our bodies and emotions.

MM: That's been my experience and also what I see with people with whom I'm working. To me what's changing now in the world is that our spiritual attention is coming into the body, emotions, and nature. I've seen a lot of the lack of such attention in spiritual circles, and often there is considerable "acting out" all over the place, because there's a denial of the body and emotions. I call it "disembodied clarity." There are so many spiritual people, especially spiritual teachers, who are so charming, who are such good speakers. But if you look behind the scene, it can be a disaster or, at the least, require serious questioning.

It's actually everyone's problem. People feel so bad about who they are that they have to have these unreal models of perfection. They don't allow themselves or their teachers to be human. As a teacher, I know that there's a tremendous amount of projection. I work constantly at trying to make such projection apparent. Still, many people don't want to hear about projection, or they don't think that I'm a good teacher because I mention it. As a teacher, I'm not supposed to be human. I think that this has to do with the "ascent" that we spoke about earlier. The idea somehow is that we can ascend and no longer experience any fear. The idea is that freedom is ascending up out of the body and emotions, so that we're somehow no longer human. So many people go to retreats, do meditation practice, have all this "human" stuff come up, and think and feel that they're somehow no good. They may pretend not to have emotions, but this doesn't mean that they don't have emotions! (Laughter.)

DR: There's often a lot of emotion connected with the denial of emotion!

MM: It takes tremendous energy to resist the body and emotions, to try to ascend beyond the body and emotions. But, again, I don't think that it's good to push people. I really respect the protective nature of our defenses. I try to teach people to understand their defenses. With understanding and respect, there can be a greater feeling of safety and more of a willingness and interest in opening. Then the defenses drop away naturally as mindfulness develops.

DR: Are most of your students and peers attempting this work of integration and giving attention to many levels?

MM: Yes, there is a kind of birthing that happens on many levels. There's the development of an integrated self relating to oneself and others in the world, as well as the growth of deeper liberating insight. Any deep insight potentially transforms the self and helps it to be healthier. Of course, some people might not be genuinely interested in the relational model, being drawn more to solitude and retreat. This is especially true of some people as they get older.

Another way to look at it is to say that some people have more interest in bringing "feminine" and "masculine" values into balance in their lives, and some don't. It's silly to judge one as good and one as bad. We're all doing the best we can. (Laughter.) There are also deeper karmic reasons for whether or not people are drawn toward integration, some healthy, some probably unhealthy. Personally, however, I don't think that human beings or much of life on this exquisite planet will survive unless many of us take this approach.

Acknowledgments

I would like to thank Sean Kelly, Joanna Macy, Tony Stigliano, Roger Walsh, Diana Winston, and Michael Zimmerman for their comments on earlier drafts. April De Tally helped develop transcripts of the conversations and Joseph Goldstein, Jack Kornfield, and Michele McDonald-Smith helped with editing. An earlier version of McDonald-Smith's response to the first question appeared in the winter 1995 issue of *Blind Donkey: Journal of the Diamond Sangha*.

Notes

1. Many of the reflections in these conversations are similar, for example, to the content of the interviews of a number of contemporary Western practitioners from diverse traditions carried out by Barnard (1995).

2. Unfortunately, there is no prominent discussion of the latter two categories in Wilber's major work (1995). The central focus in this work is on the developmental logic of differentiation and hierarchical integration as the core mechanism of evolution. This has no doubt led to some confusion among Wilber's readers.

3. For a critical discussion of the plausibility of considering Kohlberg's stages as following a process of integration, see Flanagan (1991, 160–62). Kohlberg himself in his later writings distinguishes between "hard"-stage (Piagetian) and "soft"-stage models of moral development (Kohlberg and Ryncarz 1990).

4. The extent to which some of these developmental lines other than the basic structures proceed through to transpersonal stages is not clear, since Wilber's emphasis is mostly on cognitive development and the self. There is very little treatment, for example, of the meaning of transpersonal moral or "interpersonal" development or of the social context of individual development. However, in his most recent work (1995), he shows an active interest in remedying this situation, particularly through the general model of "four quadrants" of evolution.

5. This tendency to emphasize the coherent, sequential nature of spiritual development as a whole seems even more evident with some of Wilber's coauthors. Brown (1986), for example, reconstructs a stage model from three canonical Hindu and Buddhist texts

and only speaks of preliminary "ethical" development as an initial stage prior to what seems like several stages of more advanced *cognitive* development. But other Buddhist texts and approaches suggest an understanding of a more complex and interdependent relationship between what is commonly regarded as a three-fold basic training in ethics (*sila*), meditation (*samadhi*), and wisdom (*panna*). Further development in meditation or wisdom makes possible, in turn, further development in ethics, in compassionate and wise action. This point is brought out well through analyses of the multiple levels or interpretations of ethical precepts; the precepts may be seen initially as simple training precepts, while at advanced stages they may be understood in the light of "emptiness" (shunyata) (Aitken 1984, 16–18). A similar point might be made in relation to emotional and interpersonal development.

6. Whether McDonald-Smith's experiences should be labeled "regressive" or identified as an example of "regression in service of ego" is another question. Some have argued that it is important to limit the concept of regression to a kind of developmental collapse and to understand "regression in service of ego" in another way, namely as the process of giving attention, from a "base" established in one or more lines of development, to a truncated area in another developmental line (see Hunt 1995, 22).

7. A number of contemporary developmental psychologists (including Levinson and Gardner) believe that there are only hierarchical stages (following a developmental logic) for the learning of logico-mathematical competences in childhood, as identified by Piaget (Alexander, Druker, and Langer 1990, 9–10).

References

Aitken, R. 1984. *The mind of clover: Essays in Zen Buddhist ethics*. San Francisco: North Point Press.

Alexander, C., J. Davies, C. Dixon, M. Dillbeck, S. Druker, R. Oetzel, J. Muehlman, and D. Orme-Johnson. 1990. Growth of higher stages of consciousness: Maharishi's Vedic psychology of human development. In *Higher stages of human development: Perspectives on adult growth*, edited by C. Alexander and E. Langer. New York: Oxford University Press.

Alexander, C., S. Druker, and E. Langer. 1990. Introduction: Major issues in the exploration of adult growth. In *Higher stages of human development: Perspectives on adult growth*, edited by C. Alexander and E. Langer. New York: Oxford University Press.

Barnard, W. 1995. Stepping up the ladder of consciousness: An empirical assessment of the work of Ken Wilber. Paper presented at the meeting of the American Academy of Religion, Philadelphia.

Brown, D. 1986. The stages of meditation in cross-cultural perspective. In *Transformations of consciousness: Conventional and contemplative perspectives on development*, by K. Wilber, J. Engler, and D. Brown. Boston: Shambhala.

Dasen, P., ed. 1977. *Piagetian psychology: Cross-cultural contributions*. New York: Halsted.

Engler, J. 1986. Therapeutic aims in psychotherapy and meditation: Developmental stages in the representation of self. In *Transformations of consciousness: Conventional and contemplative perspectives on development*, by K. Wilber, J. Engler, and D. Brown. Boston: Shambhala.

Flanagan, O. 1991. *The science of the mind*. Rev. ed. Cambridge: MIT Press.

———. 1992. *Varieties of moral personality: Ethics and psychological realism*. Cambridge: Harvard University Press.

Gardner, H. 1983. *Frames of mind: The theory of multiple intelligences*. New York: Basic Books.

Gilligan, C. 1982. *In a different voice: Psychological theory and women's development*. Cambridge: Harvard University Press.

Goldstein, J., and J. Kornfield. 1987. *Seeking the heart of wisdom: The path of insight meditation*. Boston: Shambhala.

Hunt, H. 1995. Some developmental issues in transpersonal experience. *Journal of Mind and Behavior* 16 (Spring): 115–34.

Jaggar, A. 1989. Love and knowledge: Emotion in feminist epistemology. In *Gender/body/knowledge: Feminist reconstructions of being and knowing*, edited by A. Jaggar and S. Bordo. New Brunswick, N.J.: Rutgers University Press.

Keller, E. 1985. *Reflections on gender and science*. New Haven: Yale University Press.

Kohlberg, L. 1981. *Essays on moral development, vol. 1: The philosophy of moral development*. San Francisco: Harper & Row.

Kohlberg, L., and R. Ryncarz. 1990. Beyond justice reasoning: Moral development and consideration of a seventh stage. In *Higher stages of human development: Perspectives on adult growth*, edited by C. Alexander and E. Langer. New York: Oxford University Press.

Kornfield, J. 1977. *Living Buddhist masters*. Santa Cruz, Calif.: Unity Press.

———. 1993. *A path with heart: A guide through the perils and promises of spiritual life*. New York: Bantam Books.

Noam, G. 1990. Beyond Freud and Piaget: Biographical worlds—interpersonal self. In *The moral domain: Essays in the ongoing discussion between philosophy and the social sciences*, edited by T. Wren. Cambridge: MIT Press.

Richards, F., and M. Commons. 1990. Postformal cognitive-developmental theory and research: A review of its current status. In *Higher stages of human development: Perspectives on adult growth*, edited by C. Alexander and E. Langer. New York: Oxford University Press.

Scheman, N. 1993. *Engenderings: Constructions of knowledge, authority, and privilege*. New York: Routledge.

Schuon, F. 1984. *The transcendent unity of religions*. Rev. ed. Wheaton, Ill.: Theosophical Publishing House.

Shweder, R., M. Mahapatra, and J. Miller. 1987. Culture and moral development. In *The emergence of morality in young children*, edited by J. Kagan and S. Lamb. Chicago: University of Chicago Press.

Smith, H. 1976. *Forgotten truth: The primordial tradition*. New York: Harper & Row.

Wilber, K. 1980. *The Atman project: A transpersonal view of human development*. Wheaton, Ill.: Quest Books.

———. 1986. The spectrum of development. In *Transformations of consciousness. Conventional and contemplative perspectives on development*, by K. Wilber, J. Engler, and D. Brown. Boston: Shambhala.

———. 1990a. Structure, stage, and self. In *Eye to eye: The quest for the new paradigm*, by K. Wilber. Rev. ed. Boston: Shambhala.

———. 1990b. Two patterns of transcendence: A reply to Washburn. *Journal of Humanistic Psychology* (Summer): 113–36.

———. 1995. *Sex, ecology, spirituality: The spirit of evolution*. Boston: Shambhala.

———. 1996. *A brief history of everything*. Boston: Shambhala.

———. 1997. *The eye of spirit: An integral vision for a world gone slightly mad*. Boston: Shambhala.

Wilber, K., J. Engler, and D. Brown. 1986. *Transformations of consciousness: Conventional and contemplative perspectives on development*. Boston: Shambhala.

Winkelman, M. 1990. The evolution of consciousness: An essay review of *Up from Eden*. *Anthropology of Consciousness* 1 (3/4): 24–31.

Part Three

Transpersonal Theory and the "Other":

Nature, Women, Indigenous Traditions, and Relationships

8

Michael E. Zimmerman

At the San Francisco conference on "Ken Wilber and the Future of Transpersonal Inquiry" in January, 1997, Michael Zimmerman's clarity, balance, incisiveness, and humor were a bright spot for many attendees not familiar with his work. As in his many articles and several books, Michael brought together broad knowledge of philosophy, ecology, and spirituality, illuminating in particular the options and dangers of a spiritually based ecology.

Professor of Philosophy at Tulane University in New Orleans for many years, Zimmerman teaches courses in transpersonal philosophy, Buddhism, Heidegger, Nietzsche, feminist theory, and environmental philosophy. Early in his career, he focused on the work of Martin Heidegger, the controversial German existential philosopher (1889-1976), who gave a powerful critique of the modern world's individualism, "subjectivism," and dependence on technology. Heidegger called for the development of a kind of "meditative thinking" which might draw us closer to the "Being" which we usually ignore, in a way reminiscent of the German mystic Meister Eckhart and early Greek contemplative philosophers such as Anaximander, Heraclitus, and Parmenides. Zimmerman's work on Heidegger resulted in two well-received books, Eclipse of the Self: The Development of Heidegger's Concept of Authenticity (originally 1981), and Heidegger's Confrontation with Modernity (1990).

Over the last decade, Zimmerman has also written extensively on environmental ethics and philosophy, publishing Contesting Earth's Future: Radical Ecology and Postmodernity (1994) and editing the anthology, Environmental Philosophy (1993). He has been especially concerned with the dangers of anti-modern ecological movements and philosophies, partly in the light of his reflections on the Nazi appropriation of the language of nature mysticism (invoking, for instance, the importance of "blood and land") and of Heidegger's involvement with Nazism.

Zimmerman has also been concerned with practical questions of "inner" meaning. He has explored Buddhist contemplative practice for many years, has taught classes on Buddhism, and typically includes periods of meditation in his teaching at Tulane. He has examined the relevance of philosophical concerns for psychotherapists and has served as Clinical Professor of Psychology at Tulane University Medical School, where he teaches third- and fourth-year psychiatry residents. In recent years, he has become intrigued by widely reported anomalous phenomena, including "alien abductions," Marian apparitions, near-death experiences, and angelic visitations, which he believes may represent an increasingly insistent intrusion of the soul-realm into a materialistic culture.

In Zimmerman's recent writings, he has made considerable use of Ken Wilber's work, linking Wilber's progressive vision of human and cosmic unfolding with Heidegger's transpersonal idea that humans are the "clearing" through which things manifest themselves and thus "are," and with the concept of awakening the ever-present Buddha-nature. He has found Wilber's writings particularly useful for helping to clarify the historical context of contemporary ecological problems and responses.

In the following chapter, Zimmerman outlines Wilber's argument for understanding the ecological crisis by placing it in the context of the ancient wisdom traditions (the "perennial philosophy") and evolutionary thinking. Rather than arguing that humans should simply "re-unite" with the rest of the natural world, Wilber believes that evolution shows us that qualities of mind, culture, and spirit emerge out of and are differentiated from nature. Yet this differentiation has sometimes led to a kind of dissociation from the natural world and to extreme ecological insensitivity and crisis, as if humans could somehow live autonomously and prosper amidst concrete and technology, without attention to the well-being of the natural world.

Zimmerman helps guide the reader through Wilber's often subtle analyses of how an emphasis on "ascent" from the natural to the spiritual world has contributed to this crisis, as well as how a modern emphasis on "descending" to the natural world (in science as well as in environmentalism) has often ignored the possibility of spiritual transcendence. Wilber's solution is a balance of "ascent" (transcendence to Spirit) and "descent" (awareness of the "immanence" or immediate presence of Spirit).

Zimmerman's chapter is very sympathetic to Wilber's views. At its end, however, he questions the extent to which scientists and philosophers actually agree, as Wilber claims, that evolution has a clear direction and purpose, citing the work of biologist Stephen Jay Gould, physicist and Nobel laureate Steven Weinberg, philosopher Daniel Dennett, and scholar of religions Huston Smith. He also objects to Wilber's characterization of many ecological thinkers as "regressive"—reactionary, undemocratic, yearning to be reabsorbed in nature. By contrast, Zimmerman believes that many ecofeminists and deep ecologists are actually often "progressive" and transpersonal, and thus might be Wilber's natural allies and collaborators.

Further Readings

Zimmerman, M. 1985. The role of spiritual discipline in learning to dwell on earth. In *Dwelling, place, and environment*, edited by D. Seamons and R. Mugerauer. The Hague: Martinus Nijhoff.

———. 1986. *Eclipse of the self: The development of Heidegger's concept of authenticity*. 2nd ed. Athens: Ohio University Press.

———. 1990. *Heidegger's confrontation with modernity*. Bloomington: Indiana University Press.

————. 1994. *Contesting earth's future: Radical ecology and postmodernity.* Berkeley and
Los Angeles: University of California Press.

————. 1995. The threat of ecofascism. *Social Theory and Practice* 21: 207-38.

Zimmerman, M., ed. 1993. *Environmental philosophy.* Englewood Cliffs, N.J.: Prentice-Hall.

A Transpersonal Diagnosis
of the Ecological Crisis

ALTHOUGH IN HIS EARLIER WRITINGS KEN WILBER EXAMINED
aspects of humanity's problematic attitudes toward nature,
his most recent book, *Sex, Ecology, Spirituality: The Spirit of
Evolution* (1995), is his first systematic diagnosis of those attitudes and the ecologically destructive practices based upon
them. Affirming that there is an ecological crisis, Wilber
argues that it arose in part because patriarchal humanity dissociates itself from nature, the body, and women.[1] Such dissociation
stems not only from an inadequate understanding of humanity's dependence on biospheric processes, but also from failure to appreciate
humanity's proper relationship with the Divine, which both transcends
and is present in nature and humanity. In the short term, humanity can
best address the ecological crisis not by becoming "reunified" with
nature, which would involve psychological and social regression, but
rather by furthering on a global basis the achievement of mental-egoic
rationality. Such rationality, defined by Wilber as the mode of rationality shared by normal modern adults, can help slow ecological destruction
in two ways. First, by disclosing that human life is interconnected with
the rest of the biosphere, mental-egoic rationality recognizes the potentially suicidal consequences of despoiling the biosphere. Second, mental-
egoic rationality moves toward person-respecting, democratic political
institutions, the spread of which would decrease the militarism and
diminish the social deprivation that cause so much ecological damage
(diZerega 1995).

Wilber acknowledges that in its present form, influenced by the history of patriarchy, mental-egoic rationality reveals dissociative attitudes
toward nature. Such attitudes arise in part from ascent-oriented religions and philosophies that have often involved a death-denying, nature-
and body-repudiating search for union with the divine Spirit, understood
as wholly transcendent. The problems with the ascent tradition, however, cannot be cured by following the equally one-sided descent tradition,
which takes the form of Spirit-denying immanence or this-worldly naturalism. The descent tradition is allegedly shared by most modernists,

including two camps that are usually considered to be opposed to one another: environmentalists on the one hand and market liberals and Marxists on the other. Many environmentalists reject modernity's anthropocentrism, which justifies efforts to gain technological control of the biosphere, but they agree with modernity's this-worldly orientation. If *other*-worldly orientations neglect Creation, so Wilber argues, *this*-worldly orientations (whether environmental or industrial-progressive) neglect Spirit. Hence, he recommends reconciling ascent and descent, Spirit and Creation, in accord with the best of the perennial philosophy.

Readily acknowledging the dark side of the mental-egoic level of consciousness, Wilber asserts that humankind is experiencing the birth pangs of the final level of personal consciousness: *centauric vision-logic*. At this level of consciousness, body and mind are integrated, and the personal capacity for inhabiting multiple perspectives displaces the mental ego's monocular rationality. Vision-logic opens the way for truly transpersonal awareness, which is the *telos* of life on Earth. Wilber insists, however, that such evolution will be possible only if humankind preserves the biosphere on which all terrestrial life depends.

In the first three parts of this chapter, I examine Wilber's central ecological claims in *Sex, Ecology, Spirituality* (1995) that (1) the noosphere contains the biosphere, (2) Spirit transcends and is immanent in nature, and (3) environmentalists and modernists alike have adopted variations of this-worldly naturalism. In part four, I offer a critical evaluation of some of Wilber's claims. At the outset, however, I would like to express my admiration for this remarkable book, with the basic themes of which I find myself in agreement.

THE NOOSPHERE CONTAINS THE BIOSPHERE

Many well-intentioned environmentalists, Wilber maintains, adhere to a misguided biocentrism and hold that because humankind is contained in the interrelated whole, there is no basis for the view that humans are the most differentiated and complex form of life. Provocatively, Wilber affirms just the opposite: *the biosphere is included within the noosphere*, that is, within the domain constituted by self-conscious beings. The noosphere contains all the levels achieved by other beings in the biosphere, plus the additional level of self-awareness. Because humans have evolved with the rest of terrestrial life, and because the mass of the biosphere is obviously far larger than the mass of human beings, saying that the noosphere "contains" the biosphere does not mean that planet Earth is literally contained *within* humankind. Wilber believes that humankind represents a qualitative evolutionary advance that embraces all of the levels achieved by the previous epochs of evolution in the biosphere. The greater interiority or depth involved in human self-awareness grants humans greater intrinsic value, but this does not deny the intrinsic value accruing to *all* beings.

Wilber joins environmentalists in condemning the hierarchical attitude of anthropocentric humanists who regard all nonhuman beings instrumentally. He contrasts such a pathological hierarchy with a healthy hierarchy of the sort needed to constitute the very cosmic "wholeness" venerated by environmentalists. In their antihierarchical zeal, however, environmentalists ostensibly threaten to eliminate important hierarchical distinctions. Wilber argues that "reality" is not an undifferentiated, heterarchical heap, but instead is constituted by a "normal hierarchy" of *holons* (a term borrowed from Arthur Koestler). A holon is a whole in one context, a part in another (Wilber 1995, 18). For example, a cell is a whole that *embraces* (includes) molecules, but is also a part embraced by (included in) an organism. In holarchy, the lower is *in* the higher, but not vice versa. Hence, atoms are *in* water molecules, but water molecules are not in atoms. Even though atoms can exist without molecules, molecules cannot exist without atoms. Atoms have enormous span, in the sense that there are enormous numbers of them, and are fundamental to the cosmos, but they have very little depth and complexity and thus have less significance than more highly differentiated and complex holons.

Considered as a whole, a holon is an end in itself; considered as a part, however, a holon is a means to the end of what is higher. At a given level of reality, for example, the cell level, heterarchy prevails, that is, each element has about equal weight and contributes to the well-being of the whole level. But these elements exist within a hierarchy, and thus can simultaneously be influenced by higher level holons, and can influence lower level holons (Wilber 1995, 20). Egalitarian environmentalists claim that heterarchy makes wholeness possible, but Wilber assigns this role to the graded holarchy that "converts heaps into wholes, disjointed fragments into networks of mutual interaction." (1995, 18). Wilber recognizes that pathological hierarchy has justified needlessly harmful treatment of nonhuman beings. Like a number of other critics, however, he asserts that biocentrists who renounce a value hierarchy have no basis for making decisions in difficult moral situations, for example, when faced with saving either a child or a tiger. Many deep ecologists recommend saving the child, not because the child has higher intelligence than the tiger (perhaps an adult tiger is somehow more conscious than a two-year-old child), but because they identify more closely with the child than with the tiger. Deep ecologists, then, recommend biocentric egalitarianism only in principle, for they recognize that human interests inevitably color moral decisions. Clearly, however, deep ecologists need to continue pondering the issues raised by biocentric egalitarianism.

Asserting that the biosphere (Gaia) is both the largest and shallowest of the social holons, Wilber agrees with environmentalists that destroying Gaia would destroy humankind. But he says that environmentalists are mistaken in believing that humankind is contained "in" Gaia, for this is akin to believing that molecules are contained "in" atoms. Rather, Gaia is contained "in" humankind, because humankind not only embraces previous levels attained by life on earth, but adds "its own unique and more encompassing capacities" (Wilber 1995, 20–21). On the basis of his holarchy, Wilber advances the following "basic moral intuition": "Protect and promote the greatest depth for the greatest span," that is, encourage the fullest development and self-transcendence of all beings (1995, 613).

Many environmentalists and naturalists are suspicious of depth-hierarchical holism. Warwick Fox, for example, argues that evolutionary history should be envisioned not as a ladder atop which stands the allegedly most highly evolved species, humankind, but instead as a ramifying bush whose leaves represent species that are all *equally* evolved, no one of which is intrinsically more valuable than the others (1990, 200). According to Wilber, however, it is not anthropocentric vanity, but deeper awareness that leads nondualists to speak of humankind as a microcosm of the macrocosm. The fact that humankind stands atop the terrestrial hierarchy does not discount the "equal ground value" of other beings. Nothing is closer or farther from the Absolute Ground; hence, "All things and events, of whatever nature, are perfect manifestations of Spirit" (1995, 517).

Wilber also asserts, however, that greater complexity confers greater relative value. Hence, it is better to eat a carrot than a cow, for the latter is more complex (sentient) than the former (1995, 519). Animal rights advocates would agree that the interests and/or rights of sentient individuals trump the interests and/or rights of plants and ecosystems, which presumably are not sentient (Singer 1975; Regan 1983). Ecological holists, by way of contrast, maintain that saving animals is not always better than saving plants. When rare plants and even whole ecosystems are threatened by exotic animals that undergo rapid population growth because there are no natural predators, ecologists recommend killing the exotic animals in order to save the native plants. In terms of ecosystem ecology, species (whether plant or animal) are considered more important than individual members of those species (see Callicott 1989; Zimmerman 1993). Other environmentalists argue, however, that ecological holism, in which individual sentient beings can be sacrificed for the good of the ecological "whole," not only borders on ecofascism (Regan 1983), but is based on an outmoded theory of ecology (Warren and Cheney 1991). Ecofeminists, in particular, have done an excellent job of bringing into focus the issues of holism versus individualism, and the relative worth of plants and animals (Warren 1991; Gaard 1993).

Wilber's specific example of the carrot versus the cow implies that holarchic considerations make vegetarianism the morally preferable diet. Most Buddhists and Hindus would agree. Humans are naturally omnivorous, however, so many peoples have traditionally eaten meat, whether obtained by hunting or herding. Hunting-and-gathering cultures apparently believed that a hunter was successful only insofar as a game animal, recognizing the hunter's purity of spirit, let itself be killed out of compassion for the hunter's hungry people. Such cultures recognized that slaying another living being for food is a serious matter. The growth of the human population, made possible by agriculture and domestication of animals, gradually eradicated most of the societies in which hunting was relatively consistent with ecological stability. Today, as animal rights activists have pointed out, food animals are often raised under abominable conditions. Vegetarianism seems a less noble option, however, if one consumes plants grown on giant farms whose exploitative, chemically dependent operations threaten the long-term viability of entire ecosystems. The rising prices of organic fruits, grains, and vegetables put them out of reach of many ordinary families. Moreover, many higher mammals (including primates) are being exterminated as their habitats are cleared for the farms needed to feed more and more people. Even though at first glance one may agree with Wilber's conclusion that it is better to eat a carrot than a cow, further reflection reveals that that conclusion raises a host of complex issues.

DIVINE SPIRIT AS IMMANENT AND TRANSCENDENT

Wilber agrees with deep ecologists and many ecofeminists that religious and philosophical otherworldliness has contributed to humankind's mistreatment of nature, but he argues that otherworldliness belongs to the patriarchal version of the ascent tradition, according to which the immortal soul can gain salvation only by leaving the inferior corporeal domain of "mother nature" and ascending to the Divine One (1995, 363). This introverted and pessimistic soteriological strategy, based on a perverted view of the Great Chain of Being that despises the material realm and regards worldly involvement as pointless, is inconsistent with the life-affirming attitude needed to avoid ecological calamity. To curtail such otherworldliness, Wilber calls not for abandoning the ascent tradition altogether, as do many environmentalists, but instead calls for coupling it with descent, as do the best exponents of the nondual perennial philosophy.

Wilber acknowledges that some perennial philosophers have been too ascent-oriented, and that distorted versions of cosmic hierarchy have been used historically to justify domination of "inferior" domains. For example, insofar as some interpretations of Christianity defined God as "ontologically divorced from nature and human nature," there is *"no way that a [Christian's] final destiny could be realized in this life, in this body, on this earth"* (Wilber 1995, 350) (emphasis in original). Because this Christianity also taught that only Jesus Christ was capable of ascent, the West was "locked into a perpetually frustrated Ascent yearning—a yearning for a Goal that could *never* be officially realized, and therefore a perpetual yearning that could *never* be satisfied and let go of" (Wilber 1995, 355). Wilber argues that European "man's" military expansiveness, economic acquisitiveness, and sexual craving are efforts to quench a desire that can be satisfied *only* by union with the Divine. The West's addictive behavior may be attributable to the fact that one can never get enough of what one does not *really* want.

Wilber praises Plotinus for reconciling ascent (toward the transcendent One) with descent (toward the immanent Many). Genuine ascent culminates not in a flight to another world, but instead in descent into or embrace of Creation. The way up and the way down, then, are the "same." For nondualists, creatures are not merely a "part" of the Absolute, as in pantheism; instead, each individual "is the One Spirit in its *entirety*" (Wilber 1995, 347). Though emphasizing that dualistic Ascenders cannot discern the Divine's presence in Creation, Wilber also cautions that misguided descenders cannot discern that the Divine also transcends Creation. Opposing any view that regards creatures solely in instrumental terms, Plato and Plotinus developed a "genuinely *creation-centered* spirituality," which likens the entire universe "to a giant 'super-organism,' with all the parts interwoven with one another and with their eternal Ground" (1995, 325).

ECO CAMP VERSUS EGO CAMP

Wilber examines in detail the relation between two kinds of modernists: environmentalists who are members of the *eco camp*, and rationalists who are members of what he calls the *ego camp*. By ego camp, Wilber refers to those people affirming the achievement and aims of mental-egoic rationality. Contending that eco camp members reject the hierarchical notion that the noosphere embraces the biosphere, and that ego camp members exclude the possibility of a consciousness higher than scientific rationality, Wilber alleges that there is a hidden connection between the two camps: both are variants of this-worldly naturalism that has no room for transcendent Spirit.

Despite efforts to be fair-minded, Wilber's sympathies clearly lie more with those in the ego camp than with those in the eco camp. This is so, presumably, because those in the ego camp—despite its numerous shortcomings, including environmental destructiveness—at least adhere to the idea of progress, which is basic to Wilber's neo-Hegelian cosmology. Wilber believes that progress, properly redefined in terms of the evolution toward nondual spirituality, can encourage humankind in its struggle to protect the gains of democratic political systems and scientific rationality against dubious calls for "reuniting" with nature.

To understand Wilber's account of the ego and eco camps, we need to recall his model of the Great Holarchy of Being along with its view of the cosmos as organized into four interrelated quadrants. Each quadrant has evolved ever more differentiated and complex levels, which correspond to the levels evolved by holons in all three of the other quadrants. Any phenomenon has a foot in all four quadrants. The upper right quadrant involves the exterior structure of individual holons; the lower right involves the exterior structure of social holons; the upper left involves the interior form of individual holons; the lower left involves the interior form or structure of social holons.

Reacting against dogmatic, otherworldly religiosity, some modernists tried to eliminate both left-hand quadrants (interiority) of the holarchy and insisted that anything "real"—including human behavior—had to be explicable in empirical terms. In so doing, however, these modernists impeded the understanding of both personal and social holons. In eliminating the interior dimension, Western philosophers of science opened the way for two kinds of reductionism: gross and subtle. The former, "flatland atomism," starts by reducing all quadrants to the upper right one and then reduces all higher-order phenomena in that quadrant to atomic particles (Wilber 1995, 130). Many in the eco camp denounce such atomism as being the source of the West's nature-dominating practices, but Wilber maintains that the "fundamental Enlightenment paradigm"—which includes the ego camp—is a more subtle form of reductionism, taking the form of a "flatland holism," in which everything in the two left-hand (interior) quadrants is reduced to the two right-hand (exterior) quadrants.

Wilber stresses that many moderns viewed the cosmos as a great, interconnected, holistic system that an abstract "God" may have created, but that runs on its own. Such systemic thinking, generated by "formal-operational" rationality, eventually led to the "the first truly *ecological mode of awareness*" in the form of environmental science, which transcends the biosphere so as to grasp "the web of relationships constituting it" (1995, 233) (emphasis in original). Unfortunately, anthropocentric political ideologies have conceived of humankind as separate from the biosphere, which is portrayed as nothing but raw material for human ends. Because of the untoward ecological consequences of modernity, Wilber maintains that some in the eco camp reject scientific rationality and modern political ideologies in favor of what he calls the "retro-romantic," feeling-based ideal of reuniting with the organic whole. Yet others in the eco camp embrace the holistic views of the science of ecology in order to emphasize that humans are but one strand in the fabric of life. Since such ecological holism fails to appreciate interior depth, and since depthless holism is central to the modernity that has caused such ecological damage, Wilber concludes that the ecological crisis cannot be solved solely by appealing to such holism. Without a place for interiority, holistic theorists reduce qualities to quantities and portray individuals as functions of the overriding whole.

Wilber contends that the eco-crisis is the dark side of modernity's greatest achievement: distinguishing among the domains of (1) objects (nature), (2) persons or subjects (self), and (3) intersubjectivity (society). Claims made in each of these domains have their own validity criteria: propositional truth (accurate correspondence between statement and object) for the first, subjective truthfulness (sincerity) for the second, and normative rightness (cultural justice) for the third. In spite of the alleged autonomy of each type of rationality suitable for each of the three domains, the instrumental (scientific-technical) form of rationality soon marginalized the other two kinds. This happened for several reasons.

First, instead of transcending but integrating the prepersonal realm (nature, body, emotions) from which it had evolved and on which it was still dependent, the rational ego dissociated itself from and sought to repress that realm. As in *Up from Eden* (1981), Wilber explains such repression of nature (including by association the body, emotions, and the feminine) as an expression of the ego's denial of death.[2] In *Sex, Ecology, Spirituality*, however, he adds that "the central problem of modernity" is determining the place of the rational subject in a world of totally interconnected, but unconscious objects (1995, 431). In making its "inward" turn away from the natural system, while lacking any sense of the transpersonal, the rational ego became stuck within itself. The ego could not connect its own egoic interiority with the natural realm, for which interiority had been denied. Indeed, stripped of its interiority, nature became a projection screen first for monological rationality and later for romanticism's exalted feelings. The rational ego, thus closed in upon itself, became "a perfectly atomistic self" that sought to exteriorize everything, that is, to make everything into an aspect of natural systems that the ego could objectify, represent, and reflect upon (Wilber 1995, 262). This isolated, atomistic, rational self populates the ego camp.

Second, monological reason triumphed because the rational ego, fiercely identifying itself with its own autonomy, repudiated the transpersonal domain of Spirit that transcends but includes the ego. Modern "man's" problems can be attributed to his dissociation from nature and Spirit. Third, modernity lacked an adequate conception of *interpersonal* interiority. Hence, the hyperactive, hyperinflated, atomistic subject began treating "other humans as 'objects of information' and not 'subjects in communication' or communion." Sadly, "in aggressively pursuing intense freedom, [the rational ego] manufactured massive unfreedom" (Wilber 1995, 457). Using instrumental rationality to understand everything, the death-denying rational ego abandoned the ancient ideal that Reason (*Logos*) was to produce a substantive vision of cosmic order (Wilber 1995, 146).

Wilber himself offers such a vision, according to which human beings have the capacity to evolve to transpersonal levels of awareness on the way toward nondualism. Yet he knows that humanity is not yet prepared for the transpersonal. Indeed, "the single greatest *world transformation* would simply be the embrace of global reasonableness and pluralistic tolerance—the global embrace of [non-dissociative] egoic-rationality (on the way to centauric vision-logic)" (1995, 210). Unlike death-denying, body-despising rationality, a healthy rationality would acknowledge humanity's relation to and dependence on the biosphere. From such rationality the final level of personal awareness can emerge: eco-noetic, centauric vision-logic. Having differentiated itself from "an exclusive identification with body, persona, ego, and mind, [centauric vision-logic] can now *integrate* them in a unified fashion, in a new and higher holon with each of them as junior partners" (Wilber 1995, 262). Unhappily, the same vision-logic that can occupy all the perspectives of personal awareness is also bereft of the comforting old gods and out of touch with the Divine. Hence, vision-logic agonizes "on the brink of the transpersonal" (Wilber 1995, 264).

Let us now turn to Wilber's analysis of the eco camp. Following Charles Taylor, Wilber maintains that it was only in the space opened up by modernity's this-worldly absolutization of nature, that there could arise the romantic feelings for nature that motivate so many in the eco camp. Wilber praises romanticism for criticizing the monological rationalism that cut off humanity's relation to nature and to Spirit. He alleges, however, that because rationalists and romantics alike had abandoned the transcendent domain, romantics could only conceive of

Spirit as being identical with living nature. Instead of rationally "representing" nature, one was to participate in, commune with, and give expression to it. If rationalists celebrated the freedom that stemmed from universally objectifying nature, romantics reveled in rejoining with (for Wilber, *regressing* to) nature in all its diversity, plurality, and particularity (Wilber 1995, 445–46).

Early members of the eco and ego camps operated from within the same framework of modern universalism, but with very different emphases. An Enlightenment rationalist like Kant emphasized universal uniformitarianism: all humans share the same rationality. Romantics emphasized universal diversitarianism: every perspective is to be honored (Wilber 1995, 460). Though acknowledging the eco camp's respect for difference, Wilber alleges that in seeking unique emotional experiences and heightened individuality, ecoromantics slid "into forms of ego absorption that no Ego camp would even dream of! In fact, this divine egoism was precisely the heteronomy that the Ego camps were fighting" (1995, 464). Ecoromantic egoism pulls one away from universal compassion and from other positive achievements of egoic rationality and leads one toward ever narrower engagements that represent enslavement to one's own sickly "me-ness." Focusing solely on the pathological, dissociative, and dualistic aspects of mental-egoic rationality, ecoromantics regard any differentiation as "the sign, not of a newly emerging integration, but of a lost paradise" (Wilber 1995, 448).

According to Wilber, ecofeminists such as Starhawk and Charlene Spretnak and "ecomasculinists" such as Dave Foreman and Gary Snyder misguidedly praise prehistoric tribal social forms that were often socially repressive, ecologically uninformed, and lacking an adequate understanding of Spirit as simultaneously immanent and transcendent. Wilber discerns a death wish operative in such ecoromantic descenders, who allegedly scrape

> layers and layers of depth off the universe in search of the
> primal ground where [reinsertion into nature] could occur.
> . . . In search of a larger life, they found only a greater
> death, a rancid leveling of just those differentiations that
> allowed their search in the first place. (1995, 453)

Though ecoromantics often criticize rational-egoic subjectivity, Wilber argues that the longing for nature amounts to infantile narcissism, the most primitive form of egoism, in which the self and world remain undifferentiated. The ecoromantics' effort to "feel" their way into the interlocking natural system forms the photographic negative of the rationalists' attempt to "think" their way into that same system. In effect, ecoromantics first reduced the Divine to material nature and then reduced nature itself to their own inner nature, as their own pure and unmediated feelings, which then became the source for "spiritual" sentiment and salvation from alienating modern life. Nature was known

> by the impact that [it] released in me. Nature was valued because of the thrill it sent swishing through the ego in "pristine" wilderness encounters. Not a transparency to the Divine, but the divine ego reflected to itself in monological feeling. (Wilber 1995, 470)

Insofar as the ecoromantic idea of reuniting with nature involves narcissistic absorption in infantile feeling states, ecoromantics commit what Wilber calls the *pre/trans fallacy*, which involves the failure to distinguish between prepersonal awareness (self and other not yet distinguished), interpersonal awareness (self and other distinguished), and transpersonal awareness (self and other reintegrated without being obliterated). According to the perennial philosophy, reunion with the cosmos involves not only horizontal identification (descent) with nature, but also vertical movement (ascent) in the form of "inner transformations aspiring to the nondual One" (Wilber 1995, 467). The complementary movements of descent and ascent make possible a wider identity that clears away self-centric perception and constitutes an opening in which natural phenomena can manifest the Spirit radiating through them. In true nature mysticism, Wilber says, "nature" is understood as Nature, that is, the Spirit of which phenomena are manifestations (1995, 469).

If rationalists are guilty of a "rancid transcendence" that dissociates ego from nature, Wilber writes, then ecoromantics are guilty of a "morbid embrace" with nature in a way that reproduces the feeling-dominated egoism of childhood narcissism. Rationalism's one-sided quest for autonomy, control, and agency is an instance of pathological Ascent, which in a Godless cosmos involves "utterly futile schemes to turn this finite world into a utopian world of infinite wonderment: an infinite above collapses into an infinite ahead" (Wilber 1995, 512). The ontological thirst for the Divine can never be slaked by consuming material objects, no matter how pleasant and refined. Yet romanticism's "spiritual" quest for unity, communion, and wholeness is an instance of pathological descent, which in attempting to erase the rational ego-subject ends up validating prepersonal egoism.

Despite growing recognition that human life is inextricably connected with the biosphere, ecological problems continue to mount—for two reasons, in Wilber's view. First, the ego camp cannot "integrate the biosphere in a higher synthesis of its own interests; still leaves everywhere the corpses of its reckless repressions; still totally confuses transrational Spirit with prerational myth" (Wilber 1995, 513). Second, though correctly protesting against ecological destruction, the eco camp absolutizes the biosphere, fights pathological hierarchy by reducing everything to the same level, portrays as "anthropocentrism" the idea that the noosphere represents a "higher" level of evolutionary development, and focuses on modernity's ecologically dark side while ignoring its positive achievements. For Wilber, short-term ecological woes can be addressed by universal realization of the principled aim of mental-egoic awareness: "mutual understanding and unforced agreement as to common ends" (1995, 514). So long as subjective and intersubjective distortions prevail in socioeconomic systems, however, we will witness the egoistic craving, nationalism, militarism, and corporate greed that give rise to pollution, ozone depletion, soil erosion, habitat destruction, and other ecological problems.

Wilber contends that the eco camp's appeal to systems theory and paradigms of interconnectedness will be of little help in solving ecological problems, since those problems arise not because of a failure to grasp the external order of Gaia, but instead because of a failure to understand the interior dimension of reality, including human life. Scientific knowledge about the workings of the biosphere is widely available, but many people still behave in ecologically destructive ways. Although those in the eco camp are often "driven by a profound intuition of the World Soul, the Eco-Noetic Self," Wilber concludes that they are "completely crippled by operating within the flatland paradigm" (1995, 517). Ostensibly, their grasp of interior dynamics is "incredibly anemic, virtually nil" and "outrageously naive," for not only do they fail to appreciate the regressive potential of web-of-life ontology, but they fail to appreciate that a "change in *objective belief* [about the "interconnected" or "holistic" exterior domain] is *not* the primary driving force of *interior development*" (Wilber 1995, 514–15) (emphasis in original). As opposed to the one-dimensional "ecological self" seeking "biospheric immersion," then, Wilber calls first for the consolidation of the intersubjective rational ego and second for the development of the transpersonal econoetic self, which identifies not only with physiosphere and biosphere, but with noosphere and theosphere. Above all, we must become aware of the complexities involved in transforming human awareness from contemporary egocentrism to socio-anthropocentrism, then to worldcentrism, and finally to genuine transpersonalism (Wilber 1995, 514). Although hoping that nonpathological differentiation will lead to a transpersonal awareness that reintegrates nature, humankind, and Spirit, Wilber stresses that there are no guarantees that such awareness will arise on this planet.

CRITICAL EVALUATION

Sex, Ecology, Spirituality (1995) is noteworthy not only for its remarkable insights, but also for its enormous scope. Of course, any book with such ambitious reach can be expected to have problems, some of which are examined below.

Holarchy and Teleological Evolution

Many contemporary scientists would agree with Wilber that unexpected properties emerge in evolutionary processes and that nature can be understood as a nested hierarchy of interconnected holons. Moreover, a number of scientists are reintroducing, although with qualifications, teleological concepts into discussions about the evolution of such hierarchies. For Wilber, these trends spell the end of science's positivist-reductionistic phase and the beginning of its rediscovery that the universe involves involution (the self-emptying of the Divine into Creation) and evolution (the return of Creation to the Divine). For more than a century, Darwin's theory "allowed science to ignore any sort of Eros, any sort of 'gentle persuasion' or transcendent/emergent drive" in evolution (1995, 492). But, Wilber goes on to say,

> It is now almost universally recognized by scientists that although natural selection can account quite well for "microevolution" . . . , it can account not at all for macroevolution (or the emergence of new ranges of possibility). Add to that the fact that the Big Bang has made Idealists out of virtually anybody who thinks about it, and the result is that most philosophers of science now openly admit—and even champion—the fact that evolution has some sort of self-transcending drive [Eros] tucked within its own processes. (1995, 492)

Although agreeing that science is moving in the direction described by Wilber, I believe that he overestimates how many scientists and philosophers have jumped on the bandwagon of cosmological hierarchy and the teleological evolution of consciousness. Many scientists remain skeptical both about whether there are levels of consciousness that are "higher" or "more integrated" than mental-egoic rationality, and about whether humans can achieve such levels, even if they do happen to exist. Further, Wilber's claim that virtually anyone who thinks about the big bang has become an idealist is contentious. Physicists such as Paul Davies argue eloquently for cosmic teleology (Davies 1983, 1988, 1992), but scientists such as Stephen Jay Gould (1989) and Nobel laureate

Steven Weinberg (1977), as well as philosophers such as Daniel Dennett (1995), continue to deny that the universe has any special direction.[3]

In important respects, the antiteleological views of scientists like Gould and Weinberg reflect the cosmic absurdism that arose in the late nineteenth century as a consequence of (1) Darwin's theory of evolution, according to which evolution lacks any purpose, and (2) the Second Law of Thermodynamics (entropy), according to which the universe is headed to "heat death." A number of important scientific trends, including chaos theory, complexity theory, autopoeisis, and dissipative structures, support Wilber's contention that teleology is making a significant reappearance both in evolutionary theory and cosmology (see Depew and Weber 1995). But caution is needed with respect to how far these new sciences go even in supporting, much less in demonstrating, the idea that eros guides cosmological evolution.

In a recent essay in *Scientific American* (1995), John Horgan maintains that some scientists are becoming impatient with the "sciences of complexity." When, he asks, will these sciences pay their large promissory notes? Further, even though a number of philosophers of science are intrigued by the return of teleology, most of them are far too cautious professionally to "champion" Wilber's idea that eros guides cosmic evolution. Wilber himself, along with a good many astrophysicists and theologians, may need to exercise a bit more caution in hanging his cosmology on theories, including the big bang, that may eventually be supplanted. The Hubble Space Telescope's recent revelation that a number of stars appear to be older than the age of the universe, for example, has tempered the enthusiasm of big bang theorists who had been elated by the announcement of the apparent discovery of a black hole, the existence of which supposedly confirmed the big bang theory. Contrary to prevailing trends in cosmology, as well as to Wilber's view of the connection between the big bang and cosmic evolution, Eric Lerner (1992) has argued in a most interesting way not only that the big bang never happened, but also that big bang cosmology is *inimical* to progressive ideologies and cosmologies.

Let us focus more on Wilber's idea that hierarchical levels emerge not only in the evolution of matter and life, but also in the evolution of consciousness and culture. Although I am sympathetic to Wilber's evolutionary scheme, in the past several decades there have been a number of factors that challenge the credibility of ideas about progressive evolution, including the social consequences of Soviet Marxism, the ecological consequences of industrial modernity, and the cultural consequences of First World ethnocentrism. Though well aware of such consequences, Wilber insists on the superiority of societies in which slavery has been abolished, in which rights for all persons are universally recognized (at least in principle), and in which material well-being for humankind has increased. Weaving together Schelling, Hegel, Habermas, Piaget, Kohlberg, and Gebser, along with Eastern theorists such as Aurobindo, Wilber contends that achievements of mental-egoic personhood and constitutional democracies represent significant progress in the painful process whereby Spirit—having emptied itself into matter-energy in the big bang—regains consciousness and self-consciousness.

But critics of various stripes have questioned the developmental schemes to which Wilber appeals. Many thinkers associated with the major world religions, including Huston Smith, question the idea of human moral progress. Rather, for many Christians, the sorry condition of the world manifests God's judgment in relation to growing human sinfulness. According to Hinduism, the world—including human society—has fallen from the highest to the lowest possible state, the *Kali Yuga*. Further, in opposition to Wilber's reinterpretation of the Eden myth as a fall "upward" for humankind, many Buddhists argue that humankind has fallen into ever greater darkness since the appearance of the Buddha twenty-six hundred years ago.

On the other hand, many Christian theologians have interpreted Jesus' admonition, "Come, follow me," as an indication that humans can grow spiritually. Moreover, Christian eschatology has provided the basis for progressive ideologies, such as Marxism. Further, Buddhism can easily be read as affirming a procession from confused to ever clearer levels of awareness. Indeed, Beni Madhab Barua remarks that "in the progressive path of life" followed by the aspirant, there are "sixteen or seventeen successive stages" (cited by Sangharakshita 1987, 140). Such citations could be expanded indefinitely. Clearly, then, there is at least some significant religious basis for Wilber's contention that humankind can progress, morally and intellectually.

Still, because Wilber does minimize the widespread notion that humanity has fallen from a higher level and does emphasize claims supporting progressive evolution, he leaves himself open to the charge that he favors the ascent tradition (diZerega 1995b and personal communication). In his analysis of Plotinus, for instance, Wilber tends to ignore passages in which Plotinus describes matter as "evil" (when deprived of formative intelligence), nonbeing, phantom, shadow, inactive, and veritable delusion (Brehier 1958, 170). According to one commentator, Plotinus believed that "If the evil in the sensible world is irremediable, the good for the sage will not consist in submitting to it but in escaping from it in order to return to his real home, to the perfect order of the intelligible world" (Brehier 1958, 180). But Wilber replies that despite some lapses, Plotinus shows his true colors by condemning the Gnostic revilement of the Creation, which manifests the glories of the One. Given Wilber's developmental orientation, which leads to his concerns about regressive ecoromanticism, it would be somewhat surprising if he did not favor the ascent tradition. Nevertheless, his commitment to nondualism produces an impressive effort to reconcile ascent and descent, divine Spirit and Creation.

In recent decades, the ideas of progress and progressive evolution have also been attacked by secular critics from various perspectives. Many feminists, for example, maintain that the schemes of moral and consciousness development devised by Kohlberg and Habermas reflect a masculinist bias (Gilligan 1982). Furthermore, despite Wilber's claim that "not a sentence that follows is not open to confirmation or rejection by a community of the adequate" (Wilber 1995, x), postmodern theorists and environmental thinkers would join feminists in expressing concern that Wilber's developmental scheme is another instance of the "One True Story" that has justified exclusion, marginalization, and domination of the humans (and nonhumans) that have only minor roles in that story. In the quest to realize allegedly universal goals, contemporary critics charge, totalizing "progressive" ideologies have eradicated social differences and devastated the biosphere.

Wilber's entire book can be read as a reply to these important concerns, especially the ones raised by ecofeminists. Indeed, the second volume of his planned trilogy will be devoted to his appraisal of the promise and problems of ecofeminism. Wilber maintains that his views on human development and evolution, far from contributing to further social oppression and ecological damage, are consistent with the politically emancipatory and ecological aims of most ecofeminists. Further, he argues that the ecocrisis results not from rationality as such, but rather from a dissociated rationality, from a "rationality (and its technical know-how) in the service of ethnocentric dominance or tribal power ploys" (1995, 664). He insists that only the personal freedoms, democratic institutions, and scientific understanding made possible by such rationality can stave off the ecological crisis long enough to permit the emergence of centauric vision-logic, the final personal level that will integrate humankind and nature (1995, 201, 513–14). Even though joining ecofeminists in condemning the ecologically destructive and socially repressive dimensions of patriarchal history, Wilber refuses to concede that there is no *telos* in human history. The death and destruction suffered by human and nonhuman alike in world history can be redeemed in part because they contributed to a transcendent purpose. Wilber would agree with Hegel's dictum that many an innocent flower is trampled underfoot as Spirit moves toward self-consciousness. Sentimental attachment to existing social or ecological formations is understandable, but naive. Rather than focusing solely on the undeniable social and eco- logical problems posed by liberal capitalism, then, Wilber prefers to emphasize the extent to which it has furthered—however imperfectly— the emancipatory ideals of Enlightenment humanism. But while sup- porting modernity's emancipatory ideals, Wilber claims that his spiritu- al cosmology goes well beyond the secular limits of modern ideologies.

Affirming modernity's ideals of universal human rights, Wilber also warns against resurgent tribalism. As I have argued elsewhere (1995), the fact that National Socialism involved a perverted "green" dimension, including celebration of racial blood ties with the sacred land, should send up warning flags to every environmentalist tempted to condemn modernity wholesale. Legitimate concerns about the revival of regressive social movements, however, may lead Wilber to posit an overly linear model of human psychological and cultural development, a model that cannot readily take into account the implications of variations in such development.

Individual Development

In personal development, individuals often reenter previous levels of consciousness, without remaining there and without undoing the achievements necessary to arrive at mental-egoic personhood. Indeed, exploring and "completing" those earlier levels (as Wilber himself sug- gests) may be necessary for further personal development. A person can affirm the political and intellectual achievements of mental-egoic per- sonhood, while temporarily suspending such personhood in order to explore earlier levels of awareness. Obviously such explorations can go too far, especially if they take place in the context of regressive political views. Consider the case, however, of someone at the mental-egoic level who is not yet prepared to attain centauric vision-logic, but who has an agonizing sense of being disconnected from nature. In order to establish a felt unity with nature, and thus to heal the dissociative tendencies of mental-egoic consciousness, this person may engage in practices that reawaken levels of consciousness in which the self-nature split is less intensive. Arguably, such practices, if undertaken within a supportive and conscious framework, could actually assist that person in the process of consolidating mental-egoic consciousness.

But Wilber seems to prefer experiential efforts to reintegrate humanity and nature to occur within the centauric level of awareness, which he believes reflects a more developed consciousness than, and is thus superior to, the "felt unity" experienced at prepersonal levels. He is concerned that pagan rituals, goddess worship, shamanism, and various New Age practices loosely linked with environmentalism represent a dangerous regression to the "magical-typhonic" level of consciousness. In some cases, such concern may be justified, but in other cases there may be legitimate reasons for such exploration, if carried out in appropriate circumstances. In still other cases, people engaging in practices that seem prepersonal may in fact be exploring the first *transpersonal* level of consciousness, the psychic level. In *Up from Eden* (1981), Wilber says that the psychic level (Nirmanakaya) involves shamanistic trance, shakti, psychic capacities, siddhis, driyas, elemental forces (nature gods and goddesses), emotional-sexual transmutation, body ecstasy, kundalini, and hatha yoga (253).

As Wilber himself argues, people taking part in the same practices, for example, goddess worship or shamanistic trance, may be at quite different levels of awareness. In the same setting, a person with relatively tenuous mental-egoic awareness may be exploring (perhaps in a risky manner) the magical-typhonic realm, whereas a person who has consolidated centauric awareness may be exploring the psychic realm. Again, during the same ritual, one person may be worshipping the Great Mother, which involves prepersonal awareness, while another person may be worshipping the Great Goddess, which involves transpersonal awareness. Hence, one should not lump all such practitioners into an undifferentiated prepersonal heap, though everyone involved in such practices should be aware of the pre/trans fallacy and the danger of confusing prepersonal with transpersonal states.

At the psychic and subtle levels, as reported by people from many spiritual traditions, people encounter all sorts of entities, ranging from angels and demons to the Great Goddess. According to the traditional Great Chain of Being, these entities have ontological status. Hence, medieval theologians posited a host of angelic beings whose ontological status is higher than humankind's. But the diagram of Wilber's Great Holarchy shows no such beings (angels, gods, demons, or *bodhisattvas*) above, beyond, or parallel with humankind. Wilber accuses ecoromantics of being prepersonalists who are scraping off the personal levels of the Great Chain of Being. In turn, however, some explorers of the psychic and subtle realms may accuse Wilber of being a personalist who is depopulating the transpersonal levels. Concluding that talk of angels and demons is an embarrassment to "higher" levels of spirituality, Wilber might argue that such "entities" have no independent reality, but are anthropomorphized expressions of experiences undergone at the psychic level. By following this approach, however, one could argue that *all* entities encountered in *whatever* levels are simply anthropomorphic projections. But this goes too far. Perhaps the ontological status of entities encountered at these levels will receive further examination in the next two volumes of Wilber's trilogy.

Wilber's Critique of the Eco Camp

Turning now to Wilber's depiction of the eco camp, I believe that he often paints with too broad a brush. To be sure, in such an enterprising work, one can expect sweeping generalizations, but in view of the work's frequent erudition, I expected it to differentiate more carefully among the varieties of romanticism, as well as among today's ecotheorists, instead of lumping most of them together. Wilber suggests that most ecophilosophers yearn to become reabsorbed in nature, are personally underdeveloped, and are prone to ecofascism and other reactionary views. Certainly, the utterances of a few radical environmentalists may be read in this way, but the large majority of ecophilosophers and environmental activists have broadly democratic political views, just as did many early romantics. That certain kinds of ecoromanticism may be interpreted as justifying regressive political goals is not evidence that environmentalism in particular or romanticism in general are inherently regressive either socially or psychologically.

Most romanticists, as even Habermas admits, originally had broadly democratic views, despite criticizing many aspects of industrial modernity (1987, 92). Their longing to regain a lost unity with "nature" may have sometimes represented a regressive yearning for infantile bliss, but at other times represented an impulse toward unity with "Nature," defined as Spirit that both manifests itself in and transcends material "nature." In making the distinction between nature and Nature, Wilber himself cites (1995, 470–71) Wordsworth, but he might well have quoted a number of other representatives of romanticism, the complexity of which is notorious.

Contemporary ecophilosophy is also complex, with representatives ranging from "weak anthropocentrists" who acknowledge the worth of nonhuman beings while affirming the centrality of human life, to biocentrists who repudiate anthropocentric ideologies. Wilber, however, says that

> with a few notable exceptions . . . most approaches [to environmental ethics] center exclusively on the principle of "bioequality," a reworking of the very old tenets of the Descending path of Plenitude (divorced and dissociated from any true Ascent). (1995, 517)

Bioequality or biocentric egalitarianism is most often associated with deep ecologists, according to whom no organism (and no ecosystem) has more intrinsic value than any other organism (or ecosystem). As noted earlier, however, environmental ethicists have criticized such biocentric egalitarianism for lacking the distinctions needed for guidance in situations of moral conflict, for example, if one were faced with the dilemma of being able to save either a child or a rare species. Warwick Fox, however, denies that deep ecology is an example of environmental ethics, since the latter requires ascribing some kind of "intrinsic value" to nonhuman beings in order to include them in the domain of morally considerable objects (1990, 1995). Deep ecologists, in contrast, call for a transpersonal "ecological Self" with a "wider sense of identification." Such a Self, no longer identifying so closely either with its own ego or body, or with its narrow circle of family and friends, would spontaneously exhibit compassion for all beings (Fox 1990; Macy 1991). Normally, one's human identification with the child would lead one to save it rather than the endangered species, but some deep ecologists can imagine situations in which one would save the endangered species.

In some ways, Fox's ecological Self resembles Wilber's econoetic awareness, a post-egocentric and post-anthropocentric level in the evolutionary sequence of moral development (Wilber 1995, 291). In a passage that could have been taken directly from Naess or Fox, Wilber writes that for the econoetic self "treating others as one's Self is not a moral imperative that has to be enforced as an ought or a should or a difficult imposition, but comes as easily and as naturally as the rising of the sun or the shining of the moon" (1995, 291). Fox and Wilber agree that transpersonal awareness leads someone spontaneously to act to protect a rainforest just as he or she would act to prevent harm to his or her own body, or to his or her own family. No moral compulsion would be at work here, but instead compassion grounded in a transpersonal or wider sense of identification. Many ecofeminists, however, would criticize Fox, Naess, and Wilber precisely because the universalistic and disinterested transpersonal approach betrays an abstractness characteristic of masculinist thinking.

Wilber distinguishes between himself and deep ecologists by insisting that the latter are not really transpersonalists, but instead are ecoromantic prepersonalists for whom "nature" is little more than a reflecting screen for unintegrated emotional states. Wilber himself may sound like an ecoromantic in saying that psychic transpersonal awareness "directly and immediately breathes the common air and beats the common blood of a Heart and Body that is one in all beings" (1995, 291), but he maintains that people at the psychic level can experience the interconnection of all life without regressing to the prepersonal level, for they recognize that life itself is a manifestation of the Spirit, toward reintegration with which all evolutionary processes move.

Fox insists, however, that the transpersonal-ecological Self identifies with a far wider array of beings than do either those modern selves who identify solely with egoic states or with other humans, or those romantic selves who identify with their own projected emotions and thus have little genuine concern for nonhuman beings. Wilber would reply that Fox's ecological Self identifies so closely with manifest entities that it fails to recognize transcendent Spirit. The compassion of which Fox speaks, so Wilber argues, can arise only at a higher and deeper level of awareness, based on adequate differentiation among the various levels of reality. Only such differentiation enables compassion to be informed enough that one knows that saving a horse is better than saving a plant, even though recognizing that each being has a worth of its own.

Even assuming the validity of Wilber's critique of Fox, however, Arne Naess's version of deep ecology can be read as consistent with the transpersonal and nondual traditions on which Wilber himself draws. Informed by Mahayana Buddhism and Advaita Vedanta, Naess's ecosophy theory distinguishes between the phenomenal domain (spatio-temporal "span") and the noumenal domain (non-spatio-temporal "depth" or "emptiness") (see Zimmerman 1994). Like many critics, then, Wilber sometimes either discounts the best work of deep ecology theory, or else confuses such theory with foolish pronouncements made by environmental activists who manifest regressive tendencies. Moreover, even if many deep ecology theorists fail adequately to integrate the immanent and transcendent moments of Spirit, Wilber would win a more careful hearing if he offered a fairer presentation and critique of their work.

Regarding ecofeminism, Wilber reveals the same disconcerting tendency to toss distinct positions onto the same undifferentiated heap, although the in-depth coverage of ecofeminism promised in volume two of the Kosmos trilogy may correct this problem. Some ecofeminist positions may resemble the nature-loving, tribal-favoring, ego-surrendering viewpoint indicted by Wilber, but many other versions of ecofeminism cannot be so criticized. Despite having argued in *Up from Eden* (1981) that Great Goddess spirituality represents the next level beyond egoic rationality, in *Sex, Ecology, Spirituality* (1995) Wilber interprets most ecofeminist devotion to the Great Goddess not as ascent, but rather as descent-oriented and regressive worship of the Great Mother. Far from unanimously opposing the ascent tradition, however, ecofeminist theologians such as Rosemary Radford Ruether (1992) and Catherine Keller (1986) affirm that the Divine must be understood as both immanent and transcendent. Furthermore, ecofeminists such as Karen Warren (in Zimmerman 1993), Riane Eisler (1987) (whom Wilber himself cites on this point), and others recognize the dangers involved in abandoning the liberties achieved by modernity. Likewise, years before Wilber, Val Plumwood (in Zimmerman 1993) criticized deep ecologists for mistakenly believing that atomism is the real source of the ecocrisis and for recommending that atomism be overcome by undifferentiated "identification" with all beings. Yet according to Plumwood, again anticipating Wilber, the real problem with patriarchal modernity is not atomism (Wilber's gross reductionism), but subject-object dualism (Wilber's subtle reductionism).

I would have expected Wilber to discuss the neo-Hegelian, evolutionary cosmology most notably associated with the social ecology of Murray Bookchin, but no such discussion is to be found. Elsewhere (Zimmerman 1994), I have argued that Bookchin and Wilber agree on the following: (1) that science reveals that the cosmos has a telos leading to ever greater differentiation and complexity; (2) that life and self-conscious life, including human beings, are not cosmic accidents, but important and even inevitable moments in cosmic evolution; (3) that despite its dark sides, Enlightenment modernity represents an important level of human development, not least because it emphasizes the importance of personal freedom and autonomy; (4) that those environmentalists calling for re-immersion in nature represent regressive psychological and social tendencies that must be resisted; and (5) that humankind is capable of evolving modes of awareness and social institutions that not only harmonize humankind and nature, but also help nature to give expression to its own internal striving.

There are important differences between the two thinkers, however, the major one being that Wilber affirms the transcendent Divine, whereas Bookchin regards such an idea as reactionary and obscurantist. Bookchin affirms a deep debt to Aristotle and Hegel, but omits the metaphysical ground (the Divine) required by the cosmologies of these illustrious predecessors (see Zimmerman 1994). Despite this important lacuna in Bookchin's work, Wilber would have provided a more balanced critical appraisal of the eco camp had he discussed social ecology as presented by thinkers such as Bookchin, John Clark, Joel Kovel, and others (see the social ecology section in Zimmerman 1993). Equally puzzling is why Wilber chose not to mention the provocative and inspiring evolutionary narratives developed by thinkers such as Thomas Berry, Brian Swimme, and Duane Elgin (Swimme and Berry 1992; Elgin 1993). Although disagreeing in certain respects with Wilber's vision, these authors have much in common with his view that Spirit is at work in the evolutionary processes whereby the universe generates ever more complex levels of reality and consciousness.

Rhetorical Style

Finally, let me mention what is to me the most disturbing aspect of Wilber's admirable book: its rhetorical style. Despite his commitment to nondualism, Wilber sometimes resorts to divisive, even contemptuous rhetoric when discussing views with which, and people with whom, he disagrees. He uses the term *flatlanders*, for example, to name modernists, and he speaks of the "Shadows" when referring to nature as understood by those naturalists. Though he criticizes otherworldly ascenders, he saves his harshest words for this-worldly descenders, who supposedly believe that

> By becoming one with the Shadows and seamlessly inserting ourselves into a denatured nature, salvation will be found— and if it doesn't seem to be working, just insert harder.

> The idea still seems to be that if I can just French-kiss the Shadows, I will see the light. (1995, 521)

In a work that reflects such insight into nonduality, I see no reason to speak so disdainfully of others who are doing their best in speaking of serious matters. Wilber may successfully address all the criticisms discussed above, but his position will be weakened unless he adopts a more charitable rhetorical style when examining the views of his opponents. Failure to do so would be a shame, since he has gone further than anyone else in recent history in developing an affirmative vision of humanity's evolutionary history and future. His achievement is conspicuous enough that it should provoke all thoughtful ecologists and modernists alike to reevaluate their positions, perhaps in a way that will improve the future both for humankind and for the biosphere on which such life depends.

Acknowledgments

My thanks to Gus diZerega, Donald Rothberg, and Sean Kelly for their very helpful critical suggestions, which improved this essay.

Notes

1. In some ways, Wilber would seem more sympathetic with those who deny that there is an ecological crisis and instead predict a new era of human prosperity consistent with ecological well-being. See Stock 1993, Kelly 1994, Kaufmann 1994, Bailey 1995, and Easterbrook 1995. Even as the debate rages between eco-optimists and eco-pessimists, however, Wilber believes that ecological calamity might halt humanity's evolution to more integrated levels of awareness.

2. In *Up from Eden*, Wilber argues in much greater detail that *death-denial* motivated the rational ego's efforts to conquer nature through science and industry. By focusing less in *Sex, Ecology, Spirituality* on the dark consequences of technological modernity, even while stating them, Wilber tries to avoid the technophobia that he associates with the eco camp.

3. In favorably reviewing Daniel Dennett's book, *Darwin's Dangerous Idea* (1995), the evolutionary biologist John Maynard Smith agrees with Dennett that "In essence . . . , no matter how mindless the processes of evolution may be, they have, in fact produced a world of astonishing diversity and beauty, which we can enjoy, and ought to protect" (1995, 48).

References

Bailey, R., ed. 1995. *The true state of the planet*. New York: The Free Press.

Brehier, E. 1958. *The philosophy of Plotinus*. Translated by J. Thomas. Chicago: University of Chicago Press.

Callicott, B. 1989. *In defense of the land ethic*. Albany: State University of New York Press.

Davies, P. 1983. *God and the new physics*. New York: Simon and Schuster.

———. 1988. *The cosmic blueprint*. New York: Simon and Schuster.

———. 1992. *The mind of God*. New York: Simon and Schuster.

Dennett, D. 1995. *Darwin's dangerous idea*. New York: Simon and Schuster.

Depew, D., and B. Weber. 1995. *Darwinism evolving*. Cambridge: MIT Press.

diZerega, G. 1995. Democracies and peace. *The Review of Politics* 57:279 308.

diZerega, G., and R. Smoley. 1995. Up the down staircase. *Gnosis* (Fall): 86-87.

Easterbrook, G. 1995. *A moment on the Earth*. New York: Viking.

Eisler, R. 1987. *The chalice and the blade*. San Francisco: Harper and Row.

Elgin, D. 1993. *Awakening Earth*. New York: Morrow.

Fox, W. 1990. *Toward a transpersonal ecology*. Boston: Shambhala.

———. 1995. A critical overview of environmental ethics. *World Futures* 46:1–21.

Gaard, G. 1993. *Ecofeminism: Women, animals, nature*. Philadelphia: Temple University Press.

Gilligan, C. 1982. *In a different voice: Psychological theory and women's development*. Cambridge: Harvard University Press.

Gould, S. 1989. *Wonderful life*. New York: Norton.

Habermas, J. [1985] 1987. *The philosophical discourse of modernity*. Translated by F. Lawrence. Cambridge: MIT Press.

Horgan, J. 1995. From complexity to perplexity. *Scientific American* 272:104–09.

Kaufmann, S. 1994. *No turning back*. New York: Basic Books.

Keller, C. 1986. *From a broken web*. Boston: Beacon Press.

Kelly, K. 1994. *Out of control*. Reading, Mass.: Addison-Wesley.

Lerner, E. 1992. *The big bang never happened*. New York: Times Mirror.

Macy, J. 1991. *World as lover, world as self*. Berkeley: Parallax Press.

Regan, T. 1983. *The case for animal rights*. Berkeley: University of California Press.

Ruether, R. 1992. *Gaia and God*. San Francisco: HarperSanFrancisco.

Sangharakshita. 1987. *A survey of Buddhism*. London: Tharpa Publications.

Singer, P. 1975. *Animal liberation*. New York: Avon.

Smith, J. 1995. Genes, memes, and minds. *The New York Review of Books* 42 (19): 46-48.

Stock, G. 1993. *Metaman*. Toronto: Doubleday Canada.

Swimme, B., and T. Berry. 1992. *The universe story*. San Francisco: Harper.

Warren, K., ed. 1991. *Hypatia* 6 (special issue on ecofeminism): 1–224.

Warren, K., and J. Cheney. 1991. Ecological feminism and ecosystem ecology. *Hypatia* 6:179–97.

Weinberg, S. 1977. *The first three minutes*. New York: Basic Books.

Wilber, K. 1981. *Up from Eden: A transpersonal view of human evolution*. Boston: Shambhala.

———. 1995. *Sex, ecology, spirituality: The spirit of evolution*. Boston: Shambhala.

Zimmerman, M. 1994. *Contesting Earth's future*. Berkeley and Los Angeles: University of California Press.

———. 1995. The threat of ecofascism. *Social Theory and Practice* 21: 207–38.

Zimmerman, M., ed. 1993. *Environmental philosophy*. Englewood Cliffs, N.J.: Prentice Hall.

9

Peggy A. Wright

Peggy Wright is a pioneer in articulating feminist voices in transpersonal studies. In her writing and teaching at Lesley College in Cambridge, Massachusetts, she has developed integrative models of education, human development, and spirituality, much like Ken Wilber has done. In seeking ways of knowing linked both culturally and historically with women's voices, her goal is to balance mainstream ideas and learning styles with personal, subjective (or in Wilber's terminology, "interior"), intuitive, empathic, "connected," and embodied dimensions of knowledge.

Wright's initial work was in science and nutrition, and she earned degrees in nutrition from the University of California, Berkeley (B.S.), and Tufts University (M.Ed.). For many years, she taught and had a private practice in clinical nutrition (with a holistic health emphasis) in the Boston area, offering workshops and lectures.

In 1982, she began teaching at Lesley College. Her students, 90 percent women and primarily adult learners returning to school, have been, she says, her primary teachers about women's developmental pathways and "connected" ways of knowing. Her work chiefly consists of mentoring independent-study graduate students in integrating theory, research, and practice, mainly in psychology, alternative healing methods, education, and women's studies, including women's spirituality.

Wright has also immersed herself in indigenous ways of knowing. For many years, she studied the method of shamanic journeying developed by Michael Harner of the New School in New York. This led to a period of organizing and then leading sweat lodge ceremonies, primarily for women. She learned from a number of indigenous teachers, particularly Lakota, including Wallace Black Elk, Archie Lame Deer, and Oyate. From 1986 to 1992, she attended many Native American ceremonies, including those of noted yuwipi healer Godfrey Chips. Her interest in indigenous spirituality has led to a number of publications, particularly on shamanic altered states of consciousness. She describes her own spiritual orientation, following Joan Halifax, as that of "bodhishamanism," combining the radical nondualism of Buddhism with indigenous spirituality.

Wright's background in feminism and gender issues also is long standing, dating from her work at the Berkeley Women's Health Collective in the early 1970s. Over the years, she has been deeply influenced by feminist theories of knowledge, such as in Women's Ways of Knowing *(Belenky, Clinchy, Goldberger, and Tarule 1997) and*

Transforming Knowledge *(Minnich 1990). She also emphasizes the "connected" and "relational" models of self articulated by Carol Gilligan and the theorists at the Stone Center of Wellesley College (Jordan, Kaplan, Miller, Stiver, and Surrey 1990). The many explorations of women's spirituality, especially goddess-centered cultures, contemporary goddess-centered spirituality, indigenous traditions, and Buddhism, also inform her work.*

Wright's recent work in many ways brings together these varied interests. Her dissertation, to be completed in 1998 at the Saybrook Institute, is an important investigation of "intimate committed relationship" as a spiritual path, based on numerous in-depth interviews. Her 1995 ReVision *essay on "Bringing Women's Voices to Transpersonal Theory" is one of the first explicit attempts to connect feminist and transpersonal theories. In that essay, to which Wilber comments in detail in his response to Wright in this book (chapter 14), Wright gives what she takes to be a sympathetic yet vigorous critique of Wilber's writings published at the time of her writing (prior to* Sex, Ecology, Spirituality*). She argues that the transpersonal experiences of indigenous peoples, children, and women have been largely neglected in the formation of his transpersonal theory, and that Wilber has used primarily male-centered material from Asian and Western spiritual traditions of the last 2500 years.*

Basing her work on that of Nancy Chodorow and Jean Baker Miller and their development of the model of a "connected self" or "self-in-relation," which predominates in women, Wright emphasizes that to be basically in relation to others (as opposed to basically separate) is to have "permeable" boundaries, which allow one to experience simultaneously both self and other. She goes on to argue that such permeability is often mistaken as indicating a lower level of development and the lack of appropriate self-boundaries. She speaks of this confusion, following Wilber's naming of the "pre/trans" fallacy, as a "pre/perm" fallacy. Yet such permeability seems to be a fundamental aspect of women's experience, including transpersonal experience. However, Wright believes, transpersonal theory has not yet integrated an understanding of permeability and the connected self and thus of the gender dimensions of transpersonal experiences.

In her contribution to this volume, Wright continues her study of Wilber's work, focusing especially on the treatment of gender in Sex, Ecology, Spirituality. *Although she agrees with much of Wilber's innovative work, she outlines ways in which she believes that his theory is nevertheless continuous with—and indeed perpetuates—male-centered themes. The problem, Wright argues, is that Wilber bases his theoretical constructs on traditions and values which take men's experience in general and spiritual experience in particular as the norm for both genders. As a result, those values which seem typical of women's experience—especially empathic connection, relationship, and permeability of boundaries—tend to be misunderstood and even denigrated. Though she commends many of Wilber's core intentions, she points to what she sees as the great need to integrate the perspective of the connected self into transpersonal theory.*

Further Readings

Belenky, M., B. Clinchy, N. Goldberger, and J. Tarule. [1986] 1997. *Women's ways of knowing: The development of self, voice, and mind*. New York: Basic Books.

Jordan, J., A. Kaplan, J. Miller, I. Stiver, and J. Surrey, eds. 1991. *Women's growth in connection: Writings from the Stone Center*. New York: Guilford Press.

Marler, J., and P. Wright, eds. 1998. *Cultures of the goddess*. ReVision 21 (3).

Minnich, E. 1990. *Transforming knowledge*. Philadelphia: Temple University Press.

Wright, P. 1989. The nature of the shamanic state of consciousness: A review. *Journal of Psychoactive Drugs* 21 (1): 25-33.

———. 1992. Rhythmic drumming in contemporary shamanism and its relationship to auditory driving and risk of seizure precipitation in epileptics. *Anthropology of Consciousness* (March).

———. 1994. A psychobiological approach to shamanic altered states of consciousness. *ReVision* 16 (Spring): 164-72.

———. 1995a. Bringing women's voices to transpersonal theory. *ReVision* 17 (Winter): 3-10.

———. 1995b. The interconnectivity of mind, brain, and behavior in altered states of consciousness: Focus on shamanism. *Alternative Therapies in Health and Medicine* 1 (3): 50-56.

———. 1997. History and concepts of dissociation. In *Broken images, broken selves: Dissociative narratives in clinical practice*, edited by S. Krippner and S. Powers. New York: Brunner/Mazel.

Gender Issues in Ken Wilber's Transpersonal Theory

ONE OF THE ONGOING ISSUES IN TRANSPERSONAL THEORY CONCERNS how little of women's experience has been incorporated into its foundations. Transpersonal theory primarily draws from Eastern and Western psychological, philosophical, and spiritual traditions. Unfortunately, the cultures underlying these traditions share a long history of the oppression of women, which has affected how these cultures make sense of the world around them. For example, although their deepest teachings are usually gender inclusive, the majority of the maps, models, and social and political structures of Eastern and Western spiritual traditions are not (Saiving 1992). Another example is Western psychology, in which many of the foremost theorists (e.g., Freud, Erikson, Kohlberg, Piaget) have used male behavior as a developmental norm for both genders (Gilligan 1993). Usually, women's failure to fit neatly into these theories has been interpreted as a sign of inherent problems in women's development.

The process of basing cultural or personal values on male-centered norms is known as *androcentrism* (Humm 1990, 8). In Western culture, androcentrism has deeply affected how inquiry is conducted and how theories are built. Searching for and examining the origins of gender biases in inquiries and theories are important tasks of feminist criticism. By "feminist," I am referring to the voices of our culture, female and male, that call for the inclusion of women's experiences in forming the models of reality that affect us all. According to Humm (1990): "Criticism is feminist if it critiques existing disciplines, traditional paradigms about women, nature or social roles, or documents such work by others, from the point of view of women" (40).

As I (1995) noted in a previous essay, Wilber's earlier work (1981; Wilber, Engler, and Brown 1986) primarily relies upon androcentric psychological and spiritual models for the fundamental building blocks of its theories. This has led to a developmental theory more attuned to the experiences and values of the men, rather than of the women, of Western and Eastern cultures. Left out of or minimized in his schema have been values, qualities, and perspectives that are often connected with women's psychological and spiritual development. These include the effect of women's more permeable ego-boundaries on their patterns of personal and spiritual development; an emphasis on developing personal "wholeness" over attaining a specific level or type of consciousness; preferences for circular and web-like models of development and reality that emphasize mutual interconnectedness; and the importance of body, nature, and/or Goddess-oriented experiences of spirituality. I also voiced the concern that Wilber's attempts to fit the breadth of women's experience into his model could easily truncate the very essence of these values and experiences.

Lately, Wilber (1995) has been seeking to develop a theory of human evolution and spirituality that incorporates various theories about gender, including material from some feminist works. He promises a detailed examination of gender issues in a future work, but lays the groundwork for it in his latest book, *Sex, Ecology, Spirituality: The Spirit of Evolution* (*SES*). An evaluation of his efforts forms an important part of furthering a feminist critique of, and continuing the integration of women's experience into, transpersonal theory. How does Wilber approach, evaluate, and present information on gender issues? To what degree does Wilber incorporate current feminist theory and the feminine value sphere? Does Wilber continue to privilege androcentric models of consciousness? In other words, how well does Wilber connect with the "feminine"?

THE CONNECTED SELF AND THE FEMININE VALUE SPHERE

First, however, we need to explore the meaning of the term *feminine*.

Fundamental to women's development is the centrality of relationship and connection, rather than a more masculine focus on the attainment of independence and autonomy (Miller 1991; Gilligan 1982). Although both men and women develop as "selves-in-relation," in Western culture women are more likely to experience a "connected self," while men mostly experience an autonomous "separate self." Chodorow (1978) postulates that these differences stem from a male's psychological need to radically separate from his mother in order to achieve a stable gender identity. In contrast, a female does not experience such radical separation and consequently develops a more permeable ego and a self-structure that is oriented toward relationship. Miller takes a different perspective and faults the culturally defined, gender-based psychosocial shaping that infants undergo from the moment they are born. She points to research that indicates that infants are subtly reinforced for certain behavior patterns, depending on whether the infant is perceived to be a boy or a girl—despite the real sex of the infant. Regardless of the cause, men in Western culture are seen as developing a self that emphasizes separation and autonomy in relationships, rather than connection. Currently, the connected self is considered to belong to the "feminine value sphere," although this categorization is very simplistic.[1]

What are the effects of experiencing a more connected sense of self? A whole value system or "value sphere" arises when connection, rather than autonomy, becomes the central principle of social organization, the development of knowledge and scientific inquiry, and of spiritual development. Feminist approaches to epistemology (Belenky et al. 1997), science (Keller 1985), psychology (Chodorow 1978; Gilligan 1982; Miller 1991), critical discourse (Chambers 1995) and spirituality (Christ 1980; Spretnak 1982), have identified qualities and values that flow from a connected sense of self. These include qualities, values, or concepts that our culture has either ignored, devalued, or repressed, and which provide a balance to our culture's androcentric biases. For example, the qualities of connection, relationship, and communion are presented as a balance to the masculine qualities of autonomy, independence, and agency (Chodorow 1978; Miller 1991). A moral ethic of care is advanced to balance the ethic of justice (Gilligan 1982). Modes of social discourse that honor emotions and the ability to respond to others are introduced to balance the use of reason and procedural rules (Chambers 1995). Research methods that emphasize connection and mutual dialogue, and/or recognize and utilize our inherent subjectivity are used to provide a necessary balance to methods that emphasize detachment and objectivity (Bleier 1984; Brown and Gilligan 1992; Keller 1985). In education, the value of personal experience in creating knowledge is recognized, in contrast to approaches that systematically exclude such experience (Belenky et al. 1997). In spirituality, an emphasis on embodiment, nature, descent, immanence, and the feminine faces of divinity provides a balance to an emphasis on detachment from the physical or the earthly, ascent, transcendence, and masculine forms of divinity (Christ 1980; Spretnak 1982). In addition, wholeness and healing are emphasized over spiritual perfection (Hopkins in Kornfield 1990). In general, less hierarchical models of society, science, spirituality, and reality are considered and serve to balance the hegemony of hierarchical models.

THREE AREAS OF CRITIQUE

In *SES*, Wilber (1995) provides a complex and fascinating example of how gender-related issues "play out" in developing transpersonal theory. Although he offers many valuable ideas, a number of problems arise when he addresses issues of concern to feminists, ecofeminists, and the proponents of women's spirituality. Due to space constraints, I will critique—from a feminist perspective—only three of these areas, moving from his most helpful to his most problematic contributions to gender issues. I begin with Wilber's descriptions of four related concepts: hierarchy, heterarchy, agency, and communion. Here Wilber makes many excellent points; however, his presentation regarding heterarchy bears some examination.

The next area covers Wilber's approach to our ecological problems and what is needed to solve them. His presentation is often astute; however, there are significant problems with his conclusions about the majority of people involved in the ecology movement—conclusions that are fueled by a questionable evaluation of ancient and/or simpler societies and a lack of attention to the contributions of the connected self.

Finally, I address Wilber's theory of the evolution of feminine and masculine value spheres. As I will show, his treatment of this area is highly problematic as it relies on outdated and androcentric models of early human evolution. This leads to a theory that does not hold up when confronted with the data from more recent and less androcentric material. As mentioned, however, the discussion will continue; Wilber promises to examine this topic in more detail in his next volume.

HETERARCHY—HIERARCHY/COMMUNION—AGENCY

Since Wilber's (1981, 1995; Wilber, Engler, and Brown 1986) theories of personal development, human evolution, and reality are integrated into one hierarchical model, the issue of defining hierarchy assumes major significance in explicating his paradigm. Overall, his presentation on hierarchy offers a larger, wider scope with which to understand both human social hierarchies and the evolutionary hierarchies of the natural world. His presentation of the related terms *agency* and *communion* also adds some valuable clarifications, which are particularly relevant to issues in women's psychology. However, Wilber misses an opportunity to convey the ideas of "heterarchists" (including most feminists) in a clear and meaningful way, leaving in his wake a series of avoidable misunderstandings.

Heterarchy—Hierarchy

Briefly, Wilber (1995) begins by rescuing the term "hierarchy" from the social and ecological egalitarians' wastebaskets, pointing to its positive meaning in the areas of science, linguistics, ecology, systems theory, and social theory. He affirms a "sacred" nature of hierarchy, citing both its Greek root meaning of "sacred rule" and its usage by the Christian mystic Dionysius in sixth-century Rome. He points out the inherently hierarchical aspects of pattern emergence in the natural world and equates the concept of hierarchy with the concept of "holarchy" (21). As observed in general systems theory, holarchy is simply an "asymmetrical order of increasing wholeness" (19). Each order of wholeness is a *holon*— "that which, being a whole in one context, is simultaneously a part in another" (18). Within a holarchy, "the elements of that level operate by heterarchy. That is, no one element seems to be especially more important or more dominant, and each contributes more or less equally to the health of the whole level" (20).

Wilber (1995) also details the problems with the extreme or "pathological" forms of both heterarchy and hierarchy. The weakness of taking a "heterarchy only" approach is that one cannot make sense of the connections among the parts—there are only "heaps, not wholes" (21). Pathological heterarchy occurs "when there is a blurring or fusion of that level with its environment . . . it loses itself in others—and all distinctions, of value or identity, are lost" (23). Pathological hierarchy occurs when "a particular holon assumes a repressive, oppressive, arrogant role of dominance over other holons (whether in individual or social development)" (23). Wilber, after Eisler (1987), distinguishes pathological hierarchies from the positive, or as Eisler calls them, "realization" hierarchies, of systems theory. Taken together, these distinctions and terms should provide a useful way to bridge the semantic gap that occurs, as Wilber notes, between social heterarchists and realization hierarchists.

Ironically, Wilber's (1995) attempts to clarify the semantic disagreements between social heterarchists and systems theory hierarchists begin by obscuring the very conceptual distinctions he seeks to clarify.

He writes:

> In a heterarchy, rule or governance is established by a plu-
> ralistic and egalitarian interplay of all parties; in a hierar-
> chy, rule or governance is established by a set of priorities
> that establish those things that are more important and
> those that are less. (16)

Here Wilber (1995) confuses the issue of who has the *power to set priorities* with the *act of having priorities*. He misses the point that in governance, one may set priorities either through a more *heterarchical*
approach, in which the *power to establish values is distributed more or
less equally among all the affected parties*, or through a more *hierarchical* approach, in which the *power to establish values is concentrated in
the hands of a few*. Value hierarchies can become oppressive when the
values created by a circumscribed group are used to judge the values of
those who were not included in the defining group.[2] By defining heterarchy as being incapable of establishing priorities and hierarchy as a
model based on priorities, Wilber (1995) effectively sets the stage to
ridicule and diminish the concerns of the heterarchists.

Wilber's (1995) questionable interpretation of heterarchy seems to
color much of his subsequent discussions concerning this and related
issues. For example, Wilber believes that heterarchists typically espouse
a "flatland" of equal values, while denying that they themselves have a
hierarchy of values (e.g., equal values over prioritized values). He caps
his questionable interpretations with the overgeneralization that "the
social champions of the web of life deny hierarchy in any form" (16).[3]
Basically, Wilber reduces a diverse group of writers and theorists to a
caricature, then interprets their work as if they were writing from his
framework of systems theory, rather than from their own frameworks,
which tend to be set within the context of an evaluation of social power
relationships (Diamond and Orenstein 1990).[4]

In portraying hierarchy as sacred, Wilber (1995) omits any mention
of a sacred nature of heterarchy. Does this mean that while hierarchy
(the deep structural aspects of a holon) is sacred, heterarchy (the specific instances and qualities of the part-to-part interactions) is not?
Perhaps it's time to reframe the meaning of heterarchy, as well as to
rename it, so its positive aspects may become more apparent.[5] I believe
that the root meaning of heterarchy ("other rule") is an inadequate
reflection of the nature of a positive or normal heterarchy, and I propose
replacing the term heterarchy with *synarchy*. This word incorporates the
Greek root *syn* or "with"; thus synarchy means "rule with." It supports
the notion of the mutual relations or intercommunion of the parts, as

opposed to Wilber's depiction of heterarchy as disparate objects or unconnected threads. It draws attention to the relationships within the interior of a holon (part-to-part relations), rather than to a holon's integrative structural pattern (part-to-whole-relations). It shows, contrary to Wilber's assertion, that hierarchy alone is synonymous with neither holarchy nor wholeness. If you destroy either hierarchy or synarchy, you destroy holarchy. It also becomes clear that both synarchy and hierarchy reflect the sacred, perhaps in the related guises of immanence and transcendence.

While Wilber has not examined the positive aspects of synarchy, many women have taken great pains to identify and utilize synarchy's healthy aspects, including egalitarianism and an ethic of caring in social rule. Eisler's (1987) "partnership" model of female-male relationships can be viewed as an example of positive synarchy. Various feminists have been experimenting with social synarchy in a number of arenas, including politics (Chambers 1995) and spirituality (McCallum 1994), while chronicling both the strengths and weaknesses of such an approach. A discussion of these approaches may take place in Wilber's second volume. However, in *SES* an excellent opportunity to integrate certain synarchical concepts as a foundation for future work is bypassed, and a true integration of these concepts is, at best, delayed.

Fortunately, by the end of his presentation, Wilber (1995) redefines holarchy to mean "the balance of normal hierarchy and normal heterarchy," which "undercuts both extreme hierarchy and extreme heterarchy, and allows the discussion to move forward with, I believe, the best of both worlds kept firmly in mind" (25). With this reform, I am in full accord. However, I remain concerned about Wilber's oversimplified portrayal of heterarchists. Wilber's stated intention was to "give normal femininity and normal heterarchy an exaggerated emphasis and a greater value, simply because we are trying to balance the scales [of pathological hierarchy]" (25). I believe his presentation often works contrary to his intentions, which suggests that his work still reflects many androcentric biases, however unintentional they may be.

Communion—Agency

Related to the concepts of synarchy and hierarchy are the concepts of communion and agency. Wilber (1995) explains: "Its [a holon's] agency—its self-asserting, self-preserving, assimilating tendencies—expresses its wholeness, its relative autonomy; whereas its communion—its participatory, bonding, joining tendencies—expresses its partness, its relationship to something larger" (41). Although these particular terms are not used commonly by feminists, clearly the concepts behind them are quite important, especially as regards women's psychological development. Wilber's elaboration of these terms provides a useful way to connect psycho-social issues to more abstract and structurally encompassing frameworks, such as that of systems theory.

Wilber (1995) observes that agency and communion are coexistent and, given their polarity, dwell in perpetual tension. He introduces the concept of "agency-in-communion" to portray the idea that agency and communion are always in relation to each other and that neither can exist in isolation. He depicts the nature of their tension through the following question: "In short, how can I be both my own wholeness and a part of something larger, without sacrificing one or the other?" (45). Imbalances in either direction can lead to either pathological agency ("alienation and repression") or pathological communion ("fusion and dissociation") (41). He associates pathological agency and pathological communion with the pathological manifestations of the masculine and the feminine value spheres, respectively.

Wilber's (1995) treatment of these issues is astute and useful for feminist theory. However, I wish to correct one misconception on his part. He writes that "feminists center on the male pathologies of dominance and miss the equally catastrophic pathologies of fusion" (24–25). Yet, from feminism's first stirrings, feminists have directed enormous attention to the problems of pathological communion. For example, during feminism's consciousness-raising period women began to question the feminine role of "selflessness," in which—in its extreme form—one loses one's identity by merging it into another's identity (Attanucci 1988). From its inception, feminist psychology has been struggling both to validate the female need for healthy communion and to balance it with the self-assertion of agency. Maintaining girls' natural sense of agency (as well as communion) as they enter and transit through adolescence, when their sense of agency is most at risk, is viewed as a crucial developmental issue (Brown and Gilligan 1992; Miller 1991). Women are often at the forefront of developing new conceptions of healthy communion in a culture that is tipped towards pathological agency. For example, psychologist Josselson (1992) has developed a model of a healthy self-in-relation, in which she recognizes the extremes of pathological communion and pathological agency or isolation.

Ultimately, I believe that pathological communion and pathological agency are best recognized as being mutually supportive processes— they are "co-dependent," if you will. Pathological agency depends on pathological communion for a full expression of totalitarianism (as in Nazi Germany). Also, the co-dependence between pathological communion and pathological agency is a major reason why many feminists turned their attention to pathological agency—attempts to deal with pathological communion alone are futile. Given our culture's relative lack of healthy communion, considerable experimentation may be needed in order to understand not just the theory of healthy communion, but its experience and embodiment on both social and individual levels.

ECOLOGICAL CONCERNS

Ecological concerns are central to both cultural and radical feminism and to the women's spirituality movement (Humm 1990). As Wilber (1995) demonstrates, there are a number of theoretical issues that are relevant to the very practical problem of how best to heal the earth. The following section presents some of Wilber's views on this issue, and offers a critique from a feminist developmental perspective.

Wilber contends that an inner psycho-spiritual transformation is needed in order to respond fully to the ecological crises and that understanding how the biosphere works, in and of itself, is insufficient for this task. For Wilber, the task is especially not to regress to the level of premodern traditions, but to integrate that which has been differentiated in modernity, the "Big Three" of "person, culture, [and] nature" (455). According to Wilber, the self-structure (e.g., ego, mode of cognition, etc.) of early humans existed in a state of undifferentiated, fused oneness with nature and with the others in their social system—a primitive condition replete with magical thinking and a lack of individuality. Over the millennia, then, humans differentiated from the natural environment, in ways analogous to how the psyches of infants differentiate from their mothers, as well as from their own bodies. If this differentiation is pushed too far—as has been the case in Western culture—it can lead to dissociation, in which a part that has been differentiated becomes overly repressed by a newly emergent part (e.g., the body is repressed by the mind). Ultimately, Wilber says, the goal is an integration that retains the new differentiation, not a movement back to a more primitive, merged stage. Wilber contends that we are at a unique point of human evolution, one in which both men and women have completed their differentiation from nature, and that reintegration is about to begin. For Wilber, this integration will take place in a cognitive developmental stage called *vision-logic*, which follows our current stage of rational or formal operational thinking. Contrary to the limitations of rational thinking, vision-logic can "hold in mind contradictions, it can unify opposites, it is dialectical and nonlinear" (185). In vision-logic, Wilber sees the possibilities of a "truly planetary culture" (186).

At the same time, Wilber (1995) acknowledges that the current eco-problem is due to a "dissociation" between mind and body, and between noosphere and biosphere. He indicates that we do need "regression in the service of the ego," (664)—a "recontacting [of] the lower structure that has been alienated and distorted" (688–89)—to heal the split. This involves a retreat, which is accomplished *from the level of the higher structure*, to the personal and cultural point prior to the dissociation, but not prior to the differentiation. According to Wilber (1981), our cultural dissociation already was established by about the sixth century B.C.E.— the beginnings of Western thought and the differentiation of noosphere from the biosphere (or culture from nature). This dissociation has continued on through the most recent cultural stage of differentiation (e.g., the Enlightenment period), up through the modern era (Wilber 1995).

Our dissociation from nature also entails a dissociation from the Great Mother archetype: "Once the Great Mother myths were transcended by the Hero Myths, the Great Mother was not integrated into subsequent mythology. . . . Rather the themes, moods, and structures of the Great Mother corpus were simply *left out* of the subsequent mythology" (emphasis in original) (Wilber 1981, 189). The desired differentiation from the Great Mother with her subsequent integration was replaced by differentiation, repression, and dissociation. These dual dissociations affected both society and the individual: "the alienation of the self from nature (and the Great Mother) is the alienation of the self from body" (191).

Healing the Split: Connection or Regression?

I basically agree with Wilber's assertion that we need a mutual understanding about how best to proceed with ecological healing and that this depends in large part "on individual growth and transformation" (143). However, the issue now becomes, what actually needs to be done to make this happen on the individual and collective levels? This leads to other important questions: If Western thought has carried mind-body and male-female dissociations from its inception, which aspects of Western thought represent healthy differentiation and which represent pathological dissociation? Since we have all been enculturated within this milieu, how can we detect the subtler manifestations of these pathologies in "higher" developmental levels, including vision-logic? Until we actively take part in the work needed to heal this dissociation, how do we know where to draw the line? If we do not address these issues, we become in effect spiritual "bypassers" who substitute transcendence for the darker and less "heroic" work of regression.

Unfortunately, Wilber (1995) does not address these issues on a practical level. His approach to the issue of regression remains abstract, lacking a discussion of which actions and experiences such a regression might entail, on both personal and social levels. Instead, he prefers to focus on transcendence and ascent, in part because "recontacting the lower is not at all the same as discovering the higher: and it is in the higher that the true healing, and the true integration, can occur" (689). Perhaps as a result of his focus on, and preference for, the "higher," Wilber primarily frames these issues in terms of regression versus ascent. This overlooks, or at best minimizes, the importance of the positive, integrative actions currently taking place within the cognitive levels of the rational, and, to a lesser degree, of vision-logic. As discussed below, this includes actions that involve an integration of masculine and feminine value spheres within the rational level and the manifestation of the connected self across both rational and vision-logic levels. It also involves the reintegration of the knowledge from older and/or less structurally complex (i.e., matrifocal and tribal/indigenous) cultures. However, from Wilber's perspective, such actions often are interpreted as being unwisely regressive.

For example, Wilber spends considerable energy chastising those whom he labels regressive (e.g., deep ecologists and ecofeminists). According to him, their concept of the interconnected "web of life" does virtually nothing to affect the needed interior transformation:

> Not only is the web-of-life ontology regressive (its end limit is always biocentric feeling in divine egoism), but, more telling—and this is the only point I would like to emphasize—even if the web-of-life ontology were absolutely true, nonetheless change in *objective belief* is *not* the primary driving force of *interior development*. (emphasis in the original) (514)

Here, in what I take to be Wilber's (1995) misunderstanding of what is being asked for by ecofeminists, is where I believe his prescription for change begins to fall short. *What is being asked for by ecofeminists is not simply a change in objective beliefs, but an actual change in the way we experience ourselves and our relations with nature.* It *does* require interior development—development based on a more connected sense of self. What Wilber labels regressive "biocentric feeling in divine egoism" (514) may be better interpreted as an interior change flowing from an *empathic* connection to nature. Spretnak (in Diamond and Orenstein 1990) writes: "To care empathetically about the person, the species, and the great family of all beings, about the bioregion, the biosphere, and the universe is the framework within which ecofeminists wish to address the issues of our time" (12).

This empathy is an important aspect of the connected self, whose permeable self-boundaries allow one to experience "self-and-other," not

just "self-or-other." Attending to and nurturing these permeable boundaries in women and supporting their development in men is one step (but
not the last step) in developing a less egocentric self. It is also a practical step toward developing a more ecologically oriented mode of being. I
interpret the development of this empathic, connected self, specifically
as it relates to the natural world, to be a part of what Macy (1990) calls
"the greening of the self" (53) or the development of the ecological self.
Like Macy, I believe that the actions that many deep ecologists and
ecofeminists currently advocate and engage in contribute to the interior
transformations needed to heal the ecosystem.

By failing to recognize the contributions of the connected self and
by framing the debate as regression versus ascent, Wilber falls into
what I (1995) call the "prepersonal self/permeable self fallacy" or
"pre/perm fallacy" (6). This concept is modeled, in part, after Wilber's
(1981, 1995; Wilber, Engler, and Brown 1986) astutely formulated
"pre/trans fallacy." In a pre/perm fallacy, however, one confuses the permeable boundaries of the connected self with the lack of boundaries of
the fused infant self. In Western psychology, this has led to the label-
ing of women's permeable self or connected self boundaries as regressive and inadequately differentiated.

Wilber (1995) essentially has taken the pre/perm fallacy of Western
psychology and carried it into transpersonal theory. This causes a number of problems for Wilber, including a misunderstanding of ecofeminism. It is also a factor in Wilber's confusing the transpersonal/bios-
pheric permeability spoken of in ecofeminism and tribal cultures with
prepersonal magical thinking, child-like egocentric regression, and/or a
fusion between self and environment.[6] The pre/perm fallacy is an example of how unexamined androcentric biases can lead to a subtle domination hierarchy in which a part of women's (and indigenous people's) reality is devalued and/or eclipsed.

Some of the changes leading to an improved ecological perspective
may be interpreted as taking place within the rational or formal operational thinking stage of Wilber's (1995) developmental model. At this
stage, one manifestation of the female-male and body-mind split can be
seen in the dissociation between the emotional/subjective/experiential
and the rational/objective modes of knowing. A healing takes place
through their integration. An example of this integration is the "constructed" knowing described by Belenky et al. (1997), in which subjective
and objective ways of knowing are integrated into a way of knowing that
judiciously incorporates both. As Swimme (in Diamond and Orenstein
1990) observes, incorporating emotional, empathic responses with more
objective, scientific information can form a stronger and more encom-

passing approach to ecology. However, this type of integrated knowing requires actual *experience* on the part of the knowers—otherwise the experiential contributions are apt to be reduced by the rational knower into another body of objectified information. In this case, we do get what Wilber calls "a bunch of egos with holistic concepts" (498).

This particular integration does not necessarily reflect a move to a new developmental level of vision-logic; instead, it is a *healthy expression* of the rational level in that it integrates both feminine and masculine value spheres. If, as Wilber (1995) presents, the emergence of developmental levels operates according to a "holonic" paradigm, there is no need to postulate a separate vision-logic stage for the reintegration of the body with the mind, nature with culture, and the feminine with the masculine. The potential for reintegration should be inherent within the holon or stage in which the dissociation first developed, as well as within each holonic stage that emerges thereafter. The anatomy of the brain provides a simplified analogy: we do not need to develop a newer, higher, "integrative," additional brain structure simply because the cerebral cortex (rational) has trouble integrating (e.g., overly represses) the messages from the older limbic (emotional) system. Instead, the connections that already contribute to the integration of the two systems can be enhanced.

If the dissociations currently exhibited at the rational level are not fully healed, the next stage, vision-logic, also will be fragmented. For Wilber (1981, 1995), the stage of vision-logic is symbolized by the centaur, which portrays the integration of the biosphere or nature (horse) and the noosphere or culture (human). However, the image of the centaur also can be interpreted as symbolizing a fragmentation occurring at the vision-logic level. As McIntyre (1995) points out, the centaur is a profoundly male symbol; it does *not* represent an integration of male and female.[7] From the standpoint of Greek mythology, only Cheiron—half-horse and half-god, and a healer, scholar, and prophet—offers a true representation of Wilber's vision-logic stage. But, as a masculine symbol, Cheiron denotes a vision-logic dissociated from the feminine. Notably, Cheiron was dealt an incurable wound and retired to his cave in agony (Barthell 1971). Perhaps this will be the fate of vision-logic thinking if it does not incorporate more connected self or feminine ways of knowing.

Retro-Romanticism or Healing Journeys?

If we return to the idea of enacting a partial "regression" to the point at which the dissociation occurred, we are forced to ask, "What does this mean in practical terms?" Unfortunately, simply identifying the beginnings of our dissociation is a contentious issue, and we are tossed back into the arms of theory. For example, although deep ecologists (as well as Wilber 1995) see the split originating with Greek culture, many feminists view the dissociation from nature and the feminine as beginning around 4,500 B.C.E. (Spretnak in Diamond and Orenstein 1990). They assert that at this time the peaceful, horticultural, Goddess-oriented, Neolithic societies—in which men and women apparently lived in relative harmony with each other and with nature—were invaded by aggressive and patriarchal Indo-European pastoralists from the north (Eisler 1987). According to Wilber (1995), others assert that the split began much earlier, with the development of horticulture. Certainly by the time of Greek culture, the related female-male dissociation was already quite firmly established and the discord between Goddess and God was in full swing (as exemplified by the relationships of Hera and Zeus, and Demeter and Hades). This suggests that the origins of our nature-culture and feminine-masculine dissociation occurred quite a bit earlier than the sixth century B.C.E.

Since we come from an admittedly dissociated culture, how are we to judge if the Neolithic cultures—or even contemporary hunting and gathering cultures—were fused, differentiated, or dissociated from nature? Our dissociation affects our very perceptions of other cultures; dissociation is "normal" to us and differentiation may look like fusion. Without a careful attempt to identify and compensate for the dissociation-related cultural biases in past and present anthropological and archaelogical theories, we simply perpetuate long-held, but distorted, evaluations of other cultures. For example, perhaps a close examination of our biases would reveal that (contrary to Wilber's viewpoint) matrifocal Neolithic cultures either exhibited or were developing a healthy differentiation between nature and culture, which was pushed into dissociation, and even regression, by the nomadic invasions. In this case, we might find that reconnecting with our roots from that era is a very necessary part of individual, social, and ecological healing processes.

For Wilber (1995), turning to tribal cultures or ancient matrifocal cultures is typically a form of regressive "retro-Romanticism" to be studiously avoided. Wilber's (1981, 1995) own developmental phylogeny equates tribal cultures with a particular childlike developmental stage of egocentrism, magical thinking, and biospheric fusion (for the bulk of their populations), and a journey for a chosen few (e.g., shamans) primarily into the lower transpersonal levels of nature mysticism and psychic phenomena. Also according to Wilber's (1995) theory, women did not fully differentiate from the biosphere and begin to develop sociocultural agency until the mid-eighteenth century in the West. For this reason, any desire to uncover or resurrect aspects of matrifocal ancient and/or non-Western cultures, in which women enjoyed considerable power and authority (usually identified as horticultural societies), is also regressive and shallow. In contrast to Wilber, many ecologists, feminists, and/or spiritually minded people believe valuable insights can be gained not only by an intellectual investigation, but also through a lived experience, of these older forms of spirituality. Halifax (1993) writes: "The wisdom of the peoples of elder cultures can make an important contribution to the postmodern world, one that we must begin to accept as the crisis of self, society, and the environment deepens" (148). Why is there such a rift between Wilber and the many advocates of tribal and ancient wisdom?

This rift is formed partially by differences in developmental models. A different interpretation of both the developmental stages of indigenous and/or prepatriarchal ancient societies and of the history of female social agency leads to conclusions that are quite different from Wilber's. These different interpretations rest on the following two points.

First, from the standpoint of contemporary anthropological theory, Wilber's (1981, 1995) model of human evolution is highly questionable. *Up from Eden* (Wilber 1981) has been criticized for its interpretation of and reliance on a mixture of outdated and ethnocentric nonanthropological literature. According to Winkelman (1990), the current anthropological and archaeological data simply do not fit Wilber's developmental model. Thus, Wilber's evaluations of the cognitive abilities of current and past tribal and/or matrifocal societies is severely flawed. Wilber (1995) has attempted to defend his theory by attacking Winkelman's review. He also has attempted to bolster his argument by drawing on the phylogenic theories of sociologist and critical theorist Jürgen Habermas (1979). However, in my opinion neither of these attempts at defense is very successful, at least in terms of the question of whether the data support Wilber's theory. Wilber still relies on outdated sources, and my review of Habermas (1979) indicates that this shortcoming is true of his writing as well.[8]

It is important to realize that our judgments of these cultures were originally based upon observations from researchers who projected their own theoretical constructs and meanings onto these cultures. Their outmoded ideas are being challenged from a number of directions, including writers from indigenous cultures (Deloria 1993; Underwood-Spencer 1990), anthropologists who have embraced the traditions of indigenous cultures (Halifax 1993; Katz 1993), and Western theorists who are reexamining the concepts of "Native science" (Harman 1991; Kremer 1996).[9]

Second, Wilber's (1981) earlier presentation of ancient Goddess-oriented cultures and his (1995) current developmental history of women's social agency also are based on flawed data; the latter topic is covered in the next section of this chapter. In terms of the former, many feminists believe that the peaceful, egalitarian, and Goddess-centered societies were invaded by patriarchal, Father-God worshipping northern invaders (Eisler 1987; Spretnak 1990). Thus the worship of a Mother Goddess was supplanted by worship of a Father God. Wilber disagrees mightily with this interpretation for at least two major reasons.

One part of Wilber's disagreement is only sketchily introduced in *SES*. Put simply, Wilber (1995) asserts that due to humankind's previous inability to differentiate itself from biospheric demands, when horticulture predominated, God was a woman and when plow agriculture predominated, God was a man. Wilber promises to offer his full support of these assertions in Volume Two, and so I will defer my comments on this particular aspect of his theory until the full explanation is available for evaluation. The other component of this rests on Wilber's differentiation of the ancient Great Mother from the Great Goddess. Zimmerman (in Diamond and Orenstein 1990) aptly summarizes this differentiation:

> Wilber sees the Great Mother as representing early humanity's conception of "Mother Nature" as the now-bountiful, now-withholding source of life and death, who must be placated by ritual and blood sacrifice, while the Great Goddess represents the insight of a few into the transcendent Divine Unity that constitutes the creative source of all things. (144)

Wilber's (1981, 1995) version of early humanity's Great Mother is quite bloodthirsty. He writes (1995) that women in that era "handsomely oversaw the central rite in horticultural society, that of the ritual human sacrifice (which drew 'equalitarianly' on men, women, and children; one such site revealed eighty-one one-year-old infant girls sacrificed to the Great Mother)" (450). Given these rites, what could contemporary women possibly find of value in this era, now that higher forms of the Great Goddess who requires the sacrifice of the separate self instead of blood are available?

Fortunately, Wilber's (1981, 1995) statement about the centrality of human sacrifice, when applied to early matrifocal societies, is a myth. There is practically no archaeological evidence that human sacrifice existed in early Neolithic cultures, such as those at Catal Huyuk and Minoan Crete (Rorlich 1980; Joan Marler, personal communication, 2 January 1996). Significantly, the sacrificial Great Mother cultures that Wilber (1981) presents in *Up From Eden* represent transitional patriarchies (e.g., Sumer, Egypt). It is in the later Bronze Age cultures that evidence of large-scale human sacrifice is found (Joan Marler, personal communication, 2 January 1996). As Eisler (1987) points out, the strongest evidence of ritual human sacrifice is found among the later imperialistic societies (e.g., Aztecs, Carthaginians). Wilber (1995) has voiced concern about ecofeminists "wildly interpret[ing] the past in order to find hope for the future" (184). However, it appears that Wilber may be the one making the wild interpretations.

Wilber's (1981, 1995) questionable construction of the Great Mother in early, matrifocal Neolithic cultures provides fuel for his preference for ascent. For him, "the cure is no longer regression to horticultural mythology, but progression to Goddess embodiment in the forms of tomorrow's integrations" (1995, 666). What Wilber overlooks in this statement is that the cultural forms of the Great Goddess that exist in current Eastern and Western patriarchal cultures do not exhaust all the reflections of the Goddess. Some cultural reflections, qualities, and images from matrifocal Goddess-centered times, as well as from contemporary indigenous cultures, speak to many women, and some men, on a profoundly deep level; they cry out to be reintegrated into our conscious experience of women's and men's spirituality. This does not mean that we uncritically accept the past; it does mean that we remain open to what the past has to offer.

A diagnosis of what needs to be healed in our culture and the process of healing can be clarified through theoretical models, but the healing itself requires lived experience. This healing is sometimes an exceedingly difficult and unpleasant process. Coming back into the individual and collective bodies to heal trauma often means reliving our suffering. Without healing, we may "ascend," but we cannot be whole. For example, Ram Dass (1992) describes a personal regression that carried him into his sensual, emotional, infant self, and ultimately helped him confront a (false) "charismatic, charming, spiritual" identity (19). Halifax (1993) offers an example of a collective, simultaneous regression and ascent during a Native American ceremony where participants confronted their emotional pain and isolation, renewed their connection to Spirit and nature, and witnessed the end of a three-year drought. Healing the split at times requires messy, emotive, and nonrational "regressive" experiences. In addition, it requires developing personal, empathic relationships with the elements of the biosphere and with each other, as well as with Spirit. Ultimately, individual and social healings facilitate our spiritual development.

I share Wilber's (1995) concern regarding the proper "unpacking" or interpretation of knowledge, which is essential to an understanding of the ecological crisis and, furthermore, of spiritual matters. I recognize that individuals may be unclear at times about how their own perspectives and actions stand in relation to paradigms that lie outside of, or even encompass, their own areas of expertise. Such a lack of clarity complicates the process of developing an intersubjective understanding between those with different viewpoints. Wilber pointedly directs our attention to this problem and offers potential solutions (i.e., the concept of holarchy), which, by moving the collective dialogue forward in certain areas, should aid in resolving this problem. However, androcentric (and Eurocentric) biases also interfere with the process of unpacking the gifts of Spirit, and many elements of Wilber's work reflect such biases. A primary concentration on ascent and hierarchy, a position that is syntonic with most Western and Eastern cultures and spiritual approaches, may serve to inhibit one's understanding of unfamiliar and culturally discordant perspectives, and, thereby, muddle the unpacking process.

I believe we will be well served by the knowledge flowing from an extensive range of biospheric-inclusive, so-called "regressive" experiences from ancient and tribal/indigenous cultures. We need a full exploration of healthy synarchy and the connected self perspective on all levels, incorporating the biosphere (body and nature) and the noosphere (mind and culture), to complement our knowledge of hierarchy. *A full healing of the dissociation between body and mind, nature and culture requires sustained embodied experience, both individually and collectively.* Otherwise, we will not have the full knowledge and understanding that a truly comprehensive, collective dialogue on how to heal our world requires. Keeping the dialogue open and inclusive on this topic is of utmost importance. If left unchecked, androcentric (and Eurocentric) biases could shut the door on individuals—such as those who have experienced the ways of contemporary indigenous cultures and those who value the knowledge from ancient matrifocal cultures and have attempted to put this knowledge into practice within a modern context—with a tremendous amount to contribute to this dialogue.

THE EVOLUTION OF GENDER STRATIFICATION

In this section, I critique a portion of Wilber's (1995) theories of human female and male individual development and of social evolution. Since in *SES* he merely sets a stage for further work, I will limit my commentary accordingly.

One of Wilber's aims is to "follow the course of the male and female value spheres" (154). According to Wilber (based on Habermas 1979), "even in archaic hominid societies, these two spheres were already beginning to differentiate, and often sharply" (154). This is portrayed as having led to two subsystems, the social sphere of male hunters and the private sphere of female gatherers/child-raisers. The male-as-father provided the link between the social and private spheres. Men became the noospheric agent; women were the biospheric agent, "embodied in communion" (182). Not until the completion of the noospheric and biospheric differentiation in the eighteenth century would women move beyond fusion with the biosphere and fully be able to act in the noosphere. In this process, women would incorporate their biospheric "roots" from the reproductive sphere and simultaneously take their place as historical agents, which gives them a special role in the integration and healing of our time. (Wilber sees the noosphere or mind as "gender neutral" with no "fundamental gender bias in the deep structures themselves" [157].)

Wilber (1995) holds that women's emergence into the noosphere coincided with the end of the agrarian period, during which great strength was needed for plowing,[10] and the beginning of the industrial period, during which work required less strength, thus allowing women to enter the social labor market. Therefore, in industrial cultures, in which biological strength is not a crucial factor in employment, the oppositions of female-male and nature-culture can be transcended. In this modern period, furthermore, the male-as-father no longer bears the weight of integrating the male social and the female private/domestic sphere. Instead, a new and remarkable integration of male and female finally can take place in the noosphere at the developmental stage of vision-logic.

As a consequence of the preceding analysis, Wilber (1995) views (1) the emergence of patriarchy as necessary due to "biological givens" (e.g., greater male physical strength, women's pregnancy and childbirth) (162); (2) the interest in contemporary and ancient matrifocal societies as regressive; (3) the modern female as having been embedded in nature (unlike men) until fairly recently and as retaining a special connection with nature and the body; (4) the disagreements between radical and liberal feminists as being due to their championing the biosphere and the noosphere, respectively; and (5) today's resistance to feminism primarily as a resistance to the emergence of the new, postrational stage of vision-logic. I will return in a moment to a critical consideration of these claims. First, however, it is helpful to review some of the issues that underlie a discussion of gender and social development.

Wilber's (1995) presentation and analysis require a close investigation as to their historical and cultural roots and the unexamined androcentric biases of their sources (e.g., Habermas 1979; Wilber 1981). We need to take into account the historical biases against women when reviewing data about human evolution. These biases have included ideas such as Aristotle's views of women as being only biological incubators for human males (Lange in Harding and Hintikka 1983); Rousseau's (and other Enlightenment philosophers') conception of women as being close to nature, which was also considered an explanation of their inferiority (Bloch and Bloch in MacCormack and Strathern 1980); and Levi-Strauss's application of Rousseau's ideas in his formulation of social structures, upon which assumptions about the universality of male and female behaviors were made (MacCormack in MacCormack and Strathern 1980). These and similar perspectives have found their way into much of our Western anthropological, sociological, and scientific literature, including material on the genesis of human culture, as has been noted by various feminist and nonfeminist scholars. In terms of anthropological models of gender relationships, Bleier (1984) cautions:

> It has been customary in anthropology, with notable exceptions in the past two decades or so, to assume (rather than demonstrate) certain universals and to record observations of other cultures and make interpretations that appear to confirm the (assumed) universals. (139)

Since the seventies, a growing number of feminist and nontraditional anthropologists have challenged androcentric, universalist assumptions, supported by fieldwork data and a rising feminist political consciousness (Bleier 1984; Bourguignon 1980; Haraway 1989; Rogers 1978). They have questioned the "man-the-hunter" hypothesis and the axiom that women are considered inferior to men in every known culture (MacCormack in MacCormack and Strathern 1980).[11] They have criticized the unwarranted projections of Western values, dichotomies, and family structures onto other cultures. These dichotomies include those of nature-culture (Strathern and MacCormack in MacCormack and Strathern 1980) and social-private (e.g., domestic) (Leacock 1978). They have contested the hegemony of the idea of male-female gender stratification, citing numerous instances of male-female gender complementarity (Strathern in MacCormack and Strathern 1980). They have disputed the belief that cultures have "a single monolithic outlook on male and female" composed of only two uniform and opposing categories (Meigs in Sanday and Goodenough 1990, 99).

As it now stands, Wilber's (1995) theory of the initial development of feminine and masculine value spheres may owe more to traditional Western cultural biases than it owes to contemporary anthropological theory. The "man-the-hunter" hypothesis has been critiqued extensively; it does not fit the evidence that currently is available. Our hominid ancestors likely were gatherers and scavengers, not hunters and gatherers (Fausto-Sterling 1985). The earliest social bonds may have been fostered through the sharing of gathered food between mothers and children (Eisler 1987). Later hunting and gathering subsistence activities probably involved males and females (a) in an interdependent social realm (Bleier 1984), (b) ranging widely for food (Slocum in Reiter 1975), and (c) with somewhat mutable labor roles (Hubbard in Harding and Hintikka 1983). In other words, social agency existed for both women and men. Fertility was probably low and children widely spaced (Blumberg 1984). This scenario holds for all but a tiny fraction of human evolution. As to current societies, which include a variety of levels of social development, "women have been making culture, political decisions, and babies simultaneously and without structural conflicts in all parts of the world" (Sachs in Bleier 1984, 138).[12]

On the basis of the preceding information, we can analyze and evaluate Wilber's claims as described above about the evolution of gender.

1. Patriarchy is not an evolutionary necessity based on biology, as Wilber presents it, but is the result of just one in a number of cultural bifurcations occurring throughout human development. This doesn't mean that men only are at fault for initiating patriarchal gender stratification. As Wilber (1995) points out, various cultures have gravitated towards gender stratification because of environmental and biological circumstances and the "agreement" of both sexes. Environmental stress may be a factor in the development of social hierarchy among both humans and primates (Fausto-Sterling 1985). The need for societies to expand or defend territory has been cited as a factor in the decline of women's status (Sanday 1981; Chafetz 1984). Yet, Sanday notes that "male oppression of women, however, is neither an automatic nor an immediate response to stress" (210). There are many nonindustrialized cultures in which women have struggled for and retained their social authority. In addition, cultures ruled by pathological hierarchies have invaded and dominated more egalitarian peoples throughout history, imposing upon the latter the former's hierarchical structures and related cultural beliefs (Eisler 1987).

Although the exigencies of survival, as well as other factors, may have moved some cultures toward hierarchy, this does not mean that anyone would have been aware of the extent of the repercussions—including women. It is not, as Wilber (1995) suggests, that women never were cultural agents; rather, women *lost* their status as cultural agents. In many cases the legal code made them property or objects. Wilber asserts that men and women have co-created their social structures at every stage of human development. However, Chafetz (1984) states that there comes a point when women as a group are no longer equal co-creators of their conditions. For example, with male control in place over a social structure, such as the contemporary patriarchal family, the men can arrange the structure to be of maximum convenience to themselves.

Even though the women may have decision-making control, it is in a sphere defined by men.

2. In this context, interest in contemporary and ancient matrifocal cultures is revealed as a potentially healing journey to reincorporate the social and spiritual agency that was repressed during patriarchy, rather than as an imprudent regression.

3. The idea that *only* women have natural biospheric roots can be seen for the cultural artifact that it is—a continuance of the Enlightenment's portrayal of women as "closer to nature," passed down through the years by androcentric philosophers and scientists (MacCormack and Bloch in MacCormack and Strathern 1980).

Western men also can be honored in their desire to rediscover their roots in biospheric communion. Wilber (1995) suggests that women may be concerned with "regression" in the men's movement, due to memories and fears of physical domination. However, Chafetz (1984) notes that physical size has not been a factor in human social (including gender) stratification. Rather, in humans the incidence of assault is related to imbalances in formal power relations.[13]

Scientific data also reveal the mythic nature of testosterone's role in siring the supposedly violence-prone "malevolent male" (Blumberg 1978; Fausto-Sterling 1985). Wilber's "might makes right" interpretation of social relationships in the biosphere also echoes older, simplistic approaches to biology. Intraspecies and interspecies interactions are complex. For example, blood studies of chimpanzees show that nondominant chimps have an unexpected number of offspring (Fausto-Sterling 1985).

4. Wilber's proposed solution to the conflict between the radical and the liberal feminists unfortunately fades away. Under closer scrutiny, this solution would have been problematic at best. Feminist debates are rooted in more than simple biases toward either the biosphere or the noosphere (see Diamond and Orenstein 1990). Even within a dialogue about nature and culture, there is a question of where to draw the line between the two. For example, primates show evidence of intentionally teaching learned cultural behaviors (such as tool use) to their young, and some primate species are more likely to form social hierarchies in response to environmental stress (Fausto-Sterling 1985). However, perhaps essentialist[14] and nonessentialist feminists could come together on some points, with essentialists championing the full appreciation and manifestation of communion in our society and nonessentialists supporting the full realization of female agency (regardless of how they distinguish between the biosphere and the noosphere).

5. The outlooks for women's future are not as assuredly positive as Wilber's (1995) schema portrays. Although Wilber presents Chafetz's (1984) work as a support for his claims about social evolution, there are clear differences between them. For instance, Wilber presents biology as the primary factor in industrialization's effect on female liberation as "industry made individual physical strength less and less important" (648). Notably, Chafetz does *not* posit physical strength as a contributing factor in her treatment of industrialization and female liberation. Instead she posits an economic cause—the greatly expanded work force needed to create the unprecedented increase of material surplus ushered in by the industrial revolution.

According to Chafetz (1984), it is the need for surplus labor, not a decreasing need for strength, that changed the face of the workplace and set the stage for women's liberation in the West. During both the industrial revolution and the early 1950s, women were pulled into the work force because of the demand for workers. Chafetz points out the backslide that occurred as men came home from World War II and women became surplus labor. She (1990) paints both optimistic and depressing future scenarios for gender stratification with the outcome depending on economic variables. She cautions that "until women consolidate their power, they constitute an expendable labor force to be used according to the perceived needs and interests of the mostly male elites" (231).[15]

Finally, a mundane reason is most likely responsible for the current opposition to female social agency. The opposition may not involve, as Wilber (1995) suggests, a collective resistance to a social birthing of vision-logic. Instead, it may be due solely to the usual struggles any group undergoes when exhorted to confront its past and present injustices and relinquish its special privileges. We need to deal skillfully with the defense mechanisms—denial, projection, rationalization, etc.—that inevitably arise during this process. Differentiating and integrating the emotional sphere, rather than either repressing it or acting it out (either consciously or unconsciously), is an important part of this work. We are unlikely to act on the insights of vision-logic or transpersonal wisdom successfully if we sidestep these issues.

CONCLUSION

Wilber (1995) offers a number of very valuable concepts such as holarchy and agency-in-communion which may further a truly interdisciplinary dialogue. He also draws our attention to some important problems in ecological theory. However, in his presentations, Wilber appears limited in his ability to accurately portray the views and the concerns of heterarchists and feminist theorists. Despite his efforts to open the way for an understanding of the "feminine value sphere," he appears restricted in his ability to integrate the more experiential understandings and values of the connected self into his paradigm. He still attempts to fit the concepts and values related to the connected self into his predetermined developmental schema. He continues to offer his readers a story of human consciousness emergence that relies heavily on androcentric, and often outdated, sources.

I take these attempts to be well intentioned. However, in these attempts the very essence of the values of the connected self is in danger of being lost. Perhaps Wilber's use of the centaur as a symbol for a level of evolution that supposedly integrates nature-culture and female-male best illustrates this danger. What the centaur, in part, may represent is a co-optation of the feminine value sphere by androcentric thinking. I would prefer, however, to believe that the centaur represents androcentric thinking that has perceived its limitations and now is reaching toward a more balanced approach. Regardless of the cause, I take the weaknesses in Wilber's model as confirming the need for alternative models of transpersonal development, especially models that inherently embody the feminine or connected self perspective in their deep structures, while still addressing the wide, interdisciplinary scope that Wilber so energetically embraces.

Notes

1. In the context of this essay, "feminine" and "masculine" refer to culturally constructed gender-based categories, while female and male refer to biological sex distinctions. For an excellent discussion of gender and identity in America, as compared to other cultures, see Kopytoff (1990).

2. According to Minnich (1990), the intentional or unintentional noninclusion of the knowledge of certain groups leads to a cycle of faulty generalization, circular reasoning, partial knowledge, and "hierarchically invidious monism" (HIM). In HIM, one category is set up as the highest and most significant category, and over time, this category becomes accepted as if it was the only category—as often has been the case with the category of "man" in Western thought.

3. Wilber (1995) also reduces the ecofeminist "web of life" to an androcentric version of a web. His depiction of a web is based upon his interpretation of certain Enlightenment concepts. According to Wilber, "the dominant theme of the Enlightenment was the 'harmony' of an interlocking order of being" (131). It also involves "a perfectly holistic world that leaves a perfectly atomistic self" (262). I find Wilber's interpretation of a web to be closer in metaphor to a chain-link fence than to a web in that it is composed of orderly, interlocking threads. It is the antithesis of the meaning of "web" as encountered in a feminine value sphere, where a mutuality of communication, flexibility, and change are emphasized.

4. Other species can be seen as a part of our larger bio-social community. Proponents of heterarchy seek to balance the power relations among humans and other species in part by taking on the representation of those species through both justice (e.g., legal

representation for endangered species) and caring/response orientations (e.g., Joanna Macy's [Macy et al. 1988] "Council of All Beings").

5. Feminists, as well as others, point out that words have the power to shape our reality. According to Humm (1990), "the power of naming defines the *quality* and value of that which is named and denies reality to that which is not named—often women's lives and experience in our own terms" (146). In "naming" synarchy, I am re-describing reality in a way that calls attention to "feminine" qualities that, otherwise, might be overlooked.

6. A pre/perm fallacy may also account for Wilber's (1995) assertion that "nature immersion and nature worship prevent the realization of Nature, or Spirit" (288). For Wilber, the road to the lower, shallower realms of biospheric, lowercase *n* nature lies in the opposite direction from the higher, deeper realms of the spiritual uppercase *N* Nature. To only revel in the beauty of or empathically connect with biospheric nature is, thus, regressive and cannot lead one to a developmental ascent, which involves an experience and appreciation of the Spirit that underlies Nature. I can appreciate Wilber's developmental distinction between a simple appreciation of the beauty of nature and a more mystical experience of Nature. However, the appreciation of the beauty of and empathic connections to nature are often the doorways to more mystical experiences. For many people, the path to nature is the doorway to Nature. What Wilber views as a developmental regression, may lead, in fact, to developmental progress.

7. From a mythological standpoint, the centaurs (except for distantly related Cheiron) were a "savage race of bull killers" (Barthell 1971, 59). They provide an excellent symbol for the pastoral nomads reputed to have swept in and decimated the Neolithic matrifocal cultures. From a biological standpoint, stallions have harems of mares and are aggressive toward other males—an apt symbol of man's supposed inherent aggressiveness and sexual possessiveness.

8. I see only one major weakness in Winkelman's (1990) critique of *Up from Eden* (Wilber 1981), which Wilber (1995) exploits in his rebuttal. Winkelman maintains that the primary flaw in Wilber's work is using an "ontogeny recapitulates phylogeny" model. Drawing from Habermas (1979), Wilber (1995) argues that such a model is potentially valid. However, even if one acknowledges its potential validity, the data may not fit an "ontology recapitulates phylogeny" theory. As Winkelman has amply demonstrated, this is not the case. Instead, Wilber's (1981) "effort to force the phylogenetic facts to fit an ontogenetic model has biased the selection, assessment and interpretation of the data" (Winkelman 1990, 29).

9. Western followers of tribal ways generally look toward the visionary aspects of tribal epistemology, such as shamanism, and not the magical-thinking that abounds in all cultures. Wilber (1995) asserts that neoshamanism reflects the "Western male's warrior-ethic" (576). Yet, many women have found shamanism to be *antithetical* to a "male warrior-ethic" and an important way of enacting agency-in-communion for the benefit of all sentient beings.

10. Wilber, referencing Chafetz (1984) also points to "devastating" (Wilber 1995, 386) rates of miscarriage as being a factor in the change to male-dominance during the plow-based agrarian period. This claim requires some correction. Chafetz's assertion regarding "higher rates of miscarriage" (16) is not attributed to any source. In the surrounding paragraph, Chafetz cites Blumberg (1978), in which there is no mention of miscarriage. Chafetz (personal communication, 16 November 1995) does not recall the statement's origins, therefore the statement currently has no known foundation in the

literature. This is another example—as we have seen in our examination of the anthropological data—of Wilber's basing a claim (and in this case, an exaggerated claim) on an unsubstantiated secondary source.

11. MacCormack (MacCormack and Strathern 1980) notes, "There would not be the social ferment over gender roles in Western industrial societies today if a substantial number of men and women did not subscribe to the thesis of universal female subordination" (18).

12. Given the availability of more current and/or less androcentric sources, including those listed in the bibliography of *SES* (i.e., Blumberg 1984; Eisler 1987; Fausto-Sterling 1985; Reiter 1975; Sanday and Goodenough 1990; Sanday 1981), I am interested in Wilber's rationale for choosing work based on outdated anthropological material (i.e., Habermas 1979) as the basis for this portion of his theory.

13. A complete reading of *Iron John* (Bly 1992) reveals another possible reason for women's concerns: some women fear that these men will remain stuck in the primal, wild, or "hairy man" phase, remain *eternal puers*, and never complete the developmental process of contacting and integrating their "inner female." At the end of *Iron John*, it is the sacred marriage of male and female that finally transforms the wild man, unveiling him as a previously enchanted king.

14. Essentialist feminists believe in a unique female nature (Humm 1990).

15. In his footnotes, Wilber (1995) asserts that given the exigencies of childbearing, "a 'parity' in the public/productive domain would be around 60-40 male/female" (649). He assures his readers that his ideas have feminist support, writing that "Chafetz reports this from several feminist researchers, and she herself feels that is fairly reasonable" (649). However, Chafetz (personal communication, 16 November 1995) herself *does not* support such a split, and is actually at a loss as to what Wilber means by it in practical terms.

References

Attanucci, J. 1988. In whose terms: A new perspective on self, role, and relationship. In *Mapping the moral domain*, edited by C. Gilligan, J. Ward, and J. Taylor. Cambridge, Mass.: Harvard University Press.

Barthell, E. 1971. *Gods and goddesses of ancient Greece*. Coral Gables, Fla.: University of Miami Press.

Belenky, M., B. Clinchy, N. Goldberger, and J. Tarule. [1986] 1997. *Women's ways of knowing: The development of self, voice, and mind*. New York: Basic Books.

Bleier, R. 1984. *Science and gender: A critique of biology and its theories on women*. New York: Pergamon Press.

Blumberg, R. 1978. *Stratification: Socioeconomic and sexual stratification*. Dubuque, Iowa: William C. Brown.

———. 1984. A general theory of gender stratification. In *Sociological theory*, edited by R. Collins. San Francisco: Jossey-Bass.

Bly, R. 1992. *Iron John: A book about men*. New York: Vintage.

Brown, L., and C. Gilligan. 1992. *Meeting at the crossroads*. New York: Ballentine.

Bourguignon, E. 1980. *A world of women: Anthropological studies of women in the societies of the world*. New York: J. F. Bergin.

Chafetz, J. 1984. *Sex and advantage: A comparative macro-structural theory of sex stratification*. Totowa, N.J.: Rowman & Allanheld.

————. 1990. *Gender equity: An integrated theory of stability and change*. Newbury Park, Calif.: Sage.

Chambers, S. 1995. Feminist discourse/ practical discourse. In *Feminists read Habermas: Gendering the subject of discourse*, edited by J. Meehan. New York: Routledge.

Chodorow, N. 1978. *The reproduction of mothering*. Berkeley: University of California Press.

Christ, C. 1980. *Diving deep and surfacing: Women writers on spiritual quest*. Boston: Beacon.

Deloria, V. 1993. If you think about it, you will see that it is true. *Noetic Sciences Review* 27:62–66.

Diamond, I., and G. Orenstein, eds. 1990. *Reweaving the world: The emergence of ecofeminism*. San Francisco: Sierra Club Books.

Eisler, R. 1987. *The chalice and the blade: Our history, our future*. San Francisco: Harper & Row.

Fausto-Sterling, A. 1985. *Myths of gender*. New York: Basics.

Gilligan, C. 1993. *In a different voice: Psychological theory and women's development*. Cambridge: Harvard University Press.

Habermas, J. [1976] 1979. *Communications and the evolution of society*. Translated by T. McCarthy. Boston: Beacon.

Halifax, J. 1993. *The fruitful darkness: Reconnecting with the body of the Earth*. San Francisco: Harper.

Haraway, D. 1989. *Primate visions: Gender, race and nature in the world of modern science*. New York: Routledge.

Harding, S., and M. Hintikka, eds. 1983. *Discovering reality: Feminist perspectives on epistemology, metaphysics, methodology, and philosophy of science*. Boston: D. Reidel.

Harman, W. 1991. *A re-examination of the metaphysical foundations of modern science*. Sausalito, Calif.: Institute of Noetic Sciences.

Humm, M. 1990. *The dictionary of feminist theory*. Columbus: Ohio State University Press.

Josselson, R. 1992. *The space between us: Exploring the dimensions of human relationships*. San Francisco: Jossey-Bass.

Katz, R. 1993. *The straight path: A story of healing and transformation in Fiji*. Reading, Mass.: Addison-Wesley.

Keller, E. 1985. *Reflections on gender and science*. New Haven, Conn.: Yale University Press.

Kornfield, J. 1990. *Buddhist meditation and consciousness research*. Sausalito, Calif.: Institute of Noetic Sciences.

Kremer, J. 1996. Introduction (Indigenous Science). *ReVision* 18 (Winter). 2–5.

Leacock, E. 1978. Women's status in egalitarian society: Implications for social evolution. *Current Anthropology* 19 (2): 247–75.

MacCormack, C., and M. Strathern, eds. 1980. *Nature, culture and gender*. Cambridge, England: Cambridge University Press.

Macy, J., A. Naess, J. Fleming, and J. Seed. 1988. *Thinking like a mountain: Towards a council of all beings*. Philadelphia: New Society.

————. 1990. *The greening of the self*. In *Dharma Gaia: A harvest of essays in Buddhism and ecology*, edited by A. Badiner. Berkeley: Parallax.

McCallum, B. 1994. Re-worlding toward solidarity: Healing and empowerment in feminist spiritual community. Doctoral dissertation, Harvard University. DAI, Vol 55-06A, 1586 (accession # AAG9428726).

McIntyre, J. 1995. [Review of *Sex, Ecology, Spirituality: The spirit of evolution.*] *Tricycle* 5 (2): 117–19.

Miller, J. 1991. The development of women's sense of self. In *Women's growth in connection: Writings from the Stone Center*, edited by J. Jordan, A. Kaplan, J. Miller, I. Stiver, and J. Surrey. New York: Guilford Press.

Minnich, E. 1990. *Transforming knowledge*. Philadelphia: Temple University Press.

Ram Dass. 1992. *Compassion in action*. New York: Bell Tower.

Reiter, R. ed. 1975. *Toward an anthropology of women*. New York: Monthly Review.

Rogers, S. 1978. Woman's place: A critical review of anthropological theory. *Comparative Studies in Society and History* 20:123–62.

Rorlich, R. 1980. State formation in Sumer and the subjugation of women. *Feminist Studies* 6 (1): 77–102.

Saiving, V. 1992. The human situation: A feminine view. In *Womenspirit rising*, edited by C. Christ and J. Plaskow. San Francisco: Harper.

Sanday, P. 1981. *Female power and male dominance: On the origins of sexual inequality*. Cambridge: Cambridge University Press.

Sanday, P. and R. Goodenough, eds. 1990. *Beyond the second sex: New directions in the anthropology of gender*. Philadelphia: University of Pennsylvania Press.

Spretnak, C. 1990. Ecofeminism: Our roots and flowering. In *Reweaving the world: The emergence of ecofeminism*, edited by I. Diamond and G. Orenstein. San Francisco: Sierra Club Books.

Spretnak, C., ed. 1982. *The politics of women's spirituality: Essays on the rise of spiritual power within the feminist movement*. Garden City, N.Y.: Anchor.

Underwood-Spencer, P. 1990. A Native American worldview. In *Noetic Sciences Collection, 1980-1990: Ten years of consciousness research*, edited by B. McNeil and C. Guion. Sausalito, Calif.: Institute of Noetic Sciences.

Wilber, K. [1981] 1983. *Up from Eden: A transpersonal view of human evolution*. Boston: Shambhala.

———. 1995. *Sex, ecology, spirituality: The spirit of evolution*. Boston: Shambhala.

Wilber, K., J. Engler, and D. Brown, 1986. *Transformations of consciousness: Conventional and contemplative perspectives on development*. Boston: Shambhala.

Winkelman, M. 1990. The evolution of consciousness: An essay review of *Up from Eden* (Wilber 1981). *Anthropology of Consciousness* 1 (3–4): 24–31.

Wright, P. 1995. Bringing women's voices to transpersonal theory. *ReVision* 17 (Winter): 3–10.

10

Jürgen W. Kremer

Jürgen Kremer focuses his practical and theoretical work on the importance of traditional indigenous ways of knowing within Western cultures. His writing and teaching is devoted to revitalizing what he calls the "tribal mind" for the future, exploring the nature of "indigenous science," and commenting critically on conventional Western models of evolution, science, and discourse.

Kremer was born in 1949 in Hamburg, Germany. As an adolescent, he won a scholarship at school to visit Sapmi, the northernmost part of Scandinavia, a place he had dreamed of since childhood. Encompassing the northern parts of Norway, Sweden, Finland, and Russia, Sapmi is the home of the last remaining indigenous European people. He was prevented from making this trip, however, because of surgery for a benign bone tumor. He went on to become a clinical psychologist and lecturer in Hamburg, where he worked to integrate humanistic (especially Rogerian) and transpersonal approaches into his clinical practice, teaching, and research. He also worked extensively with the critical social theory of the Frankfurt School, particularly the work of Adorno and Habermas.

During this period in Hamburg, Kremer had an out-of-body experience during which he seemed to be the agent in the relief of another person's physical suffering. This experience set him back on the course that had been blocked in his adolescence. He embarked on an extensive exploration of alternate forms of healing and traveled to meet with and learn from shamans and medicine people from various cultures, including the Navajo, Cherokee, Pomo-Miwok, Japanese, and Cambodian. This exploration eventually led him to inquire more deeply into his own indigenous—German and Nordic— roots, and brought him finally to Sapmi, the land of his childhood dreams, where he has spent a part of most of the years of the last decade.

Kremer came to the United States in 1982. He has taught in a wide range of transpersonally oriented programs at the Saybrook Institute, John F. Kennedy University, and the California Institute of Integral Studies, where he currently teaches in the Ph.D. program on Traditional Knowledge and Recovery of Indigenous Mind. He also helps to guide groups in northern California interested in shamanism.

Kremer has published dozens of articles on humanistic and transpersonal psychology, critical theory and philosophy, shamanism, and indigenous mind and its recovery. He is currently writing a philosophical memoir on the disappearance of the white man, entitled Wing of Memory. *For several years he has been an executive editor of* ReVision *and has edited issues on* Culture and Ways of Knowing *(Spring and Summer, 1992) and on* Indigenous Science *(Winter 1996, Winter 1997).*

In his contribution to this volume, Kremer argues that Wilber's model, along with all evolutionary models which presuppose the notion of "progress," is complicit with the fact that all supposed "advances" have come at the price of the genocide and exploitation of indigenous peoples. One cannot, he maintains, speak of cultural evolution without addressing the "shadow" that has accompanied it, a reflection which Kremer believes is largely absent from Wilber's work.

Kremer points out further the absence of contemporary indigenous voices in Wilber's account, which seems instead to reproduce the voices and projections of nineteenth- and twentieth-century anthropologists concerning the "primitive" mind. He draws attention to massive and widespread data which call into question Wilber's characterization of indigenous mind as "pre-rational." By contrast, Kremer sees the indigenous mind process—or "participatory concourse," as he also calls it—as providing alternative frames for understanding history, evolution, and universality through engagement in ongoing conversation with the past and with the surrounding community, both human and natural.

Further Readings

Kremer, J. 1986. The human science approach as discourse. *Saybrook Review* 6 (Spring): 65-105.

_____. 1992a. *Prolegomena Shamanica*. Red Bluff, Calif.: Falkenflug Press (P.O. Box 8783, Red Bluff, Calif. 96080).

_____. 1992b. The dark night of the scholar: Reflections on culture and ways of knowing. *ReVision* 14 (Spring): 169-78.

_____. 1992c. Whither dark night of the scholar? Further reflections on culture and ways of knowing. *ReVision* 15 (Summer): 4-12.

_____. 1994a. *Looking for Dame Yggdrasil*. Red Bluff, Calif.: Falkenflug Press (P.O. Box 8783, Red Bluff, Calif. 96080).

_____. 1994b. Shamanic tales of power: Trance narrative in traditional and modern settings. In *Trance, possession, healing rituals, and psychotherapy: Yearbook of cross-cultural medicine and psychotherapy*, Vol. 6, edited by R. van Quekelberghe. Mainz, Germany: Verlag für Wissenschaft und Bildung.

_____. 1995. Perspectives on indigenous healing. *Noetic Sciences Review* (33) (Spring): 13-18.

_____. 1996. Evolving into what and for whose purpose? Reading Bateson. *ReVision* 18 (Winter): 27-36.

_____. 1997a. Mind on fire. *ReVision* 19 (Winter): 42-48.

_____. 1997b. Recovering indigenous mind. *ReVision* 19 (Spring): 32-46.

The Shadow of Evolutionary Thinking

> *To all my ancestors!*
> *To all my ancestral relations!*
> *To all my relations!*

 WHEN I TRY TO FATHOM WHAT IT MEANS TO BE ALIVE THESE DAYS, what my obligation as an individual may be, then I have to be present in a variety of ways. Let me first speak more personally before I explicate my major points in a more theoretical way. I have made an attempt in the style of this article to reflect my understanding of the indigenous mind process as I am recovering it (see Kremer 1994, 1995a, b, c). This is why I begin with an honoring, continue with a personal story as an evocation of the recovery of the indigenous mind process identifying the specific place from which I speak, and proceed to a description of indigenous consciousness in a contemporary society. I finish the article with yet more descriptions of the indigenous mind process. In this sense the article is a compromise between the more common academic writing style (of the middle part of the paper) and indigenous presentations, including my own attempt to speak from a recovering indigenous perspective.

I. RECOVERING MY INDIGENOUS CONSCIOUSNESS PROCESS

At the threshold of this coming-to-be-present I encounter a variety of guardians: The land I live on is not my ancestral land—it is the ancestral land of the Ramaytush-speaking people of the San Francisco peninsula, the first people of this particular land with a name we still remember; for the purposes of dealing with the shadow of evolutionary thinking, the original keepers of this land. The beauty of the land I live on has suffered from the devastating consequences of technological progress: overpopulation, overbuilding, pollution of the waters, pollution of the air. I live in a society the destruction of whose aboriginal cultures is scarcely acknowledged and is not mourned by the majority of people; living in this society I am in a certain way complicit in the ongoing perpetration of racism and cultural genocide. Yet, I also live in a city which seems to be among the most comfortably and richly multicultural places in the United States, with less pollution than in many other metropolitan areas.

My Germanic ancestry puts me in the gateway of the Holocaust. I recall Hitler's perversions of mythology in the service of genocide; I will never forget the image of the Germanic goddess Nerthus drawn by cattle past Hitler, which I saw in the Holocaust Museum in Washington, D.C.; I

recall the aberrations of the Vikings, their vicious slaughters and con-
quering—another guardian at the threshold. Passing these and more
guardians, witnessing what they hold, is to heal old collective wounds as
they have been passed down to me as an individual, passed down con-
sciously and unconsciously. These guardians don't stand at the threshold
simply to propagate guilt. The guardians are medicine for the collective
shadow of the Western world. They are the medicine of remembrance with
all that it entails, be it fear, pain, guilt, anger. . . .

Having taken this medicine I see the outlines of an old tree, the tree of
the Nordic and Eurasian traditions that is spoken about in a language
simultaneously poetic and scientifically precise: At this tree stories are
told of the Great Return, the great round of the precession of the equinox-
es, the Ragnaroks *of the past;[1] these stories contain the native scientific*
star knowledge of my traditions. The spakona *and the* spamadhr, *the*
women and men seers and healers, travel along this tree across the rain-
bow bridge, across the Milky Way—Bifrost—to the ancestral souls of the
past and future. These seers place those in need of healing at this center
of the universe, one of many known to them, to see if they can help the sick
find their place of balance. Stories are told at the tree of ancestors, trade,
and migrations. Ceremonies are held to honor the great and the small
cycles of the season, to honor the law of balance, of fridr. *Community*
gathers at the tree. I hold ceremony to honor the protective spirits, the
disir, *and the* mattr og megin *or gift which they hold for me; I hold cere-*
mony to find balance and to honor balance. I look at the stars and see the
image of a deerlike animal, and I look at the rock carvings by the tree and
see images of various deer. And I see boats, boats filled with ancestors
traveling the skies and traveling the seas. Across the stream three spirits
appear. In the rock I see the deer carrying the sun. My conversation, which
is also a prayer or chant, is with all these relations within fridr. *I offer*
amber as I am held by all these beings and by the guardians.

The only way to reach the tree for somebody like me is to pass the
guardians at the threshold and to take the medicine they offer. They offer
their painful medicine kindly.

All this helps me understand what my obligation is as I recover
today ancient memory for the future. (For background information on
this section, see Bonnefoy 1993a, b; Davidson 1988; Metzner 1994.)

II. NURTURING AND BEING NURTURED—A CONTEMPORARY INDIGENOUS CONSCIOUSNESS PROCESS

The contemporary Andean peoples of Peru have their own way of
talking about their obligation. This is how it has been described:

The ayllu *is a group of related persons living in a particular place. The* ayllu *consists not only of a group of related humans but of other beings of that place: the animals, the mountains, streams and rocks, and the local deities. The* ayllu *should therefore not be considered simply a sphere of kinship. Rather one could say that kinship in the Andes extends to the nonhuman realm.*

The conversations held between persons and the other inhabitants of the world are not primarily engaged in for the purpose of "knowing reality." They are engaged in it as part of the activity of criar y dejarse criar, *of nurturing (raising) and letting oneself be nurtured (raised). The verb* criar *is used to speak of raising children, animals, plants, relationships, etc. It is the activity that fosters the growth and development of any potentiality or generativity. It is a fundamentally mutual or reciprocal activity: as one nurtures one is simultaneously nurtured. The action in the world does not leave the actor untransformed; acting in the world is being in relationship with that world, so the language of conversation is more appropriate than the language of knowledge. There is here no knower and known, no subject and object. Rather there are actors in relationships of mutuality. By acting one transforms not only the world but oneself as well. Therefore it is a fundamentally dynamic world, always moving, always changing, always in flux. There is, as it were, no simple act of knowing as we moderns understand the term, for such knowledge-acquiring activity presupposes that there is something to be known irrespective of who knows it.*

This is not to say that conversing with the world does not involve cognitive faculties; it of course does, but that the activity is not primarily and certainly not exclusively a cognitive one. Criar *demands not only understanding but love, tenderness, patience. But it is to say that the point of conversation is not the attainment of knowledge through the interrogation of nature, it is rather to generate and regenerate the world and be generated and regenerated by it in the process.* (Apffel-Marglin 1994, 9)

III. WILBER'S EVOLUTIONARY THINKING IN THE LIGHT OF AVAILABLE EVIDENCE

The above descriptions of *fridr* and the knowing and nurturing conversation in the *ayllu* are illustrations of what can be called rather inadequately *the indigenous mind process* (the reader may consult Valkeapää [1985 and 1996] for a Saami description of *siida* life, or Colorado [1988] for an Iroquois description of *skanagoah*). They describe an integral way of knowing and being which is difficult to capture in its richness and subtleties. They circumscribe my place of analysis and point of departure for dialogue with Ken Wilber's books.

I am writing this article as somebody who is remembering his indigenous roots without any claim to being native or having shared native experiences of discrimination and colonialism; I grew up as part of the dominant culture in Germany (see Kremer [1994, 1995a] for further discussions of my stance). The endeavor which I call *recovery of indigenous mind* is a process which does not invite romanticism or nostalgia—it is a painful process of remembering back in order to go forward. There is no going back. My way into the future moves through the integration of historical wounds, painful memories, and seemingly senseless events in order to work out a future based on *ayllu* or *fridr*, based on an ecologically specific notion of balance.

The indigenous mind or consciousness process I am referring to is not based on an essentialist understanding of tribalism or indigenism,[2] but on a discourse view in which individuals understand themselves in an ongoing conversation with the surrounding community, in which the local animals, plants, ancestors, and other spirits take as much part as the humans (cf. Apffel-Marglin 1994; Rengifo 1993). This conversation is carried on as a part of unfolding one's own gifts while paying attention to the ceremonial and seasonal cycles as well as the larger astronomical cycles. This is a world view of total immanence.

My primary focus in this article is on Wilber's *Sex, Ecology, Spirituality* (1995), and *Up from Eden* (1981). My central question in looking at social evolutionary theories such as Wilber's is: How do evolutionary theorists deal with contemporary indigenous peoples? Or, to return to my initial descriptions: How would Wilber conceptualize the conversational process of the *ayllu* in the Andes?

My discussion of Wilber's more recent work focuses on two major aspects of this broad issue:

1. What is the nature of the indigenous mind process, and are Wilber's descriptions consistent with the available data? My point below is that closer attention to the indigenous consciousness

process suggests a different model of history than do Eurocentered conceptualizations and cannot be subsumed under stage models without being made invisible (discussed below in this section).

2. If Wilber's conceptualizations of evolutionary stages imply "losers" (those of the so-called lower stages and their contemporary "remnants"), then how does his theory deal with this shadow of evolutionary theorizing? The stance which I take is that we can no longer afford to think about the evolution of consciousness and so-called civilizations without *explicitly* addressing the shadow of these purported advances (discussed below in section IV).

I conclude this article with a continuation of the indigenous mind process descriptions given at the beginning of this article, which suggest alternate conceptualizations of universality, evolution, and knowledge exchange (section V below). It is beyond the scope of this article to explicate these alternate conceptualizations fully; all I can do is give the rough outlines and some general parameters.

At the root of my concerns is the question of cultural ownership of evolutionary thinking which I have raised in a recent *ReVision* article (Kremer 1996) and the call for theorists of human evolution to reflect consciously and explicitly on the cultural biases inherent in their thinking.

Wilber's model of social evolution is in the tradition of nineteenth-century evolutionary conceptualizations (cf. Winkelman 1993, 5). Julian Huxley gives a good example of this thinking in the field of biology:

> If we accept the doctrine of evolution, we are bound to believe that man has arisen from mammals, terrestrial from aquatic forms, vertebrates from invertebrates, multi-cellular from unicellular, and in general the larger and the more complex from the smaller and simpler. To the average man it will be indisputable that a man is *higher* than a worm or a polyp, an insect is *higher* than a protozoan, even if he cannot exactly define in what resides this highness or lowness of organic types. (Julian Huxley, *Evolution: The Modern Synthesis*; quoted from Barlow 1994)

Of course, if this type of evolutionary thinking is extrapolated into the field of the evolution of consciousness and societies, then we can see how the prehistoric peoples of all continents and the contemporary remaining indigenous peoples can be classed as "lower" and the Eurocentered as "higher" (even if there are yet higher stages to come). In E. B. Tylor's words:

Human life may be roughly classified into three great stages, Savage, Barbaric, Civilized, which may be defined as follows. The lowest or *savage* state is that in which man subsists on wild plants and animals, neither tilling the soil nor domesticating creatures for his food. . . . Men may be considered to have risen into the next or *barbaric* state when they take to agriculture. . . . Lastly, *civilized* life may be taken as beginning with the art of writing, which, by recording history, law, knowledge, and religion for the service of ages to come, binds together the past and the future in an unbroken chain of intellectual and moral progress. (1881, quoted from Wenke 1980, 32–33) (italics in original)

Evolutionary thinking concerns itself with development according to the inherent tendencies of anything that may be compared to a living organism (*Compact Oxford English Dictionary*). Theories of evolution, whether in the fields of biology, consciousness, or culture, fundamentally have a monocausal structure, where things unfold from some point of origin basically in a linear fashion (however complex and multidimensional the descriptions of this causal line may be) toward some future or utopian stage that represents the unfoldment of the inherent tendencies, particularly of human beings and their cultures.

Let me give a very brief overview of Wilber's model as it appears to pertain to contemporary indigenous peoples. In *Up from Eden* (1981), Wilber delineated dates for the stages of the evolution of human consciousness, and he has updated his descriptions since then.

• Hominids appear during the *uroboric stage* which lasted roughly from three to six million years ago to two hundred thousand years ago (Wilber 1981, 28). "Simple sensorimotor intelligence and emotional-sexual drives" are seen as characteristic for the early hominids of this epoch (Wilber 1983, 240; see also Wilber 1987, 239 for descriptions of the "archaic"; and 1995, 153ff.).

• The subsequent *typhonic stage* lasted roughly from two hundred thousand years ago to 10,000 B.C.E. (Wilber 1981, 39 and 87). Here we find "the first symbolic cognitive mode, the primary process, which confuses inside and outside, whole and part, subject and predicate, image and reality" (Wilber 1983, 240). "Magical thinking" is an important characteristic of the mental process of the *typhonic epoch* which Wilber describes as follows: "This includes simple images, symbols, and the first rudimentary concepts, or the first and lowest mental productions, which are 'magical' in the sense that they display condensation, displacement, 'omnipotence of thought,' etc. . . . The magic realm is the beginning of *mind*" (1987, 239) (italics in original).

• The more recent *mythic-membership stage* lasted from about 12,000 to 2,500 B.C.E., with the high membership period dating from about 4,500 to 1,500 B.C.E. (1981, 87). According to Wilber, "this stage is more advanced than magic, but not yet capable of clear rationality or hypthetico-deductive reasoning" (1987, 239).

• And the current *solar ego stage* began about 2,500 B.C.E. (with the low ego period dating from 2,500 to 500 B.C.E., the middle ego period dating from 500 B.C.E. to 1,500 C.E., and the high ego period dating from 1,500 C.E. to the present [Wilber 1981, 179–80]). Wilber more recently has set the incipient egoic-rational phase at about 500 B.C.E. (1995, 179). "Egoic rationality and formal-operational logic" (1983, 240) are some of the central characteristics in the individuals of this epoch.

Wilber clarifies (1995, 172–73) the meaning of his stage descriptions by stating that

These various "epochs" . . . refer only to the *average* mode of consciousness achieved at that particular time in evolution—a certain "center of gravity" around which the society as a whole orbited. In any given epoch, some individuals will fall below the norm in their own development, and others will reach quite beyond it.

Wilber comments in regard to the contemporary situation that

the majority of individuals in rational societies still settle in somewhere around the mythic-rational, using all the formidable powers of rationality to prop up a particular, divisive, imperialistic mythology and an aggressively fundamentalistic program of systematic intolerance (1995, 252).

The statement that "the majority of individuals in rational societies still settle somewhere around the mythic-rational" is somewhat inconsistent with the definition that this is the epoch where "the average mode of consciousness achieved" is the rational mode; this implies that at least fifty percent of the population is functioning in that mode, particularly if the "high egoic period" is dated to the present. Wilber's statement that "the majority of individuals in rational societies still settle somewhere around the mythic-rational" suggests more the "low ego period" rather than the time when the next epoch is beginning to emerge, even if only as the low vision-logic period. In any case, Wilber appears to put contemporary Eurocentered societies (the modern state) at the rational stage, and he places "the rough beginning of this new emergence (egoic-rational) in the middle of the first millennium B.C.E. . . . it reaches its fruition with the rise of the modern state, roughly the sixteenth century in Europe" (1995, 179; similarly on 396). All this "brings us up to the present, and the new integration that is struggling to emerge" (1995, 184), namely "vision-logic."

Wilber never concerns himself explicitly with the indigenous peoples who remain. He primarily discusses the anthropological construct "shamanism" and "shaman" when elaborating the earlier evolutionary stages. This isolation of shamans and the "shamanic state of consciousness" inappropriately focuses only on certain aspects of the holistic and integral process of indigenous conversation described at the beginning of this article. How this particular lens may be related to some of the problems which I identify in Wilber's theory should become apparent below. Since contemporary indigenous peoples continue to use ceremonies, for example, in which, according to anthropologists and in Wilber's value-laden words, "mental intentions are believed to be able to 'magically' alter the physical world," (1995, 165), they could be considered contemporary remnants of the typhonic stage, or at best the mythic stage. In any event, contemporary indigenous peoples still engaged in their traditional cultural practices would *not* fit Wilber's various descriptions of the mythic-rational stage or more recent epochs. Nevertheless, as previously quoted, he would concede that some of their authentic spiritual practitioners may be able to reach the psychic or subtle levels.

Wilber is reluctant (1995, 571) to use anthropological material about contemporary indigenous peoples in order to discuss past evolutionary stages (such as the magical or mythological stages), yet much of the understanding of the past evolutionary stages is based on projection of the anthropological literature of this century into the past (see e.g., Cazeneuve [1972] or McGrane [1989]). He also does not include the direct voice of indigenous peoples in his discussions of the contemporary situation.[3] I am assuming that this is either because he does not see them as significant for, or part of the cutting edge of, the evolutionary arc he describes, or that they don't offer descriptions which illuminate this evolutionary arc. Whatever his reasoning, contemporary indigenous peoples end up de facto as a negligible quantity in his writings.

The following is a brief listing of some examples from past and continuing indigenous cultures, which by all appearances not only require, if they are to be integrated, a fine-tuning of Wilber's theory, but, if taken seriously, a rethinking of the entire model (see Winkelman [1990] for a first extensive list of objections). All these brief descriptions highlight the cognitive aspects of the indigenous mind process in order to show the limitations in Wilber's descriptions and interpretations; the integral nature of this process is implied in each of the examples, but is not explicated here. Readers may use their own imagination to see how the various sacred sites mentioned below, for example, represent the indigenous conversation I have described at the beginning of this paper using the examples of *fridr* and *ayllu*.

- The first example is the Aztec and Mayan calendars (which can be dated back to the Olmec times), with the calendar of the great pyramid in Chichen Itza as an elaborate example of the thinking and architectural skills of these peoples. We can add to this example Mayan mathematics in general (according to Wilber these civilizations are part of the mythic stage [1981, 92]). All of these instances presuppose cognitive skills that do not fit his descriptions of any of the stages before the rational (Aveni 1980; Closs 1986; Men 1990).

- The alignments of the pyramids in Teotihuacan (just outside of Mexico City) and the knowledge of the number pi are other examples that do not fit Wilber's scheme (Aveni 1980; Hancock 1995; Tompkins 1976).

- The Egyptian pyramids, their alignments and architecture, are yet another example of similar feats on a different continent (see, e.g., Bauval and Gilbert [1994] or Hancock [1995].

- The architecture and alignments of Stonehenge, dating to about 3,000 B.C.E., and Newgrange, dating to about 3,200 B.C.E. are European examples (Aveni 1993; Brennan 1980, 1983; Burenhult 1993).

- Finch (1996, 25) points out that

  the Dogon have known (probably for seven hundred years) that Sirius B was a mostly invisible white dwarf that periodically underwent nova explosions which spewed matter ("grains") into space that ultimately became the stuff from which other heavenly bodies— including our solar system—were made.

This traditional knowledge of an ancient African tribe, which is consistent with the findings of contemporary astronomy, questions definitions of "primitive" and Wilber's descriptions of the stages prior to the rational (see also Finch 1991, 1995; de Santillana and v. Dechend 1969).

• And most recently the rock art of Chauvet, thought to be
about 30,000 years old (Chauvet, Dechamps, and Hillaire
1995), points to cognitive skills akin to our own.

We could argue in each single instance given in my list above that these
feats were accomplished by the most advanced individuals of those times,
but to my mind this argument is increasingly difficult to sustain with all
the examples given (and this list is not complete). And this argument could
hardly be made for the following instances, which represent widespread
skills, rather than skills conceivably attributable solely to an elite:

• The cognitive skills required for flintknapping provide an
example for the mentations of early hominids. Gowlett (1993,
54–5) gives a detailed analysis of the sophisticated cognitive
skills the making of the stone tools of the Oldowan people (in
Wilber's scheme of uroboric times) imply.

> Many activities of early man [sic!] which have left
> traces were co-operative, social ones. Does this then
> imply the use of language from the time of early tool-
> making? (55)

Lewin (1988) suggests that the behavior of early hominids increasingly was governed by complex rules, and that these abstractions seem
impossible in the absence of language.

• Additionally, Wilber has yet to answer the various points
Winkelman (1990) makes regarding evidence for language
use among the earliest hominids, the similarities in cognitive
capabilities in humans of today and humans of forty thousand
to one hundred thousand years ago, the nonexistence of the
uroboric stage, and astronomical observations as early as
thirty thousand to thirty-two thousand years ago (see also
Aveni 1993, 23). Marshak (1991) provides extensive discussions and illustrations of the complexity of cognitive processes of paleolithic hominids from 35,000 to 10,000 B.C.E.

All of these examples presuppose complex cognitive processes supposedly unavailable to humans during those time periods. They suggest
that a stage model may *not* be the most appropriate way to take these
data into account.

The pieces of evidence which don't fit easily with Wilber's timelines
and descriptions lead me to doubt that his model adequately represents
contemporary and past indigenous peoples and their mind processes. His
abstract descriptions and the available data don't match sufficiently, and
if Wilber continues to think that they do, then he is under an obligation

to explicate this more fully than he has done in response to Winkelman. His descriptions of the "earlier evolutionary stages" render the integral mind and being process of past and present indigenous people invisible in his model and devalue it in these distorted representations.

IV. THE SHADOW AND PROJECTIVE IDENTIFICATION

From a native perspective, evolutionary thinking in general has always been problematic because of its (at least implicit) notion of progress toward some better, more complete, or more actualized way of being, some *outopos* (Greek: utopia) or nonexistent place to be realized in the future.

> European utopian visions have been used to rationalize a range of criminal behaviors including the enslavement of millions of Africans and the annihilation of entire American Indian peoples as the (sometimes) regrettable but necessary consequence of the construction of some kind of future state of human perfection. (Dion-Buffalo and Mohawk 1994, 33)

This statement cannot be taken seriously enough and should be a clear warning signal to pay attention to the shadow of evolutionary thinking. Unless we do so, evolutionary thinking will remain misguided and dangerous. There is no reason to assume that it is different now than it was in the past when—at least implicitly—evolutionary thinking was used to justify cultural and physical genocides. In order to step outside of this intellectual history, it is necessary to address explicitly shadow material issues such as the ones Dion-Buffalo and Mohawk mention in their quote. Otherwise whatever is written is at least an unconscious continuation of Eurocentered dominance and (cultural) genocide. McGrane (1989) in his critical analysis of the history of "the Other" and anthropology comments that

> When the "sun" of civilization dawns on the virgin forest of the Other, instead of nourishing him, it chars and blackens him. . . . *At the very instant they (primitive societies) become known to us they are doomed.* (108, last sentence quoted from Bastian)

This would mean that one of the most important current historic tasks of Eurocentered cultures is to retract its attention and periodic obsession with other cultures and to focus on its own history, including the shadow of its own history.

Wilber talks about the emergence of a global market economy and acknowledges that it is "tinged, *initially*, by remnants of imperialism, which indicated not an excess of reason but a lack of it" (1995, 178) (emphasis added)—an acknowledgment which is far from sufficient, given the ways in which the rise of what he considers to be evolutionarily positive is entwined with rather lethal shadow material. The words genocide, colonialism, imperialism do not show up in the index of the book, and they do not seem to warrant special analysis within his evolutionary scheme. The phrase "tinged, initially, by remnants of imperialism" implies that this is in the past—a denial of the ongoing destruction of native cultures (Bodley 1982; Berger 1990). It is also a denial of such continuing imperialism (biocolonialism) as is exemplified by the hunt among native people for certain nutritional plants and plant medicine, which then are patented and resold to the indigenous peoples they were taken from (Abya Yala News 1994; Mies and Shiva 1993; Shiva 1993). Imperialism and colonialism have taken on the mantle of economic developmental thinking, under which they continue their contemporary expression and continue to have a destructive effect on indigenous peoples (see Sachs [1995] for a history of the term and a critical discussion in terms of sustainability). All of these destructive events are, of course, a result of the increasingly global market economy and the expansiveness of Eurocentered ways. While Wilber may label these events pathological within his system, *their effect on new emergent and purportedly desirable qualities still needs to be critically reviewed.*

Looking at the historical shadow material created by what the dominant discourse of Eurocentered cultures (Wilber's rational societies) calls "evolutionary advances" or "achievements" is not just a question of intellectual honesty or integrity; it is much more a question of doing one's best to avoid inflation, ethnocentricity, and prejudice. If Eurocentered societies are to step out of the *continuing* history of colonialism, then the evolutionary thinking produced by the intellectuals of these societies needs to grapple with the fact that so-called evolutionary advances have come at a price, and that this price is even now being paid by peoples who can be identified as the "primitive," "archaic," or "mythic" peoples of contemporary "backward" societies.

The nineteenth century saw the height of colonialism and imperialism. It was also when evolutionary theories were first proposed. McGrane shows how this notion of the "primitive" is entwined with the idea of progress:

> The very identification of and naming of the non-European
> Other as "primitive," as "primitive mentality," as "primitive
> culture," presupposed a theory (language) of rational
> progress, of progress in and by reason (Enlightenment)
> and/or progress in and by history (nineteenth century). The

very possibility of the conception of "primitive" presupposed the prior commitment to a conception of progress.
(1989, 99)

The notion of progress implies that there is something at least insufficient or even bad in the past and that the good lies in the future. The
historical connection between the arising of enlightenment philosophy
and colonialism is not just accidental.

Anthropology has been an extremely subtle and spiritual
kind of cognitive imperialism, a power-based monologue
about alien cultures rather than, and in active avoidance
of, a dialogue with them in terms of sovereignty, i.e., the
untranslatability and irreducibility of one "culture" to the
being and language of the other. (McGrane 1989, 127) (italics in original)

Until we understand the impact of this connection, cultural shadow
material will determine what Eurocentered cultures are as "rational
societies" to an extent difficult to fathom.

In keeping with one brand of rather conventional wisdom, Wilber
describes the process of Hawaii becoming one of the United States of
America—its annexation—as follows:

All the *basic structures* and functions are preserved and
taken up in a larger identity, but all the *exclusivity* structures and functions that existed because of isolation, set-
apartness, partialness, exclusiveness, separative agency—
these are simply dropped and replaced with a deeper
agency that reaches a wider communion. (1995, 52; see also
245) (italics in original)

I doubt that traditionally spiritual Hawaiians (let alone political
activists) would agree with this statement as an appropriate abstract
principle derived from this specific historical example. Not only is his
theoretical statement racist and colonialist, it also lends itself to the justification of genocide in the service of the emergence of higher order
holons. After all, "each emergent holon transcends but includes its pre-
decessor(s)" (1995, 51). Wilber may consider such use of his theories as
abuse. However, his *model* adds to a justificatory context that facilitates
this kind of thinking in contemporary Eurocentered cultures. To my
mind the Hawaii illustration of his eighth tenet does not hold, and his
model would be invalidated if it is based on similar examples.

When I analyze other instances that Wilber's tenet should cover (and
the above quote of his principle), then his model becomes increasingly

questionable in the form stated. If we look, for example, at the reality of the relationship between Native American tribes and the dominant society and apply his abstract statement to the specifics of an ongoing history, then his statement is simply ludicrous. The history of invasion and colonization has destroyed native ceremonies, instituted boarding schools, and used missionary activity as a major avenue to genocide (all these are things that are still happening in the *present* in one form or another); in the process the reservation system was created. Wilber's statement has a certain compelling logic in its abstractness (if we agree with the implicit assumptions of progress and universalization as he defines it), but this generality obfuscates the inflated stance hidden in it. This inflation is based on the culturally narcissistic assumption that we have truly understood peoples who live in an entirely different consciousness.

My basic point is that we need to ban the concept of progress from descriptions of the evolution of consciousness and civilizations, because they are entirely Eurocentric. McGrane succinctly states that "if the rather deeply sedimented, institutionalized belief in 'progress' disappeared, the 'primitive' would vanish" (1989, 99). Progress is part of Wilber's thinking, and the "primitives" are alive even if not so well within his model.

Wilber recommends "regression in service of higher integration—a regression that allows evolution to move forward more harmoniously by healing and wholing a previously alienated holon" (1995, 105). This is a somewhat unfortunate analogy to individual psychological theory, since it presupposes the ego constructed by modernity, an ego—as I have pointed out elsewhere (see Kremer 1995a)—that is constructed dissociatively (from nature, community, ancestry, from what I have described as the conversation in the *ayllu* above). Consequently, this ego is likely to project from its personality makeup into the past whatever it has dissociated from. In fact, projective identification may be the most apt clinical term to point to the psycho-emotional process Eurocentered cultures are engaged in with contemporary indigenous peoples (This term also acknowledges that history is carried and handed down specifically in the process of socialization in each individual.) Projective identification means that other people are made to feel the highly conflicted and split-off material dominant cultures unconsciously injected into them, so that they feel and experience it as if it is their own. Natives feel the Eurocentered dissociation from prehistory, ancestry, nature, et cetera, as self-hatred ("primitives") that is so destructive to their cultures. Of course, self-hatred as an effect of internalized colonization warrants a much longer statement than I can offer here. Notably, in individual psychotherapy, projective identification is known to be a pathological process, oftentimes quite resistant to change because of its strongly self-reinforcing nature. This would seem to imply that we can assume strong resistance to the healing of the history of colonialism in the relationship between indigenous and Eurocentered cultures. I would think that the retraction of these projections is the first order of business. For this we need a different metaphor than "regression in the service of the ego" (an adequate statement in the psychotherapeutic context, of course). The reintegration of cultural shadow material presupposes the possibility of an ego—the indigenous ego in communal conversation, if you wish—which would be so differently constructed that our contemporary ego cannot easily imagine it (see Kremer 1994 for descriptions).[4]

We know from individual psychology that the shadow, the aspect of the self that is most troublesome and inimical to the ego-ideal, has a significant impact on the conscious awareness of the individual. Individual psychotherapy is in many ways the process of integration of this shadow material. Just as denial of the personal shadow distorts development of self, denial of the cultural shadow—indigenous peoples' past and present—distorts the development of our understanding of history and consciousness. My point is that evolutionary thinking needs to grapple with the fact that there are not only parts of history that have been denied (which we are or can easily be conscious of), but that there may be parts of history, just as with the individual shadow, which we are not aware of and which we need to struggle to become aware of and integrate. The fundamental question is this one: Is somebody who publishes *A Brief History of Everything* (Wilber 1996) under an obligation to struggle with the nonmediated voices of contemporary indigenous peoples?[5]

V. ALTERNATE FRAMES

Let me return to the beginning of this paper and add some descriptions, which point to alternate frames for history, evolution, and universality through grounding conversations in the astronomical cycles and facilitating universality through equitable knowledge exchange within a consciousness of the same indigenous quality. The constraints of this article don't allow for the elaboration of these practices of being and knowing, but I will briefly sketch some of the fundamental assumptions. The knowledge exchange between peoples in a dissociated consciousness process and peoples in an integral, nondissociated consciousness process is likely to be governed by a paradigm of domination (driven by the dissociative process), while knowledge exchanges among peoples in an integral, nondissociated consciousness process have a greater chance of being equitable. Universality is created in the latter exchanges through the specific understanding of relatedness and the sharing of the specific conversations engaging each other; the ceremonial context of such exchanges supports equity and reaches for global connections and universality in a different way than the process of abstraction. Deloria gives a succinct description of such an indigenous perspective from one strand of the Native American traditions:

> The Plains Indians arranged their knowledge in a circular format—which is to say, there were no ultimate terms or constituents of their universe, only sets of relationships which sought to describe phenomena. No concept could stand alone in the way that time, space, and matter once stood as absolute entities in Western science. All concepts not only had content but were themselves composed of the elements of other ideas to which they were related. Thus it was possible to begin with one idea, thoroughly examine it by relating it to other concepts and arrive back at the starting point with the assurance that a person could properly interpret what constituted the idea and how it might manifest itself in concrete physical experiences. (Deloria 1996, 40ff.)

Returning to the Andean peoples of Peru we find the following descriptions of the indigenous mind process:

> What happens between the Andean communities of humans, deities and nature is reciprocal dialogue, a relationship which does not assume any distancing and objectification between those dialoguing, but rather an attitude of tenderness and understanding towards the life of the other. Such dialogue does not lead one to a *knowledge about the other*, but rather to empathize and attune oneself with its mode of being, and in company with that other, to generate and regenerate life. (Rengifo 1993, 168, translation by Apffel-Marglin) (italics in original)

These are descriptions of a process of an immanently present, visionary, socially constructed being, which is sustained without a need to progress or overcome some insufficient state—conversations are held for balance's sake. These descriptions are different from Wilber's definition of vision-logic. Let me just briefly sketch some coordinates. The two quotes and my initial sections above describe the immanent, ongoing conversation with everything, including spirits, that constitutes the community for human beings. Within this framework, if individuals do not know their ancestry, their place in the community, their cultural stories, the land they live on, the cycles of the seasons, the stars, et cetera, then these persons are lost to who they are, and pathology ensues—these individuals are in need of healing or balancing. These indigenous models, which to my mind require cognitive skills akin to Wilber's vision-logic, allow for an alternate understanding of time, history, and the variety of cultures; they also allow people to be in participation or conversation while exercising high-level rational skills. Part of this conversation is the observation of the precession of the equinoxes and other larger historical cycles.[6] This indigenous conceptualization allows each culture to understand its historic spiritual mission in its own ecological niche, so to speak. It is not just that this type of model is preferable; I would suggest that it has greater accuracy because it is more complete and integral. It facilitates cultural exchange because it establishes equality among prospective partners in the exchange of knowledge and avoids implicit or explicit imperialistic thinking. From this particular perspective Wilber's evolutionary story is a sad one, because it seems so desperately to seek that place of balance and the healing of dissociation, but sadly continues to speak from a place of dissociation from parts of the self that indigenous consciousness considers essential for well-being; it continues to perpetrate the splits from participatory or conversational self, shadow, and historical roots. As long as there is a trajectory of progress and as long as vision-logic is described without full attention to all aspects of the conversation in the *ayllu* (Wilber 1995, 185), we further the dissociation from the ancient conversation of balance, and Wilber's grand scheme remains additive holism still in need of further integration.

This article is dedicated to the memory of Eduardo Grillo, one of the founding members of PRATEC and their primus inter pares, who unexpectedly passed away on April 23, 1996.

Notes

1. The precession of the equinoxes (the westward drift of the vernal equinox through the zodiac) is caused by the wobble of the earth; as a result her axis points to different parts of the sky at different times (e.g., while Polaris is the current North Star, Vega will have that position thirteen thousand years from now). See Kyselka and Lanterman (1976) for a basic overview of this astronomical phenomenon. De Santillana and v. Dechend (1969) have written the fundamental work—from the European perspective—for an interpretation of myths in astronomical terms, demonstrating how the language of ancient stories can be simultaneously poetic and scientifically precise (especially in regards to the example just given in my text).

2. Cf. Warrior (1995) for a discussion of these positions; cf. Vizenor (1989, 1994a, b) for an example of Native American discourse stance.

3. In scanning the approximately 640 references listed in Wilber (1995), I found two—Lake and McGaa—where indigenous peoples speak with a voice of their own (problematic

as they are to some traditional natives); I was unable to determine during my reading or with the help of the index how these references actually have been used.

4. Thanks to Betty Bastien for our conversations about internalized colonization which led me to conceptualize the dynamic in terms of projective identification.

5. Dion-Buffalo and Mohawk (1994) have discussed the discourse between dominant societies and indigenous peoples in terms of "non-subjects" as one possible strategy. I have developed the notion of participatory or shamanic concourse (1992a, b) which can be used to discuss problems and possibilities of conversations and cultural exchanges between peoples of fundamentally and qualitatively different paradigms (see Kremer 1995a for some more detail). Application of these two notions in the context of discussion with Wilber could be illuminating.

6. The indigenous understandings of calendrics and time keeping in terms of the precession of the equinoxes are receiving increasing attention in Eurocentered discourse. It began with de Santillana's and v. Dechend's (1969) groundbreaking work; recent examples of such interpretations are Sullivan (1996) and Hancock (1995).

References

Abya Yala News. 1994. *Confronting biocolonialism*. Oakland, Calif.: South and Meso American Rights Center.

Apffel-Marglin, F. 1994. Development or decolonization in the Andes. *Daybreak* 4 (3): 6–10.

Aveni, A. 1980. *Skywatchers of ancient Mexico*. Austin: University of Texas Press.

———. 1993. Washington, D.C.: Smithsonian.

Barlow, C., ed. 1994. *Evolution extended*. Cambridge: MIT Press.

Bauval, R., and A. Gilbert. 1994. *The Orion mystery*. London: Heineman.

Berger, J. 1990. *The Gaia atlas of first peoples*. New York: Doubleday.

Bodley, J. H. 1982. *Victims of progress*. Mountain View, Calif.: Mayfield.

Bonnefoy, Y. 1993a. *Asian mythologies*. Chicago: University of Chicago Press.

———. 1993b. *American, African, and Old European mythologies*. Chicago: University of Chicago Press.

Brennan, M. 1980. *The Boyne Valley vision*. Dublin, Ireland: The Dolmen Press.

———. 1983. *The stars and the stones*. New York: Thames and Hudson.

Burenhult, G. 1993. Newgrange: Temple of the sun. In *People of the stone age*, by G. Burenhult. San Francisco: Harper.

Chauvet, J. M., E. Deschamps, and C. Hillaire. 1995. *Grotte Chauvet*. Sigmaringen, Germany: Thorbecke.

Closs, M., ed. 1986. *Native American mathematics*. Austin: University of Texas Press.

Colorado, P. 1988. Bridging native and western science. *Convergence* 21 (2/3): 49–67.

Davidson, H. 1988. *Myths and symbols in pagan Europe*. Syracuse, N.Y.: Syracuse University.

de Santillana, G., and H. v. Dechend. 1969. *Hamlet's mill*. Boston, Mass.: Nonpareil.

Deloria, V. 1996. If you think about it, you will see that it is true. *ReVision* 18 (Winter): 37–44.

Dion-Buffalo, Y., and J. Mohawk. 1994. Thoughts from an autochthonous center. *Cultural Survival* (Winter): 33–35.

Finch, C. 1991. *Echoes of the old darkland*. Decatur, Ga.: Khenti.

————. 1995. *Science and civilization in Africa*. Decatur, Ga: Khenti.

————. 1996. New perspectives on ancient African science. *ReVision* 18 (Winter): 17–26.

Gowlett, J. 1993. *Ascent to civilization*. New York: McGraw-Hill.

Hancock, G. 1995. *Fingerprints of the gods*. New York: Crown.

Kremer, J. 1992a. Whither dark night of the scholar? *ReVision* 15 (Summer): 4–12.

————. 1992b. The dark night of the scholar. *ReVision* 14 (Spring): 169–78.

————. 1994. *Looking for Dame Yggdrasil*. Red Bluff, Calif.: Falkenflug Press (P.O. Box 8783, Red Bluff, Calif. 96080).

————. 1995a. Shamanic tales of power: Trance narrative in traditional and modern settings. In *Jahrbuch für transkulturelle Medizin und Psychotherapie. Trance, Besessenheit, Heilrituale und Psychotherapie* (Trance, possession, healing rituals, and psychotherapy: Yearbook of cross-cultural medicine and psychotherapy), edited by R. van Quekelberghe and D. Eigner. Berlin: Verlag für Wissenschaft und Bildung.

————. 1995b. On understanding indigenous healing practices. *Ethnopsychologische Mitteilungen* 4 (1): 3–36.

————. 1995c. Perspectives on indigenous healing. *Noetic Sciences Review* (33) (Spring): 13–18.

————. 1996. Evolving into what, and for whose purposes? *ReVision* 18 (Winter): 27–36.

Kyselka, W., and R. Lanterman. 1976. *North star to southern cross*. Honolulu: University of Hawaii Press.

Lewin, R. 1988. *In the age of mankind*. Washington, D.C.: Smithsonian.

Marshak, A. 1991. *The roots of civilization*. Mount Kisco, N.Y.: Moyer Bell.

McGrane, B. 1989. *Beyond anthropology*. New York: Columbia University Press.

Men, H. 1990. *Secrets of Mayan science/religion*. Santa Fe, N.M.: Bear.

Metzner, R. 1994. *The well of remembrance*. Boston: Shambhala.

Mies, M., and V. Shiva. 1993. *Ecofeminism*. London: Zed.

Rengifo Vasquez, G. 1993. Educacion en Occidente Moderno y en la Cultura Andina. (Education in the modern west and the culture of the Andes.) In *¿Desarrollo o descolonizacion en los Andes?* (Development or decolonization in the Andes?) by PRATEC. Lima: PRATEC.

Sachs, W. 1995. Global ecology and the shadow of "development." In *Deep ecology for the 21st century*, edited by G. Sessions. Boston: Shambhala.

Shiva, V. 1993. *Monocultures of the mind*. New Jersey: Zed Books.

Sullivan, W. 1996. *The secret of the Incas*. New York: Crown.

Tompkins, P. 1976. *Mysteries of the Mexican pyramids*. London: Thames & Hudson.

Valkeapää, N. A. 1985. *Trekways of the wind*. Guovdageaidnu, Norway: DAT.

————. 1996. Poems from *Trekways of the wind*. *ReVision* 18 (Winter): 45–48.

Vizenor, G. 1994a. *Manifest manners*. London: Wesleyan University Press.

————. 1994b. *Shadow distance*. London: Wesleyan University Press.

Vizenor, G., ed. 1989. *Narrative chance*. Albuquerque: University of New Mexico Press.

Warrior, R. 1995. *Tribal secrets*. Minneapolis: University of Minnesota Press.

Wenke, R. 1980. *Patterns in prehistory*. New York: Oxford University Press.

Wilber, K. 1981. *Up from Eden: A transpersonal view of human evolution*. Boston: Shambhala.

————. 1983. *Eye to eye: The quest for the new paradigm*. Garden City, N.Y.: Anchor Press.

————. 1987. The spectrum model. In *Spiritual choices*, by D. Anthony, B. Ecker, and K. Wilber. New York: Paragon.

————. 1995. *Sex, ecology, spirituality: The spirit of evolution*. Boston: Shambhala.

————. 1996. *A brief history of everything*. Boston: Shambhala.

Winkelman, M. 1990. The evolution of consciousness: An essay review of *Up from Eden* (Wilber 1981). *Anthropology of Consciousness* 1 (3/4): 24–30.

————. 1993. The evolution of consciousness? Transpersonal theories in light of cultural relativism. *Anthropology of Consciousness* 4 (3): 3–9.

11

Jeanne Achterberg

Jeanne Achterberg has been one of the pioneers in the development of a transpersonal perspective in healing. She is known for her work on the use of imagery in healing, psychoimmunology, behavioral strategies for the reduction of pain and anxiety, the role of women in healing, and healing rituals. She brings to her research and practice a wide background, including a doctorate in experimental psychology, with an emphasis in physiology; many years of work in medical settings, notably with cancer patients; a license as a practicing psychologist; training in biofeedback; and extensive experience in developing healing communities and in exploring ritual and the spiritual dimensions of health in workshops and training programs.

Raised as an "Army brat," Achterberg attended high school in Germany, where she was both valedictorian and head cheerleader. Married at nineteen, she graduated in psychology from Texas A&M University (B.S.) and Texas Christian University (Ph.D.), while raising two children. She worked as a psychologist treating people with cancer, becoming research director at the Cancer Counseling and Research Center in Ft. Worth, Texas, and later codirector of the Cancer Rehabilitation Project at the University of Texas Health Science Center in Dallas. She began a collaboration with Carl and Stephanie Simonton in the mid-1970s, investigating the psychological dimensions of cancer, and has continued to work with Carl Simonton up to the present. The Simontons' work was both groundbreaking and controversial. They explored the use of guided imagery with cancer patients, claiming to find certain uses of imagery very helpful in patients' recoveries.

Achterberg continued as well a number of other projects at the University of Texas Health Science Center, while a faculty member of the Southwestern Medical School and the School of Allied Health Sciences. She researched a number of cutting-edge areas in psychology and healing, exploring the use of biofeedback in the treatment of arthritis and the psychological dimensions of reducing pain and anxiety for patients with burn injuries, spinal injuries, orthopedic trauma, cancer, diabetes, and arthritis. Her research led to numerous articles, mostly in mainstream publications, and several books on imagery, disease, and psychological approaches to health care coauthored with her husband, G. Frank Lawlis. She also was involved in the development of an award-winning film on ostomy surgery, developed from her research.

In 1985, Achterberg summarized and contextualized much of her earlier work in Imagery in Healing, which reached a considerably wider audience than her earlier writings. Her work also expanded in a number of new directions. In 1988, she moved to California, accepting a position at the Saybrook Institute, where she continues to serve as a teacher of mid-life professionals returning for advanced degrees in psychology and the human sciences. Her research and workshops increasingly explored the intersection of gender and healing, leading to Woman as Healer (1990). She also participated more fully in the area of transpersonal studies, acting as President of the Association for Transpersonal Psychology from 1990 to 1994, and serving as an Executive Editor of ReVision from 1991 to 1996, where she edited issues on Transpersonal Medicine (Winter 1992), The Foundations and Future of Transpersonal Psychology (Winter 1994), and coedited (with Jürgen Kremer) an issue on Trance and Healing: Psychology, Biology, and Culture (Spring 1994).

Achterberg has also helped in many ways to ground and legitimize alternative approaches to healing and medicine, working with the U. S. Congress' study of non-conventional cancer therapies for the Office of Technology Assessment and with the Office of Alternative Medicine of the National Institutes of Health. In 1995, she became senior editor of the peer-reviewed journal, Alternative Therapies in Health and Medicine. She also teaches and consults regularly with organizations in Japan, South America, and Germany.

More recently, Achterberg has focused on concerns of intimacy, especially in the context of healing, spirituality, community, and partnership. This has been a deep underlying interest through two long-term marriages. For many years, she was also a member of a group, described in the following chapter, in which members explored intimacy as a spiritual path. She will publish her ground-breaking work on the subject in 1998, in Uncommon Bonds.

In their contribution to this volume, Achterberg and Rothberg explore through dialogue the idea of "relational" approaches to spirituality. Their starting point is the recognition that transpersonal studies have typically focused on extraordinary experiences and the transformation of the consciousness of individuals, often considered in isolation from the larger web of their relationships. They point to the ways that Wilber's recent work contributes significantly by helping to open up conceptual space in transpersonal studies for relational approaches. They then examine two main relational modes: intimate partnerships and small groups, presenting several examples of each from their study and work experience. They conclude by appreciating both the newness of and the great need for developing further relational approaches in contemporary Western settings.

Further Readings and Resources

Achterberg, J. 1985. Imagery in healing: Shamanism and modern medicine. Boston: Shambhala.

_____. 1988. The wounded healer: Transformational journeys in modern medicine. In Shaman's path, edited by G. Doore. Boston: Shambhala.

_____. 1990. *Woman as healer*. Boston: Shambhala.

_____. 1992. Ritual: The foundation for transpersonal medicine. *ReVision* 14 (Winter): 158-64.

_____. 1994. Healing images and symbols in nonordinary states of consciousness. *ReVision* 16 (Spring): 148-56.

_____. 1996. What is medicine? *Alternative Therapies in Health and Medicine* 2 (3): 58-61.

_____. 1998. *Uncommon bonds*. New York: Putnam/Riverside.

Achterberg, J., B. Dossey, and L. Kolkmeier. 1994. *Rituals of healing: Creating health through imagery*. New York: Bantam Books.

Achterberg, J., and G. Lawlis. 1980. *Bridges of the bodymind: Behavioral approaches to health care*. Champaign, Ill.: Institute for Personality and Ability Testing.

Audio and video tapes of Jeanne Achterberg's work are available from New Era Media, P.O. Box 410685, San Francisco, Calif. 94141. She has developed "The Bodymind Audio Tapes," concerning relaxation and patient education, and "The Wellness Series," a video series, on self-improvement and habit control.

Relationship as Spiritual Practice

 RELATIONAL MODELS OF SPIRITUALITY ARE BASED ON THE IDEA that spiritual growth and transformation may occur most basically through communion with and service to other beings, particularly other human beings. Hence, relational models involve a focus on one or more of many types of relationships: friendships, intimate relationships in couples, families, small groups, communities (human and ecological), societies, and global networks. In this conversation, we explore the nature of relational spirituality, with a particular emphasis on intimate relationships and small groups.

This is an especially important concern, we believe, in the context of this conversation about the work of Ken Wilber and the future of transpersonal inquiry, in that relational models of spirituality are generally absent in transpersonal studies, including the work of Wilber. However, there are a number of signs of increasing attention to such models. Wilber himself has in his recent work created considerable conceptual space for relational approaches, although most of the practical and theoretical work remains to be done.

I. RELATIONAL MODELS IN TRANSPERSONAL STUDIES

Jeanne Achterberg: Relational models of spiritual practice have basically been either absent or loosely theorized in transpersonal psychology, although that is changing somewhat with the recent books of John Welwood (1990, 1996) and John Haule (1992). Generally, relationships are viewed as a rung on the hierarchical ladder of spiritual practice, or as one kind of door to the absolute or divine. We can contrast that approach with recent feminist thinking (such as that found in Anderson and Hopkins's [1991] *The Feminine Face of God*), according to which relationship and communion are the very substance of spiritual life. I should add, though, that transpersonal psychology grew especially from Hindu and Buddhist roots and has tended to reflect their spiritual teachings.

Donald Rothberg: In Hinduism and Buddhism, there's often an emphasis on relating *universally* to all beings, with loving-kindness, wisdom, and compassion. There's often a downplaying of the centrality of one's *particular* relationships, at least for those who are most spiritually ambitious (that is, yogis, monks, and nuns).

JA: It has taken some time for transpersonal studies to embrace other Western spiritual traditions! In the Kabbalah, for example, in both its Jewish and Christian mystical renditions, relationship between masculine and feminine, and male and female, is integral to the growth of the soul. There is also the extraordinary, erotic language of intimacy in Sufism and mystical Christianity and Judaism, although the relationships are between a human being and God, or between Christ and the Church, or between God and Israel. And in many of the Western esoteric or wisdom traditions, such as the Golden Dawn and its various offshoots, and the eighteenth-century revelatory material from Emanuel Swedenborg on what he called "conjugal" (or "married") love, the spiritual basis of relationship is very clearly articulated.

DR: Relationships are particularly important in our times because they often help us to get at aspects of our fear, grief, hatred, and ignorance, as well as our generosity, love, and insight, that are not necessarily accessible through individual spiritual practice. We can have wonderful, blissful spiritual experiences or do years of inner work without a focus on intimate and social relationships. Yet we may discover, through our intimate or social involvement with others that there are major areas of our lives which have not been touched, and which lead us to a lot of pain—both individually and collectively.

There are such strong tendencies in our culture to define and limit spirituality to the personal, the interior, the private, and the subjective (Rothberg 1993; Wilber 1995). I do think that it is quite important to be explicit when pointing out that there are new forms being developed, partly to counter the hegemony of the old forms, partly to consider and even honor the newness of these efforts. Much of our relational work is really uncharted and therefore often quite difficult in many ways.

I think that *Sex, Ecology, Spirituality* (1995) itself gives evidence of this difficulty of birthing the new forms. In this work, he points toward a different sense of spiritual needs and forms, particularly with his four quadrant model of development occurring in both "inner" and "outer" ways, both individually and socially (1995, 121ff.). At the end of this book (494ff.), and in *A Brief History of Everything* (1996, 314ff.), he speaks about the tendencies to interpret spirituality and the transpersonal only in terms of the "self," only in terms of what he would call the "individual interior" quadrant. He's very insistent that spirituality has to come out in all four of these quadrants. There are also a number of places where he suggests that the work of our time is primarily integrative, bringing the different parts of our lives together. Furthermore, he speaks of the importance of balancing "ascending" and "descending" approaches. So there are many pointers in the direction of relational models of spirituality.

However, when Wilber actually writes more specifically about transpersonal "stages" (1995, 279ff.), he uses predominantly "inner" models of spirituality, that is, the old models. He gives conceptual room for new forms, but there's not much exploration of them. Rather, the old forms are presented and explored in depth, without really integrating any significant consideration of relational models.

Yet I think that he would claim that spiritual paths occur in relation to all four quadrants. In this sense, relational models can "fit" within his theory. Relationships may open us up fully to spiritual transformation and mystical experience. In an intimate relationship, for example, there might be various kinds of "work" that would lead toward nondual experience, which might or might not be accessed in interaction with another. It may even be that the knower, the actor, the "unit" of enlightenment, is not the single person.

II. INTIMATE RELATIONSHIP AS SPIRITUAL PATH

JA: It's been very interesting to me to see how relational approaches in the West have often only taken birth outside the mainstream religious traditions. For example, I've been studying the parallel development of the romantic love tradition with Western religion. When people were not given the option of spiritual and intimate relationships within a religious tradition, they developed a literary tradition that paralleled, almost step-by-step, the religious outpouring.

Yet the romantic love tradition was an impossible tradition! The ideals of romantic love were inconceivable within a marriage. Romantic love was chaste in its original form, but quite early in its development, it became closely connected with a myth of adultery, as in the story of Tristan and Isolde. Either way, we're left with both literary and theological traditions which couldn't celebrate intimate relationship as a legitimate spiritual path. There was no "wiggle room" in either tradition.

DR: Was there tension historically between these traditions?

JA: There was probably huge tension, although there are several modern arguments that the purveyors of the romantic love stories—the troubadours or Minnesingers—were really undercover agents for the Cathars, a religious sect. Who knows? This tension between the Church and the romantic myth is very evident in the story of Abelard and Heloise. It's also very clear from the story which ideas held sway.

It's a terrible story. Abelard was perhaps the most revered humanist of his time. Heloise had an inordinately fine intellect, was highly literate, and became a major religious-theological figure. When she was about fourteen, Abelard was hired as her tutor. They fell in love and she became pregnant. To his credit, he did insist on marriage. She refused to allow the fact of the marriage to become public, because she knew that he would never again find work. There was no option for a philosopher in those times other than with the Church. Through various intrigues, her uncle had Abelard castrated, and in great shame, he retired within the church grounds. Heloise spent her life in a convent, quickly becoming one of the most powerful abbesses of the time.

In her letters, she told him in no uncertain terms that she'd rather be his whore than a queen. She saw very clearly that their relationship was spiritual practice. She saw the divine in him. She saw him as God. She was willing to sacrifice her life so that he could become the philosopher that she thought he ought to become. She held to the tradition of romantic love, as far as I can determine from her writings. He, on the other hand, moved squarely within the tradition of the Church. He recanted, repented, and said that it was certainly a mistake on his part to have granted secular love that kind of all-consuming importance.

DR: Oh my! So part of the theological critique of the romantic love tradition was that it was very limited spiritually. What were other elements of that critique?

JA: Romantic love was closely linked with lust. The other element in the romantic love tradition that still seeps into our collective bones is the moral issue of infidelity. The myth of romantic love, alive and well in *The Bridges of Madison County,* is the story of extramarital affairs. Whether or not the love is consummated, the myth is that it cannot possibly be carried into married relationships. Marriage ruins the dream. What a mess! The people today who see their intimate relationships as having spiritual dimensions, would, I think, argue with this myth and say that it no longer serves us.

DR: You've been associated with a group of couples who have attempted to understand relationship in spiritual terms.

JA: The original group was brought together by cultural anthropologist Virginia (Ginny) Hine, whom I still think of as my mentor. She networked with people who thought that they were in unusual relationships, mostly heterosexuals but some lesbians as well. Most of them had had other long-term relationships in the past, usually marriages of ten or more years length. Since then many other couples have identified themselves as what we called bonded couples.

Four years ago, Nancy Young, one of my students at the Institute for Transpersonal Psychology, tried to locate the members of the original bonded couples group. We found, much to our surprise, that all but one couple were still intact. In re-reading our old letters and transcripts, and in listening to other couples tell their stories, it's clear that all of the individuals felt connected on multiple levels: psychologically, emotionally, and spiritually. All but one couple in the original group claim that their relationships have over the years been passionately alive, full of both light and shadow, and sometimes quite difficult! No doubt quite a few have had their bags packed for all these years! [Laughter.] As with any spiritual path, as you suggested, there's a lot of learning about grief and ignorance, as well as about love and generosity. So much of the learning is both joyful and challenging, to put it mildly.

DR: Did all of them see their relationships in spiritual terms?

JA: Absolutely. Most of them were also doing spiritual practices, but the members of the original group did not have a guru and did not live within spiritual communities. Most spoke about their sexuality as a kind of spiritual practice, as a doorway leading to expanded consciousness and even touching pure consciousness. They also spoke about how they would move in and out of a sense of connection with their partners, and how they would experience a kind of "abyss" when the sense of connection was lost. The members of each couple spoke of seeing themselves as two rough diamonds doing "deep soul work" or "deep growth work," seeking and "polishing" their souls by touching another soul. They thought that this work could not happen in any other way than through the challenges of these relationships.

DR: Was there much help, other than from each other?

JA: We had each other, and we shared ideas, along with bits and pieces of history and literature. Ginny was a scribe; she circulated our letters and the transcripts of our talks. But as far as I know there are no spiritual traditions that even have the language for this type of exploration.

I should also add that a few couples explored as well the parapsychological dimension and the nonlocality of consciousness. I'll tell a personal story. In January 1995, you and I were on the phone together when my husband, Frank, had a heart attack. I was in my studio, 150 miles away, and my grandmother clock stopped at that instant. There were a series of unusual events. For instance, the day before, I'd had all of Frank's symptoms. I went back to the parapsychological literature to look for similar accounts. There are many instances, for example, of inanimate objects somehow becoming involved in a communication process between persons. I don't know how it happens; it simply does. Most of the couples could also relate stories of when they had one another's symptoms, dreams, and so forth.

DR: I wonder about the role of community and social support. In some ways, much of the recent emphasis on close relationships in our culture can be interpreted as a "subjectivization" and "privatization" of social and spiritual energies that formerly were more widely extended in nature and society. Our deeper values are often no longer expressed in our work and community; somehow everything has to be done through close relationships, the "havens in a heartless world." In such a society, it would be helpful (although difficult) for couples to have outlets beyond the couple itself.

JA: I really agree. I think that this more social dimension may be a "shadow" aspect for some of the couples in our group. The lack of this dimension may well account for those many, many "dark nights of the soul" when the members of a couple felt separate. There was simply nothing else available to cover the nakedness, to care for the wound of feeling unbonded with the partner.

DR: Let me tell you one of my own stories related to this issue of social support for couples. When my former partner Bonnie and I first met, it was unusual in many ways. After having been in contact for several months, mostly from a distance, I visited her in Vermont. For about ten days, we were together in a kind of dyadic trance. It was the depth of a Vermont winter in the countryside. We stayed on the third floor of her house and scarcely ate for those ten days.

JA: I love it!

DR: It was very powerful and profound for both of us. There were all sorts of things going on. Actually, we didn't take a lot of notes and don't remember everything that happened. But we do remember, for example, that there was often tremendous creativity. A lot of visionary states of consciousness opened up, which seemed "contagious" between us. There were movements, as it were, through many layers of our being—physically, psychologically, emotionally, sexually, and so on, often with tremendous concentration and attention. I remember one day that we didn't leave the bedroom and have anything to eat until 8 p.m. Many days we didn't come down until the afternoon.

JA: You were feeding yourselves in other ways.

DR: Afterward, we would often reflect about the individual and cultural importance of this kind of experience, both for the initial meeting and bonding of a couple, and in renewing relationships. We envisioned a kind of spiritual retreat for couples, to give them support to have such experiences. It might not be for ten days; five days or three days might be enough. We imagined that a healthy culture might regularly provide ritual retreat space and have elders available to give guidance if necessary (as there are sometimes different types of retreats for married couples in some religious traditions).

JA: People are very, very hungry for this. There are deep spiritual needs that have gone unmet for generations, not only the need for the experiences themselves, but also the need to give meaning and form to the experiences. Your story of your meeting with Bonnie reminds me of another quality reported by the couples in our group. When they came together, there were very deep recognitions of their connections, often of having been together in a past life. I am reminded of Plato's *Symposium* and the splendid speech of Aristophanes about the androgynous beings who were so powerful that the jealous gods split them in two. For the rest of their lives, generation after generation, each member of the pair seeks its other half. I've heard language so many times referring to this finding of the separated half, like, "Ah, there he is. There she is." So there can be both the great sense of wholeness and completion, connected with multiple levels of bonding and recognition, as well as the tremendous pain of feeling pulled apart and separated from the complete being.

DR: You also found that almost all members of the couples in your group had completed considerable individuation before the partners met.

JA: Yes. Later, there would sometimes be some regression and a whole lot of fear: "Oh, my God. I've lost myself. I've died." It's the classic Freudian fear of death (*thanatos*). It's the sense that the merging is too much. Then there's a pulling apart until there's some growing back, as it were, of limbs and wings and everything that has been lost. It seems to be a cyclical process. But I think that relationship as spiritual practice may not generally be possible until there's a significant level of pretty hardy individuation and ego strength.

DR: So far we've talked a lot about rather nonordinary types of experiences. But what does relationship as spiritual practice mean in terms of everyday life?

JA: [Laughter.] That's a tough question. I think that it means staying awake to the sacred nature of relationship. It means to hold in some way, perhaps through meditation or prayer or whatever, the notion that we're growing our souls through interacting with one another. Maybe all relationships do this in some ways. But if there is acknowledgment of the spiritual character of relationships by couples, families, friends, and communities, then it's different. I think that the service component of the relationship becomes clearer. It's staying awake to the way that our everyday practice with others helps to bring consciousness to another level, helps us see each other more and more as sacred beings.

Spiritual practices that are not relationship-based may sometimes represent a kind of spiritual "bypass." Often, the real development and molding of soul only occurs in these interactive ways. I would imagine, though, that both arms of spiritual practice—the inner work and the relational—are necessary, and that it may constitute a bypass if either is ignored.

DR: That reminds me of how the couples work may also be unbalanced if it is not connected to community and society, as we were saying earlier. A danger of this work is to think that it's somehow doing everything and that there's no need to engage on other levels. On the other hand, it's clear that at certain times we need to emphasize some parts of our lives more than others. But focusing so much on the couple at this point in history could be a kind of escape: The world is falling apart. The cities are becoming very nasty places. The rich and the poor are becoming increasingly polarized. And meanwhile there are wonderful peak experiences for couples. So why don't we just focus on our relationship and not look at the other parts of life? Such thinking certainly seems to constitute another danger.

JA: I think that you're absolutely correct.

DR: Yet we in many ways lack the perspectives and forms to see and work with our social relationships as spiritual practice, in ways that are similar to how we lack the language and forms for understanding intimate relationships as spiritual practice.

III. RELATIONAL SPIRITUALITY IN GROUPS, WORK, AND COMMUNITIES

DR: Some of my recent experience is in developing and working with small groups through the Buddhist Alliance for Social Engagement (BASE) program sponsored by the Buddhist Peace Fellowship (see also Rothberg 1996). With the acronym BASE, we made a deliberate reference to the base community movement of Latin America, Asia, and elsewhere. There, a base community is generally a small group led by lay persons, meeting regularly for prayer, study (including Bible study and social analysis), support, personal growth, ritual, reflection on everyday life, and action (Berryman 1987, 63ff.).

The goal of the first BASE group, which met in 1995 in Berkeley, California, was explicitly exploratory. It was a six-month training program with ten participants, including two mentors (I was one of the mentors), for people interested in having their work in social service and social change occur in the framework of "socially engaged" Buddhism. Our intention was to explore forms that can help make our lives and work in the world be fields of spiritual practice, recognizing that we might draw as well from the resources of similar approaches from various traditions.

We've thought of these groups as representing a conscious attempt to create a space where the personal, psychological, social, and spiritual dimensions of our lives, so often separated, can be woven together. Outside of groups like this, people might work with a therapist or with friends on their own individual issues, concerning interpersonal relationships or work. They might participate in secular organizations addressing social issues. They might attend classes and retreats in their spiritual communities. But rarely in any of these other contexts are these different dimensions integrated. Arguably this impoverishes each of these approaches and artificially separates them.

We met as a group two evenings a week and one to three full retreat days a month, along with weekend retreats to begin and end the program. This level of commitment permitted a significant level of bonding, shared intention, focus, and intensity. We provided opportunities for the participants to talk about their work experiences and raise issues or questions, in the context of study and training in the theory and practice of socially engaged Buddhism. The intention was to give support for them to bring the attention, energy, and wisdom of spiritual practice to their work. In this first group, two people worked with a local women's cancer support group, one person led groups on urban composting in San Francisco, and two others helped and fed homeless people. Another person worked with the Zen Hospice in San Francisco, and two others were involved in environmental activism.

At first, as with any group, we developed initial bonds. But as the group developed, our focus changed, and we came more to follow the everyday material brought up by people's lives and the members' interactions with each other. Rituals developed, as did an interest in acting together in the world. There were a number of experiments.

JA: What difficulties or shadow material did you encounter?

DR: Those (including myself) who planned the group did not take enough into consideration the need for a strong initial bonding between the members of the group as a basis for the kind of trust that permits deep exploration. We've emphasized in later programs the importance of hearing each other's stories in some depth and making general issues, skills, and norms related to group process more explicit.

Midway through the first group, for example, a number of the group members asked us to attempt a yet deeper sense of connection and interaction. That actually proved to be quite difficult for some members of the group. Some in the group, for example, were uncomfortable with the emphasis on group process, in large part, it seemed, due to concerns about the expression of anger. Of course, the expression of anger in groups (or between people in general, for that matter) is commonly a sensitive issue. For some members of the group, experiencing and especially "receiving" even a rather contained expression of anger seemed to be very difficult. This was especially interesting in relation to differences within Buddhist communities about how to understand and work with anger and other strong emotions. It's a particularly important issue to address for those active in social service and social change work.

JA: What brought the group joy?

DR: Oh! Many things. I think that many of us found joy just in the process of being together. Several people spoke of being in the group as a kind of homecoming and as meeting a need that had not been met before. They had often felt somewhat alienated in social change groups that didn't include an "inner" or spiritual dimension, as well as in Buddhist settings in which spiritual teachings are interpreted as only applying to the individual on the meditation cushion or to friends and family.

The longer periods together in retreats were particularly precious and provided opportunities to explore new forms and connect ways of inquiry not normally brought together. We would typically combine periods of silent contemplative practice, perhaps for most of a day, with stories and collective inquiries. On one retreat, for example, we focused on issues of class, catalyzed in large part by our stay at a group member's home in an exclusive oceanside community. Yet we were able to approach these sensitive and sometimes difficult issues in the context of the earlier silent practice together.

JA: Were the members of the group able to bring the spirit of the group into their work?

DR: For everyone, I think, there was an intensification in awareness at work, set in the context of spiritual practice. In the group sessions, people would bring up and discuss typical work-related difficulties: how to relate to a difficult boss, how to be with the anguish of loss, how to respond to feeling overwhelmed by exposure to suffering, how to deal with "burnout." Group support seems crucial in approaching these issues.

One member of the group who works with women with cancer spoke of feeling emotionally overwhelmed by being continually confronted with suffering and death, especially that of many young people, and contemplating the roots of such suffering in social structures and public policies. Sometimes she felt that she needed to have the kind of support and common understanding furnished by our group in her work place itself, in order to be able to stay with the difficulties with more balance.

JA: Such work as you've described is really a holy privilege. If we're not working in environments where other people realize that it's a holy privilege, burnout is inevitable.

It's interesting that the work that I've done, especially with Carl Simonton, in what we call "healing communities" of people living with cancer, is very similar, in terms of intentions and content, to your group. We say that we're in "sacred space." We're clearly teaching and healing one another. We also think of bringing together more personal, social, and spiritual aspects of transformation. It's very clear to all of us as we're working together that it is a spiritual practice, a privileged spiritual practice with people in crisis. We use various psychotherapeutic techniques, as well as imagery, relaxation, and meditation. We also use group process, particularly in our initial building of community over a seven- or eight-day period, a period which typically creates for me a rather stunning degree of synergy, openness, sharing, and family.

There's a lot of research (e.g., Pilisuk and Park 1986; Simonton, Simonton, and Creighton 1978; Spiegel, Bloom, Kraemer, et al. 1989) showing that this kind of community is life-giving; people in supportive community have more white blood cells, live longer, and so on. In fact, the presence or absence of group support can determine whether one survives or not. But such group support doesn't necessarily mean a lot of people. I think that we're in the process of redefining what support and community are.

For example, I find that women tend to make different sorts of community than men. A lot of women's community goes on in kitchens. In fact, some of the most profound community that I've experienced in the last year has been in women's kitchens. Women have visited often, talked with me, rubbed my feet, and brought me chocolate when there's been a crisis or when I'm not feeling well. That's community!

I've also noticed that many of us in my groups—the circle of women friends, the group of couples, and the healing communities of patients—are having less and less tolerance for being in settings without these kinds of spiritual support and understanding.

DR: One way that change occurs is when people are increasingly unwilling to be in settings where they spend most of their time unless those settings are continuous with their deeper values. On the other hand, this doesn't mean that one simply withdraws; in many cases, it's important to make an effort to transform the situation. Someone has to stay in our hospitals and educational institutions and political institutions and change them!

JA: It's a dance, isn't it? How long are you willing to stay in the belly of the beast?

DR: In this context, small groups can be seeds of transformation, not just in supporting individuals, but also in making accessible and tangible an alternative way of being together socially, developing a clearer sense of the values, norms, and structures that might inform other settings and institutions. In fact, small groups and communities (town meetings, neighborhood groups, councils, collectives, and affinity groups) have often had a crucial transformative role in the history of Western social and political movements. Several writers, such as Hannah Arendt (1965), have claimed that these small democratic associations were the real heart, the liberatory heart, of the Western revolutions, the French, the American, and the Russian revolutions, before they turned tyrannical or bureaucratic.

We have this great hunger to be "at home" in our relationships, in our work, in our communities. Yet it's often very hard to translate this hunger into actual practice and to know what the right forms are.

JA: It's the question of the forms again. We've seen that theme emerge in talking about couples and intimate relationships, then about small experimental groups and communities. How do I meet my homecoming needs with like-minded souls? Although we don't know exactly what forms will work, I think that we all know emotionally how we want to feel in those forms: connected, cared for, and challenged.

DR: These relationships, groups, work settings, and smaller communities can then be bases from which to respond, if we feel called to respond, to the larger society and to the planet as a whole.

Acknowledgments

The authors wish to thank April De Tally, who helped to develop a transcript of our conversation, and Sean Kelly, Inge Lembeck, and Diana Winston for their comments on earlier drafts.

References

Anderson, S., and P. Hopkins. 1991. *The feminine face of God*. New York: Bantam.

Arendt, H. 1965. *On revolution*. New York: Viking Press.

Berryman, P. 1987. *Liberation theology*. Bloomington, Ind.: Meyer Stone Books.

Haule, J. 1992. *Pilgrimage of the heart*. Boston: Shambhala.

Pilisuk, M., and S. Park. 1986. *The healing web: Social networks and human survival*. Hanover, N.H.: University Press of New England.

Rothberg, D. 1993. The crisis of modernity and the emergence of socially engaged spirituality. *ReVision* 15 (4) (Winter): 105–14.

———. 1996. What is to be done? Small groups and engaged Buddhist practice. *Turning Wheel: Journal of the Buddhist Peace Fellowship* (Winter): 43–45.

Simonton, O., S. Simonton, and J. Creighton. 1978. *Getting well again*. Los Angeles: Tarcher.

Spiegel, D., J. Bloom, H. Kraemer, et al. 1989. Effects of psychosocial treatment on survival of patients with metastatic breast cancer. *The Lancet* 2:888–91.

Welwood, J. 1990. *Journey of the heart: Intimate relationships and the path of love*. New York: HarperCollins.

———. 1996. *Love and awakening: Discovering the sacred path of intimate relationship*. New York: HarperCollins.

Wilber, K. 1995. *Sex, ecology, spirituality: The spirit of evolution*. Boston: Shambhala.

———. 1996. *A brief history of everything*. Boston: Shambhala.

Part Four

How Do We Inquire Spiritually?

12

Robert McDermott

Over the last three decades, Robert McDermott has combined innovative and productive work as a scholar, teacher, and philosopher with distinguished service in academic administration. Born in New York City, where he lived for 50 years, he moved to San Francisco in 1990 to be President of the California Institute of Integral Studies (CIIS). He and his wife Ellen, a potter and Waldorf school teacher, have two children, Darren and Deirdre.

McDermott studied classics at Queens College, City University of New York (B.A, 1962); philosophy at Emory University (M.A., 1965), and at Boston University (Ph.D., 1969). He taught philosophy and comparative religion for seven years at Manhattanville College and for twenty years at Baruch College, C.U.N.Y., where he served for nine years as Chair of the Department of Philosophy. In the 1970s he was secretary of the American Academy of Religion and secretary-treasurer of the Society for Asian and Comparative Philosophy.

McDermott was Senior Fulbright Lecturer at the Open University in England (1975-1977), where he coproduced an Open University-BBC video documentary on Sri Aurobindo, "Avatar: Concept and Example." He directed the National Endowment for the Humanities 1978-1980 Project for the Study of Hinduism and Buddhism. He is presently President of the Board of Rudolf Steiner College and from 1983 to 1994 served as President of the Rudolf Steiner (Summer) Institute at Thomas College in Waterville, Maine.

Sri Aurobindo and Rudolf Steiner are key figures in McDermott's personal, intellectual, and spiritual development, and in his movement toward transpersonal philosophy. He is author of The Essential Aurobindo, The Essential Steiner, *and numerous essays on modern Indian thought, the evolution of consciousness, and classical American thought.*

From 1991 to 1994, Professor McDermott was one of five executive editors of the journal ReVision *and edited a special double issue on* Rudolf Steiner and American Thought *(Spring-Summer 1991). Of Steiner, McDermott has stated, "More than any other single source except my family, the teaching and influence of Rudolf Steiner have proven to be a decisively positive force in my life. He offers what seems to be the most complete and careful account of individual karmic destiny in relation to higher beings (including Krishna, Buddha, and Christ), the planets and stars, the earth as a spiritu-*

al being, the evolution of language and cultural forms, modes of thought, affect and will, and the varied patterns and possibilities of one's own soul history."

McDermott lectures regularly on the evolution of consciousness, contemporary culture, the spiritual mission of America, modern spiritual masters, and classical texts of Asian and Western spiritual traditions, as well as on the teachings of Rudolph Steiner and the Waldorf approach to education. In addition to quarterly lecture series at the California Institute of Integral Studies, he has recently lectured at the Laurence Rockefeller Center for Human Values of Princeton University, the Esalen Institute, the Woodrow Wilson Fellowship Foundation, and the Fetzer Institute.

McDermott's contribution to this volume brings out well his interest in the nature of a transpersonal community of inquiry. He is concerned with articulating a model of working with differences of views in a way that manifests transpersonal values. His chapter is devoted to examining the question of Wilber's tone and style of writing, especially with respect to Wilber's Sex, Ecology, Spirituality.

McDermott readily acknowledges the groundbreaking character of this book and of Wilber's work generally, but thinks that its transpersonal intent is belied by its polemical stance toward those with whom Wilber disagrees, most of whom would consider themselves fellow transpersonalists. McDermott stresses the need for alternatives to the sometimes combative features of traditional academic discourse and calls upon Wilber to take a leading role within the transpersonal community in seeking to embody such alternatives.

Further Readings

McDermott, R., ed. 1973. *The essential Aurobindo*. New York: Schocken Books.

———, ed. 1984. *The essential Steiner: Basic writings of Rudolf Steiner*. San Francisco: Harper & Row.

———. 1986. Introduction [to William James, *Essays in psychical research*]. In *The works of William James*. Cambridge: Harvard University Press.

———. 1991a. Introduction [to *Rudolf Steiner and American thought*]. *ReVision* 13 (4): 157-160.

———. 1991b. William James and Rudolf Steiner. *ReVision* 13 (4): 161-167.

———. 1992. Philosophy and evolution of consciousness. In *Revisioning philosophy*, edited by J. Ogilvy. Albany: State University of New York Press.

———. 1993. Transpersonal worldviews: Historical and philosophical reflections. In *Paths beyond ego: The transpersonal vision*, edited by R. Walsh and F. Vaughan. Los Angeles: Tarcher/Perigree.

———. 1997. Money, sex and power: Spirituality, shadow and wonder. In *More lifeways: Finding support and inspiration in family life,* edited by P. Smith and S. Schaeffer. Hawthorn Press.

Several of Robert McDermott's lecture cycles at CIIS are available on cassette tapes through Conference Recording Service, 1308 Gilman St., Berkeley, Calif. 94706, tel.: 510-527-3600.

The Need for Philosophical
and Spiritual Dialogue:
Reflections on Ken Wilber's
Sex, Ecology, Spirituality

 I AM WRITING OUT OF A RECOGNITION OF KEN WILBER'S CONTRIBUTION to the transpersonal movement. I am delighted to join others in acknowledging the ground-breaking character of Wilber's latest work, *Sex, Ecology, Spirituality: The Spirit of Evolution* (*SES*) (1995). I am also offering suggestions concerning ways in which this work might have better served the ideals which he espouses. I believe that his readers are not well served by his style of argument against alternative perspectives and his treatment of some of his colleagues. This massive work—the fruit of enormous labor, vast knowledge, and brilliant intellect—is seriously diminished by what strikes me as caustic argumentation and overly harsh critique of contemporaries, including many contributors to the transpersonal perspective. Because I so admire Wilber's scope and precision and care so strongly about the capacity of transpersonal perspectives to revision Western thought and culture, I am taking this opportunity to plead for a less combative exchange of ideas from and within the transpersonal community.

Although I have not met Ken Wilber personally, I am positively predisposed to him and his writings. His books have been an important source of insight in my attempt to interpret and to some extent bridge my two successive teachers, Sri Aurobindo and Rudolf Steiner. I count his friends, Frances Vaughan and Roger Walsh, among my closest friends, and I had the privilege of studying *SES* with them and several others. My wife and I are especially grateful to him for his *Grace and Grit* (1991), which was helpful to us after she suffered a serious stroke two years ago.

I believe that we look in vain, however, for the healing potential of *SES*; it takes one opponent after another and argues against them, often with little apparent sympathetic understanding of their positions. The 240 pages of notes in *SES* in particular are in need of an editor and prevent the book from reaching its great potential. Let me give just a few examples. In a typical passage, Wilber criticizes "most Eco-camps"—he includes everyone from deep ecologists and ecofeminists to various exponents of the so-called "New Paradigm"—for lacking a sense of "the extensive dynamics of intersubjective communicative exchange" presupposed by their "web-of-life" theories (740). He then describes them as "some of the most quarrelsome groups around—trying to get various eco-groups together is like trying to herd cats"; he says that they amount to "a bunch of angry, monological, divine egos shouting about systems theory, and they have no idea why the world doesn't respond with gratitude to their saving graces" (740). One wonders how members of the "Eco-camp" might be expected to respond to this kind of characterization? How is Wilber's reference to ecofeminists and advocates of Great-Goddess spirituality as "power-hungry theorists" (666) calculated to further the cause of "intersubjective communicative exchange"? We should join with Wilber in objecting to the use of ad hominem attacks by many "Eco-Romantics," but not when he claims that "these critics seem to gravitate to the past phylogenetic structure that corresponds with the ontogenetic structure in themselves that is immediately prior to their failed personal integration" (665).

SES is counterproductive in its harsh evaluations of those who have, or had, reason to consider themselves Wilber's colleagues. Take Theodore Roszak, for instance, who has made many learned and insightful contributions to enlightened thinking since his *The Making of a Counter Culture* (1969). Why does Wilber denounce Roszak's recent *Voice of the Earth* (1992) for its critique of reason, as if Roszak could possibly subscribe to the simple-minded view that, as Wilber puts it, "reason is the Devil, Gaia is the God/dess" (690)? Is Roszak really attempting "to cure the human race with ecopsychology" (685)? By what criterion could it be claimed that Roszak "aggressively denies any truly transpersonal sphere" (689)?

Can we imagine this kind of attack on colleagues at the back of Plotinus's *Enneads*, Spinoza's *Ethics*, James's *Principles*, Whitehead's *Process and Reality*, Steiner's *Philosophy of Freedom*, or Sri Aurobindo's *Life Divine*? These works contain arguments, of course, but truly great thinkers, particularly those who present themselves as representing a mystical perspective, do not need to slash and burn philosophical opponents. Such ungenerous comments can only obscure the flow of significant insights for which Wilber is justly commended.

Addressing Ken Wilber more directly, let me emphasize that quotable negative remarks from a person of power not only get repeated, but effectively replace the very positive body of work to which they are attached. The tone of *SES* in the kind of passages to which I have alluded suggests to me that the author has not yet accepted the responsibility of his highly visible influence. I also resisted a similar responsibility when I was first appointed president of the California Institute of Integral Studies. During my first two years in this position, I found much that I did not admire and said so, cleverly and quotably. When the board-appointed presidential evaluator visited the institution as part of a five-year review, he heard about many positive accomplishments of my tenure (I was reappointed for another five years), but also heard about those negative comments I had made four and five years earlier. As Wilber's contentious comments are published in this major work, they will outlive all of us, and for as long as the book is read will continue to detract from its achievement.

As Ken Wilber is, along with Stanislav Grof, one of the two most influential exponents of transpersonal thinking, we should expect his writings to exhibit equanimity in the service of insight, eschewing combat, condescension, and overconfidence. The transformation of an embattled to a dialogical consciousness should be the first goal, and the enduring characteristic, of a philosophy or psychology claiming to be transpersonal.

A philosopher such as Wilber cannot represent the value of the spiritual and simultaneously be so contentious and dismissive of perspectives with which he finds fault. Doing so undermines his own claims and causes extreme reactions. Being right is not the only value—and a perspective which is so unskilled at sympathetic listening is not likely to be more right than others. Wilber has long ago, and at a very young age, established his intellectual brilliance and his role as one of the preeminent spokespersons of a transpersonal world view. It is now time for him to assume a more senior attitude, one which shows tolerance, offers encouragement, and more convincingly exemplifies the values, and more particularly the mode of discourse, of a leader of a spiritually based, transformative perspective.

I believe that such a combative and divisive mode of argumentation is destructive not only of his relations with thinkers and writers who would naturally be his colleagues, but will also prove ineffectual against mainstream thinkers. Some readers, and especially defenders, of *SES* might take its intellectual pugilism to be a tactic, a way of impressing the East Coast intellectuals and chronically contentious philosophers, or a way of "taking on" the mainstream paradigm on behalf of the wimpy West Coast. There are surely situations in which many of us might want Wilber's searing intellect to demolish Richard Rorty, Daniel Dennett, or the *New York Review of Books*. My higher, older self, however, reminds me that Gandhi is right, that belligerence is not effective, not even in combat with "nothing but" flatland materialists.

It might be helpful to remind ourselves that the *dia* of *dialogue* means "through," so that philosophical dialogue, of which there has been so little and of which Wilber could become an exemplar, means penetrating the thought of others by sympathetic imagination. At a minimum, sympathetic thinking should be a complement to critical thinking.

Ideally, given the damage wrought by too much criticism and too little tolerance, great thinkers representing the transpersonal perspective should serve as exemplars of community-based dialogue.

The idea of a community of dialogue would seem to be central to a transpersonal movement, a welcome and necessary improvement on both the model of the scholar-thinker working alone and the academic model according to which each thinker advances by discrediting the opinions of all others. In *SES* Wilber considers a contemplative community to be the best source for progress in developing a transpersonal metaphysics. Unfortunately, Wilber's mode of discourse is in tension with the mystical perspective that he applauds.

Perhaps the next two volumes of *SES* will not suffer from this tension. That Wilber has agreed to respond to the contributors to this volume devoted to his work is a convincing indication of his willingness to participate in what should prove to be a productive dialogue.

Acknowledgments

The author is grateful to both editors, Sean Kelly and Donald Rothberg, for encouragement and helpful guidelines in approaching these delicate issues, and particularly to Sean Kelly for many improvements to the text.

References

Roszak, T. 1969. *The making of a counter culture: Reflections on the technocratic society and its youthful opposition*. Garden City, N.Y.: Anchor Books.

———. 1992. *The voice of the earth*. New York: Simon and Schuster.

Wilber, K. 1991. *Grace and grit: Spirituality and healing in the life and death of Treya Killam Wilber*. Boston: Shambhala.

———. 1995. *Sex, ecology, spirituality: The spirit of evolution*. Boston: Shambhala.

Photograph of Robert McDermott by Karen Preuss.

13

Kaisa Puhakka

For many participants at the 1997 conference on "Ken Wilber and the Future of Transpersonal Inquiry," Kaisa Puhakka, a teacher and writer from the State University of West Georgia and unknown to virtually all, was the bright star. Speaking with a rare dialectical clarity, tremendous spaciousness, and considerable humor, she reminded those at the conference that systematic inquiry and thinking can be both a kind of spiritual practice and can open up and move minds and hearts from their closed and rigid patterns.

Born in Helsinki, Finland, Puhakka's child-hood years were ordinary, except that she pursued dance with a passion that she later described as connected with a kind of desire to escape the confines of bodily existence. At thirteen, she was introduced to Krishnamurti and sought, as well, she reports, to be free from the mind. Only a deep connection with nature seemed to keep her from fleeing the world altogether.

In 1965, Puhakka moved to the United States, earning graduate degrees in phi-losophy (with an emphasis on Eastern and comparative philosophy), experimental psy-chology, and clinical psychology while continuing her spiritual explorations. She was particularly drawn to the study of the work of Nagarjuna, the second-century Buddhist dialectician, and the eighth-century Advaita Vedantin Shankara, both of whom teach the limits of the forms of thought and of thinking as a way of knowing. She began a formal meditation practice that she has continued for twenty-five years, primarily in the vipassana and Zen traditions. For the past five years, she has been studying with Joshu Sasaki Roshi, a Japanese Rinzai Zen master who lives in California. She has increas-ingly rooted her reflective inquiries in more direct, experiential modes of investigation and the cultivation of awareness.

Puhakka's spiritual practice, oriented at first toward the kind of "ascent" to Spirit that Ken Wilber describes, reached a turning point nearly two decades ago, as spiritual openings were followed by a sustained period of severe physical difficulties. For a num-ber of years, she "descended" to explore and integrate more fully both her emotional and physical life, developing an appreciation for the great importance and difficulty of bringing together what Wilber calls the paths of Ascent and Descent. She worked for eight years as a psychotherapist, then, in 1990, returned to academia in the Humanistic and Transpersonal Psychology program at West Georgia, where she teaches psy-chotherapy, Buddhist thought, and meditation practice.

In her one published book and in numerous articles and chapters, Puhakka has explored transpersonal modes of knowing and being, their manifestations and transformative effects in everyday life, and the conditions that facilitate access to such modes. Her writing presents a fresh, nonacademic, and accessible way of inquiry into these issues, offering many delights and insights.

In her contribution to this book, Puhakka provides a remarkable and often very light and playful "dialectical" vantage point on Ken Wilber's work. We are invited to contemplate Wilber's theory "of everything" from several perspectives and to let some of the paradoxes and creative tensions in his work open our awareness to new modes of "seeing," particularly from the stance of what Wilber terms "vision-logic." In vision-logic, we are able to see and think in a more holistic and integrated way, understanding, for example, the interconnection and interdependence between seeming opposites. What appears often as polarization or even contradiction may, with vision-logic, appear as an integrated set, a web, a net.

Puhakka points to a basic creative tension of this kind in Wilber's work between an emphasis on purpose *and on* play. *While Wilber definitely acknowledges both purpose and play, Puhakka believes that he gives primacy to the purposeful model in his theory. Puhakka's invitation, both to the reader and to Wilber (who claims to be writing from the stance of "vision-logic"), is to enter more deeply into such a vision and to play and be purposive in what may be new ways.*

Further Readings

Puhakka, K. 1975. *Knowledge and reality: A comparative study of Quine and some Buddhist logicians.* Delhi: Motilal Banarsidass.

_____. 1980. Beyond outer and inner space. In *Dimensions of thought*: Vol. 1, edited by R. Moon and S. Randall. Berkeley: Dharma Publishing.

_____. 1991. The luminous diamond of knowing. In *Studies in Humanistic Psychology*, edited by C. Aanstoos. Carrollton, Ga.: West Georgia Studies in the Social Sciences, Vol. 29.

_____. [1990] 1993. Self and space. In *Case studies in mental health treatment*, edited by R. Kalina. Los Angeles: Pyrczak Publishing. [Originally published in *The Humanistic Psychologist* 18: 259-270.)

_____. 1995a. Religious experience: Hinduism. In *Handbook of religious experience*, edited by R. Hood. Birmingham, Al.: Religious Education Press.

_____. 1995b. Restoring connectedness in the kosmos: A healing tale of a deeper order. [Review of K. Wilber: *Sex, ecology, spirituality.*] *The Humanistic Psychologist* 23 (3): 373-391.

_____. 1997. An invitation to authentic knowing. In *Spiritual knowing: Alternative epistemic perspectives*, edited by T. Hart, P. Nelson, and K. Puhakka. Carrollton, Ga.: State University of West Georgia Studies in the Social Sciences, Vol. 34.

Contemplating Everything:
Wilber's Evolutionary Theory
in Dialectical Perspective

> Why are there essents [=existents] rather than nothing?
> That is the question.
>
>   Martin Heidegger (1961, 1)

> It is flat-out strange that something—that anything—is
> happening at all. There was nothing, then a Big Bang,
> then, here we all are. This is extremely weird. . . . This book
> is . . . about a possible Deeper Order. It is . . . about evolu-
> tion, and about religion, and, in a sense, about everything
> in between.
>
>   Ken Wilber (1995, vii-viii)

INTRODUCTION

 *SEX, ECOLOGY, SPIRITUALITY* ARTICULATES A VISION OF THE universe that claims to be more inclusive and more integrative than the views offered by any other contemporary philosopher or scientist. Wilber's aim is to be not just more inclusive and more holistic than other theorists, but to be truly all-inclusive. This means that all the various domains of knowing and being are included, and the views or theories about these domains are as well. And, finally, the theory that envisions and integrates these views and domains is itself studied, as a part of the all-encompassing whole.

Such a radically holistic stance invites the question, "How does one view a theory that is so inclusive that all views and theories become its content?" At first, the answer appears simple: assume a meta-perspective from which to view the theory of all theories. But a theory that is truly all-inclusive necessarily includes the metatheory or metaview as well. We now have an infinite regress of views of views of views. Logic has landed us in a paradox: a theory of everything cannot be viewed or thought about "from the outside" or "objectively" because the viewing or thinking itself would fall outside the theory. Hence the paradox: an all-encompassing theory cannot encompass everything. Rather than feeling disheartened, however, we can appreciate this paradox as logic's parting gift to us. It has turned our thinking into a knot that, for a moment, may silence thought's incessant flow and make room for a different kind of mental activity that is more nonlinear and contemplative, hardly a thinking at all as we ordinarily understand it but perhaps more akin to an intuitive "seeing." Heidegger's (1966) "meditative thinking" appears to be similar to this kind of contemplative "seeing." By contrast, ordinary thinking is, according to Heidegger, "calculative" and "representational"—in Wilber's terms, this is thinking in the narrow mode of egoic rationality. The paradox inherent in an all-encompassing theory invites us to shift from such narrowly rational thinking (hereafter simply "thinking") to a contemplative mode of awareness or "seeing."

Because of its radically holistic stance, Wilber's theory inspires paradoxes like these. Such paradoxes can open the horizon to what lies beyond the theorizing. Wilber writes with great passion that at times erupts in relentless, sharp criticality, at other times moves with poetic beauty. Clearly his intent is more than just to present his views; it is to stir his readers' souls and awaken them to their fullest evolutionary potential, in short, to self-transcendence (Puhakka 1995). When his theory is appreciated as being itself a manifestation of evolving consciousness, we can see that it contains within itself the potential for self-transcendence, just as do all living and evolving phenomena. This potential is held by paradoxes that emerge at the outer edge of the theory's immense scope when the theory is stretched as far as it can. And it is only because Wilber's theory lends itself to being stretched very far that paradoxes can become manifest. Theories of lesser scope and integrative power tend to invite concern and preoccupation with details, to add a little here, to improve a little there. To be sure, there is honing and working out of details still to be done in Wilber's theory as well. But the real gift of his theory lies in its self-transcending potential, made manifest by paradox. One way of stating a paradox that holds this potential is to say that, on the one hand, the theory opens to all possibilities yet, on the other hand, closes around an astonishingly rich elaboration of how everything works.

How do we approach paradox? Can we let it unfold and take delight in the impossibility it presents, remaining open to whatever may come? Or are we determined to solve the paradox "rationally" and settle the issue in one way or another? Throughout this chapter the reader may feel the tension between the purposeful stance that looks for solutions beyond the present situation and the more playful stance that joyfully embraces the situation as it is. In Wilber's theory, purposiveness and playfulness manifest as the two sides of the evolutionary movement, Ascent and Descent, Eros and Agape, wisdom and compassion. According to Wilber (1995, 347), one is not superior to the other; they are equally present, equally important in all manifestations of evolution.

"Seeing" finds kinship with playfulness, whereas ordinary "thinking" is more at home with purpose. But there is a kind of thinking that is playful in nature, yet can also reveal purposes of great depth. It is called "dialectical" thinking. Dialectic thrives on paradox, and even though it is "thinking," it can take the thinker to the verge of "seeing." According to Wilber, dialectic belongs to vision-logic, a mode of consciousness that lies just beyond the rational-egoic mode of "thinking" and represents the next cognitive step in the evolution of human consciousness. Wilber (1995) offers his work as an example of vision-logic (185, 622) in the hope that it will help accelerate the emergence of this and more subtle post-conventional modes of consciousness in people. His work is definitely purposeful. But I believe it is also playful, even though the play seems to be somewhat less emphasized. The purpose of this chapter is to appreciate the play in Wilber's theory, perhaps play with it some, and invite the reader to do the same.

The paradox contained in the previous sentence shows that, indeed, purpose and play, though seemingly opposites, move together in a dialectical dance. Dialectic moves between polarities, embracing opposites in a harmony that remains a mystery to "thinking" but reveals itself to "seeing."

FROM "THINKING" TO "SEEING"

The shift from "thinking" to "seeing"[1] begins to manifest in vision-logic, which in Wilber's developmental scheme is the prelude to the higher postconventional stages associated with genuinely transpersonal modes of consciousness. The following description of vision-logic by Wilber (1990) suggests that it utilizes both "thinking" and "seeing":

> Where the formal-mind establishes higher and creative relationships, vision-logic establishes networks of those relationships. The point is to place each proposition along-side numerous others, so as to be able to see, or "to vision," how the truth or falsity of any one proposition would affect the truth or falsity of the others. Such panoramic or vision-logic apprehends a mass network of ideas, how they influence each other, what their relationships are. It is thus the beginning of truly higher-order synthesizing capacity, of making connections, relating truths, coordinating ideas, integrating concepts. (288)

In vision-logic, "seeing" and "thinking" are both present; the objects of its envisioning are ideas and concepts, the stuff of thinking. However, in the higher postconventional stages, "seeing" becomes increasingly pure and of greater depth. That this is the case is suggested by Wilber's

(1995) description of the transition from vision-logic to the first transpersonal stage (the "psychic"): "Vision-logic gives way to direct vision, and the developmental view [which according to Wilber is characteristic of vision-logic] is supplemented by a vibratory view, where vibration is used to convey not so much a physicalistic nature as a quality of intensity of awareness" (622). "Seeing" gains yet more depth and intensity in further stages in Wilber's theory. The next stage beyond the psychic is the "subtle," and here "[v]ision gives way to intense luminosities (sometimes audible luminosities and bliss luminosities), and vibration is supplemented with a grasp of the subtle forms from which the gross domains radiate and vibrate" (622). At the "causal" stage, luminosity gives way to pure emptiness, in which the entire world of form is seen as a dream (622). Perhaps we could say that here "seeing" is seeing its own nature as void.

The shift from "thinking" to "seeing" is thus evident in Wilber's higher developmental stages. Beginning with the vision-logic of the centauric stage and moving through the psychic, subtle, and causal stages, "seeing" appears to become increasingly prominent and of greater luminosity and depth. But what is this "seeing" that can be accessed by many if not most people, perhaps only faintly and fleetingly at first, but with the possibility of increasing stability and clarity? Let me now attempt to characterize "seeing" in some detail and distinguish it from "thinking."

"Seeing" is direct and intuitive. Unlike perceiving, it does not depend on a particular sense-modality, such as the visual, even though one or sometimes simultaneously several sense-modalities may be involved (Hart, in press). It does not proceed linearly by drawing conclusions from premises as does ordinary rational "thinking" but spreads out spaciously, as it were, embracing and pervading rather than seizing or grasping at mental objects. It is important in this context to appreciate that "seeing" is not the same as "looking." "Looking" is more like "thinking" in that it is directed by internal agendas or drawn by external events. By contrast, "seeing" is not subject to the push and pull of either internal or external events. Its touch is playful and light; it does not cling to perspectives nor look for foundational truths but contemplates the forms and interrelationships of such perspectives and truths. These forms and interrelationships are the hidden presuppositions of rational thinking that become transparent to "seeing." For example, a physicist might contemplate how physical reality can be a "wave" and a "particle" at the same time. For rational thinking, the claim that reality consists of "particles" seems incongruous with the claim that it consists of "waves." But in contemplating the entire theory, the experimental procedures that yield "particle" results as well as another set of experimental procedures that yield "wave" results, the physicist may "see" how the rationales and assumptions of each procedure could not but yield the results they do, and perhaps even how these rationales and assumptions are embedded in the presuppositions of the theory. The complex structures concealed behind the seeming incongruity have now become transparent, and the physicist may "see" (as opposed to infer, surmise, or take on faith) how it is that reality is both wave and particle.

Wilber (1995) describes vision-logic as dialectical and nonlinear and as capable of unifying opposites and of "holding in mind contradictions" (185). Thinking (and perceiving) attach themselves to specific objects, whether abstract or concrete, and for this reason must abide by the principle of non-contradiction (i.e., a thing cannot at the same time be identical with itself and not identical with itself). On the other hand, the light touch of "seeing" pervades rather than seizes or grasps at an object. This means that "seeing" does not position itself as "subject" vis-a-vis the "object" but opens up a space that can hold the object even as the object is being not itself. Something being "not itself" or being "other than itself" would seem an impossibility, a self-contradiction, to linear thinking that grasps its object and demands that its identity be fixed at least for that moment of grasping. But because it can hold without grasping, "seeing" can create a transformational space in which contradictions are dialectically embraced.

According to Wilber, it is with vision-logic that consciousness first becomes aware of its fundamental structures and "finds its own operations increasingly transparent to itself" (187). Such transparency is inaccessible to "thinking" but is revealed to "seeing." "Seeing" beholds the operations of "thinking" and, depending on its depth and clarity, to a varying extent also the presuppositions of these operations.

"Seeing" should not be confused with rational self-reflection, which is also capable of taking its own operations as its object. Their difference lies in the fact that self-reflection shares the basic subject-object structure of all rational thinking. This limits its ability to penetrate the basis of its own operations. It can reflect on the object and uncover its presuppositions. But, given its identification, however subtle, with the subject, ordinary self-reflection cannot uncover its own presuppositions, and hence cannot uncover the deeper presuppositions it shares with the object. In other words, the operations that constitute the subject-object polarity are not accessible to rational self-reflection. For this reason, its attempts to turn toward this deeper presuppositional ground are doomed to an infinite regress, an endless and futile chase of object by subject, which Sartre (1988/1942) has described so well. By contrast, "seeing" is not bound to the subject-object structure. Indeed, in "seeing," this structure tends to soften, loosen up, and in some instances it may altogether dissolve.

A simple exercise may provide experiential grounding for these points about "thinking" and "seeing." Thus, to observe directly in your own experience the futility and infinite regress of subject chasing object in "thinking," take a moment to consider the question, "Who am I?" Resolve to get as clear an answer to this question as you can. All sorts of answers of the type "I am ____" will soon come, but rather than focusing attention on these, always return to the "I" that is giving the answer and looking at the answer, and try to get as clear an idea of this "I" as possible. Notice how the mind soon turns into a battleground of mounting tension. The "I" chasing after itself by looping back on itself might continue forever, were it not for the subtle but intensifying mental and physical tension that is likely soon to become unbearable enough to put an end to the exercise.

The same question, "Who am I?" will do for exploring "seeing" as well. But this time, instead of resolving to get hold of the "I," relax back into it without looking for it and without even trying to look at it, yet remaining aware. Answers may come in the form of thoughts or mental images, and the "I" may also be there looking at the thoughts and mental images. Simply let them all arise and pass away without chasing after or trying to suppress any of them. As awareness begins to detach from its familiar support, the subject-object structure, feelings of confusion and disorientation may at first be there. But let the feelings of confusion and disorientation be; accept them and relax into them while remaining alert and aware. With the increasing detachment from, or disidentification with, the thoughts and mental images, you may begin to "see" how the mental act of grasping actually constitutes the thought or image (object) being grasped, and also constitutes the "I" (subject) doing the grasping. You may also notice how this act of grasping is in a subtle way already present in the act of "looking" at thoughts and mental images. As progress is made with this exercise, thoughts and images no longer appear as "solid" mental objects before the "I" who looks at them, but they begin to arise as mental forms. Eventually, they can be "seen" in their very arising, and in this arising their own constitution tends to become increasingly transparent.[2]

How does "seeing" manifest in the human world of everyday affairs? I believe that glimpses of it occur fairly commonly in the form of insights and illuminations that may suddenly bring clarity to, or open up new perspectives on, all sorts of human problems, from mathematical quandaries and engineering design problems to interpersonal conflicts. The clarity and completeness, or depth, of the shift from "thinking" to "seeing" vary among people, and also vary for individuals at different times. In the vision-logic mode, "seeing" may be rather fleeting and sporadic.

Also, in vision-logic, "thinking" and "seeing" operate so closely together that it is easy to miss the subtle qualitative shift from one activity to the other. This shift occurs when there is a detachment or disidentification from the operative structures of consciousness, allowing contemplation of the very activity and forms of thinking. The radical holism and openness of Wilber's theory can itself nudge the reader toward this shift.

RADICAL HOLISM AND OPENNESS

Radical holism is the view that all things are connected and that "all things" means every thing; nothing should be left out. Indeed, Wilber purports to accommodate in one seamless whole both sides of all dualities whatsoever—subjectivity and objectivity, interiority and exteriority, living and nonliving, mind and body, spirit and matter, and so on. Evolutionary theories in general tend to be holistic in that they seek to integrate and find continuities where discontinuities appear in nature. But most evolutionary and developmental theories are restricted to particular domains, such as the biological, psychological, emotional, or cognitive. They therefore do not meet Wilber's standard of radical holism.

The inclusion of everything is not the only criterion of radical holism. How things are included, or what the inclusion means, is also important. True holism avoids both the reductionistic and the elevationistic forms of the pre/trans fallacy (Wilber 1990). That is, things should be included in the whole while fully respecting their integrity and reality as they are, without either reducing them to what might be presumed to be a more basic reality, such as "matter," or elevating them to what might be thought of as a more ultimate reality, e.g., "spirit." In other words, true holism, according to Wilber (1995, 33), has no bias toward either spirit or matter, or toward any other ontological category: "Reality is not composed of things or processes; it is not composed of atoms or quarks; it is not composed of wholes nor does it have any parts. Rather, it is composed of whole/parts, or holons" (Wilber 1995, 33). Holons are ontologically neutral; phenomena in all spheres of the Kosmos manifest the holonic structure, and no holon is more, or less, "real" than any other. This kind of ontological neutrality is perhaps the most radical meaning of Wilber's holism.

Open-endedness is another facet of Wilber's holism. No holons are just "whole"; all are also part of more inclusive holons that are part of more inclusive holons. We find this pattern indefinitely all the way up and all the way down the evolutionary scale. We live in systems within systems, contexts within contexts, indefinitely, says Wilber (1995, 33-40), and the systems are constantly sliding and the contexts shifting. A universe conceived as unfolding and enfolded upwards and downwards without end opens up the vision to a limitless expanse. It also effectively removes all bases for certainty and completeness. Such a vision must thus itself be necessarily open-ended and so rob itself of certainty and completeness as well. Indeed, the envisioning is part of the ongoing evolutionary process and thus can never be complete. Wilber (1995) does acknowledge that his vision is incomplete and open to revision (ix-x). As context for our further envisioning, Wilber's vision, like all contexts, is shifting.

But let us take a moment to appreciate, once again, the paradox here: a vision that purportedly includes everything is a vision so complete that it cannot complete itself. The logical impasse arrests rational thinking and in so doing may free up the inquirer again to move toward contemplation in the "seeing" mode. We might then contemplate the very incoherence and impossibility of such a vision, until it yields to a self-transcending openness that accommodates the vision as well as its ineffable horizon. This kind of openness does not stand on the same ground as the vision it opens. When the vision includes everything, includes all grounds to stand on, it appears that the openness is, ultimately, a groundless expanse that belongs to no vision at all but to the visionary consciousness that momentarily transcends its own visions. Yet it does not even belong to the visionary consciousness. We might perhaps say that when the visionary consciousness (subject) releases the vision (object) that is transcended, at that moment both belong, momentarily, to the groundless expanse.

Such a radical openness shifts the focus from the vision or the envisioning consciousness to the dialogical relationship between them. This relationship is inherently open; in structural terms, it is inherently unstable, constantly releasing its structures in acts of self-transcendence. Greater instability and openness to self-transcendence are typical of the higher noospheric levels, and in Wilber's terms, the envisioning of the entire process of evolution would seem to be quite high on the evolutionary scale. But it is not necessary to accept Wilber's interpretation of the evolutionary hypothesis to appreciate how the contemplation of everything, when such contemplation includes itself and becomes transparent to itself, can be a profoundly transformative, self-transcending act.

TOTALIZING AND EXCLUSIVITY

Openness and self-transcending engagement are the hallmarks of vision-logic that release the thinker into "seeing." But an invitation to vision-logic is not all that Wilber is offering. He also offers a rational articulation of the vision of everything. Such an articulation manifests a "totalizing" tendency that is the opposite of the openness to which radical holism calls us. Radical holism calls us to contemplate everything. By contrast, to totalize is to say what everything is or where everything is going. And this closes the vision by gathering the infinite possibilities of an open vision into a finite account. Totalizing is necessarily exclusionary, for in saying what things are or how they work, other possibilities, other ways of articulating, are excluded. The greater the scope of the totalizing claim, the more radical is the exclusion of alternatives.[3]

Totalizing has a bad reputation; it epitomizes the sins of modernity in the eyes of most postmodern critics. Indeed, these sins are many, and they are scrutinized with great clarity by Wilber himself. However, the tendency to totalize that I am concerned with here is intrinsic to all explanatory and descriptive endeavors, and as such, it is neither "good" nor "bad." Holism also has a reputation, usually "good" or "desirable." But in this chapter, such evaluations are set aside. Holism is not "good" or "desirable" and totalizing is not "bad" or undesirable." Both are equally necessary, equally fundamental, to the human endeavor of inquiry and knowing. Holism is the stance of openness to what has not yet been, and perhaps cannot be, articulated or spoken of (but is not necessarily "unknown" in the sense of not being present or accessible to awareness). Totalizing is the stance of speaking with the fullness of one's capacity of that which one's mind and intellect has grasped. The tendency to totalize, in this fundamental sense, is present as long as there is a desire to know and speak.

The totalizing tendency is evident in evolutionary theories that explain how new phenomena emerge. But few theories manifest this tendency as outrageously as Wilber's, simply because of their limited scope. Wilber's theory not only purports to include everything but in one broad sweep sets aside the possibility that anything has been left out or excluded. The theory's persuasiveness has much to do with its claim that all things are at least potentially included. But the real power of the theory has to do with its ability to convey a sense that this is necessarily so, that indeed nothing could have been left out, that everything has a place.

Such confidence can lift the human spirit and restore hope in a fragmented, relativized postmodern world, and this indeed appears to be one of Wilber's goals. The coherence and integrative power of Wilber's theory owes much to the notion of "holon." The part/whole structure of a holon constitutes the basic organizing principle, the one common feature, of all phenomena in what Wilber takes to be the four spheres of the Kosmos, from the most elementary and primitive to the most complex. There is nothing that is a whole without also being part of other, more extensive or more encompassing wholes, and vice versa; there is nothing that is just a part of something else without being a whole in and of itself.

Yet the concept of holon is an abstraction almost devoid of content. It does not tell us anything about the nature of reality or the order of things and thus does not really exclude anything. Therefore the claim that the holonic structure is ubiquitous is ethically and ontologically virtually neutral, and for this reason does not amount to a significant totalizing claim. On the other hand, abstraction is essential to totalizing. Without abstraction, totalizing would not be possible.[4] Even if it puts the viewer at some distance from what is viewed, Wilber's theory offers a single lens through which everything can be viewed. The very abstractness and lack of particular content is what allows the holonic structure to be the thread that connects all things.

A single lens as wide and well-crafted as Wilber's theory can facilitate the shift to vision-logic and beyond in a way that multiple lenses offering more limited perspectives cannot. For example, postmodern science and philosophy promote the idea of using multiple lenses. There are obvious virtues in the diversity of information and integration this allows and even celebrates. From the viewpoint of postmodern multiperspectival rationality, a single lens would seem anathema, a regressive move toward the metanarratives of modernity. Indeed, a single lens, especially when crafted for an almost perfect prescription, can reveal all things near and far with such clarity and smooth continuity as to induce forgetfulness of the fact that one is using a lens at all. But for now, I will set aside the postmodern arguments, meritorious as they may be, and simply note that awakening from such forgetfulness is possible. And when it occurs, a fine prescription lens might inspire interest in the lens itself and how it works. No longer distracted by the search for a better lens or by the task of comparing and choosing between lenses, we might become fascinated by the very activity of looking through a lens—any lens.

THE TOTALIZING CLAIM IN WILBER'S THEORY

The concept of a holon provides connections among all things and makes possible a lens of immense scope. Totalizing could be compared to the form or curvature of the lens. In Wilber's theory, the form of the lens is provided by the claim that there is a particular direction in which evolution is proceeding. The great evolutionary synthesis of modern science, notes Wilber (1995), is the realization that the "two arrows of time," entropy and evolution, have joined forces and that significant aspects of the physical universe are heading in the same direction as the biological and the mental (14). The directionality of evolution is the basic premise of Wilber's theory: "Whatever else we might say, the world does hang together, and evolution does have a direction: Eros as Spirit-in-action" (487). And what is this direction? It is toward Spirit's own self-realization. Eros is Spirit's Ascent toward higher and higher unities. Along with Hegel and Schelling, Wilber sees evolution as not simply a drive toward Spirit but as the drive of Spirit toward Spirit (487). Holons at all levels of evolution manifest a tendency toward self-transcendence, and self-transcendence manifests as the emergence of hierarchically higher level holons that are capable of integrating lower level holons, capable of greater depth and of more encompassing awareness.

The premise of Wilber's theory, simply stated, is that evolution is the journey of Spirit in the direction of greater awareness or self-knowledge. This statement is neither ontologically nor ethically neutral. It is a totalizing claim that seems to favor a certain direction while excluding others. That is, evolution is heading in the direction of greater awareness and integration, and heading in any other direction is wrong.[5] The favored direction is "right," and other directions (i.e., those that do not lead to greater awareness or integration) are "wrong." The latter result in all sorts of pathological regressions, dissolutions, developmental arrests, etc. (Wilber 1995, 67). According to Wilber, "[t]he evolution of holons is not all sweetness and light, as some proponents of 'evolutionary progress' seem to maintain. For the grim fact is that greater structural complexity—whether individual or social—means that more things can go horribly wrong" (101). The notion that things can go wrong is without a doubt the most controversial of Wilber's claims. An all-encompassing theory such as Wilber's tends not to leave margins for things that deviate from, or for people that disagree with, the vision and direction of the theory. Yet it is the very boldness of this claim that opens another doorway to vision-logic and beyond. For contemplating the totalizing claim appreciatively can bring to the fore an excluded view that, given the theory's all-inclusiveness, had to be already included in it. Thus, totalizing meets radical holism in a paradox that awakens dialectical consciousness.

PLAY AND PURPOSE:
DIALECTICAL ENGAGEMENT OF WILBER'S VISION

The dialectic moves between radical holism and totalizing to reveal the two poles, each presupposed by the other. The totalizing claim is that evolution has a particular direction. The emphasis is on where everything is heading, namely, toward awareness and integration and not anywhere else. But if everything is moving in the same direction, what does anywhere else mean? Nothing, except that it is where everything is not heading. Thus the denied possibility of other directions forms the shadow against which the beam of light makes visible the one direction where everything is going.

By contrast, radical holism embraces "everything " and spreads out the beam to light up the shadows as well and so reveals the opposite pole to Wilber's original thesis: Everything, everywhere, at all times is a manifestation of Spirit's unfoldment. Wherever it happens to be going, it is moving toward greater awareness. Any direction leads to greater awareness. So evolution really has no particular direction, at least none that could be meaningfully stated.

This opposite vision can be as big and generous as the one that posits a direction to evolution and is capable of including, without bias or favoritism, all four spheres of the Kosmos. It does not necessarily commit one to narrow empiricism, crude hedonism, or any other variation of flatland ontology. This vision is best captured in the Hindu notion of the cosmic play of Shiva, *shivalila*, in which Shiva dances the Kosmos in and out of existence through convoluted steps that have no meaning or purpose extrinsic to the dance itself. Any purposes that may appear are simply manifestations of the creative play, analogous to rules that children make up for their games just for fun. On a smaller scale, this vision has proponents among evolutionary biologists, e.g., H.G. Maturana and F. Varela (1987), whose view of evolution as a "natural drift" emphasizes the intrinsic creativity of nature that is not so much geared toward producing the "fittest" as it is toward creating anything that she can get away with.

We might call this vision the playful model, in contrast to the evolutionary or purposeful model. With the purposeful model, one views everything as incomplete and imperfect but moving toward completion and perfection. With the playful model, one views everything as always already perfect and finds that there is no particular direction to evolution and thus there are no flaws or mistakes.

The playful model has much appeal, but before adopting it as our final "position," we might contemplate the nature and bases of its appeal. There is a thrill and a sense of freedom in play. The thrill and sense of freedom have much to do with the order the play defies, the anticipations it confounds, the differences between the high and the low that it levels, and the distinction between the mundane and the sublime that it promises to transcend. Indeed, the players of the Kosmic game do not just make up rules and obstacles for fun. The game is always already going on and so the rules are in place before any of us come to play. Thus the very playfulness of the Kosmic Dance begs the seriousness it mocks, conceals samsaric suffering before it is transcended. Here the totalizing tendency is to ask, "Where is the purpose behind the play?" "What is really going on?" and discover the rules of the game, the obstacles to be overcome—in other words, that there may be serious work to be accomplished, a journey to be traveled, before true freedom can be found.

Thus the dialectic moves between play and purpose. Playfulness is celebrated in Wilber's notion of the Descent, the movement downward to embrace and celebrate the manifold of creation in all its diversity. Spirit is present in every movement of the Kosmos, says Wilber, "dancing, fully and divine in every gesture of the universe, never really lost and never really found, but present from the start and all along, a wink and a nod from the radiant Abyss" (489). The premise of his theory, however, seems to be aligned with Ascent, the movement toward self-knowledge and awareness, and the unification of diversity in this awareness. So purpose, not play, seems to be the prime mover at the outset and to be preeminent throughout the journey in Wilber's big picture of evolution. Their equal status does not become evident until the journey is over, at which point the movements upward and downward are completed and fully integrated in the nondual. Presumably we then realize that all purposes have always already been accomplished, that the evolutionary strivings of humanity and of the entire Kosmos—the Atman project—never occurred, and it is all exactly as it should be (Wilber 1997, 57). But even before such final realization, the hold of the Atman project on us can perhaps be loosened a bit by appreciating the dialectic of the purposeful and playful models.

Let us see how it works in everyday life. Our families, work environments, and communities, not to mention our beliefs and values, form systems within systems, contexts within contexts in which we live. When we are aware of them, they are objects, or the content of our consciousness; when we are not aware, they may form the context for this content (Vaughan, 1980, 1993). These systems and contexts are shifting, says Wilber. But how are they shifting? The purposeful model would have it that, as part of the big picture of evolution, they are shifting in the direction of greater integration and greater transparency. This is Spirit's movement toward greater self-awareness. But all kinds of shifts and changes occur in everyday life that do not seem to manifest increased awareness or integration. In fact, from the moment of awakening in the morning we are surrounded, inundated by such changes: the chemical additives in the breakfast cereal, the junkmail pouring out of the mailbox in ever-growing piles, the traffic jams, the pollution, the frantic pace of life—are these just changes, as opposed to evolutionary changes? If they are not genuine evolutionary changes (i.e., ultimately leading to growth and integration), they are exceptions to the evolutionary process, aberrations or mistakes, so to speak. But here radical holism comes to the fore and champions the playful model. We might contemplate the origins of the aberrations (Wilber's regressions, dissociations, developmental arrests, etc.) and the forces that propel their twisted movements.

Surely, all that is part of the Great Kosmic Dance as well! For everything is, at every moment, a manifestation of Spirit on a journey toward knowing itself. In Wilber's (1997) words, "We wish to get from where Spirit is not, to where Spirit is. But there is no place where Spirit is not." (282) The realization of Spirit's everpresence appears to bring about a shift of perspective from the purposeful (wishing to get from where Spirit is not, to where it is) to the playful model (there is no place where Spirit is not). However, if anything is Spirit, then anything goes and there is seemingly no particular direction to evolution. If a city being immersed in pollution and children dying of lead poisoning are as much evolution as is the development of multicultural tolerance and compassion, then nothing meaningful or coherent can be said about the journey. The systems and contexts are shifting, but they are, for the playful model, just shifting. So, which has the final word—the purposeful or the playful model?

How do we approach this question? The desire to settle the issues between the models and the feeling of frustration at the lack of resolution betray our predilection for purpose. The purposeful model, perhaps in the form articulated by Wilber's theory, then becomes the context of our thinking. But relaxing our grasping after resolution, we can allow this context to shift—and shift us, the thinkers, in the direction of "seeing." This is, of course, play. However, it does not lead to the conclusion that the playful model is true—that would be a resolution sought after by "thinking." The play of dialectic avoids both extremes and rides the shift in the middle, as it were.[6] From there we may contemplate deeply the meaning and implications of the playful and purposeful models and see, just behind each model, its opposite taking form. We might even see one sliding into the other, almost imperceptibly, like the fish that turn into birds and vice versa in an Escher drawing.

When seen as a manifestation of Spirit, the mindless, wasteful chaos and frustration of a morning hour spent in a traffic jam may reveal perfection in its very absurdity. Yet, however glorious and uplifting such perfection may seem, the dialectic does not end in its celebration but opens up to its opposite in an ever deeper appreciation of the suffering and imperfection—the Atman project, the nightmare of history (Wilber 1997, 56)—that now can be seen as the ground from which all perfection and glory spring.

COMPASSION AND SUFFERING

The concept of "something going wrong" is central to the purposeful model. Evolution proceeds in the direction of greater awareness and self-knowledge, and movement in any other direction manifests as a variety of pathologies, such as regressions, developmental arrests, and dissolutions. And, as we have seen earlier, Wilber emphasizes that such pathologies do occur. Indeed, "a factor of possible pathology is built into every evolutionary step. . . ." (Wilber 1995, 103), and the chance of something going profoundly wrong increases with the increasing complexity of the higher order holons. For example, atoms don't get cancer but animals and humans do (Wilber 1995, 101). At the human level, evolutionary errors or flaws manifest not just in the biological sphere but in the mental sphere as various kinds of neuroses and mental illnesses. They may even manifest as "erroneous" or "mistaken" views of evolution itself! All sorts of flaws in the social and cultural spheres are too evident to need cataloguing here.

The ubiquitousness of flaws lends urgency to the question: How does one embrace something with compassion while regarding it as flawed?

Ordinarily, compassion is understood as the capacity and willingness to feel with another (without the compulsion to change or improve the other's condition). The capacity and willingness to feel with the other is thus not conditional on being able to correct the flaw. Indeed, the call to compassion can become a real challenge precisely in those situations where nothing can be done to change things. When compassion flows out from one being to the other, what does this compassion embrace: the being in spite of and apart from its flaws, or the being with flaws and all? If the former, what is the meaning of "'compassion"? If the latter, what, if any, meaning does "pathology" or "flaw" have?

The purposeful model tells us that compassion is the embrace from above, the Descent that, because it comes from higher level holons of greater depth and inclusivity, is capable of embracing and integrating lower level holons while fully respecting their individual wholenesses (Wilber 1995, 339-41). But does compassion really manifest as an embrace from above?

Wilber's theory (the purposeful model), is not concerned with the actual manifestation of compassion as much as it is with the developmental capacities and preconditions for it. The "embrace from above" is a structural concept that refers to the greater depth and hence greater capacity to integrate lower level holons. Wilber points out emphatically—and quite correctly, I believe—that the hierarchical level-distinction is crucial for understanding the structural aspect of compassion. It is an embrace "from above" that integrates and connects lower-level holons while preserving their distinctness. On the other hand, same-level holons can enter into a "pathological communion" (Wilber 1995, 41) that may suppress or even altogether obliterate distinctions among the holons. Such a communion is not genuine compassion.

The structural account is inherently abstract and not meant to address the concrete, experiential manifestations of compassion, such as its experienced source (e.g., God), direction (e.g., from me to you or you to me), or felt power. Thus, even though Wilber might say that the compassion of Mother Teresa "embraces from above," this does not mean that, as an experiential actuality, her compassion flows from a superior position "downward." Questions like, "where is 'above'?" and "what is embracing and what is being embraced?" are relevant to the phenomenology of compassion but their meanings are very different from those they have in Wilber's abstract structural account. For example, as a devout Catholic, Mother Teresa views herself as an instrument of God, a channel through which God's compassion flows. From the viewpoint of Wilber's theory, her capabilities may in structural terms "embrace from above." But from the viewpoint of her own interiority, she probably experiences herself as "embraced from above" and sees this experience as inspiring and nurturing her compassion. On the other hand, a nontheistic practitioner of compassion (e.g., a Buddhist or an Advaita Vedantin), might not experience a vertical directionality in the flow or source of compassion.

The direction "from above" in Wilber's structural account of compassion reflects the fundamental premise of his theory concerning the direction of evolution. When compassion is viewed as an experiential actuality, on the other hand, this direction need not be assumed; in fact no direction whatever need be assumed. It is this latter meaning that is usually operative in the various spiritual traditions and their practical disciplines for cultivating compassion.

A well-known Tibetan Buddhist practice of compassion tells me to regard every being I encounter as having at some time been my mother. Seeing a person who just viciously attacked me as my mother is not easy, but doing so can certainly take the edge off of any contempt or superiority I might feel toward this person. But the practice of compassion can become much more powerful if I can see the other not just as having been my mother in the past, but as the very source and sustenance of my life and spirit now. Clearly, the point of this exercise is to disabuse the person of any notion that his or her self is embracing from above and to cultivate the realization that this self is being embraced from without by the same source that lies within it. When we see the other as God—not just as "part of God" but as God in his or her full glory, as being in no way distinct from our own perfect Self—then compassion flows effortlessly and naturally, in fact quite inevitably. And it flows not "from above" but to, and from, all directions equally. When we accept other beings just the way they are, with all their flaws, as God's creation, or as God him/herself, then compassion becomes easy and natural.

This sounds like the playful model and the view that everything manifests the glory of creation fully, that there are no mistakes and no flaws whatsoever. Indeed, the playful model celebrates the intrinsic perfection of all beings. But now we might ask, if all things are perfect simply the way they are, what is the meaning of 'perfection'? Is it not just a meaningless, empty word?

Indeed, it would be just an empty word, were it not for those blessed moments of release from our daily suffering that now and then grace us and reveal perfection right under our noses where, before such a moment, perfection had been unimaginable, perhaps quite inconceivable. It may be worth pausing here to contemplate such a moment, or to reflect on memories of such precious epiphanies in our own experience. They seem to involve a shift of consciousness more profound than what can be fully captured by conceptualizing a turn from Ascent to Descent. This shift may momentarily disengage the structures of self-transcendence as well as of "embrace from above."

When those moments are gone, we might reflect as follows: It is suffering that calls us to compassion. There is no room for suffering or for any kind of seriousness in the playful model. On the other hand, samsaric seriousness and suffering are very much honored in the purposeful model. Whenever there is incompleteness, goals not yet attained, there is suffering. In the evolutionary process, at every level there are goals not yet attained. Some of the most insightful and beautiful passages in *Sex, Ecology, Spirituality* are those that describe the course of Ascent that leaves holons at every pinnacle of self-transcendence, by virtue of their very openness to self-transcendence, necessarily incomplete or uncertain and reaching for further transcendence in the elusive quest for completeness. These are the IOU's ("incomplete or uncertain") that holons owe to the Kosmos, and, Wilber says, Kosmos will never redeem them. This is an amazing and profound contemporary interpretation of the Buddha's first and second Noble Truths concerning suffering.

Without the call of suffering, there would be no call to compassion. But without seeing the perfection of each being, compassion would not flow naturally. And true compassion can only flow naturally when the barriers to its flow are removed, when one sees the other as not something from one's evolutionary past but as one's very self in the here and now.

CONCLUSION

Is evolution a play, or does it have a purpose? Is it fish or is it birds? Or maybe some kind of fishbird? The answers that are given to these questions divide us into contending camps—the ego and the eco, the Wilberian hierarchists and the anti-Wilberian heterarchists, and so on.

But if, instead of trying to grasp and formulate the correct as opposed to the incorrect position, we were to engage the dialectic of these questions as an activity that makes salient their bases and interconnections, then we would not lose sight of the fish lurking between the birds and the birds between the fish, and we would realize how it is that neither pole in the dialectic nor even the synthesis of the two gives us the absolute truth.

Yet, far from succumbing to fragmentation and relativism, the dialectical vision of the whole begins to shine with extraordinary beauty and aliveness. The vision, to borrow Tarthang Tulku's (1978, 1987) expression, "thaws out" and becomes visioning. Like the smooth flow of in-breath and out-breath, the visioning moves between two poles without getting stuck in either, includes and moves beyond synthesis without freezing into either of its poles. The truth of "both" forever opens up to the truth of "neither," thereby becoming increasingly transparent. And the truth of "neither," seen with clarity and compassion, does not withdraw into nihilism but reveals how it is that the fish keep turning into birds and the birds into fish, the purposes into play and vice versa. In active visioning, we would not be inclined to reject either pole as absolutely false or nonexistent but might, instead, embrace them appreciatively and lightly enough to allow for the unfathomable space of transformation between them. And without yet even grasping at that space, we would remain open to the release that again and again disengages the structures of both models. It may then become possible to see that this space of transformation has no foundation at all; it is the groundless ground from which things arise and to which they return. It is the emptiness in which, Wilber says, the IOUs are finally redeemed.

Acknowledgments

I would like to thank Donald Rothberg and Sean Kelly for their comments and meticulous editorial work that helped improve the clarity and readability of this chapter. I am also grateful to Roberta Jacobs, Stacie Rayner, and Jeannette Broyles for their valuable suggestions.

Notes

1. For differentiating "thinking" from "seeing" I am much indebted to conversations with my colleagues Fred J. Hanna of Johns Hopkins University and Peter L. Nelson of Texas Instruments. Elsewhere (1996) I have described "seeing" as "authentic knowing."

2. Detailed instructions for meditations on the mind and mental objects that can help develop the capacity to "see" the structures and operations of the mental processes can be found in various Buddhist meditative traditions. See, e.g., U Pandita (1992) from the vipassana tradition of southeast Asia, Tarthang Tulku (1987) and Norbu (1987) from the Tibetan tradition, and Beck (1987) from the Zen tradition.

3. The meanings of "holism" and "totalizing" as used in this essay differ somewhat from their more common meanings. Thus "holism" commonly means "contextual knowing" or "knowing something in context." In this essay, however, "holism" refers simply to the attitude or stance of openness, or readiness to include all—a stance that is presupposed by "knowing something in context." Such an openness does not presuppose the distinction between "content" (i.e., "something") and "context." The common meaning of "totalizing" has to do with the claim that all can be articulated and accounted for. The attempt to give as full an account as possible does not, of course, amount to such a claim, but it does "tend" in the direction of such a claim. In this essay, "totalizing" is hence meant to indicate such a "tendency."

4. Buchanan (1996) has called attention to the fact that "holon" is an abstraction, not something that can be directly experienced in any of the four spheres of the Kosmos. In a thoughtful, penetrating critique from a Whiteheadian perspective, Buchanan argues that Wilber's theory is guilty of the "fallacy of misplaced concreteness" that precludes immediate experiential access to the foundational notions of the theory. Buchanan's critique, however, addresses the theory's stance toward its object (the universe), but not really what the theory says about the nature of the object.

5. A distinction between two senses of "wrong" may be recognized in this context: a) "wrong" means simply difficult or painful—in this sense things seem to go wrong but actually lead to further evolutionary growth; b) "wrong" means going against the evolutionary grain, which genuinely disrupts or arrests growth. There is plenty of room in Wilber's theory for the first sense of "wrong." It is the second sense and its implications that are being explored here.

6. For an excellent presentation of the use of dialectic in contemplative inquiry, see Fenner (1994).

References

Beck, C. 1993. *Nothing special: Living Zen*. San Francisco: Harper.

Broughton, J. 1975. The development of natural epistemology in adolescence and early adulthood. Doctoral dissertation, Harvard University.

Buchanan, J. 1996. Whitehead and Wilber: Contrasts in theory. *The Humanistic Psychologist* 24 (2): 231-256.

Fenner, P. 1994. Spiritual inquiry in Buddhism. *ReVision* 17 (2): 13-24.

Gebser, J. 1985. *The ever-present origin*. Athens: Ohio University Press.

Hart, T. In press. Inspiration: Exploring the experience and its meaning. *The Journal of Humanistic Psychology*.

Heidegger, M. [1953] 1961. *An Introduction to Metaphysics*. Translated by R. Manheim. Garden City, N. Y.: Doubleday & Co.

_____. 1966. *Discourse on thinking*. New York: Harper.

Loevinger, J. 1977. *Ego development*. San Francisco: Jossey-Bass.

Maturana, H., and F. Varela. 1987. *The tree of knowledge: The biological roots of human understanding*. Boston: Shambhala.

Norbu, N. 1987. *The cycle of day and night: An essential Tibetan text on the practice of contemplation*. Barrytown, N.Y.: Station Hill Press.

Puhakka, K. 1995. Restoring connectedness in the Kosmos: A healing tale of a deeper order. [Review of K. Wilber: *Sex, ecology, spirituality*.] *The Humanistic Psychologist* 23 (3), 373-391.

_____. 1997. An invitation to authentic knowing. In *Spiritual knowing: Alternative epistemic perspectives*, edited by T. Hart, P. Nelson, and K. Puhakka. Carrollton, Ga.: State University of West Georgia Studies in the Social Sciences, Vol. 34.

Sartre, J. P. [1942] 1966. *Being and nothingness*. Translated by H. E. Barnes. New York: Washington Square Press.

Tarthang Tulku. 1978. *Time, space and knowledge*. Berkeley: Dharma Publishing.

_____. 1987. *Love of knowledge*. Berkeley: Dharma Publishing.

U Pandita. 1992. *In this very life*. Boston: Wisdom Publications.

Varela, F., E. Thompson, and E. Rosch. 1991. *The embodied mind: Cognitive science and human experience*. Cambridge: MIT Press.

Vaughan, F. 1993. Healing and wholeness: Transpersonal psychotherapy. In *Paths beyond ego: The transpersonal vision*, edited by R. Walsh and F. Vaughan. Los Angeles.: Tarcher/Perigree.

_____. 1980. Transpersonal psychotherapy: Context, content, and process. In *Beyond ego: Transpersonal dimensions in psychology*, edited by R. Walsh and F. Vaughan. Los Angeles: Tarcher/Perigree.

Whitehead, A. [1929] 1979. *Process and reality: An essay in cosmology*. Edited by D. Griffin and D. Sherburne. New York: Free Press.

Wilber, K. 1990. *Eye to eye: The quest for the new paradigm*. Rev. ed. Boston: Shambhala.

_____. 1995. *Sex. ecology, spirituality: The spirit of evolution*. Boston: Shambhala.

_____. 1997. *The eye of spirit: An integral vision for a world gone slightly mad*. Boston: Shambhala.

Part Five

Ken Wilber
Responds

14

Ken Wilber

A More Integral Approach

I am deeply appreciative of the editors making this space available to me to respond to my critics and to otherwise join in this conversation initiated by some of my work. I have written a long response to many of the chapters in this volume, as well as to several other reviews of my work (both pro and con). This response can be found in *The Eye of Spirit: An Integral Vision for a World Gone Slightly Mad* (1997a). It deals with the work of Stan Grof, Michael Washburn, Roger Walsh, Peggy Wright, Michael Zimmerman, Donald Rothberg, Robert McDermott, Jenny Wade, Gus diZerega and Richard Smoley, Charles Alexander, Robert Kegan, and Michael Commons, among others. What follows is a condensed version of that response, along with material on those authors in this volume not treated in my book.

MICHAEL WASHBURN AND THE DYNAMIC GROUND

WE CAN BEGIN WITH THE WORK OF MICHAEL WASHBURN AND HIS concept of the Dynamic Ground. Washburn is a very clear and careful writer, whose formulations I have always appreciated, even when we disagree. I never fail to learn something interesting from his presentations, and I have always been a staunch supporter of his publications. It is therefore rather disappointing that he tends to misrepresent my overall model. Since this misunderstanding is quite common (and is found in many of the respondents in this volume), I will be as careful as I can in summarizing my view.

A Brief Summary of My Consciousness Model

As explained in *Eye to Eye* (1996c) and *Transformations of Consciousness* (1986) (and again summarized in *Brief History* [1996d]), the overall consciousness system (the upper left quadrant) has, I believe, at least *three main components*.

First, there are the relatively permanent or *enduring structures* and competences—those features that, once they emerge in development, tend to remain in existence, such as linguistic competence, cognitive capacities, spatial coordination, motor skills, and so forth. The most important of these enduring structures I call the *basic structures*, which are the basic holons of consciousness itself (e.g., sensation, perception, impulse, image, symbol, concept, rule, meta-rule, vision-logic, psychic, subtle, causal). *The basic structures of consciousness are essentially the traditional Great Holarchy of Being* (as presented by, say, Plotinus or Asanga or Aurobindo).

Second, there are those features that are relatively *transitional* or temporary; they come into existence but subsequently are phased out or replaced. The stages of moral development (according to Kohlberg and Gilligan) are prime examples. When moral stage 2 emerges, it does not so much incorporate moral stage 1 as replace it. Some of the more important *transitional structures* include *worldviews* (e.g., archaic, magical, mythic, mental, existential, psychic, and so on; cf. Gebser); *self-needs* (e.g., safety, belongingness, self-esteem, self-actualization, self-transcendence; cf. Maslow); *self-identity* (e.g., uroboros, typhon, persona, ego, centaur, soul; cf. Loevinger); and *moral stages* (e.g., preconventional, conventional, postconventional, post-postconventional; cf. Nucci, Kohlberg, Gilligan). Of course, once a particular transition structure is present, it is as important and as real as any enduring structure; it's just that transitional structures are destined mostly to pass, enduring structures mostly to remain.

The important difference between the enduring structures and the transitional structures can easily be seen in a comparison of, say, Piaget and Kohlberg. With cognitive development in general, each stage is *incorporated* into subsequent stages, so that the junior is a crucial *component* of the senior. Once images emerge, for example, the individual has full and constant access to the capacity to form images. And images themselves will be an indispensable ingredient in the higher symbolic, conceptual, and formal thought. But with moral development, the process is quite different: higher structures do not so much incorporate as *replace* previous ones. Thus, a person at moral stage 4 does not have open access to moral stage 1, for those stages are mutually incompatible (a conformist does not simultaneously act as an egocentric rebel). In fact, a moral stage-4 person cannot even think in the terms of moral stage 1; those earlier structures have long ago dissolved and been replaced (barring fixation, repression, etc.).

Now, mediating between the basic structures and the transitional structures is the *self-system* or *self-sense* (or just the *self*), which is the third major component. The self-system is, in many ways, the most important of the three, because it is "where the action is." I have suggested (1984a, 1984b, 1996d) that the self-system is the locus of several crucial capacities and operations, including: *identification* (the locus of self-identity), *organization* (that which gives cohesiveness to the psyche), *will* (the locus of choice within the constraints of the present developmental level), *defense* (the locus of defense mechanisms, phase-specific and phase-appropriate, hierarchically organized), *metabolism* (the "digestion" of experience), and *navigation* (developmental choices).

I further suggested that the self mediates between basic structures and transitional structures, and that it does so in this fashion: because the self is the locus of identification, each time the self identifies with a developmentally-unfolding basic structure, that exclusive identification generates (or is the support of) the corresponding set of transitional structures. Thus, for example, when the self identifies with preoperational thought (symbols and concepts), this supports a preconventional moral stance (Kohlberg), a set of safety needs (Maslow), and a protective self-sense (Loevinger). When higher basic structures emerge (say, concrete operational rules), then the self (barring arrest) will eventually switch its central identity to this higher and wider organization, and this will generate a new moral stance (conventional), a new set of self-needs (belongingness), and a new self-sense (conformist persona)—and so forth.

At this new and higher stage, the self will have free and perfect access to the previous basic structures, such as symbols and concepts, but not to the previous transitional structures, for those were generated precisely when the self was exclusively identified with the lower stages, an identification now outgrown. Thus, basic structures are preserved, transition structures are negated, precisely because consciousness and identity are expanding and shedding their lesser and shallower orbits.

As the self-system negotiates each unfolding basic structure and switches from the narrower to the wider identity, it undergoes a *fulcrum* or switch-point in its development. That is, each time the self steps up to a new level of consciousness (each time it identifies with a new and wider basic structure), it will go through a process of 1) merger or fusion or embeddedness, 2) differentiation or transcendence or disembedding, and 3) incorporation or integration. This 1-2-3 process is a fulcrum of self-development, and there are as many fulcrums of self-development as there are basic structures to negotiate.

Thus, at any given level of development, the self starts out identified with (or in fusion with, or embedded in) the basic structure of that level.

Its locus of identification—or its "center of gravity"—circles around that basic structure: it is identified with it. But if development continues, the self will begin to disidentify, or differentiate, or "let go of," or transcend that structure, and then identify with the next higher stage while integrating the previous basic structure into the new organization. The exclusive identity with the lower structure is dissolved (disembedded, transcended, or negated), but the capacities and competences of that basic structure itself are incorporated and integrated (preserved and included) in the new and higher organization. The center of gravity of the self is now predominantly *identified* with a higher basic structure of consciousness, and this identification and embeddedness will then generate the transitional structures of that stage (moral stance, self-needs, self-sense, etc.). For each developmental basic structure, there is thus a corresponding fulcrum of self-development, a process of 1) fusion-merger-identification-embeddedness, 2) differentiation-disidentification-transcendence, and 3) integration-incorporation-inclusion.

We can, of course, divide and subdivide development in numerous and virtually endless ways, but I have found that we need at least nine or ten basic structures of consciousness in order to account for the most pertinent facts of overall development. To each of these ten basic structures there corresponds a fulcrum of self-development, that 1-2-3 process of fusion/differentiation/integration that occurs each time the self-system steps up to a new rung in the expanding spheres of consciousness. I also suggested that the preponderance of clinical evidence strongly suggests that each fulcrum can and does generate a specific level of pathology—psychotic, borderline, neurotic, script, identity, existential, psychic, subtle, and causal.

In several publications (1996c, 1984a, 1984b, 1995) I have given extensive examples of these developmental levels of pathology with their specific subtypes. This approach is the only way I know that can even vaguely begin to take into account the vast amount of clinical data as well as altered states evidence. This model also specifically includes discrete states of consciousness; and it emphasizes *the numerous different developmental lines* that "quasi-independently" evolve through the basic levels. We will return to each of these topics—particularly the difference between lines and levels—as the discussion unfolds.

With that brief summary, we can now look at certain misunderstandings of this model. The most common is the view that my model is rigidly linear and thus tends to ignore all the amorphous and nonlinear aspects of life. But in fact, only the basic structures are linear in any fairly strict sense, in that they emerge in a sequence that cannot be significantly bypassed or reversed. Images emerge before symbols, which emerge before concepts, which emerge before rules. This is equally true in both genders; we know of no society where that sequence is bypassed; there is no amount of societal conditioning that can reverse that order; and we know of no major exceptions. In other words, research has consistently demonstrated that these basic structures, to the extent that they emerge, are gender-neutral, cross-cultural, invariant, and holarchical.

Linear is often used in a very derogatory fashion, which is contrasted with the nice holistic alternative, which is somehow supposed to be "not linear." But, of course, most organic and holistic systems actually unfold in irreversible stages of increasing inclusiveness and envelopment—acorn to oak, seed to rose—and they unavoidably do so in the linear stream of time's arrow (a point Prigogine is always emphasizing about dissipative structures).

That is the meaning of linear in developmental studies (irreversible nested envelopment), and some aspects of human development are indeed linear, as massive amounts of experimental and clinical evidence have made more than obvious. In fact, those theories that fail to take these linear aspects into account are severely deficient and inadequate theories.

There is nothing *linear* about the self-sense, however. In fact, the self can roam all over the spectrum of consciousness (or the spectrum of basic structures). This is why the self is "where the action is." It can jump ahead, regress, spiral, go sideways, or otherwise dialectically spin on its heels. *Precisely because the basic structures themselves have no inherent self-sense, the self can identify with any of them.* And, in my model, each time the self does so, it will generate a set of transitional structures. It will see the world from its presently-identified-with basic structure (which acts as its center of gravity), and the basic limiting principles of that dimension will govern what it sees, and what it can see, from that vantage point. Growth will involve the relinquishing of a narrower and shallower level of awareness in favor of an expansion into wider and deeper and higher modes.

Thus, while the basic structures unfold in a linear (but still quite holarchical) fashion, with each senior dimension nesting and enfolding and including its juniors, the self's journey through those expanding spheres of consciousness is nowhere near that "linear." The self can be, and usually is, all over the place. This means that, on the long view, there will be a discernible progression of the self's development from narrower to wider, from shallower to deeper—an overall expansion of identity from matter to body to mind to soul to spirit. Nonetheless, in the short view, the self's journey is altogether tumultuous, much more of a roller coaster than a linear ladder.

This is why the transitional structures, although they, too, show a broad progression on the long view, nonetheless tend to be fairly unstable. For example, research shows that somebody who is at, say, moral stage 3, actually only gives 50 percent of her responses from that level; 25 percent of her responses are from *higher* levels, and 25 percent are from *lower* levels (Loevinger 1977). In other words, her center of gravity is at moral stage 3, but the self is still "all over the place."

I believe that only by taking all three of these components into account—"linear" basic structures, the self-system all over the place, and unstable but generally progressing transitional structures—can we even vaguely begin to honor, acknowledge, and incorporate the massive amounts of evidence from clinical, meditative, altered states, phenomenological, and empirical studies, both East and West. And I have found that any models that do less than that are severely deficient.

The Romantic Agenda

Since I maintain that repression or defenses in general can and do occur at all fulcrums of development (except the end limits), I obviously believe that defensive repression can occur in the preegoic period. The major difference between Washburn and me is thus whether something like a Dynamic Ground is actually forced out of the consciousness of the infant in the first year of life, as Washburn maintains. We can now turn to a close examination of this issue.

I myself was once an advocate of the Romantic model. In this general view, the infant at birth (and humanity in its dawn state) is the noble savage, fully in touch with a perfectly holistic and unified Ground, "harmoniously one with the whole world." But then through the activity of the analytic and divisive ego, this Ground is historically lost, actually repressed or alienated as a past historical event (as opposed to an involutional event happening now). This historical loss—the loss of a *past actual*—is nonetheless necessary, according to the Romantic view, in order for the ego to develop its own powers of mature independence. And then, in the third great movement (after initial union and subsequent fragmentation), the ego and the Ground are *reunited* in a regenerative homecoming and spiritual marriage, so that the Ground is *recaptured*, but now "on a higher level" or "in a mature form."

Such is the general Romantic view. And, indeed, I began writing both *The Atman Project* (1996a) and *Up from Eden* (1996b) in an attempt to validate that view ontogenetically (*Atman Project*) and phylogenetically (*Eden*). I even fancy that I brought some new ideas to this old notion. In ontogenetic development, for example, I postulated that the infant begins in a state of almost pure adualism, fully in touch with the primal Ground and the true Self (Atman), so that subject and object are one; the self and the "whole world" are united. Then through what I called "primary repression," the subject and object are split, the self and the world (as the Great Mother) are fragmented and alienated from each other, and the world of duality crashes onto the scene, with all the tragedy and terror inherent in that divisive nightmare (Wilber 1979).

But the developmental damage does not stop there. Once the body-ego is split from the world and the Great Mother, the body-ego has two basic but contradictory desires, my early Romantic account continued. There is the desire to reunite with the Great Mother and thus recapture that pure oneness and paradisiacal state that it had known before subject and object were brutally split. But in order to reunite with the Great Mother, the body-ego self would have to die to its own separate existence, and this it is terrified of doing. It therefore wants reunion but is also terrified of it, and these conflicting desires drive subsequent development. I called the amalgam of these two drives "the Atman project"—the desire to attain unity (Atman) but the intense fear of it as well, which forces the self to seek substitute gratifications and substitute objects.

(The Atman project is a very real project and a very valid concept, I firmly believe, but the state of unity that is desired is not that of the infant at the mother's breast, but of the self at primordial Emptiness. As we will see, I had wildly "elevated" the nature of the early infantile and prepersonal structure to some sort of transpersonal ground and glory, and so I mistakenly believed that the drive to unity was a drive to recapture that infantile structure, but of course "in a mature form," instead of understanding that the drive to unity is an attempt to capture something lost in prior involution—as I will explain in a moment.)

Once the body-ego has split from the Great Mother or Great Surround, my early Romantic account continued, then because of this primary repression it suffers primary alienation and a deformation of its own libidinal energies. All of the libidinal organizations are thus simply reduced and restricted versions of a consciousness that was once actually "one with the whole world." I therefore ended one of these early published chapters with the conclusion: "God-consciousness is not sublimated sexuality; sexuality is repressed God-consciousness" (Wilber 1979).

But the more I tried to make this Romantic model work—and believe me, I tried very, very hard—the more I realized its central inadequacies and confusions, which I will outline in a moment. I thus furiously reworked the early drafts of both *The Atman Project* and *Up from Eden*—neither had yet been published in book form—explaining this shift in my thinking, which I also explained at length in "Odyssey" (1982). Incidentally, when I wrote "The Pre/Trans Fallacy" (1980), I was in effect cataloging all of the errors that I myself had made in this regard, which is why I seemed to understand them with an all-too-alarming familiarity.

Anyway, let us call my early model Romantic/Jungian/Wilber-I, and the later model, Wilber-II.

Now the odd thing about Wilber-I and Wilber-II is that they aren't really all that different. They both move from preegoic to egoic to transegoic. They both agree on the great domains of prepersonal to personal to transpersonal. They both see development ultimately driven by the attempt to regain Spirit. They both see involution and evolution occurring. That is why both Wilber-I and Wilber-II can handle virtually the same type and amount of available clinical and experimental evidence. The big difference—the crucial difference—is that Romantic/Wilber-I *must* see the infantile preegoic structure as being, in some sense, a primal Ground, a perfect wholeness, a direct God-union, a complete immersion in Self, a oneness with the whole world. Since the perfection of enlightenment is a *recontacting* of something present in the infantile structure, then that infantile structure must therefore itself fully possess that utter Perfection (even if unconscious). Thus, if God is not *fully* present in the infantile structure, the entire scheme collapses.

And here, of course, the Romantic/Wilber-I model runs into a series of absolutely fatal difficulties, as is probably quite obvious. The traditional Romantic view is that the infantile structure is one with the entire Ground or Self, but in an *unconscious* fashion. The self then divides and splits from this Ground, actually represses this Ground, alienates it and loses touch with it. Then, in the third great movement (transegoic), the self and the Ground *reunite*, the Ground is resurrected ("on a higher level," whatever that might actually mean), and a spiritual renewal and regeneration occurs.

Thus, what we might call the *traditional Romantic view* is that development moves from unconscious Heaven (preegoic) to conscious Hell (egoic) to conscious Heaven (transegoic). The self is totally one with the Ground in *both* the first and the third stage, but in the first the union is unconscious, in the third, conscious.

The fatal problem with that version is that the second step (the loss of unconscious union) is an absolute impossibility. As the Romantics themselves soon acknowledged, all things are one with Ground; if you actually lost your union with Ground, you would cease to exist. Rather, there are only two options you have with regard to Ground: you can be aware of your union with Ground, or you can be unaware of it. The union itself is always present, but it can be either conscious or unconscious.

Now, as we saw, according to the traditional Romantic view, the preegoic state is one with Ground but in an *unconscious* fashion. But if that is so, then the next step—the move from preegoic to egoic—*cannot* therefore be the loss of that unconscious union. If that happened, you would cease to exist. You can either be conscious or unconscious of the union with Ground; if you are *already* unconscious of the union, you can't get any lower! The real loss has *already* occurred. The preegoic structure or original embedment is *already* fallen, alienated, lost. Involution has priorly occurred. And this the Romantics, very slowly, began to realize, which, of course, fatally undermined their entire project.

The precariousness of their position becomes even more obvious when the standard Romantic notion of "original wholeness" is carefully examined. The infantile structure is supposed to be "one with the whole world in love and bliss," as Norman O. Brown put it. But what is the neonate actually one with? Is the infantile self fully one with the world of poetry, or logic, or economics, or history, or mathematics, or morals and ethics? Of course not, for these have not yet emerged: the alleged "whole world" of the infantile self is a pitifully small slice of reality. The subject and object of the infantile structure are indeed predifferentiated to a large extent (which is simply the oceanic or fusion phase of fulcrum-1), but that fused world excludes and is ignorant of an extraordinary amount of the Kosmos. It certainly is not one with the whole world; it is one with a very small slice of the whole world.

The one-month-old self might come "trailing clouds of glory" (from the rebirth Bardo, which I believe it does, and will explain below), but it is still actually immersed and embedded, not in nirvana, but in samsara. It has all the intense seeds of grasping, avoiding, ignoring, hunger, and thirst. The flames of samsaric hell are *already* all around the infantile self, and if this is occasionally a relatively peaceful time, it is the peace of prepersonal ignorance, not transpersonal wisdom. The infantile self is fully immersed in samsara; it just doesn't have enough awareness to register that burning fact. But as the ego develops and gains in consciousness, it will increasingly realize its already fallen state—*realize* the fact that it is *already* living in the fires of samsara.

This shocking realization, this conscious initiation into the fact that the phenomenal world is inherently marked with tears and terror, sin and suffering, *trishna* (craving) and *duhkha* (suffering), is a profound trauma to the self. This *waking-up trauma* begins, in its earliest forms, during the first or second year of life (particularly during fulcrum-2), and that is what has confused the Romantic/Wilber-I theorists: they imagine that at this point the infant is passing from nirvana into samsara, whereas the infant, born in samsara, is simply waking up to that shattering fact.

Original Embedment and the Dynamic Ground

Washburn in many essential respects echoes the Wilber-I model. He uses the same general stages, with the same general terminology. Many

of his conclusions are direct echoes of my earlier model, and he generously acknowledges as much—as he (1995) puts it, "Wilber (1979) once
held a view similar to this but later abandoned it" (249).

At the same time, Washburn has built upon this view and enormously expanded and sophisticated it. He has, after all, based two long
books on it. Moreover, Washburn has at least realized some of the profound difficulties with the *traditional* Romantic version, and he has
attempted to bypass some of its central and fatal difficulties. But this, in
my opinion, simply takes him out of the frying pan and into the fire.

To begin with, Washburn realized early on that if the preegoic structure (more specifically, the "original embedment") is one with Ground,
then that union with Ground *must be fully conscious and unrestrictedly
present in the infant*. Remember, the traditional view was that the original state was a union with the Ground but in an *unconscious* fashion,
but Washburn realizes that if that is so, then that original state is
already fallen, it is already as low as you can go (it is, in fact, not unconscious Heaven but unconscious Hell). So Washburn is forced to maintain
that the one-month-old infant is fully open to, and fully conscious of, the
unrestricted Dynamic Ground. There is "the unrestricted power of the
Ground within the newborn's body," evidenced in "dynamic plenitude
and blissful well-being characteristic of original embedment," marked by
"wholeness, fullness, and bliss . . . undivided, boundless fullness" (48, 50,
49). Washburn maintains that the Ground is "unrestrictedly present"; of
course, if it were unconscious, it would be restricted in some sense, and
this cannot be. Washburn acknowledges that the Ground itself *cannot* be
lost or the ego would cease to be (25). So the only item that can actually
be lost is the consciousness of Ground, and this means that the one-
month-old infant must *fully possess* that consciousness of unrestricted
Ground, or the entire scheme falls apart.

Now a more coherent view of involution/evolution (as found in, say,
Plotinus, Asanga, Schelling, Aurobindo, Garab Dorje, *The Lankavatara
Sutra*, or, I believe, Wilber-II) would maintain something like this: Spirit
manifests as the entire world in a series of increasingly holistic and holarchic spheres, stretching from matter to body to mind to soul to spirit
itself. But all of these different dimensions are actually just forms of
Spirit, in various degrees of self-realization and self-actualization. Thus,
there is really spirit-as-matter, spirit-as-prana, spirit-as-mind, spirit-as-
soul, and spirit-as-spirit.

Involution (or efflux), this general view continues, is the process
whereby these dimensions are manifested as forms of spirit, and *evolution*
(or reflux) is the process of recollection and remembrance, moving from
spirit-as-matter to a final remembrance of spirit-as-spirit: a recognition of
spirit, by spirit, as spirit—the traditional realization of enlightenment.

In this scheme, the infantile self might indeed be trailing clouds of glory (which I will discuss in a moment), but it is primarily adapting to the dimensions of spirit-as-matter and spirit-as-prana (sensuality, emotional-sexual energies, elan vital, diffuse polymorphous life, and vital force) as well as the very early forms of spirit-as-mind (images, symbols, protoconcepts). Developmental evolution continues with the further unfolding of the mental dimensions (spirit-as-mind) and then the beginning of the consciously spiritual dimensions (spirit-as-soul), culminating in enlightenment or the direct recognition of spirit-as-spirit, which, transcending all, embraces all.

So the infant is indeed immersed in spirit and is one with Ground— as all things are!—but it is primarily spirit-as-matter and spirit-as-prana, not spirit-as-spirit. (Not even according to the Bardo view is the infantile or neonatal self in touch with spirit-as-spirit!) Thus, in all of these views, the infantile self is not conscious of spirit-as-spirit, or the pure nirvanic state altogether free of karmic tendencies and desires and hunger and thirst.

But this general view is completely blocked to Washburn (and Wilber-I), because for Washburn, the Ground *must be fully conscious and unrestrictedly present* in the one-month-old infantile structure. This forces Washburn into a series of increasingly incoherent stances in an attempt to defend this awkward assertion.

To begin with, Washburn must first separate Ground and spirit. (Since spirit is *not fully manifest* in the infantile structure, which Washburn seems to realize, then *something else* must be fully present in order to drive his scheme, and this something else will be the Dynamic Ground.) Thus, for Washburn, Ground and spirit are not the same thing. Ground, he says, can appear as libido, as free psychic energy, and as spirit. I myself will refer to these different organizations of Washburn's Ground with the shorthand phrases Ground-as-prana, Ground-as-psyche, and Ground-as-spirit (Washburn's terminology, for example, is "the power of the Ground as spirit"). Notice that Ground is somehow more than spirit, because it can appear in forms that apparently spirit cannot.

But there is one thing Ground is not: Ground is not the mental ego. Strangely, the Ground can appear as libido, and the Ground can appear as free psyche, and the Ground can appear as all-encompassing spirit, but the Ground is not strong enough to appear as the poor ego. In fact, the ego and the Ground are dramatically separate entities, says Washburn. But in the higher stages of development, Ground somehow appears as spirit (what I am calling Ground-as-spirit) and then Ground-as-spirit and the ego unite, according to Washburn, and thus a *superentity* (which he never really names or specifies) then emerges: the Ground-as-spirit/one with the ego.

But, says Washburn, this is not a novel state: it is in some sense a *reunion* with the Ground that was directly repressed by the two-year-old. That, of course, is the absolutely crucial point: according to Washburn, the Ground of spiritual realization is essentially the same Ground repressed by the child's ego, which is exactly why Washburn *must* postulate that this Ground is *fully present and conscious* in the infantile structure.

This is where Washburn's very slippery definition of "Ground" becomes crucial. As we saw, Ground can appear as libido, as psyche, and as spirit. Washburn can therefore claim that the child represses the Ground *without ever claiming that the child represses spirit* (because Ground and spirit are not the same). But in order for Washburn's scheme *actually* to work, the Ground that is repressed by the young ego *must* be the Ground-as-spirit, because, Washburn makes clear, the higher union is a union *specifically with Ground-as-spirit.*

But Washburn, apparently realizing that simply will not work, therefore never *explicitly* claims the infantile self is actually in touch with Ground-as-spirit, nor does he ever claim that the young ego represses Ground-as-spirit. In fact, he consistently maintains (in the text and in his tables) that Ground-as-spirit appears *only* in the transegoic stages.

At this point, Washburn's model is starting to look suspiciously like Wilber-II in disguise. But Washburn wants it both ways: he wants to acknowledge that spirit actualizes *only* in the transegoic stages, but he also wants to say that the *same* reality was somehow *fully* present in the infantile structure and was then actually repressed by the ego.

The only way he can do this is to create a notion, "the dynamic Ground," that has the power of *all three great domains at once* (the libido of the prepersonal, the psychic energy of the personal, and the spirit of the transpersonal), and then he can use the Ground in virtually any way he wishes. Thus, when the young ego represses Ground in its form as prana or vital bodily energy, which it certainly might, Washburn will simply claim that the *entire Ground* itself has been repressed, thus *implicitly* claiming a spiritual repression without *explicitly* ever having to say so, which he realizes will not work. Then, when the ego enters the transpersonal domain, Washburn *simply begins calling the Ground by the name "spirit,"* without ever explaining why all of a sudden the dynamic Ground turns explicitly spiritual—and yet that is, of course, the central problem to be addressed. Instead, in the transpersonal stages Ground is now simply called "the power of the Ground as spirit," which is then *claimed* to be the *same* Ground the infant repressed, whereas in fact (and even according to the actual evidence that Washburn presents), what the infant basically repressed was Ground-as-prana, not Ground-as-spirit.

But Washburn wants it both ways, and therefore, in those rare instances when he actually attempts to define Ground, he must define it in a way that will not challenge his reductionism. Thus, he simply defines the Ground as "physicodynamic processes" (no further explanation is given for that term). Since Washburn loosely identifies Ground with physicodynamism, then he can hide his reductionism and his pre/trans fallacies in this rather nebulous concept, having his preegoic spiritual cake and eating it too.

There is, I believe, a fairly straightforward reason that Washburn attempts to identify the entire Dynamic Ground with "physicodynamic" processes, and it relates directly to his pre/trans fallacy worldview (ptf-2). Chogyam Trungpa pointed out in *Shambhala: Sacred Path of the Warrior* (1988), as did Huston Smith in *Forgotten Truth* (1976), that the great wisdom traditions without exception—from the shamanic to the Vedantic, in the East as well as the West—maintain that reality consists of at least three great realms: earth, human, and sky, correlated with body, mind, and spirit (gross, subtle, and causal), and these are further correlated with the three great states of human consciousness: waking (gross, body), dream (subtle, mind), and deep sleep (causal, spirit).

These are, of course, the three great domains of prepersonal, personal, and transpersonal. *But Washburn refuses to clearly acknowledge these three domains.* Under the burden of his pre/trans collapse, he keeps the ego-mind as one domain, but he then *fuses the gross-body with causal-spirit*: this lump he calls the "Ground," which he then contrasts with the ego-mind. Thus, instead of the three great domains of body, mind, and spirit, he simply has his "two poles" of ego-mind and Ground.[1] And since he has collapsed causal-spirit into gross-body and its vitality, then of course he will refer to the entire Ground as physiological energy or "physicodynamic processes," thus completing his pre/trans plunge. By reducing the Ground of Being to physiology, he can elevate infancy to God.

Yet it is in the highest stages that Washburn's Romantic/Wilber-I model faces even worse difficulties. According to Washburn, once the ego has necessarily and rather fully repressed the Ground, then it can reunite with the Ground. Since the Dynamic Ground "is originally lost via repression, it can be restored only via regression" (1995, 171). More than one critic has puzzled over what that could possibly mean. Does the adult have to regress to preverbal babbling? If not, then what?

Nonetheless, according to Washburn, the ego must regress back to the Ground which was present but repressed in the infantile period, and then these "two poles of the psyche"—namely, Ground and ego—"can be integrated to form a single, perfected, psychic whole" (1995, 171). This means, rather bizarrely, that Ground is now a *subset* of the whole psyche (an altogether incoherent point I will return to below).

But what, according to Washburn, is actually *recontacted*? It is not Ground-as-spirit, since that manifests, he says, only in the transegoic. Since it can't be spirit that is recontacted, Washburn reverts to his catchall concept—the physicodynamic potentials are recontacted: "Primal repression is lifted and physicodynamic potentials are reawakened" (1995, 201). That somehow means spirit is now manifest. In any event, it is at this transegoic point that Ground can manifest as spirit.

But this means that a *completely new entity* therefore comes into being with this awakening: namely, the "single, perfected, psychic whole"—the union of ego and Ground. The real conclusion is obvious: *this whole was never repressed or lost, because it never existed before.* It is an emergent, a newly realized entity. Thus, according to Washburn's own presentation, the infantile self is actually in touch with *neither* Ground-as-spirit nor the Ground-and-ego unified state, from which it follows that enlightenment or spiritual awakening is not in any essential fashion a recontacting of something fully or unrestrictedly present in the infantile structure but subsequently lost. That being the case, Washburn/Wilber-I immediately reverts to Wilber-II.

Thus, for Washburn/Wilber-I, primal repression of Ground is the way development proceeds *by necessity*, and thus spiritual awakening requires the recapture of something actually and fully present in the infantile structure. Repression is part of the actual mechanism of development. For Wilber-II, repression is something that may or may not occur, but in any event it is not the mechanism of growth, and when it does occur in these early stages, it is a repression essentially of spirit-as-prana, not spirit-as-spirit. But if this repression is moderate to severe, then in the higher stages of growth, regression might have to occur in order to reintegrate these lower potentials. Whether this regression does occur will vary from person to person, and the amount of this regression will vary from person to person, but it is not a wholesale necessity for all cases, and it is not a recontacting of an infantile but repressed spirit-as-spirit.

There are, of course, numerous cases of enlightenment occurring without wholesale infantile regression, which *prima facie* condemns the Washburn model. In the one carefully conducted investigation of the merits of Washburn versus Wilber, L. Eugene Thomas et. al. (1993) conclude that, of those individuals who had reached transpersonal stages of development, "only about half gave indications of having undergone a regressive transition period. On the basis of this, and other internal evidence, support was found for Wilber's theory" (67).

STAN GROF AND PERINATAL REDUX

Stan Grof is arguably the world's greatest living psychologist. He is certainly a pioneer in every sense of the word and one of the most comprehensive psychological thinkers of our era. Fortunately, Stan and I are in substantial agreement about many of the central issues in human psychology, the spectrum of consciousness, and the "realms of the human unconscious."

But we are here, of course, to discuss our differences. In *Sex, Ecology, Spirituality* (1995) I offer a sustained criticism of Grof's position, highlighting a half-dozen of what I believe are severe weaknesses in his model (particularly its profoundly monological bias). I repeat and summarize these criticisms in *The Eye of Spirit* (1997a). Here I will focus only on what I believe are specific confusions surrounding the perinatal level.

Grof (1985) defines the word *perinatal* as follows: "The prefix *peri-* means literally 'around' or 'near,' and *natalis* translates as 'pertaining to delivery.' It suggests events that immediately precede, are associated with, or follow biological birth" (435). In Grof's early psychedelic research, he consistently found that as a typical session unfolded, individuals would in some sense contact successively earlier stages of their own development, moving first from surface abstract or aesthetic patterns, to earlier biographical (and Freudian) material, and eventually to what appeared to be an actual reliving of biological birth. Grof named the entire spectrum of experiences that seemed organized around the imprints of the actual delivery process "perinatal." Once this perinatal level was contacted, it often acted as a doorway to transpersonal and spiritual experiences.

Further observations suggested that perinatal experiences in general, although not merely a reliving of biological birth, nonetheless organized themselves in four fairly distinct classes that in many important ways seemed to parallel the clinical stages of childbirth. Grof therefore postulated that "basic perinatal matrices" (BPM) were laid down during the actual biological delivery. Although not all perinatal experiences can be reduced to an actual reliving of biological birth, nonetheless these matrices, as deeply imprinted structures in the total bodymind, act as formative patterns in perinatal experiences in general.

"The connection between biological birth and perinatal experiences is quite deep and specific," says Grof (1988, 9). He believes that "This makes it possible to use the clinical stages of delivery in constructing a conceptual model that helps us to understand the dynamics of the perinatal level of the unconscious" (9). The general stages of clinical delivery cement the blueprints of the four basic perinatal matrices: BPM I, the oceanic or amniotic universe; BPM II, cosmic engulfment and no exit; BPM III, the death-rebirth struggle; and BPM IV, the death-rebirth experience. These blueprints, stencils, or matrices "have deep roots in the biological aspects of birth" (9).

Nonetheless, Grof points out that perinatal experiences rarely involve a simple reliving of the birth trauma. Rather, perinatal experiences tend to be *the doorway to transpersonal experiences in general*. Thus, Grof (1988) is at pains to point out that "In spite of its close connection to childbirth, the perinatal process transcends biology and has important psychological, philosophical, and spiritual dimensions. . . . Certain important characteristics of the perinatal process clearly suggest that it is a much broader phenomenon than reliving of biological birth" (9).

That very well might be true, but nonetheless, right there, I believe, Grof has begun to lose track of his definitions. He deliberately introduced the term *perinatal* because it pertained specifically to experiences surrounding the actual biological birth process. But when aspects of these experiences "clearly suggest that it is a much broader phenomenon than reliving of biological birth," he explicitly rejects the reduction of these experiences to biological birth but keeps the term *perinatal*.

Thus, any time an intense death-rebirth struggle occurs, of any sort, at any age, under any circumstance, Grof will tend to do a dual analysis, reflecting his hidden, dual definition of perinatal. He will first claim that a reliving of the actual birth trauma is the central core of the death-rebirth phenomenon; then he will disavow reduction to that specific trauma and open his analysis to all sorts of other levels, factors, and dimensions. In doing so, he will deny reductionism to biological birth, but he will keep the term *perinatal* to describe any and all intense experiences of death-rebirth, experiences that he nevertheless continues to insist are anchored to, if not reducible to, blueprints laid down in actual childbirth.

This is typical: "On this [perinatal] level of the unconscious, the issue of death is universal and entirely dominates the picture" (1985, 99). So far, this demonstrates that all deep perinatal experiences involve intense life-and-death issues; it does not in the least demonstrate that all life-and-death issues are perinatal. So it is necessary for Grof to move from this broad and general account of perinatal as involving death, to perinatal in the specific sense of being directly related to childbirth. This he does in the next step: "The connection between biological birth and perinatal experiences is quite deep and specific" (1988, 9). "Experiential confrontation with death at this depth of self-exploration tends to be intimately interwoven with a variety of phenomena related to the birth process. . . . Subjects often experience themselves as fetuses and can relive various aspects of their biological birth . . . many of the accompanying physiological changes that take place make sense as typical concomitants of birth" (1985, 99).

Now Grof might be correct that intense life-and-death issues have at their core a biological birth stencil, but his evidence in no fashion establishes this. Rather, those particular observations stem primarily from intense LSD sessions, where individuals might indeed regress to an actual reliving of the clinical delivery process. But on the face of it, those observations do not in any way describe, for example, the transpersonal stages of vipassana meditation as one enters *nirvikalpa samadhi* (the *necessity* of first experiencing oneself as a fetus is found in none of the traditional texts). Grof is referring to a specific nexus of phenomena that occur under intense LSD sessions and, occasionally, under other intense forms of physiological stress.

I am not denying Grof's data; it very well might be quite accurate. What I am questioning is the immediate and massive generalization from this very specific and narrow situation, where intense life-and-death issues appear to coalesce around childbirth, to issues of death and rebirth in general, not all of which appear to involve a reliving of clinical delivery.

I will return to that point in a moment, because it's crucial. But in the meantime, notice that Grof immediately makes that unwarranted and generalized leap (and he will do so using exactly his hidden, dual definition of perinatal). Thus: "The central element in the complex dynamics of the death-rebirth process seems to be reliving the biological birth trauma" (1985, 140). He always adds that death-rebirth is more than a mere reliving of the birth trauma, but nonetheless the core and *necessary element* is a reliving of biological birth: "Although the entire spectrum of experiences occurring on this level cannot be reduced to a reliving of biological birth, the birth trauma seems to represent an important core of the process. For this reason, I refer to this domain of the unconscious as *perinatal*" (1985, 99).

And here exactly we have the hidden dual definition. What actually is "this level of self-exploration?" It is the confrontation with death and rebirth. What is an important *core* of this confrontation—that is, a *necessary* ingredient? The reliving of biological birth, which is why it is called perinatal. But what does the *perinatal level* itself consist of? Any intense existential death-rebirth experiences. But that moves from the first definition (biological birth) to the second (any intense existential crisis in general), and does so in a fashion that is not in the least supported by Grof's evidence or arguments. There is, as he puts it, "the entire spectrum of experiences occurring on this [life-death] level," and there is the "process of biological birth," and his dual definition refers to *both* of them as perinatal.

At this point, Grof's definition of "perinatal" has slipped completely loose from its original mooring and is running indiscriminately through the existential world at large: "Deep experiential encounter with birth and death is typically associated with an existential crisis of extraordinary proportions during which the individual seriously questions the meaning of his or her life and existence in general" (1988, 10).

But all that follows from Grof's actually presented evidence is that perinatal experience can be profoundly existential; it does not follow in the least that all existential crises are perinatal. But with that elemental confusion, Grof resorts to his dual definition and anchors all *existential* death-rebirth phenomena squarely in the actual *childbirth* stencils, so much so that he begins referring to any death-rebirth experience as THE death-rebirth experience, and this monolithic death-rebirth blueprint is, of course, biological birth: "The experiences of the death-rebirth process . . . can be . . . derived from certain anatomical, physiological, and biochemical aspects of the corresponding stages of childbirth with which they are associated" (1985, 99).

When it is necessary to use his dual definition in order to expand the role of childbirth trauma beyond that warranted by his evidence, Grof will switch from biological birth to "the perinatal level," because, as we have seen, by his dual definition they are now not the same thing at all. This dual definition (childbirth/existential) allows him to implicitly keep his reductionism while explicitly denying it.

Thus, says Grof, the perinatal level of the unconscious is at the intersection between the personal and the transpersonal. But all that actually means is that *an existential death-rebirth lies between personal and transpersonal development*. Grof has not in any fashion demonstrated that a reliving of biological birth is necessary in all or even most cases in order for that development to occur. Intense LSD and holotropic sessions might indeed involve an actual reliving of childbirth; but in attempting to generalize beyond those quite specific situations to existential and transpersonal dimensions in general, Grof has stepped quite beyond the warrant of his evidence.

In fact, it is my own opinion that with this hidden, dual definition of perinatal (it means both existential and childbirth), Grof has rather completely confused chronology with ontology. With intense LSD sessions—which formed and still form the core of Grof's model—individuals might regress in a chronological sequence: from present-day to early childhood (Freudian) to birth trauma (Rankian), beyond which, once the individual has dropped an exclusive identification with the gross bodymind, properly transpersonal experiences do indeed disclose themselves.

But by confusing this chronology with an actual ontology of dimensions of awareness, Grof must insert the actual biological birth process between the personal and the transpersonal domains, and that is the only fashion in which he can generalize his model beyond the specific and rather narrow conditions in which it was developed. And thus he is forced generally to postulate that a reliving of specific biological birth, in one form or another, is generally necessary for transpersonal development.

At that point, Grof's model, I believe, is profoundly out of touch with the great preponderance of evidence from the meditative and contemplative traditions, from Western depth psychology (including Jungian), and from most of the evidence generated in nonordinary states of consciousness (NOSC) research. The issue, to state it rather crudely, is not whether an existential level exists between the personal and the transpersonal domains. Virtually all parties (including me) agree that is the case. Rather, the question is, does that existential level necessarily involve, in part, the actual reliving of the clinical birth delivery? Not might it occasionally, but must it as a rule, do so? Grof basically says yes; virtually everybody else says no.

You do not find the necessity to relive clinical birth in any of the major spiritual manuals and techniques. It is rarely if ever mentioned in any of the ascetic practices, shamanic techniques, or contemplative yogas. You do not find it in the great classics of the perennial philosophy or in any of the major wisdom tradition texts. Nor do you find it in the vast majority of the Western depth psychologists, including James and Jung and the general Jungian tradition. (You don't even find it in Washburn, who, as a regressivist, might be expected to concur; he does not.)

Huston Smith (1976, 155-73) has given what is still perhaps the definitive critique of Grof's model from the view of the great wisdom traditions. Of the many crucial points Smith makes—and I am in substantial agreement with all of them—especially relevant are the charges that 1) Grof confuses chronological regression with ontological modes of being and consciousness, thus fundamentally misunderstanding their actual origin; 2) this leads Grof to misunderstand the actual role of clinical birth in existential and spiritual domains, since they are "influenced only, not caused" by such; 3) this leads Grof to fail to appreciate that "birth and death are not physical only" (165).

On the other hand, Huston has always acknowledged that the holarchy of basic structures as I have outlined them is in substantial agreement with the perennial traditions as he summarizes them in *Forgotten Truth*. Massive amounts of meditative and phenomenological evidence from the great traditions squarely and unequivocally support this view, which Grof's model simply cannot handle in its present and rather limited form.

Grof tends to respond to such criticism by saying that all of those wisdom traditions do in fact recognize death-rebirth phenomena, and they all agree that such existential crises are the crucial transition from personal bondage to transpersonal liberation. This is quite true, but Grof goes further and, in the same breath, equates existential death-rebirth with perinatal/birth, which is exactly the equation that is altogether unwarranted by the preponderance of evidence, and an equation that gains currency *only* by his hidden dual definition of perinatal. Grof is assuming exactly that which he is supposed to demonstrate—namely, not that there exists an existential level lying between all personal and transpersonal development (all parties agree that is so), but that the essential core of that existential level is a stencil of clinical childbirth (which virtually nobody but Grof maintains, and for which he has presented no generalized evidence).

Thus, in my opinion, what may be typical in intense LSD and holotropic sessions has been unjustifiably made paradigmatic for all forms of transpersonal development, an extension for which there is no evidential warrant whatsoever. The net result is that, in my opinion, this remains an extremely important and fruitful, but quite limited, model of overall consciousness and its development.

Fulcrum-0 (Pre- and Perinatal) and Fulcrum-6 (Existential)

I am not denying the existence of the basic perinatal matrices, nor the possibility that they might play a formative role in certain psychospiritual developments. I will now briefly indicate how I believe Grof's data, shorn of their hidden dual definitions, can find resonance with my own model.

Let me begin with what I call the actual *existential level*. In my model, the basic structure of this level is called vision-logic, the self-need is that for "self-actualization," the moral sense is postconventional, and the self-sense or self-identity is called *centauric* or *existential* (fulcrum-6).

I have consistently, from my first book to my latest, maintained that the vast majority of evidence, culled from hundreds of sources East and West (which I have cited), clearly suggests that an existential level (by whatever name) is the great doorway to the spiritual and transpersonal dimensions. *The existential level is, as it were, the intersection between the personal and the transpersonal* (or, more technically, between the gross-oriented bodymind and the transegoic subtle and causal domains). Accordingly, in order for development to continue beyond the individual and existential level, the self (or consciousness) must break or deconstruct its exclusive identification with the gross bodymind and all its relations.

This is a "death," to be sure, but in my model, as Stan acknowledges, every fulcrum possesses a signature death-rebirth struggle. Nonetheless, the death-rebirth struggle of the centaur/existential level is, in some ways, the most dramatic, simply because, as we noted, it is the great transition from the personal to the transpersonal domains.

Accordingly, the real question is, Does this great death-rebirth transition necessarily involve the actual reliving of the clinical delivery? I maintain, contrary to Grof, that in *some* cases this *might* indeed happen, just as Grof recounts, but it is *not necessary*, and, not being necessary, *it cannot be the actual mechanism of the great transition to the transpersonal*.

Here is what I believe we can say on the basis of more enduring evidence: a general existential level (by whatever name) lies between personal and transpersonal developments. On this, Washburn, Grof, the great traditions, and I all agree. In my model, this is fulcrum-6. This does not mean that transpersonal experiences cannot occur prior to fulcrum-6; they can and often do, but only as temporary states of consciousness (NOSC), or as a peak experience, or as part of the "trailing clouds of glory" (as I will explain in more detail below). Washburn, Grof, and I also agree that this existential transition is something of a total life/death confrontation (or series of them), often difficult and brutal, but in all cases profoundly transformative.

At that point, our accounts diverge. Both Washburn and Grof see this as (in part) a literal and necessary regression: Washburn, to fulcrum-1; Grof, further back into the intrauterine state of fulcrum-0. I myself maintain that such regression *might* occur, but it is *not* the defining or essential core and doorway to the transpersonal.

Thus, the crucial point, as I see it, is that this model can handle all of the evidence and data of both the Grof and Washburn models, but the reverse is not true. If, in any individual case, actual regression occurs, either to fulcrum-1 (Washburn) or fulcrum-0 (Grof), there is ample room for such phenomena in my model.[2] But if such massive regression does *not* occur in some cases, both of their models fail rather dramatically. And since the total web of cross-cultural evidence clearly indicates that regression and direct recontacting of the infantile state is simply not a necessary prerequisite for, say, *sahaj samadhi*, then these models have already failed directly and profoundly.

As it is now, there are vast amounts of clinical, experimental, phenomenological, intersubjective, meditative, and psychotherapeutic evidence and data (from perennial to modern sources) that Grof's model, by itself, fails to take into account. I agree entirely with Grof that models must be based on extensive evidence and on their match with facts. I will conclude by affirming that I am more than willing to let that judgment fall where it will.

Nevertheless, I would like to end on the same note with which I began: in terms of the overall "big picture" of the spectrum of consciousness and the realms of the human unconscious, there is an extraordinary amount of overlap and agreement between Washburn, Grof, and myself. I prefer to think in terms of those extraordinary similarities, even as we continue to hash out the details.

SEAN KELLY: STRUCTURES AND STATES

Sean Kelly makes a series of very interesting and important observations, with which I generally agree.[3] But most of his criticisms, in my opinion, do not quite apply to my own work because they do not specifically take into account the differences between enduring and transitional, nor between levels and lines. Likewise, I believe Kelly does not give enough emphasis to the distinction I make between *structures* (enduring and transitional) and *states*. Since individuals, starting from the earliest months after conception, have access to the three broad states (of waking, dreaming, sleep), they therefore have general access to the three great domains of gross, subtle, and causal (although not in any permanently accessible and continuous fashion!). But influx from these states can therefore occur at any developmental (frontal) stage, simply because all individuals wake, dream, and sleep. Moreover, every individual, at no matter what age, goes through an entire "round" every twenty-four hours, plunging from waking (gross) into dream (subtle) into deep sleep (causal), and then around again. I have fully acknowledged that point from my earliest to my most recent books.

I have simply pointed out that the great preponderance of evidence indicates that these *states* are converted to stable and enduring *traits* only through a process of incorporative structuration, which of necessity includes and builds upon previous enduring structures. Furthermore, as consciousness grows and evolves and gains in strength—precisely through the ongoing march of developmental structuration—it will increasingly remain "awake" under all possible states, *a constant state of witnessing carried unbroken through waking, dream, and deep sleep states*, a constancy which is prerequisite and mandatory to full realization of nondual Suchness (and a constancy which, if you have experienced it, is unmistakable, self-referential, postrepresentational, nondual, self-validating, self-existing, and self-liberating).

Thus, in the advanced stages of spiritual practice, the self will remain fully conscious in waking, dream, and deep sleep, and thus it will eventually recognize *that which remains the same under all possible changes of state*. In other words, it will recognize the changeless, the timeless, the spaceless—it will recognize, or re-cognize, its own Original Face, its own primordial nature, the ever present Emptiness in which and through which all states arise, remain a bit, and pass. God-consciousness has become, not a changing state, but a timeless trait.

DONALD ROTHBERG:
LEVELS AND LINES, WAVES AND STREAMS

I earlier mentioned that, in my own theoretical work, I had moved from a Romantic/Wilber-I to a Wilber-II model because of certain profound difficulties in the Jungian and retro-Romantic orientations. And, as I indicated, the Wilber-II model was first presented in *The Atman Project*—a model with seventeen carefully outlined stages, from birth to enlightenment; it also specifically included the bardo stages of prenatal, preconception, and postlife states (the frontal/soul or evolution/involution lines). I gave rather brief but fairly comprehensive summaries of each of the seventeen stages. I especially focused on the changes in motivation, cognition, sense of self, modes of space and time, affect, types of wholeness, self-control, socialization, morality, angst-guilt, perceptual clarity, and death-terror as *they all developed and evolved through the seventeen stages*.

I usually condense these seventeen levels into nine or ten basic levels (the basic structures of consciousness), along with the various lines developing through those basic levels. This Wilber-II model (nine or ten basic levels of frontal development plus a deeper/psychic involutional line) is still fairly widespread. (Jenny Wade's *Changes of Mind* [1996] gives yet another version of this model.)

But exactly the relation of levels and lines was a point that demanded clarification. Thus, almost as soon as I had published the Atman Project/Wilber-II model, I realized that it needed to be refined in a very specific direction. The basic stages were still generally valid, but that model did not *fully differentiate the various lines of development through each of those stages*, nor did that model carefully distinguish between, for example, the enduring structures and the transitional structures.

Thus, less than one year after I published Wilber-II, I published its refinement (1981), which we might as well call Wilber-III. Wilber-II and Wilber-III still share the same general stages or basic structures of consciousness, but Wilber-III explicitly distinguishes *the different developmental lines that unfold through those basic levels*. These different developmental lines include affective, cognitive, moral, interpersonal, object-relations, self-identity, and so on, *each of which develops in a quasi-independent fashion through the general levels or basic structures of consciousness*.[4] There is no single, monolithic line that governs all of these developments (as I will carefully explain below).

I also distinguished between the enduring and the transitional features of each of those developmental sequences, outlined the six major characteristics of the self-system navigating those stages in its own frontal development (in addition to the "indestructible drop" of its own involutionary arc), and added the existence of temporary *states* (e.g., waking/dreaming/sleep) to the more directional and structural frontal unfolding.

That is the model I have consistently presented since its first publication (Wilber 1981, 1996d, 1997a; Wilber, Engler, and Brown 1986). Unfortunately, most people, when they "critique" my model, are referring to the earlier Wilber-II model, which is not an accurate reflection of my overall view. And this relates directly to the conversations with the American Buddhist teachers.

Are There Stages of Spiritual Development?

In *SES* I describe Donald Rothberg as "one of the very brightest of lights in the transpersonal field," and it is always a gift to have his clarity grace a discussion. Donald contributed three excellent chapters (chapters 1, 7, 11) to the present volume. His introduction ("Ken Wilber and the Future of Transpersonal Inquiry: An Introduction to the Conversation") contains a good overview of my work. The only negative comment I have on it is that to repeat irresponsible criticism is itself irresponsible.

Donald's second piece, "How Straight Is the Spiritual Path? Conversations with Three Buddhist Teachers," begins with a very good summary of the psychological quadrant of my model. As such, Rothberg's accurate summary, despite its briefness, already goes a long way to defuse and correct common misrepresentations of my model (such as its being unilinear). Donald then conducts a series of interesting discussions with three American Buddhist teachers on the general theme of spiritual stages.

My overall view on "stages" is exactly as Rothberg summarizes it: "Development doesn't somehow proceed in some simple way through a series of a few comprehensive stages which unify all aspects of growth . . . . The [different] developmental lines may in fact be in tension with each other at times. Futhermore some lines do not typically show evidence, Wilber believes, of coherent stages. . . . There might be a high level of development cognitively, a medium level interpersonally or morally, and a low level emotionally" (pp. 136, 137, 139). He adds, and I quite agree, that "These disparities of development seem especially conditioned by general cultural values and styles" (p. 139).

As we have briefly seen, in my overall model (Wilber-III), there are the basic structures of consciousness, as a type of central skeletal frame, but through those basic structures there move at least a dozen different developmental lines, involving both enduring and transitional structures. These developmental lines include affective, moral, interpersonal, spatiotemporal, death-seizure, object relations, cognitive, self-identity, self-needs, worldview, psychosexual, conative, aesthetic, intimacy, creativity, altruism, various specific talents (musical, dance, artistic), and so forth. These are relatively independent ("quasi-independent") lines of development, loosely held together by, of course, the self-system.

The immediate question then becomes: Is spirituality itself a separate developmental line? Or is spirituality simply the highest level(s)—the deepest or highest reaches—of the other lines?

In other words, the meaning of the word *spiritual* becomes crucial in this discussion, because all of the arguments in this area tend to reduce to two different definitions of that word. There are those who define *spiritual* as a *separate developmental line* (in which case spiritual development is alongside or parallel to psychological and emotional and interpersonal development). And there are those who define *spiritual* as the *highest reaches* of all of those lines (in which case spiritual development can only occur after psychological development is mostly completed).

I believe that both of those stances are correct, but in each case we must indicate exactly what we mean by *spiritual*. If, for example, we define *spiritual* specifically as transmental, then clearly the transmental cannot stably emerge until the mental has in some rudimentary sense been solidified. Likewise, if we define *spiritual* as transverbal, or as transegoic, or as specifically transpersonal, then the spiritual domain cannot stably emerge until there is a verbal, mental, egoic self to transcend in the first place.

On the other hand, if we define spirituality as a separate developmental line, then clearly it can develop alongside, or behind, or parallel with developments in the other lines (affective, interpersonal, moral, etc.). I myself believe this is also an appropriate way to proceed (as long as we are clear about what we are doing), since my own model is precisely that of different developmental lines proceeding through the same general basic structures.

Thus, for example, in the affective line, we have preconventional affect (e.g., narcissistic rage), conventional affect (feelings of belongingness), postconventional affect (global concern, universal love), and post-postconventional affect (*ananda*, transcendental love-bliss). In the moral line, we have preconventional morals (what I wish is what is right), conventional morals (my country right or wrong), postconventional morals (universal social contract), and post-postconventional morals (*bodhisattvic* vows). In the interpersonal line, we likewise have preconventional, conventional, postconventional, post-postconventional, and so on.

In my view, the common axis (of which precon, con, postcon, and post-postcon are all measures) is simply *consciousness* as such (the basic structures themselves, the Great Holarchy of Being, the spectrum of consciousness—gross to subtle to causal—which I usually present as nine or ten basic levels of consciousness, through which the dozen or so developmental lines quasi-independently proceed). The levels of the spectrum constitute the stages or *waves* of developmental unfolding, the various lines are the different *streams* that move through those waves, and the self-system is that which attempts to juggle and balance those quasi-independent streams with their cascading waves of development.

Now, if we allow that spirituality is a relatively *separate developmental line* (and I believe this is one legitimate approach), nonetheless we are immediately faced with several very real difficulties. To begin with, how can we then define *spiritual* such that it is *not* defined using only the terms of higher, transpersonal, transmental levels? You see, if we define *spiritual* using any of those *trans* terms—transverbal, transmental, transconventional, transegoic—then we revert to the other model (where spirituality exists only in the higher domains and thus can develop only *after* the lower domains). Nor can we define spirituality using only the terms of *other* developmental lines (affective, moral, interpersonal, cognitive, etc.). In order to make spirituality a separate line of development, we cannot define spirituality as emotional openness, or as love, or as moral compassion, or as affective bliss, or as cognitive intuition and insight, and so on (for all of those already have their own developmental lines).

Defining the "spiritual line," you see, becomes extremely tricky, and most people who maintain that spiritual development is parallel to psychological and other lines, do so only by not defining *spiritual* in any specific sense at all.

So I will simply state my own preference. I will follow Paul Tillich in defining the spiritual line as that line of development in which the subject holds its *ultimate concern*. That is, the spiritual line of development is the developmental line of ultimate concern, regardless of its content. And, like almost all other developmental lines, the line of ultimate concern will itself unfold through the general expanding spheres of consciousness, from preconventional concern (egocentric), to conventional concern (sociocentric), to postconventional concern (worldcentric), to post-postconventional concern (*bodhisattvic*). Or again, in more detail, using the terms of the associated worldviews: archaic concern to magical concern to mythic concern to mental concern to psychic concern to subtle concern to causal concern.

The question then becomes, are those really stages? Are there actually stages of spiritual unfolding in some general sense? I believe they are indeed *transitional stages*, and as such, they are stages in a "soft" sense (responses span several levels). But they show important stage-like aspects because they unavoidably build upon previous competences, while adding new and defining features that replace the narrower and shallower orientations.

Thus, for example, in order to move from preconventional spirituality (archaic, magical, egocentric) to conventional spirituality (mythic-membership), it is *necessary* to learn to take the role of other. Care and concern simply cannot expand from the self to the group without that growth, and there is no corresponding unfolding of a deeper spiritual concern without it.

That is exactly an example of why the general stage conception is so important, and why I believe it is crucial in the spiritual line as well. It does not tell the whole story by any means, but rather a very important part of the whole story. Moreover, no alternative account whatsoever that completely leaves out the stage aspect has yet been credibly advanced. (I keep hearing alternative metaphors like a flower unfolding, but flowers unfold in stages.) Even in Joseph Goldstein's simplified account, development moves from what he calls gross to subtle (to very subtle).

Thus, although many details need to be refined, the stage conception itself unequivocally continues to match the great preponderance of available evidence. In Alexander and Langer's (1990) thoughtful book, *Higher Stages of Human Development*, the editors present a rather comprehensive overview of the models of development that acknowledge higher or deeper domains than the typical egoic state, and of the twelve major models that are presented, the editors point out in their introduction that all except one are partially or totally based on hierarchical stages (including those of Carol Gilligan, Daniel Levinson, Michael Commons, Pascual-Leone, and Charles Alexander). This is the baby that we must not toss with the bathwater. And given the American climate of hostility to "stages" (and anything "higher" than the ego), it is a baby whose life we must rather aggressively defend.

Greater Depth, Less Span

This brings us to yet another rather delicate issue. Rothberg points out that some research indicates that no more than one to two percent of the population reach Loevinger's highest stage. This is true. One careful study (Alexander and Langer 1990) showed that one to two percent reach the autonomous stage (next to highest), and less than 0.5 percent reach the highest stage in the scale, the integrated (those two stages correspond to early and late centauric). Similar studies have shown that less than four percent reach Kohlberg's stage 6; Fowler found less than one percent reached his highest stage; and so on. Let us simply accept, for argument's sake, that those are generally true statistics.

The question then becomes: Does this mean that people have to pass through those stages (postconventional, centauric, integrated, etc.) in order to make genuine spiritual progress?

Once again, you see, it depends upon the meaning of *spiritual*. If we define spirituality as postformal and post-postconventional, the answer is yes, definitely. But if we define *spiritual* as being a separate line of development, the answer is no, definitely not. In this case, spiritual development is occurring alongside or behind or parallel to those other lines of development, and thus it may race ahead of, or lag behind, those other lines.

But that simply pushes the question back: Does stable postconventional spiritual development depend upon passing from its preconventional wave to its conventional wave to its postconventional wave? And I believe the answer, backed by the preponderance of evidence, is most definitely "Yes."

To say the same thing using other terms, the spiritual line moves from a *prepersonal* wave (archaic, food, safety, preconventional) to a *personal* wave (from belongingness and conventional concern to postconventional/global) to a *transpersonal* wave (post-postconventional, psychic, subtle, causal, *bodhisattvic*). In short, the spiritual stream runs through subconscious to conscious to superconscious waves, by whatever name.

These spiritual stages, I believe, are transitional stages (stages in the "soft" sense); of course, the self-system can still be "all over the place." This is not a rigid and mechanical clunk-and-grind view, as I said. At the same time, it does show, on the long haul, a general unfolding through the expanding waves of consciousness, with developments in the spiritual stream depending upon previously established competences in that stream itself.

Thus, for example, you simply *cannot* get from preconventional concern to conventional concern without learning to take the role of other. And you *cannot* get from conventional concern to postconventional or global concern without learning to establish perspectivism. In that sense, spiritual development most definitely progresses through these broad and general levels in a stage-like fashion. The spiritual stream runs through the same general waves as any other skill acquisition, if it is to be a stable adaptation and not merely a peak experience or temporary state.

At the same time, those developments are occurring quasi-independently from the other developmental lines, so that one's spiritual development (as a separate stream) may forge ahead, or it may lag behind, one's development in affective, interpersonal, artistic, object-relations, defense mechanisms, and other lines.

If we focus now specifically on the spiritual line—and given the fact that postconventional *anything* is very rare (one to two percent or so)—does that mean that even less than one percent of the general population will actually develop to the *post-postconventional* or transpersonal wave of spirituality (psychic, subtle, causal)? In my opinion, yes, definitely. (No real surprise, in that evolution produces greater depth, less span.) In fact, I would even say that not much more than one percent of the *meditating* population develops stably to the post-postconventional levels of the spiritual line. But this, of course, is a matter for empirical research (see below).

Discriminating Wisdom

This is a particularly delicate issue for spiritual teachers of any persuasion. A large number of individuals who come to, say, a meditation retreat, might be at a preconventional level of moral, self, and interpersonal development. They might make strides in the spiritual line of concern or in the cognitive line of insight, only to see those insights gobbled up by the low center of gravity operating in the rest of the psyche. Spiritual teachers constantly find themselves having to cater to these lowest common denominator trends, where, no matter how much development one might accomplish in the spiritual line, it is not enough to pull the other lines along with it, and might itself be merely dragged down.

At the same time, we all know spiritual teachers who have glimpsed very high stages of spiritual and/or cognitive development, while their moral, affective, defense, object-relations, and interpersonal lines are very poorly developed—often with disastrous consequences. Moreover, the great traditions themselves often emphasize the spiritual line alone (particularly in its ascending mode), and thus they severely neglect the interpersonal, affective, and psychological lines, so that they remain, as it were, the last place to look for help in these areas.

My suggestion for an "all-level, all-quadrant" approach is a suggestion for a more integral orientation, drawing on the strengths of the various approaches (psychological to interpersonal to spiritual to social) in an attempt to fill in the very big gaps left by each alone. I am by no means alone in this call; but it is disappointing to see the intense and widespread resistance to a more integral and balanced approach.

Another difficulty for spiritual teachers in America is that, as Jack Engler noted, a disproportionately large number of people who are drawn to transpersonal spirituality are often at a preconventional level of self-development. This means that much of what American teachers have to do is actually engage in supportive psychotherapy, not transformative and transpersonal spirituality. Needless to say, these teachers will rarely see stages of development of anything.

As I earlier suggested, for the post-postconventional stages of spiritual awareness, I would say that, in any given meditation retreat—and speaking very generally—less than one percent will actually reach a profound *satori* or *rigpa* cognition (stable causal or nondual access). I have been in retreats of several hundred dedicated and long-term practitioners where only two people strongly accessed *rigpa* and had it fully confirmed by the Tibetan teacher. Two people is not exactly a huge pool from which to draw data, and yet it is only from such a pool that the full dimensions of the stage conception will stand forth.

Is This Trip Really Necessary?

Some people, I believe, are put off by the notion that rationality (and vision-logic) might somehow be a *necessary* prerequisite for higher or transpersonal development. And these folks especially do not trust this notion when it comes from egghead theorists.

Rothberg himself raises this issue (in chapter 7) as what I take to be perhaps the most thorny of his objections, namely, does the transpersonal really "integrate" the rational, and if so, what about nontechnological cultures that do not seem to access rationality? Do we deny them spirituality?

Developmental psychologists (such as Kegan) and philosophers (such as Habermas) tend to use "rational" in a very broad and general fashion, which sometimes confuses people. The simple capacity to *take the perspective of another person*, for example, is a rational capacity. You must be able mentally to step out of your own perspective, cognitively picture the way the world looks to the other person, and then place yourself in the other's shoes, as it were—all extremely complicated cognitive capacities, and all referred to as "rational" in the very general sense.

Thus, as I explain in *SES*, rational in this broad sense means, among other things, the capacity for perspectivism, for sustained introspection, and for imagining "as-if" and "what-if" possibilities. Rationality, to put it simply, is the sustained capacity for cognitive *pluralism* and *perspectivism*.

Some theorists have claimed that "rationality" (as used by Piaget or Habermas) might actually be, in effect, Eurocentric, and that its "lack" in other cultures might reflect Western biases. But, as Alexander and Langer (1990) point out, several researchers "have convincingly argued that formal operational capacities are evident within nontechnological societies when tasks appropriate to the culture are employed" (8). Rationality doesn't mean you have to be Aristotle; it means you can take perspectives. This is why Habermas maintains that even in foraging societies, formal operations were available to a significant number of men and women. You are operating within reason when you operate within perspective. You don't have to be doing calculus.

Likewise, vision-logic does not mean that you have to be Hegel or Whitehead. Rationality means perspective; vision-logic means integrating or coordinating different perspectives. Even in the earliest foraging tribes, it is quite likely that a chieftain would have to take multiple perspectives in order to coordinate them: vision-logic. The Western forms of reason and vision-logic are just that: Western forms, but the deep capacities themselves are not.

But you can't coordinate perspectives if you can't take perspective in the first place; and you can't take perspective if you can't take the role of other. And there, once again, is the limited but crucial role of the stage conception.

And yes, I most definitely believe that *postconventional spirituality* depends upon the capacity to coordinate different perspectives. *I do not believe the* bodhisattva *vow can operate fully without it*—without, that is, vision-logic. I believe it is the gateway through which stable psychic, subtle, causal, and nondual waves of spirituality must pass, and upon which they rest. Indeed, by definition, the *bodhisattva* vow rests upon vision-logic, and if you have ever vowed to liberate all perspectives, you have operated with vision-logic.

Nevertheless, you certainly can have spiritual development without perspectival reason and without integral-aperspectival vision-logic, for the simple reason that the spiritual line is a quasi-independent line of development. The spiritual line goes right down to the archaic, sensorimotor level, where one's religion—one's ultimate concern—is food. And the spiritual line will continue through the early prerational realms (magical, egocentric). With the capacity to take the role of other, the spiritual line will begin to expand its ultimate concern from the self to the group and its beliefs (mythic-membership). From there it will learn to take a more universal perspective (mythic-rational, rational), where its ultimate concern will begin to include the welfare of a global humanity, regardless of race, gender, creed. That awareness will flower into a global vision-logic, with its concern for *all sentient beings as such*, and that will be the platform of the transpersonal spiritual stages themselves, which take as their foundation the liberation of the consciousness of all sentient beings without exception.

Thus, you can have all sorts of spirituality without "integrating reason." But you cannot have a global spirituality, a *bodhisattvic* spirituality, a post-postconventional spirituality, an authentically transpersonal spirituality, unless the perspectives of all sentient beings are taken into account and fully honored. Unless, that is, you integrate the deep capacities of reason and vision-logic, and then proceed from there.

Anybody can claim to be "spiritual"—and can be such, because everybody has some type and level of concern. Let us therefore see the actual conception, in thought and action, and see how many perspectives it is in fact concerned with, and how many perspectives it actually takes into account, and thus see how deep and how wide runs that *bodhisattva* vow to refuse rest until all perspectives whatsoever are liberated into their own primordial nature.

MICHAEL MURPHY: THE NEW CANON

Mike Murphy is a visionary. As the name implies, a visionary is one who possesses vision—and, I would add, often expresses it with vision-logic. This is certainly evident in Murphy's chapter. Mike sees entire forests, instead of obsessing about one or two leaves on one or two branches on one or two trees (important as those are). At the level of vision-logic, Mike has zeroed in on what is surely one of the most profound worldview transformations of the last three hundred years: the shift from a static (or, at best, devolutionary) worldview to a process-oriented, developmental, dynamic, holarchical, evolutionary worldview. This evolutionary arch-view is indeed the new canon, in the very best sense of that word, and it has rendered the "old paradigms" old indeed. It handles more evidence, across more disciplines, in more fruitful ways, than any of the alternatives.

In the Upper Right quadrant, the evolutionary view is almost entirely uncontested by serious scientific researchers. That evolution has moved from atoms to molecules to cells to multicellular organisms is a generally accepted fact; what is being hotly argued is not the that and the what of evolution, but the how and the why. Mutation plus natural selection is not enough, many scientists now agree, to give a full account of evolutionary unfolding (which is where a transcendental Eros has much to offer in an explanatory fashion)—but evolution itself is the accepted paradigm. Likewise, in the Upper Left quadrant, the general notion of developmental unfolding is largely uncontested: from Freud's psychosexual stages to Gilligan's moral stages to Piaget's cognitive stages to Maslow's needs hierarchy—are grounded in the notion of dynamically evolving and developing systems of interaction. Not all aspects of the psyche show specific development, and not all theorists agree on the types and extent of development itself, but few would dispute its profoundly significant role in the unfolding of interior life.

Likewise for the collective or communal domains. There is little argument that the social (Lower Right) domain shows a pattern of asymmetrical development. In Gerhard Lenski's formulation, for example, which is largely uncontested, the social structure generally evolves from foraging to horticultural to agrarian to industrial to informational. As Jantsch and Laszlo have pointed out, these types of sequences are asymmetrical, hierarchical, and irreversible (i.e., just as apes do not evolve into amoebas, steam engines do not evolve into plows—although with regression or dissolution, the reverse path is often followed). The cultural domain (Lower Left) likewise shows some significant types of development, at least according to theorists as diverse as Gebser and Habermas and Heard (1963). (All of their formulations show a substantial if general agreement, which, to use Gebser's terminology, is that cultural worldviews evolve or mutate from archaic to magical to mythic to mental.) Although it is politically incorrect to discuss cultural development, those who contest it have had a rather difficult time explaining why evolution, in their view, touches all other domains but manages to bypass the cultural.

There are several immediate repercussions of the new canon. First, it is perhaps the only arch-view with a genuine chance of integrating science and spirituality (modern science is wedded to an evolutionary worldview; the Great Chain of Being, if temporalized, is quite consistent with that evolutionary view). I explore this theme in *The Marriage of Sense and Soul: Integrating Science and Religion* (Wilber 1998).

Second, the new canon dramatically, even fatally, undermines the essence of the retro-Romantic alternatives, which fit no known mechanisms of evolutionary unfolding. Mature oaks do not attempt to return to their acornness in order to realize that they are one with the forest.

Third, the new canon gives strong credence to Plotinus's notion that sin is not a "no" but a "not yet." That is, it is not the case that we were phylogenetically or ontogenetically immersed in Spirit but subsequently lost that union (by saying "no" to it), but rather we are in the process of growing into Spirit (which is therefore a "not yet"), even though Spirit is, paradoxically, fully present at each and every point of the growth. But involution itself occurs prior to the Big Bang, not after it (whether the big bang is of the cosmos or of human birth).

Fourth, the new canon promises a truly integral approach across numerous disciplines and practices. Mike has mentioned only the pioneers of the new canon; but even the shortest possible list of other Western theorists who have contributed substantially to the new canon would include Freud, Piaget, Kohlberg, Gilligan, Loevinger, Maslow, Erikson, Dennett, Bellah, Habermas—covering fields from psychology to philosophy to sociology to religion. And as theorists such as Daniel P. Brown (1986) and Chogyam Trungpa (1976) have pointed out, the great Eastern traditions—from the skandhas and vijnanas of Buddhism to the koshas and chakras of Vedanta—are to be understood, in part, as developmentally unfolding fields. No wonder the great Abraham Isaac Kook could state: "The theory of evolution accords with the secrets of Kabbalah better than any other theory" (Matt 1994, 31). For it is the new canon alone, I believe, that can tie all of these great traditions—East and West, North and South—together into a coherent and persuasive holism. An "all-level, all-quadrant" approach is simply my way of working with a genuinely integral overview; others, no doubt, are possible. But it will be very difficult to retreat to earlier, less integrative and less holistic stances.

Fifth, the new canon supports the validity of the general notion of the pre/trans fallacy with a massive amount of cross-cultural and interdisciplinary evidence. And proponents of the canon point out that a great deal of what is called "integral," "integrative," and "new paradigm" studies—centering on Romanticized and regressive currents—is actually old canon in disguise.

Sixth, the new canon is the only way, I believe, that we can integrate first-person (I, subjective), second-person (we, intersubjective), and third-person (it, objective) accounts of consciousness. Each is linked through a holarchical, interwoven, developmental unfolding (Wilber 1997b).

Seventh—and this is Mike's particular interest—the new canon translates directly into a genuinely integral spiritual practice, covering self and culture and nature. Murphy and Leonard's "Integral Transformative Practice" is but one of what I believe will be an increasingly widespread adoption of integral spiritual practice, uniting the best of premodern wisdom with the brightest of modern knowledge.

I very much appreciate Mike Murphy's use of vision-logic to elevate this topic to a plane it deserves.

MICHAEL ZIMMERMAN AND RADICAL ECOLOGY

As usual, I am in substantial and widespread agreement with much of Zimmerman's presentation, and I am glad to again have the opportunity to publicly express appreciation for the clarity, care, and brilliance he always brings to the task at hand. I cannot speak too highly of his expositions of Heidegger (*Eclipse of the Self* [1981] and *Heidegger's Confrontation with Modernity* [1990]), as well as his *Contesting Earth's Future* (1994).

Zimmerman's main point is that, whether one agrees with all the details in *SES*, it constitutes a genuinely transpersonal approach to ecophilosophy, an approach that simultaneously challenges most of the standard ecophilosophies (including deep ecology and ecofeminism). Zimmerman then raises a handful of criticisms.

First, Zimmerman (in chapter 8 of this volume) believes I have "over-estimated how many scientists and philosophers have jumped on the bandwagon of . . . teleological evolution" (p. 194). He is quite right that this is still a minority opinion in orthodox circles. I was simply drawing attention to the fact that several serious cracks have begun to appear in orthodoxy itself (especially around the recalcitrant problem of emergence and mutational transformations), and that an impressive number of orthodox scientists are increasingly open to nonreductionistic modes of explanation. As Zimmerman himself summarizes the available evidence, "A number of important scientific trends . . . support Wilber's contention that teleology is making a significant reappearance both in evolutionary theory and cosmology" (p. 195). But we both very much agree, as Zimmerman also summarizes it, that "Caution is needed with respect to how far these new sciences go. . ." (p. 195).

Second, Zimmerman calls into question certain aspects of cultural evolution. I have elaborately responded to such criticisms in *The Eye of Spirit* (1997a), and I will not repeat my observations here. Let me simply say that the "dialectic of progress" means the growth of both new potentials and new horrors, and I have never shied away from calling attention to both.

Third, Zimmerman feels that my treatment in *SES* of the actual schools of ecophilosophy is short and sometimes overgeneralized. But, as Zimmerman knows, Volume Two is devoted to a full discussion, with all the appropriate differences and distinctions, of the major schools of this broad and varied movement (including the work of Fox, Naess, Swimme, Berry, Warren, Eckersley, Merchant, Spretnak, Bookchin, etc.) Zimmerman also knows, from personal correspondence, that I have relied on his wonderful *Contesting Earth's Future* as a superb source, and that in many ways I am in substantial and widespread agreement with the important views he advances therein.

Zimmerman nonetheless maintains that my treatment of the ecophilosophers in *SES* is occasionally distorted and misrepresenting, that I have not been fair to the deeper aspects of ecophilosophy, and that I simply lump them all together in the worst way. I disagree, and I think Volume Two will bear this out amply.

Zimmerman gives as an example of my alleged misrepresentation the work of Arne Naess, whose philosophy Zimmerman maintains is compatible with the great nondual traditions of Mahayana Buddhism and Advaita Vedanta (which Naess also claims). But this "similarity" or "compatibility," I believe, is itself true in only the most superficial and shallowest sense. In Volume Two, I present an in-depth fifty-page analysis of Naess's Ecosophy T and find it lacking in almost every respect when compared with the great nondual traditions. Even Naess himself, when attempting to present the similarities, fails to account for even the simplest and most crucial issues—for example, the notion of unity-in-multiplicity, a hallmark of nondual realization. Naess fumbles in the worst of ways: "The widening and deepening of the individual selves *somehow* never makes them into one 'mass'. . . . How to work this out in a fairly precise way I do not know" (1989, 173) (his italics). And as soon as we do get precise (as Volume Two does), the similarities evaporate. I demonstrate precisely the same problems for representatives of each of the major ecophilosophies, and thus their "compatibility" with the nondual traditions likewise is exposed as largely superficial.

Thus, the generalizations I make in *SES* about ecofeminism, deep ecology, and the general ecophilosophies, far from being "distorted" or "lumped together," are based on a deep level of analysis which reveals that they are all variously caught in profound flatland orientations, and the detailed analysis of Volume Two supports just that strong conclusion. These are not wild overgeneralizations, but the summary of a series of very specific and detailed analyses.

Fourth, Zimmerman, in what seems to be a rare nod to political correctness for its own sake, implies that all "big pictures" command totalizing agendas that inherently marginalize social differences. Since *SES* is a big picture, could not it be marginalizing?

Some "totalizing" schemes are indeed marginalizing; others offer dramatically different incentives. My "big picture" explicitly does the following: it simply says, here are some areas of research and theory and evidence that perhaps you should look at. I am not trying to cram all differences into monological uniformitarianism, as I carefully explain. I thoroughly condemn that approach. Rather, my "big picture" is simply an explicit offer to take a larger view of things, a view that precisely invites researchers to stop any marginalization that they might otherwise be involved with. It's open-ended; it is not a "foregone conclusion" nor a conceptual straightjacket.

There is nothing inherently alienating in open-ended big pictures. And, in fact, it is increasingly becoming obvious that those critics, such as Lyotard or Rorty, who rail against metanarratives and big pictures, do so only under severe performative contradictions. Ask them why big pictures are not desirable or even possible, and they will give you a very big picture of why big pictures don't work. This performative contradiction has been pointed out by theorists from Charles Taylor to Quentin Skinner to Gellner to Habermas. Karl-Otto Apel (1994) is simply the most recent theorist to point out that "Rorty himself confirms this structure by the validity claims raised by each one of his own verdicts against all universal validity claims of philosophy. He thus ends up with the novel rhetorical figure of constantly committing a *performative self-contradiction*" (ix) (his italics).

PEGGY WRIGHT: A FEMINIST PERSPECTIVE

Peggy Wright (1995, and in this volume) has published two feminist chapters about my work. I must say, alas, that Wright's overall treatment is one of the most extensive distortions of my work that I have seen published, and I can only warn readers that, in my opinion, she does not in any substantial fashion represent my overall view, nor, therefore, a believable critique of it.

This is altogether typical of a Wright argument: "Representing any theory as describing deep invariant human structures rather than culturally shaped experience involves the responsibility to identify the cultural assumptions inherent in the model itself" (1995, 3). But I do not, and have never, portrayed my model as describing invariant structures rather than culturally shaped experiences. I have frequently used the analogy of the human body: it universally has 208 bones, 2 lungs, 1 heart—those deep structures appear to be universal—but societies everywhere differ on the modes of play, sex, culture, and work engaged in by the body—those surface structures are contingent, historically molded, and culturally relative. I have consistently called for an understanding that carefully balances universal deep structures with culturally variant surface structures.

But in both of Wright's chapters, as we will see, she tends to ignore that explicit balance in my work; she presents a very lopsided and at times ludicrous caricature of my views; and she then triumphantly corrects them with a "more balanced view" that is often nothing but a variation of my actual view before Wright distorted it. She simply reintroduces my actual conclusions, changing terminology if necessary to hide the sleight of hand, and then presents this as a "feminist" correction of my "androcentric" views.[5]

I do not have the space to address all of Wright's major distortions; I will outline only a few of them in endnotes as we proceed. I believe Wright's distortions are typical of a certain unfortunate trend in a number of feminist writers, and clarifying these general issues is crucial, in my opinion, if any sort of genuinely integral feminism is to emerge that can actually command the respect of both male and female theoreticians.

Carol Gilligan

We can start with Carol Gilligan's work and the notion of hierarchy. As will become obvious in this section, I believe that Wright misunderstands the nature of hierarchy, which leads her to misrepresent not only my model but also Carol Gilligan's, which is a deeply hierarchical model.

Gilligan (1982) found that men and women both move through three broad hierarchical stages of moral development, but that men tend to progress through these stages based on judgments of rights and justice, whereas women tend to negotiate these hierarchical stages based on judgments of care and responsibility. Thus, Kohlberg's mistake was *not* the broad hierarchical stage conception itself (which Gilligan accepts[6]), but the belief that, *within* those stages, male ranking represented a higher stage than female linking, which is simply not true. (This is the confusing of permeable with prepersonal, a fallacy we most definitely want to avoid.) But notice: each successive stage of female judgement is indeed superior in its capacity to express and manifest care. Each female stage is hierarchically ranked, but within each stage, judgments occur by linking and connection. So the same vertical, hierarchical, developmental ranking of stages occurs in both men and women.

I have summarized the large amount of research in this area by saying that both men and women exist as agency-in-communion (as do all holons), but men tend to *translate* with an emphasis on *agency*, women with an emphasis on *communion*. But both of them *transform* through the same broad, gender-neutral, holarchical stages of consciousness unfolding (holarchy itself includes both hierarchy and heterarchy).

Thus, for Gilligan (1982), women move through three general stages: selfishness to care to universal care (which she also calls selfish to conventional ethical to postconventional metaethical). These are the three broad stages of preconventional, conventional, and postconventional, which I have also termed *egocentric*, *sociocentric*, and *worldcentric* (and, in my model, the worldcentric or global stage is the platform and the gateway to higher spiritual domains). For Gilligan, each of those successive stages is *higher and more valuable* precisely because, as I would word it, the woman can extend the *circle of care* to more and more people (just as when men move through those same stages, they extend the *circle of justice* to more and more people, from egocentric to ethnocentric to worldcentric modes).

Gilligan has also suggested that "these two distinct moral orientations . . . can be further integrated in a hierarchical moral stage beyond the formal operational level."[7]

Note also: besides being hierarchical, Gilligan's model is linear, in the sense meant by developmentalists. That is, her three (or four) major stages unfold in a linear fashion that cannot be reversed or bypassed, because each stage depends upon certain competences provided by the previous stages (you cannot get to universal care without the previous stage of care, for example). The first two things to note about Gilligan's model, then, is that it is linear and *hierarchical* for *both* men and women.

All of this unfortunately tends to be ignored or overlooked by many feminists, who somehow imagine that Gilligan was saying women are altogether free of that nasty "ranking." I believe this is typical of a certain feminist approach that tends to ignore and deny any sort of female ranking hierarchy, under the performative contradiction of web-only models. By focusing essentially on heterarchy in women's experience, advocates of this approach ignore and devalue the important aspects of women's experience that are also hierarchical, which, I believe, badly distorts this entire approach, and makes it virtually impossible to give a coherent account of female development at all. In other words, it is deeply involved in what I call pathological heterarchy.

The Permeable Self

Wright agrees with the extensive research that suggests that men tend to emphasize agency (which she rather derogatorily calls "separation") and women communion (which she glowingly calls "connection" and the "permeable" self). However, I believe that because she tends to devalue and marginalize hierarchical integration in females, she does not present any coherent explanation of the development of the permeable self. My approach does so, or at least attempts to do so, in the following way.

We saw that men and women both develop through the same gender-neutral basic structures or expanding spheres of consciousness, but men tend to develop through these expanding spheres with an emphasis on agency, rights, justice, and autonomy, whereas women tend to develop through the same holarchical spheres based more on communion, responsibility, relationship, care, and connection. Thus, in my model, the "permeable" self of women develops through the same general stages of egocentric, sociocentric, worldcentric, and spiritual domains as the male, but with a different emphasis ("in a different voice"), a different set of priorities, a different mood, and a rather different set of spiritual disciplines (see below).

Accordingly, for the female, there is egocentric permeable (selfish), sociocentric permeable (care), worldcentric permeable (universal care), and spiritual permeable (universal union), precisely as the male negotiates those same general spheres with a somewhat more agentic emphasis (agentic egocentric, agentic sociocentric, and so on).

Thus, it is absolutely not the case, as Wright supposes, that in my model the prepersonal stages are simply equated with "permeable" boundaries, thus intrinsically devaluing the female orientation.[8] Rather, the prepersonal stages—in both male and female—involve self-boundaries that, *within the context of their own gender standards*, are fragile, noncohesive, broken and fused (not simply permeable, but fractured). As we saw, the permeable self in the female develops through the same general realms (but with a different voice), so that there is prepersonal permeable, personal permeable, and transpersonal permeable. Thus, in overall development, the female self becomes permeable to deeper and wider spheres of consciousness, right up to and including a permeability to Spirit or Ground—the same basic spheres through which the male develops with a more agentic orientation. Neither gender orientation is in any fashion privileged or made paradigmatic.

Integral Feminism: All-Level, All-Quadrant

Since, in reading both of Wright's chapters on my work, you would get little idea of what my published views on feminism actually are, perhaps a short summary is in order.

There are today at least a dozen major schools of feminism (liberal, socialist, spiritual, eco, womanist, radical, anarchist, lesbian, Marxist, cultural, constructivist, power), and the only thing they all agree on is that females exist. There simply is no consensus view on "the" voice of women, despite the claim of some feminists, including Wright, to be speaking for such.[9]

Rather, I believe that what we need is a much more integral approach, an approach that, in acknowledging the truly different perspectives of a dozen different feminist schools, might actually find a scheme that would be more accommodating to each of them.

This more integral approach is indeed part of what *SES* attempts to develop, at least in rough and outline form. In Volume Two of the *Kosmos* trilogy (tentatively entitled *Sex, God, and Gender: The Ecology of Men and Women*), I expand and fill in the details of this general model of sex and gender. Here is a brief summary (evidence and references can be found in *SES* and Volume Two).

The idea, I believe, is to bring an "all-quadrant, all-level" approach to sex and gender issues—an integral feminism. For example, each of the different theories of sex and gender (orthodox as well as feminist) has tended to focus on only one quadrant (and usually only one level in one quadrant), with an attempt to make it paradigmatic and exclusionary. I'll go around the four quadrants and give examples from each, and then suggest how their crucial insights might be honored and acknowledged.

Upper Right (Behavioral). These are the objective aspects of individual holons, which, in the case of human beings, include biological and hormonal factors, such as the effects of testosterone, oxytocin, and estrogen on individual human behavior. These factors, most researchers agree, *influence* (but do not strictly *cause*) sometimes quite different behavioral patterns in the sexes (sexual profligacy in the male being a typical example).

The *radical feminists* have particularly embraced the notion that there are dramatic, biologically based differences between the sexes, as have their strange bedfellows, the sociobiologists. This approach also forms an important part of the increasingly influential school of evolutionary psychology.

As I would summarize all of their conclusions, there is a *biological basis* for males to tend toward agency, women toward communion, and these tendencies are the product of perhaps several million years of natural selection, which is why we find them *crossculturally*—there is nothing "androcentric" about these sex differences, as many radical feminists have made quite clear. However, the actual value attached to these sex differences does indeed *vary from culture to culture* (on this, see the next section).

These upper right factors also include the macrobiological constants that researchers also agree are present universally and crossculturally. For example, women give birth and lactate, while men have an average advantage in physical strength and mobility. Both second- and third-wave feminists, as well as orthodox researchers, agree on the existence and importance of most of these factors. (They are crucial, for example, in explaining the statistically different roles of men and women in the productive and private spheres, once oppression fails as a causal category.)

Lower Left (Cultural). Nevertheless, the reason that these biological factors are *tendencies*, not *causes*, is that whatever biological factors are present, they nonetheless are taken up and reworked by powerful cultural factors, which can in many cases increase, neutralize, or reverse the biological tendencies.

Most researchers refer to these *biological* differences as *sex*, and the *cultural* differences as *gender*. Likewise, researchers usually refer to the biological sexes as *male* and *female*, and the cultural differences as *masculine* and *feminine*.

There are, in my opinion, two flagrant errors that are constantly being made in the study of sex and gender. The first (common with conservatives) is to assume that all gender issues are totally determined by sex differences (so that biology is destiny). The second (common with liberals) is that all sexual differences are merely culturally constructed (so that biology can be ignored). Both of these stances are profoundly distorted and almost always driven by ideology.

What we want to do instead, it seems to me, is to acknowledge and honor both moments of truth in those positions: biologically constant sex differences (such as the fact that women give birth and lactate, males have higher levels of testosterone) are taken up and reworked, often in dramatic ways, by cultural factors and influences.

In this regard, I particularly focus on the role of *worldviews* in the formation of gender. These worldviews (archaic, magical, mythic, mental, existential, etc.) are, recall, part of the *intersubjective cultural patterns* within which individual subjects and objects arise. As such, they play a decisive role in helping to *select which factors from the male and female value spheres will in fact be honored in any given society*.[10] The point is that women and men co-create (sometimes intentionally, sometimes unintentionally) the intersubjective patterns within which their own subjects and objects will be manifest and recognized, and these cultural patterns are sometimes decisive in sex and gender issues as well.

The *constructivist* and *cultural feminists* have furthered to a great degree our understanding of the important role of this lower left quadrant, and their voices are desperately needed in the choir. Unfortunately, they sometimes go beyond the warrant of their own evidence and claim that this quadrant is the only important quadrant in existence, which not only lands them in performative self-contradictions, but also distorts the equally important voices of the other quadrants (and the other schools of feminism). What then happens is that the *influence* of those other quadrants, since they are not fully acknowledged on their own terms, must be ascribed to *oppression*, because the constructivists can figure out no other way to explain how they got there. Thus, for example, biological differences in function must be ascribed to male imposition of ideology. Giving birth and lactating are somehow a male plot of the patriarchy, since all differences are culturally constructed.

This approach, of course, *defines* women as primarily molded by an Other (precisely the definition these feminists say they wish to overcome). And it defines males as essentially oppressors of one sort or another—"All men are rapists" being the most typical and outrageous example. All men are not rapists; as everybody knows, all men are horse thieves.

But we can ignore those differences of emphasis for the moment and simply note that all of these important lower left approaches are united in the affirmation of the strong and crucial role played by intersubjective cultural factors in the unfolding of sex and gender.

Lower Right (Social). Nonetheless, worldviews are not disembodied structures, hanging in idealistic midair. That is, all worldviews—indeed, all cultural factors in general—are strongly anchored in the material components of the society—such as the forces of production, modes of technology, architectural structures, economic base, geopolitical locations, and so forth, all of which I refer to as "social." In other words, all cultural factors have social correlates. (All four quadrants have correlates in all the others, and this applies to the cultural and social as well.) The social system and cultural worldviews are intimately interwoven, and this, of course, directly relates to gender issues.

In particular, there is now almost overwhelming evidence that, as I would put it, *worldviews follow the base*, not in any strong Marxist or deterministic fashion, but in the general sense that the techno-economic base sets certain broad limits within which worldviews tend to unfold. Thus, with regard to sex and gender issues, the discussion at this point turns to an analysis of *the types of gender roles available to men and women at each of the five or six major stages of techno-economic development in the formation of the human species*. These stages include foraging (scavenging, hunting, gathering), early and late horticultural, early and late agrarian, early and late industrial, and early informational. (The five broad technological stages correlate respectively with archaic, magical, mythic, mental, and existential worldviews.)

What we find, with this more integral approach, is that the techno-economic base has a profound influence in *selecting those factors from the male and female value spheres that will be evolutionarily advantageous for a given society*. For example, horse and herding societies place a premium on physical strength and mobility, which selects for the male value sphere in the public and productive domain. (Indeed, 97 percent of such societies are strongly patriarchal, with oppression playing no explanatory *causal* role.) Likewise, horticultural societies, whose primary force of production is the digging stick or hoe, place a premium on the female work force, because pregnant women can easily handle a hoe with no serious side effects. (Indeed, 80 percent of the foodstuffs in all horticultural societies are produced by women.) Not surprisingly, one-third of these societies have female-only deities (so that wherever you find the Great Mother religions, you find a horticultural base, with only one or two maritime exceptions). In Volume Two, I outline and summarize these various factors and the extensive evidence for each of these conclusions.

The *Marxist feminists* and *social feminists* have contributed much to our understanding of the importance of this lower right quadrant for an overall view. Likewise, one of my favorite writers, Janet Chafetz, has contributed a social systems-oriented analysis that is brilliant and thorough. And the *ecofeminists* have emphasized the role of Gaia as the ultimate social system. (On the possible meanings of "Gaia" and its actual role in living systems, see *SES*, chapters 4 and 5.)

All of those factors—behavioral, cultural, and social (at each of their developmental levels)—will have a strong hand in determining how *individual* men and women experience their own embodiment, engenderment, and gender status. Which brings us to the upper left quadrant.

Upper Left (Intentional). The upper left quadrant is the interior of the individual, the site of consciousness itself, which is composed of (at least) the three main components of basic structures, self-system, and transitional structures.

Within this spectrum of consciousness, it is important to examine both the horizontal dimension—that of *translation*—and the vertical dimension—that of *transformation*. Translation is a process of agency-in-communion, or the relational exchange between any holon and its interwoven environs. Transformation is the shift to a higher or deeper domain altogether (a different level of agency-in-communion).

Where agency and communion operate horizontally on every level, Eros and Agape operate between levels, as it were. Eros is ascending or evolving transformation; Agape is descending or involving transformation (which I will explain in a moment). The important point is simply that both the horizontal or translative dimension and the vertical or transformative dimension need to be taken into account.

If we do so, with regard to sex and gender differences, I believe we will find the following: Men translate with an emphasis on agency, women with an emphasis on communion. And men transform with an emphasis on Eros, women with an emphasis on Agape.

This is where the Gilligan/Tannen approach becomes an important (if limited) part of the overall picture and where the extensive research on male agency and female communion needs to be taken into account. But it is not enough simply to contrast male and female in the translative dimension (agency/separation versus communion/relationship), because men and women tend to transform with a different emphasis as well—namely, Eros/ascending versus Agape/descending.

This tends to confuse some people, because they imagine it means that men only ascend and women only descend, which is not the case at all. Rather, it means that, in any stage of vertical growth and development, men and women tend to face in different directions when they negotiate these stages, and these directions are not explainable merely in terms of agency and communion, but of ascending and descending *orientations in the nested holarchy of their own being*. Eros tends to reach up, as it were, and assault the heavens, whereas Agape tends to reach down and embrace the earth. Eros is much more transcendental, Agape much more immanent (and each has its own agency and communion, which refer to horizontal, not vertical, orientations).

These are not airy abstractions but a rather precise summary of much of the cross-cultural research on modes of transformative (or developmental) orientation in men and women. Thus, to give only one brief example, Phil Zimbardo, in his widely acclaimed psychology series on public television, summarized the cross-cultural differences in the behavioral patterns already demonstrated in young boys and girls—differences that show up in everything from eating habits to types of friendships to styles of play: "Girls have roots, boys have wings."

Roots and wings. Agape and Eros. It is this vertical dimension of depth that needs to be added to the horizontal dimension of agency and communion in order to take into account the multidimensional differences in the native styles of men and women.

Thus, in my view, men and women develop through the same gender-neutral basic structures, but they tend to do so with somewhat different values and styles in both the translative and transformative domains: men tend toward agency and Eros, women toward communion and Agape. (Of course, any specific individual will show a unique proportion of those four factors, and all four factors are decisively present in men and women alike. These are simple tendencies and average probabilities, not causal determinants!)

Nonetheless, and most significantly, these simple sex-class probabilities allow us immediately to stop interpreting females as being deficient males, or the more recent trend of trying to interpret males as being deficient females. Neither the male nor female disposition is itself higher or lower, or deeper or wider, on the nested holarchy of basic structures.

Moreover, this approach prevents the more recent attempts, by various spiritual feminists, to remove female spirituality from any sort of transformational requirements at all. This attempt simply paints women as the "permeable" (communion) self, which is fine, but it then rather straightforwardly equates this permeable self with a spiritual self and an ecological self, thus effectively denying the demand for any hierarchical transformation in women whatsoever. This catastrophically ignores not only Gilligan's female hierarchy but all others as well, which effectively aborts any sort of transformation in women at all.

What that flatland approach fails to take into account is that the permeable self (or the self-in-connection) itself undergoes growth, development, and transformation. The permeable self holarchically unfolds and transforms through the same expanding spheres of consciousness that the male agentic self must also negotiate in its own fashion. The permeable self is not, in itself, a spiritual self at all. In fact, the lower stages of the permeable self (the prepersonal stages) are just as egocentric, narcissistic, and altogether unpleasant as the shallower stages of the male agentic self. Both of them are equally locked into the orbit of their own endless self-regard, which is, by any definition, the antithesis of all things spiritual.

And as for the permeable self and its alleged regard for ecological connections, it is often quite the opposite. The lower stages of the permeable self (like the lower stages of the agentic self), are altogether prepersonal, preconventional, and egocentric in their stance—which is precisely the stance that is the prime contributor to ecological despoliation in general. Simple communion or permeability will, in itself, do nothing to alleviate this: it simply extends its own narcissism, permeably spreads its own egocentricity, shares its own disease.

Communion is the interwoven, web-like relationship of all of the elements in a given domain, but Agape is the capacity to embrace deeper domains altogether. When we understand that communion and Agape are not simply the same thing, then it becomes obvious that merely possessing a permeable self is not, as these feminists imagine, enough to bring moral light and salvation into the wretched world of male agency. Rather, the shallower and egocentric stages of the permeable self, along with the shallower stages of the agentic self, are the twin faces of evil in this world, and one of those smiling faces has female written all over it.

Female Spirituality

It is precisely the two basic native differences in the male and female value spheres (males tending toward agency and Eros, females toward communion and Agape) that, when they unfold through the basic structures of consciousness, under the influence of different worldviews and different stages of techno-economic development, generate the various modes of gender that have historically been observed in men and women. The burden of Volume Two is to render that thesis plausible.

This "all-quadrant, all-level" approach gives us a chance, I believe, to bring together an enormous number of very important, indeed crucial, factors in the discussion of sex and gender. Thus, the gender-neutral basic structures play themselves out differently for men and women, dependent on factors in all four quadrants, from hormonal differences to worldviews to modes of production to translative/transformative differences. Since all four quadrants intimately interact, none of those factors can be overlooked in a genuinely comprehensive theory of sex and gender.

And this relates directly, I believe, to spiritual development as well. Volume Two is a sustained look at the different types of spiritual development—in many cases, decisively different from male patterns—that certain highly original women saints, shamans, and yogis have pioneered over the centuries. These female practices uniformly and cross-culturally involve an intense mode, not merely of *translative* communion and permeability, but of *transformative* Agape (incarnational, body-centered, immanent, descended, involutional, and profoundly embodied mysticism). They offer a stunning contrast to the more traditionally ascending, transcendental, agentic, and Eros-driven modes of spirituality typical of males.

But these more female-oriented spiritual practices are still practices in profound *transformation*, not mere translation. As such, these women offer a stinging criticism of the merely "permeable" self theories that find permeability in itself to be spiritual (as if communion and Agape were simply the same).

In other words, in order to manifest a genuine spiritual consciousness, women have just as much hard work to do as the men. As we noted, "permeable" and "spiritual" are not even remotely the same thing. Rather, only the deepest stages of the permeable self are genuinely spiritual ("spirit-as-spirit"), and these deeper developments require intense and sustained spiritual practice. But where the men need to transform their agentic selves, the women need to transform their permeable selves (from selfish to care to universal care to spiritual recognition). These are the same expanding spheres of consciousness (egocentric to sociocentric to worldcentric to authentic spiritual), but negotiated with different styles.

What too many "permeable self" theorists actually mean is, "I am a woman, and by virtue of my permeable self, I am already more spiritual than men." What these genuine female mystics demonstrate, on the contrary, is that for women actually to transform their permeable selves, and not merely translate differently, requires an enormous amount of intense and profound work (just as it does in the men). These extraordinary women mystics say to their sisters, in effect: "Fine, you have a relational, embodied, permeable self. But within those givens, here is what you still must do—with intensity and fire and unrelenting dedication—in order to actually transform that self and render it fully transparent to the Depths of the Divine."

Indeed, some of the transformative practices of these remarkable women—which almost always involve wrenching bodily ordeals as they bring spirit down and into the bodily being via descending or incarnational Agape and its unrelenting compassion—are so intense that they even make for difficult reading; in any event, they are not for the faint-hearted, and they put to shame the "wonderful permeable self" assumptions of merely translative female spirituality. These extraordinary women practitioners are blazing beacons of what a woman actually has to do if she is genuinely to transform in depth and not merely claim a superiority based on translative permeability.

At the same time, we simply cannot forget that both men and women have decisive access to both agency and communion, as well as to Eros and Agape. That they might inherently tend to emphasize one or the other does not mean that they are different species altogether. This is why, I believe, we need constantly to keep our eye on both the profound similarities as well as the significant differences between men and women and resist the urge to sink our discussion in an ideological fervor to promote one at the expense of the other.

Male and Female Moral Depth

Which brings us to our last and somewhat delicate area, that of actual moral development itself. Many radical feminists and ecofeminists constantly claim, explicitly or implicitly, that the general female mode is in some profound sense more moral or ethical than the male mode. But actual feminist research itself demonstrates something quite different— and much more fascinating.

Radical feminists and ecofeminists emphasize, quite correctly it seems to me, that women do indeed tend to stress embodied personal relationship (the "connected self"). And this very fact, it seems, makes it rather difficult for women to develop to Gilligan's third and highest stage of female moral development—that is, from the stage Gilligan (1982) calls "conventional ethical" to what she calls "postconventional metaethical." (She also calls this moving from care to universal care.)

In other words, precisely because women tend to remain attached to personal and conventional relationships, they find it harder to reach the postconventional and universal stages *in their own female development* (based on their own relational terms, not on male agentic terms). Thus, even if we use the Jane Loevinger test originally developed using solely women, more men reach the higher stages. Men, being less personally attached to sociocentric relationships, find it easier to take a universal and postconventional "big picture" view, and thus more men make it into the universal, postconventional moral stages than do women (even when the women are judged by their own scales and values).

On balance, male and female moral development display an interesting split. Just as in IQ tests, more males score both lower and higher than females (most of the really dumb, and really brilliant, are male), so men score both lower and higher than women in most scales of generalized moral development. Again, women seem to gravitate to personal, embedded, conventional relationships, and thus they have a harder time moving from *conventional communion* (care) to *postconventional communion* (universal care, Gilligan's "postconventional metaethical").

Men, on the other hand, due to their predominantly agentic outlook, tend to gravitate *to either side of that conventional divide*: more of them reach the postconventional worldcentric stage of universal embrace, but more of them also remain at the preconventional and egocentric mode. For every Abraham Lincoln and Mahatma Gandhi, there is a Charles Manson and Son-of-Sam. Historically, this has made men both truly stunning moral and spiritual beacons, as well as the most viciously evil animals, without exception, to walk the face of the earth.

But the point, once again, is that simply possessing female communion, as opposed to male agency, is not enough to make you spiritual or moral. In fact, it might slow your growth into universal and global domains (spiritual as well as moral), and it might actually cripple anything resembling a genuine global ecological stance (which calls into question one of the central tenets of many schools of ecofeminism, namely, the native superiority of the female when it comes to developing an ecological stance to the global biosphere).

But the central conclusion, in all cases, is that the communion self needs just as much work, sometimes more, as the agentic self, in order to move from egocentric selfish, to sociocentric care, to worldcentric universal care, there to stand open to the radiance of the Divine. Women, just like men, face years, and often decades, of blood, sweat, tears, and toil, in order to claim their birthright.

ROBERT MCDERMOTT: SHAKING THE SPIRITUAL TREE

Robert McDermott, in his chapter "The Need for Physical and Spiritual Dialogue: Reflections on Ken Wilber's *Sex, Ecology, Spirituality*," raises the issue of whether polemical discourse is ever appropriate for academic and especially spiritual dialogue. He ends up rather strongly condemning polemic, his major point being that it isn't "spiritual." But I believe that this, too, reflects an impoverished and narrow view of spirit—what it is, and where it is located.

McDermott asks if we would ever hear polemic from the great spiritual philosophers, such as Aurobindo or James or Plotinus. The answer, of course, is yes. In fact, the vast majority of spiritual philosophers have engaged at one time or another in intense polemical discourse—Plato, Hegel, Kierkegaard, Nietzsche, Fichte, Schopenhauer, Schelling, Augustine, Origen, Plotinus, to name a very few. They do so, I believe, precisely because they understand the difference between what Chogyam Trungpa Rinpoche used to call "compassion" and "idiot compassion." This is perhaps the hardest lesson to learn in politically correct America, where idiot compassion—the abdication of discriminating wisdom and the loss of the moral fiber to voice it—is too often equated with "spirituality."

I think, on the contrary, that we admire these spiritual philosophers because idiot compassion was foreign to them, because they all had the moral courage to speak out in the most acerbic of terms when necessary, to make the hard calls and make them loud and clear. People too often imagine that "choiceless awareness" means making "no judgments" at all. But that itself is a judging activity. Rather, "choiceless awareness" means that both judging and no judging are allowed to arise, appropriate to circumstances. I think this is exactly why so many great spiritual philosophers engaged in such incredibly *intense* polemic, Plotinus being a quite typical example. Plotinus so aggressively attacked the astrologers that Dante felt it necessary to consign the entire lot of them to the eighth ring of hell, and Plotinus unrelentingly tore into the Gnostics as having "no right to even speak of the Divine."

I used to think that if somebody engaged in that type of forceful polemic, he or she could not be very enlightened. I see now it is exactly the opposite. We tend to believe genuine spirituality should avoid all that, whereas in fact it quite often engages in such polemic passionately as a manifestation of its capacity to judge depth (i.e., its capacity for discriminating wisdom). Plotinus's acerbic and occasionally sarcastic attacks on the astrologers and Gnostics is paradigmatic: they were a politically powerful and unpleasant lot, and it took courage to claim they had no right to even speak of the Divine. If McDermott is sincere about his pronouncements, then he would have been there to publicly condemn Plotinus, no doubt; but the point is that right or wrong Plotinus stood up to be counted, and it is a service to us that he did so in no uncertain terms. Moreover, Plotinus is not saying one thing in public and another in private; you know exactly where he stands.

The question is thus not whether these great spiritual philosophers engaged in polemic, for they did; the question is why. When such sages engage in intense polemic, I suppose we sometimes get nothing but their lingering neuroses; but we often get the full force of the overall judgment of their entire being, a shout from the heart in a sharp scream. It takes no effort at all to act out the former; it takes enormous courage to stand up and voice the latter, and this is what I have come to admire in all the sages and philosophers I have mentioned who have left us the full force of their summary judgments.

Contrary to McDermott's sincere but misplaced pronouncements, such polemic comes not from this side of equanimity, but from the other side.

One taste is the ground of intense judgments, not their abdication. These are not lunatics blathering prejudices; they evidence more like what the Tibetans would call the wrathful aspect of enlightened awareness.

McDermott tells us that he used to publicly and passionately voice his own judgments of qualitative distinctions and discriminating wisdom, but that he quit doing so in order to become a better administrator. I accept his choice. But I think it would be catastrophic for everybody in the transpersonal field to adopt that same stance and abdicate the public voicing of one's discriminating wisdom.[11]

There are many who see all too clearly the sad shape our field is in. They talk about it often in private. They tell me about it all the time. They are truly alarmed by the reactionary, antiprogressive, and regressive fog thickly creeping over the entire field. Yet most of them are not willing to stand up and be counted, precisely because the countercultural police await, poised and ready to sanctimoniously damn them. A little less administrative juggling, and a little more discriminating wisdom backed with occasional polemic, is exactly what the entire field could use, in my opinion. I, at any rate, can no longer sit by and smile numbly as depth takes a vacation. And in a more honest process, where our public pronouncements actually match our private statements, we just might find that spiritual awareness includes, not excludes, the fiercest of judgments.

KAISA PUHAKKA: DIALECTICAL APERSPECTIVE

Kaisa Puhakka's (1995) review/summary of SES (1995) entitled "Restoring Connectedness in the Kosmos: A Healing Tale of a Deeper Order," is (along with Roger Walsh's) the finest and most accurate summary of SES that I have ever seen. She is not necessarily agreeing with the book; she is simply summarizing and explaining it, and she does so brilliantly. It is rare that I can read an explanation of my work and feel that there are no inaccuracies or misrepresentations, but such is the case with Kaisa's summary, which proves that it most definitely can be done. It would have been a great service to have included that extraordinary summary in this volume, so readers would have advantage of that accurate overview; in any event, I hope that her review is reprinted elsewhere, and often, for those who would like a superb summary of SES.

Kaisa's present chapter is a delightful play on the impossibility of finally saying anything about anything, and yet having to do so all the time. She invokes the dialectic of vision-logic, which includes both play and purpose, and dances gracefully with this theme.

In that regard, perhaps I might mention that there were two dialectical modes that I had in mind when working with SES. One is the dialectic most famous in the West, which runs in various forms from Plato to Hegel. The other is the dialectic most famous in the East, which runs from Nagarjuna to Mahayana Buddhism and Vedanta Hinduism. In a sense, we could say that the former is the dialectic of Form, the latter, the dialectic of Emptiness.

Kaisa tends to over-identify me with purposeful rather than playful; and when she sets my position up as one of a duality (as when she states [p. 301], "The answers that are given to these questions divide us into contending camps—the ego and the eco, the Wilberian hierarchists and the anti-Wilberian heterarchists, and so on"), she has completely misreported my position, an extremely rare lapse for Kaisa. The aim of *SES* is to make room for both ego and eco, hierarchy and heterarchy, purpose and play, etc. But behind all of those nondualities, there lies the granddaddy of all nondualities, that between the dialectic of the West and that of the East: and that is exactly the single major message of *SES*.

So important is that nonduality, that I end the first part of *SES* with this conclusion: "Abide as Emptiness, embrace all Form." The world of Form is the world of evolution, in both its purposeful and playful modes. (Even evolution, as Mike Murphy points out, meanders more than it progresses—or plays more than it advances.) This dialogical, developmental, dialectical world has been dealt with by Western theorists (such as Schiller with play and Hegel with purpose), and I had all of that in mind when I was working on the dynamics of both the Ascending and Descending currents.

But Emptiness is neither purposeful nor playful, neither Ascending nor Descending, neither Eros nor Agape. It has absolutely nothing to do with right or wrong, progression or regression, holistic or analytic, connected or fragmented, hierarchy or heterarchy, calculating or dancing. There are no holons, abstract or concrete; there is no evolution or devolution or anything in between. More precisely, as Nagarjuna demonstrated, with regard to any possible polarities (such as right and wrong, play and purpose, ascending and descending, true and false), the absolute cannot be characterized as one, or the other, or both, or neither. The absolute, rather, is simply but profoundly disclosed in contemplative awareness invoked by the injunctions of meditation, but what is disclosed cannot, without profound confusions, be further stated (unless you have *already* completed the injunction). The dialectic of Nagarjuna, unlike the dialectic of the West, is a relentless attack on any mental forms whatsoever—playful, purposeful, analytic, or holistic—pointing out that all are radically powerless to grasp the absolute.

It is very like the taste of a pecan pie. If you want me to tell you what a pecan pie tastes like, all I can really do is give you the recipe and have you make it and then taste it yourself. Other than telling you the recipe (the injunctions that, if followed, will invoke the experience), I can't really say what the pie tastes like. Just so with Emptiness. All I can do is give you the injunctions for meditation, let you follow them and thus taste the experience yourself. But once we step down into the manifest world of form, all our mental concepts, dialectical or otherwise, miss the point altogether.

(But yes, playing at the edge of the dialectic of Form—with vision-logic—as Kaisa wonderfully does, can on occasion give one a glimpse of the dialectic of Emptiness, and I sometimes attempt to do just that in my writings, as Kaisa points out. But both of us would agree: a glimpse is one thing, a stable realization, quite another. And the latter usually takes the better part of a decade, at least, of meditative injunctions, apprehensions, and confirmations. Emptiness can be briefly glimpsed, but rarely stabilized, with the dialectic of Form.)

In the world of Form, making love is better than being brutally tortured; and yet each is equally, fully, perfectly a manifestation of Spirit or Emptiness. As explained in the last chapter of *SES*, this is the difference between intrinsic value and Ground value; the former requires a yardstick, such as ethics or Eros; the latter recognizes no yardsticks whatsoever, for all forms are always already the Great Perfection—although right there I have said too much, and Nagarjuna would slap me hard across the face for that breach of the dialectics of Emptiness. But the point is simply that, in real life, we have to swim in both oceans, as it were—that of relative gradation and absolute emptiness.

So in *SES* I was attempting to make room for both of these great dialectics—the dialectic of Form (especially operative in vision-logic) and the dialectic of Emptiness (operative in prajna), with the further understanding that, once you successfully complete the contemplative injunction, *you will see exactly how these two are related* (see *The Eye of Spirit* [1997a] for a full discussion of this theme). But the fact that, as stated in the book itself, I deliberately wrote *SES* at and from the level of vision-logic, and therefore of necessity gave emphasis to the dialectic of Form (in both its playful and purposeful aspects), should not detract from its clearly stated conclusion: "Rest in Emptiness, embrace all Form."

COMMENTS ON OTHER CONTRIBUTORS

Roger Walsh: I would like particularly to express a deep appreciation for Roger Walsh's superb summary of some of the central themes of *Sex, Ecology, Spirituality*. Given that his chapter, in its various forms, has now been read by approximately three times the number of people who have read *SES* itself, you will understand that I am altogether relieved that it is fair, accurate, and informative, and, beyond that, a model of academic exposition and excellence.

Jürgen Kremer: Although I have an enormous sympathy with the inclusionary intent of Jürgen Kremer's chapter, and with the great heart he clearly expresses, I am sorry to say that I find his actual argument rather confused. I will briefly respond by saying: a) I have, in *The Eye of Spirit* (1997a), given an extensive outline of the shadow side of evolutionary thinking; b) Kremer refers to Winkelman's criticism of *Up from Eden* (1996b), but Kremer gives no response at all to my extensive critique in *SES* of Winkelman's approach (the performative contradiction embodied in Winkelman's stance is shared, in my opinion, by Kremer); c) any individual can be above or below a society's center of gravity, and thus remarkable accomplishments are open to virtually any society[12]; d) Volume Two deals with many of Kremer's issues in great detail; e) despite Kremer's disclaimer that he is engaged in a process "which does not invite romanticism or nostalgia" (p. 242), I find Kremer does just that, evidenced in the fact that his entire chapter is full of examples of allegedly "integral, nondissociated consciousness" (p. 253) of the indigenous mind, and yet *only one sentence* is given to a specific example of the often extreme and brutal shadow side of many indigenous cultures. I do not consider this fair, balanced, or anthropologically representative.

Jeanne Achterberg and Donald Rothberg: "Relationship as Spiritual Practice" is a wonderful piece. I could simply say "ditto" and that would cover my response! These types of issues are so important as we all struggle toward a genuinely integral practice.

Donald says (p. 263) that "I think that [Wilber] would claim that spiritual paths occur in relation to all four quadrants. In this sense, relational models can fit within his theory." That is indeed the point of what I'm trying to do, namely, make room for various authentic approaches in a more integral view. At the same time, I tend deliberately to leave the details open and fluid, so that those more competent than me can fill them in (or correct them altogether!).[13] In fact, I basically publish only my broad and orienting conclusions. I have thousands of note pages of evidence and arguments, often in frighteningly boring detail, and although I sometimes present those details in elaborate footnotes, for the most part they never see publication (unless one of my conclusions is challenged, and then I am happy to drag out all the evidence). But I offer none of these generalizations lightly, nor without what I consider to be very substantial evidence.

Thus, when the authors state that "Wilber himself has in his recent work created considerable conceptual space for relational approaches, although most of the practical and theoretical work remains to be done" (p. 261), I could not agree more.

Many of the chapters carried in this "conversation" understandably focused on various criticisms and negative reactions, but the great preponderance of responses have been more in line with those of Jeanne's and Donald's, namely, finding my orienting outline to be useful in furthering their own substantial contributions. It is unfortunate that we could not have focused on more of these positive responses to my work, but that, perhaps, is for yet another round in yet another forum.

NOTES

1. Incidentally, Washburn's "ptf-3," mentioned in his essay in this volume, is indeed a fallacy: it is simply another name for Washburn's inability to recognize the Trikaya (the existence of gross, subtle, and causal realms). His collapse of tripartite into bipartite thus forces him to view any renormalization as a fallacy.

Washburn states this fallacy as "inferring separateness from difference" (see p. 79 in this volume); in fact, all I do is infer separateness from separateness (waking, dream, and deep sleep are separate; I simply say, do not equate waking and deep sleep on the basis of the fact that they are both nondreaming). Moreover, even if I did infer separateness from difference, the separateness still might actually be there. Washburn does not in any way demonstrate otherwise; his thesis, on the contrary, rests on the conflation of relatively different and separate dimensions (the collapse of the Trikaya), and this can be demonstrated with much more confidence than his contrary suggestions.

Washburn also raises the issue of mind/body in relation to ego and centaur. Why do I say that it is only centauric vision-logic that can integrate mind and body? This is, of course, a relative affair and a matter of degrees. One might even make the argument that the mind and body are not truly integrated until radical Enlightenment, and I would not argue with that. But generally speaking, I describe the centaur as an integration of mind and body because 1) this directly follows the evidence of Loevinger, Broughton, Graves, and others; and 2) the centaur, as the great transition from the gross bodymind to the subtle bodymind, represents the "final" integration of that gross bodymind.

More technically, because vision-logic is on the edge of the transmental, the self of vision-logic is increasingly disidentifying with the mind itself. Because vision-logic transcends formal rationality, it can more easily integrate formal reason and body.

It is true that each stage generally transcends and includes its predecessors, but that refers most specifically to the basic structures themselves (which are without inherent self-sense). But we must never forget that the basic structures are negotiated by the self, and the leading edge of self-development is the home of the death-terror. Thus, whatever the leading level of development with which the self's center of gravity is identified, just that level is the central nexus of the death-seizure. While the basic structures can be rather cleanly integrated, the self-stages, with their boundary of death-terror, cannot. Only as each basic structure is transcended and stripped of self-identity, can the self cease defending it against death. Thus, when the self is identified with formop, it cannot let go of formop and effect a "clean" integration with previous levels. This is nothing new with formop, but is true of every level appropriated by self-development. (This is, in fact, the dynamic of the repression barrier at each and every level of development: the boundary of defenses, in their many forms and levels, are instituted from the embedded-unconscious of any level, with its inherent death-terror.)

The first stage beyond identification with formop is, of course, vision-logic, at which point the formop mind, now basically stripped of self-sense, can be more cleanly integrated with the previous levels, including the bodily realms. And this, whatever the explanation, is what the actual clinical evidence shows at this level, where "mind and body are both experiences of an integrated self."

The evidence, in short, clearly shows that this postformal integrated personal stage (centaur) is significantly distinct from the previous, formal, egoic stage. There is nothing ad hoc in any of this.

2. The fact that fulcrum-0 is the "beginning of the line" in terms of this life, does not mean it is the beginning of the line for consciousness itself. We must hold open the possibility that, prior to fulcrum-0, there are the entire Bardo (and past-life) realms. I extensively outlined this possibility in *The Atman Project* (1996a)—in fact, I devoted the entire last chapter to it.

As I point out in that chapter, prior to conception in the gross bodymind, consciousness has traversed the causal Dharmakaya and then the subtle Sambhogakaya, and then finally takes gross form with conception (where it then begins fulcrum-0). This is why, since *The Atman Project*, I have always used Wordsworth's "Not in entire forgetfulness . . . But trailing clouds of glory do we come" to describe this situation. This is also why I have never denied that transpersonal experiences of various sorts are available during the preegoic period; I have simply denied that they are due to any preegoic structures.

In *The Atman Project*, I carefully describe the prior Bardo domains through which this soul-drop travels on its way to rebirth in the gross bodymind (i.e., the *involutionary* journey from causal to subtle to gross bodymind), where it then ends up in the prenatal state. In other words, this prenatal state is then the beginning of fulcrum-0, or the *beginning of frontal consciousness development* (the beginning of the lifetime indestructible drop), a development which occurs through the nine or ten basic structures of (frontal) consciousness and their associated self-fulcrums.

I believe that much of Stan's perinatal data in fact applies to these "trailing clouds." Unfortunately, space prevents me from discussing this important topic, but a full treatment of this issue can be found in chapter 7 of *The Eye of Spirit* (Wilber, 1997a).

3. For a discussion of how implicate and explicate orders relate to my model, see *The Eye of Spirit* (1997a, 209ff).

4. For a discussion of why the basic structures are not strictly or merely cognitive in any conventional sense, see *The Eye of Spirit* (1997a), chapter 9.

5. Take, for example, her critique of my use of the terms "hierarchy" and "heterarchy." These terms have a long and established usage in the literature, which I represent carefully and fairly. I then add the understanding that each of these modes of governance has a *pathological* form. My entire discussion concerns all four modes: normal and pathological hierarchy, normal and pathological heterarchy.

I point out that "In a heterarchy, rule or governance is established by a pluralistic and egalitarian interplay of all parties" (1995, 16). Wright (in her essay in this volume, p. 214) immediately claims that I am therefore "defining heterarchy as being incapable of establishing priorities," that I am in effect denying that heterarchy has any priorities at all. But of course "rule or governance" means a set of directions, guidelines, or priorities, or else there would be no rule or governance whatsoever (which would in fact be *pathological* heterarchy, as I make quite clear). But normal heterarchy's governance or priority, I point out, is based on "pluralistic and egalitarian interplay of all parties."

Wright will then "correct" my view by saying, "No, heterarchy really means 'rule with,' which is governed by 'mutual relations and intercommunion of parts'"—in other words, exactly the way I actually define heterarchy.

Wright thus totally caricatures my view as saying that natural heterarchy has no governance at all, and as examples of this, she gives what I clearly identify as *pathological* heterarchy, which is indeed a failure of priorities altogether. She then claims that I have ridiculed heterarchy by proclaiming it to be incapable of any governance or priorities or rules at all, and then she sets about to fix my faulty and demeaning (and "androcentric") thesis.

She does this by simply *renaming* my heterarchy ("mutual equivalence and communion of all parties") as "synarchy" ("mutual relations or intercommunion of the parts") [p. 214]. And all of a sudden we are on a strange Gilligan's Island, where there is the constant background implication that all the nice linking and communion and healing connections belong to females, and all the nasty ranking and dominance belongs to males. Males will then be the major possessors of hierarchy—which Wright narrowly interprets, quite against the massive literature on the subject, as being power "concentrated in the hands of a few" (which is in fact *pathological* hierarchy)—and females are the main bearers of the wonderful synarchy. This is called correcting androcentrism.

My actual conclusion in that discussion was stated very clearly: "Beware any theorist who pushes solely hierarchy or solely heterarchy, or attempts to give greater value to one or the other in an ontological sense. When I use the term 'holarchy,' I will especially mean the balance of normal hierarchy and normal heterarchy. Holarchy undercuts both extreme hierarchy and extreme heterarchy, and allows the discussion to move forward with, I believe, the best of both worlds kept firmly in mind" (1995, 24).

The fact that I point out that hierarchy originally meant "sacred rule" does not mean heterarchy is *not* sacred. (I was rehabilitating hierarchy from theorists such as Wright, and so I needed a more accurate historical reconstruction.) My actual conclusion was that the sacred exists in and as a balance and partnership of hierarchy (traditionally male) and heterarchy (traditionally female).

But that conclusion, of course, Wright simply coopts under the name "synarchy," and so again she has simply taken my conclusion, presented it first inaccurately as androcentric, then added the gynocentric aspects of my view that she herself has ignored or distorted, and then presented my conclusion, renamed, as her contribution to the discussion.

6. Alexander and Langer (1990, Introduction) have an excellent discussion of the centrality of hierarchy in Gilligan and a contribution by Gilligan herself that highlights this importance.

7. Alexander and Langer (1990, 10). Gilligan refers to this higher stage of moral integration as involving "a cognitive transformation from a *formal* to a *dialectical* mode of reasoning that can encompass the contradictions out of which moral problems often arise" (my italics, ibid., 223), which is what I have called the shift from formop to vision-logic, a vision-logic which Gilligan also calls "more encompassing," "dialectical,"

and "polyphonic"—a vision-logic that will "reunite intelligence and affectivity" (centauric) and, especially, integrate "the different voices of justice and care" (224)—that is, achieve a balance within each individual of male and female, which Gilligan also calls a "paradoxical interdependence of self and relationship" (agency and communion) (224). *All of those points were explicitly mentioned in my definition of centauric vision-logic*, a stage that included the beginning integration of masculine and feminine within each individual.

8. Wright maintains this distortion in both of her essays. She claims that "Wilber has essentially taken the pre/perm fallacy . . . and carried it into transpersonal theory" (in this volume, p. 220). The fact that I clearly distinguish between prepersonal permeable, personal permeable, and transpersonal permeable, demonstrates that I do not in any fashion equate prepersonal with permeable, which is the entire crux of Wright's charge that I commit the "pre/perm" fallacy, the centerpiece of her charge of sexism. The fact that I clearly do no such thing does not stop Wright from making that bizarre charge.

Wright divides her critique of my position into three main sections. The first is her "hierarchy/heterarchy" discussion, which I dealt with above. The second she calls "ecological," and it concerns two main issues. One is her claim that, because I commit the pre/perm fallacy, my discussion of ecological issues is flawed. But I do not commit the pre/perm fallacy, as we saw. This massive misconstrual is directly related to the other major ecological issue Wright focuses on. She feels, for example, that I underrate the contributions that rationality itself can make to world healing. But in truth, I make it quite clear that all of the positive contributions of all of the previous stages need to be honored, integrated, and incorporated, and this most definitely includes both prerational and rational modes. Wright incomprehensibly maintains that my view "overlooks, or at best minimizes, the importance of the positive, integrative actions [that can] take place within the cognitive levels of the rational. . ." (p. 219). But in fact, after pointing out the extraordinary integrative capacity of rationality and reasonableness, here is my actual conclusion: "Thus, the single greatest world transformation would simply be the embrace of a global reasonableness and pluralistic tolerance—the global embrace of egoic-rationality. . ." (1995, 201). Once again, Wright has reached a similar conclusion—the importance of what can be achieved within rationality—claimed it for herself, denied it to me, and then presented my position as androcentric, outmoded, and fallacious.

Wright's third main area of critique is the claim that my anthropological sources are "outmoded." She points to my use of Habermas as an example. But I did not rely on Habermas as a main anthropological source. The bibliography of *SES* contains almost one hundred contemporary anthropological sources (and Volume Two contains over five hundred), all of which are listed for a reason. Thus, Wright claims that my earliest technological stage is hunting and gathering, and she says this conception is outmoded because scavenging was quite prevalent. Actually, my earliest technological stage is foraging, which includes scavenging, hunting, gathering. I clearly list the actual stages on page 157 as "foraging, horticultural, agrarian, industrial, informational," and I explicitly tie this discussion to Lenski, not Habermas (for a long discussion of these technological stages in my model, see Wilber 1996d). For Wright to claim that my approach is based on outdated anthropological research is irresponsible in the extreme.

Here are further examples of Wright's "arguments": In *SES* I mention that Janet Chafetz has made the significant point that women who operated a heavy plow had higher rates of miscarriage, and therefore it was to their Darwinian advantage not to engage in such activity. Chafetz herself does not cite a source for this information. Wright leaps at this as evidence that I often use "unsubstantiated secondary sources" (p. 234, note 10). But the fact that heavy physical labor in the third trimester increases the rates of miscarriage—sometimes dramatically—is a common medical fact. It is uncontested, and therefore Chafetz does not need to reference a source for this, nor do I. But Wright offers this as evidence that I don't cite sources well and that they are often "secondary."

Wright especially jumps on my use of the term "centaur." The meaning of a word, semanticists agree, is simply how you use it. Jane Loevinger's highest stage of development, for both men and women, is one that she summarizes (with reference to Broughton) as: "both mind and body are experiences of an integrated self." Hubert Benoit, Jane Alexander, and Erik Erikson had used the term "centaur" to describe such an integrated state, because the human (mind) is not a rider divorced from the horse (body) but one with it. I thought that was an interesting use of the term, and so I adopted it, and defined it precisely using Jane Loevinger's summary. The way I define and use the term is, of course, precisely its actual meaning.

But Wright pounces on the fact that in ancient Greek mythology, the centaurs were male. Wright takes this as yet further evidence that my approach is androcentric. But why not go all the way? In ancient Greek mythology, the centaurs were male, it is true; but many were also filthy, stupid, vulgar, and general idiots. Why not be consistent and accuse me of male bashing at the same time?

If it were widespread knowledge that centaurs were male, and if the use of that term could be shown to disenfranchise women in some significant ways, then its continued use might be sexist. But not only does the fact that centaurs were male come as news to most people, to claim its use is sexist, based on archaic mythology, is like claiming that since Gaia is female, the very use of the term "Gaia" is sexist, biased, and prejudiced.

9. Wright will, she implies, as a feminist represent "the point of view of women" (in this volume, p. 210).

10. I intentionally say "select from *male* and *female* value spheres" because different aspects of these biological givens are variably *selected* (e.g., plow societies select for male physical strength). I always refer to the male and female value spheres (not masculine and feminine), for these are biologically based and thus quasi-universal. "Masculine" and "feminine" are not so much "selected for" as "constructed from"—that is, upon this selection from biological factors will be built culturally specific styles of masculine and feminine. Both techno-economic factors and cultural worldviews will play a hand in the selection from the male and female value spheres, which will then be elaborated and constructed in culturally specific ways to generate particular masculine and feminine styles.

11. McDermott chastises me for several polemical endnotes in *SES*. For various reasons I did indeed decide that a certain polemical stance was required in a few cases. After consultation with several editors, publishers, and colleagues, I decided to include several endnotes with a polemical/humorous tone, sharply critical of perhaps nine or ten theorists (out of several hundred discussed). These theorists themselves often use polemical, and in some cases even vitriolic prose. They aggressively condemn entire cultures and civilizations, or engage in unrelenting male bashing, or declare, without irony, that they alone boast the new paradigm. Those who disagree with them are often viciously dismissed. I simply chose in these endnotes to address their arguments by using a bit of their own polemical medicine.

Specifically, from each of the dozen or so movements that are particularly regressive or flatland—or that are merely Descended or merely Ascended—I chose one or two typical representatives. These fractious movements include some of the merely Descended (and regressive) aspects of ecofeminism, deep ecology, ecoholism, and eco-primitivism; some of the regressive aspects of Jungian, archetypal, and mythopoetic movements; astrology and astro-logic as mythic-membership; monological physics equals mysticism; monological systems theory; positivism; and merely Ascended gnosticism (East and West).

I chose a representative example from each and responded polemically. McDermott laments this; I consider it an integral part of the book, without which it would have abdicated its duty. (I have had several opportunities to change those notes; I have seen no reason to do so.) At the same time, I am more than willing to meet any of these theorists in dialogue, as witness the present book. *Sex, Ecology, Spirituality* has become a focal point for just this discussion, and the good in all this, as I see it, is that indeed the conversation has been jolted into high gear. This has also forced certain theorists to actually show their cards. McDermott opines that the tone of these endnotes has hindered the conversation, whereas exactly the opposite is the case. People have been galvanized, both for and against, pro and con, and this is a profound good, it seems to me.

12. The fact that a culture's center of gravity is, for example, at moral stage 3, does not prevent any specific individual from being above or below that average. Likewise, a foraging culture can have *individuals* at any number of stages of actual development. I simply suggested that, based on extensive evidence, the *average* level of self-development was typhonic, and the *highest* level of development tended to be psychic/shamanic, with a few rare higher exceptions. (This was also the conclusion of Walsh's [1990] *The Spirit of Shamanism.*) Nobody has to "skip" stages for this to occur.

Thus, for example, in today's society, where many of the basic organizing principles of public discourse are organized around moral stage 5 (rational social contract), some individuals will fall above, some below, that average. Some will remain at moral stage 1. Most will reach stages 3, 4, and 5. A very, very few will proceed into the post-post-conventional or genuinely transpersonal stages (stage 7 and higher). *But in all of these cases*, the same basic structures of consciousness will still have to be negotiated as growth continues; nobody skips major basic structures (images, symbols, concepts, rules, etc.).

13. Rothberg correctly states that I am "very insistent spirituality has to come out in all four of these quadrants" (p. 263). Nonetheless he believes that when I "write more specifically about transpersonal 'stages,' he [Wilber] uses . . . the old models" (p. 263). The discussion he references does so, but only because it is in fact discussing the old models (which generally address only the individual quadrant). At the same time, I will be the first to admit that my call for a more integral approach covering all four quadrants (in both ascending and descending modes) is introductory; but it is not, in my opinion, nearly as anemic as Rothberg seems to present it.

References

Alexander, C., and E. Langer, eds. 1990. *Higher stages of human development*. New York: Oxford University Press.

Apel, K. 1994. *Selected essays, vol. 1*. Atlantic Highlands, NJ: Humanities Press.

Brown, D. 1986. The stages of meditation in cross-cultural perspective. In *Transformations of consciousness: Conventional and contemplative perspectives on development*, by K. Wilber, J. Engler, and D. Brown. Boston: Shambhala.

Gilligan, C. 1982. *In a different voice*. Cambridge: Harvard University Press.

Grof, S. 1985. *Beyond the brain*. Albany: State University of New York Press.

———. 1988. *The adventure of self-discovery*. Albany: State University of New York Press.

Heard, G. 1963. *The five stages of man*. New York: Julian Press.

Loevinger, J. 1977. *Ego development*. San Francisco: Jossey-Bass.

Matt, D., ed. 1994. *The essential Kabbalah*. San Francisco: Harper.

Naess, A. 1989. *Ecology, community and lifestyle*. Cambridge: Cambridge University Press.

Puhakka, K. 1995. Restoring connectedness in the kosmos: A healing tale of a deeper order. [Review of K. Wilber: *Sex, ecology, spirituality*.] *The Humanistic Psychologist* 23 (3): 373-391.

Smith, H. 1976. *Forgotten truth*. New York: Harper & Row.

Thomas, L., S. Brewer, P. Kraus, and B. Rosen. 1993. Two patterns of transcendence: An empirical examination of Wilber's and Washburn's theories. *Journal of Humanistic Psychology* 33 (3): 66–81.

Trungpa, C. 1976. *The myth of freedom and the path of meditation*. Berkeley: Shambhala.

———. 1988. *Shambhala: Sacred path of the warrior*. Boston: Shambhala.

Wade, J. 1996. *Changes of mind*. Albany: State University of New York Press.

Walsh, R. 1990. *The spirit of shamanism*. Los Angeles: Tarcher.

Washburn, M. 1995. *The ego and the dynamic ground*. Rev. ed. Albany: State University of New York Press. (First edition published in 1988.)

Wilber, K. 1979. Are the chakras real? In *Kundalini, evolution and enlightenment*, edited by J. White. Garden City, N.Y.: Doubleday Anchor.

———. 1980. The pre/trans fallacy. *ReVision* 3 (Fall): 51-72. (Reprinted in K. Wilber, 1996, *Eye to eye*, 3rd ed. Boston: Shambhala.)

———. 1981. Ontogenetic development: Two fundamental patterns. *Journal of Transpersonal Psychology* 13 (1): 33–58.

———. 1982. Odyssey. *Journal of Humanistic Psychology* 22 (1): 57–90.

———. 1984a. The developmental spectrum and psychopathology: Part 1, stages and types of pathology. *Journal of Transpersonal Psychology* 16 (1): 75–118.

———. 1984b. The developmental spectrum and psychopathology: Part 2, Treatment modalities. *Journal of Transpersonal Psychology* 16 (2): 137–66.

———. 1995. *Sex, ecology, spirituality: The spirit of evolution*. Boston: Shambhala.

———. [1980] 1996a. *The Atman project*. 2nd ed. Wheaton, Ill.: Quest Books.

———. [1981] 1996b. *Up from Eden*. 2nd ed. Wheaton, Ill.: Quest Books.

———. [1983] 1996c. *Eye to eye*. 3rd ed. Boston: Shambhala.

———. 1996d. *A brief history of everything*. Boston: Shambhala.

———. 1997a. *The eye of spirit: An integral vision for a world gone slightly mad*. Boston: Shambhala.

———. 1997b. An integral theory of consciousness. *Journal of Consciousness Studies* 4 (1): 71-92.

———. 1998. *The marriage of sense and soul: Integrating science and religion*. New York: Random House.

Wilber, K., J. Engler, and D. Brown. 1986. *Transformations of consciousness: Conventional and contemplative perspectives on development*. Boston: Shambhala.

Wright, P. 1995. Bringing's women's voices to transpersonal theory. *ReVision* 17 (Winter): 3-11.

Zimmerman, M. 1981. *Eclipse of the self*. Athens: Ohio University Press.

———. 1990. *Heidegger's confrontation with modernity*. Bloomington: Indiana University Press.

———. 1994. *Contesting earth's future*. Berkeley and Los Angeles: University of California Press.

Part Six

The
Conversation
Continues

15

Responses to Ken Wilber

Roger Walsh

Ken Wilber's Integral Vision

 IF WE STEP BACK AND LOOK AT ALL OF KEN WILBER'S WORKS WE see that what he offers us is an integral vision: a vision of human nature, development, potential, pathology, therapy, and evolution; a vision of human society and culture, the cosmos and its evolution, and of the nature and relationship of consciousness and matter. Obviously this is a vision of enormous scope, being integral, multidisciplinary, developmental, evolutionary, epistemologically pluralistic and nonreductionistic.

Most visions are expressed in images, stories, or myths. Wilber's is a logical argument based on and integrating scientific data, philosophical analysis, and contemplation: an example of vision-logic, grounded in, but significantly updating, the perennial philosophy.

How are we to assess this vision? It seems we need at least two levels. The first, which is discussed later, is to determine the validity of the constitutive elements: the scientific data, logical and hermeneutical processes, and contemplative insights. The second level is to assay the value of the vision as a whole, or at least its major dimensions. What criteria are we to use for this?

We might begin with Plato's classic triad of the Good, the True, and the Beautiful. We might also add Joseph Campbell's four functions of mythic vision (envisioning and supporting the cosmos, religion, society, and individual development), Aldous Huxley's four features of the perennial philosophy (existence of a divine ground, human unity with this ground, the possibility of realizing this unity, and the overriding value of doing so), and Lewis Mumford's three characteristics of major intellectual and social transformations (broad syntheses of knowledge, acknowledgment of a hierarchy of existence, and evolution toward the good).

THE GOOD

Wilber affirms the reality of both the mystical and ethical Good, the possibility and value of realizing them, and a means (spiritual practice) to do so. His vision challenges the reigning scientistic, materialistic, reductionistic world view which has so effectively rendered the world foreign (Hegel), disqualified (Mumford), disenchanted (Weber), meaningless (Whitehead) and desacralized (Maslow), leaving us uprooted (Heidegger) and adrift. Wilber is effectively reenchanting the world and thereby offering a metaphysical-developmental-evolutionary grounding for the ethical Good, which is seen as (apparent) movement up the Great Chain of Being toward, and fuller expression of, the mystical Good.

His vision also encourages us to similar efforts: to enlarge the scope of our vision, to seek for integration and coherence, to intensify our scholarship, to deepen our contemplative practices (which are essential for transpersonal vision and understanding), and to approach our intellectual work as jnana yoga.

THE TRUE

The appropriate question is not "Is Wilber's vision true?" (there are far too many elements and topics to evaluate with an answer to a single question), but rather, "How much of his vision is true and what parts are true?" It may take decades to decide this and the process will require scientific testing, philosophical analysis, and contemplative insight. Nothing less than the combination of all three epistemological approaches (the "three eyes" of flesh, reason, and contemplation as Wilber, following St. Bonaventure, calls them) will finally be adequate.

At this stage, my own overall assessment of his work is that the great majority of his claims are backed by significant data and are integrated into a coherent system, thus at least partially satisfying both correspondence and coherence theories of truth. Several critics have raised valuable questions about specific elements of the system. However, overall, Wilber seems to have held his own in the debates. Importantly, none of the critiques seem to have seriously threatened the vision as a whole.

THE BEAUTIFUL

There are diverse aspects of Wilber's vision that many people find beautiful. To begin with, the sheer scope and degree of integration can be inspiring and refreshing in an age of intellectual and social fragmentation.

The vision offers a beautiful view of the Infinite/the Divine/the Tao/God, whose nature is inexpressible (transverbal, transrational) *shunyata* (emptiness), and *satchitananda* (boundless consciousness-being-bliss). The cosmos is seen as a creation of the Divine, as not separate from the Divine, and as evolving toward recognition of the Divine.

Similarly for humans. For Wilber, we are spirit, creations of, loved by, and not separate from the Divine, though lost in maya and illusions of being separate, limited, material, and mortal. But we can awaken from these illusions; enlightenment, salvation, or liberation are real developmental possibilities for us all. The suffering and agony of the world are partially transformable and ultimately transcendable, though in the interim extremely painful and tragic. We are called to relieve this suffering and to serve all beings as both a means to, and an expression of, our own awakening. Thus we have a role to play in the evolution and awakening of the cosmos.

There is beauty also in the manner in which this vision has been created. It is generously inclusive; its many disciplines, four quadrants, multiple ontological, developmental, and evolutionary levels, and epistemological pluralism acknowledge the potential value of each discipline and approach. Each can be honored, provided only that it does not overstep its limits and claim to be the only true way to knowledge (e.g., scientism) or to offer the whole picture (e.g., systems theory). The major jarring note has been the tone, which some people find overly harsh, of certain critical footnotes in *Sex, Ecology, Spirituality*, but these constitute far less than one percent of Wilber's writings.

SUMMARY

Wilber's vision seems to approximate Plato's criteria. How does it fare against the other criteria discussed earlier? The above discussion suggests that it seems to embody and update the essential elements of the perennial philosophy, to fulfill Campbell's four functions of myth, and to match Mumford's three requirements for transformative syntheses.

By their own theories of human nature and the cosmos, researchers either uplift or crush that nature. Our challenge is to create theories that envision and express the Good, the True, and the Beautiful, and thereby uplift our nature. Wilber seems to offer us such a vision.

Michael Murphy

The Natural History of
Extraordinary Experience
in Relation to the New Canon

IF WE TAKE SPECULATIVE PHILOSOPHIES SUCH AS THOSE OF FICHTE, HEGEL, Schelling, Bergson, Whitehead, Hartshorne, Aurobindo, and Wilber to comprise a new canon, then, as Wilber suggests, it is clear that many scientists, thinkers, and visionaries have also contributed to it, among them Freud, Piaget, Kohlberg, Maslow, and Habermas, as well as count-less philosophers and contemplatives from all the sacred traditions. One such contributing stream of work, which might be called the "natural history" or "anthropology" of extraordinary human experience, involves the collection and comparison of metanormal experiences from religious discipline, sport, adventure, the arts, childbirth, erotic relationships, and other walks of life. With the founding of the (British) Society for Psychical Research in 1882, such work accelerated in Great Britain, Europe, and America, became more systematic, and gave birth to land-mark collections of case studies such as Edmund Gurney's *Phantasms of the Living* (1886) and Frederic Myers's *Human Personality*. Such work is represented by, among others, William James in his *Varieties of Religious Experience* and other explorations of the "margins of consciousness"; by Abraham Maslow in his investigations of peak experience; by Marghanita Laski, who studied secular and religious ecstasies; by Herbert Thurston, a leading Catholic authority on the psychical and physical phenomena of mysticism; by Oxford University's Religious Experience Research Unit; by the Esalen Institute's Study of Extraordinary Experience (which contributed to my work on *The Future of the Body*); and by Rhea White, who has assembled what is possibly the world's largest collection of studies related to metanormal functioning. Each of these people or groups has assembled case studies, subjective reports, and experimental investigations regarding the transpersonal dimensions of human nature. Their work is empirical, in the spirit of the synoptic, integral, or multi-disciplinary empiricism implicit in Wilber's four-quadrant approach. All of it is subject to verification. In *The Future of the Body*, I presented a wide range of data produced by such work, and proposed that it shows that most, if not all, human attributes are capa-ble of extraordinary development. Writing that book, I became more and more convinced that the study of human metanormality is immensely fruitful and will develop more fully in the decades ahead.

The evidence for high level human change resulting from such research is brought into coherent purview by the central ideas of "evolu-tionary panentheism"—for example, by the notion that because divinity is latent everywhere it can flower in all our capacities. In *The Future of the Body*, I gave examples of metanormal sensorimotor, kinesthetic, com-munication, and cognitive abilities; of extraordinary pleasures and ecstasies; of self-surpassing love, vitality, volition, and sense of identity. Since the book's publication in 1992, many more examples of this kind have come my way, convincing me that the study and cultivation of extraordinary human experience is just getting started.

References

Gurney, E. 1886. *Phantasms of the living*. New York: Scholars Facsimiles and Reports.

Myers, F. [1903] 1954. *Human personality*. London: Longmans, Green.

Michael Washburn

Linearity, Theoretical Economy, and the Pre/Trans Fallacy

WILBER STRESSES THAT HIS CONCEPTION OF DEVELOPMENT ALLOWS FOR THE following kinds of exceptions to a strictly linear climb up his hierarchy of basic structures: loops at stage transitions, regressions, relocations of the sense of self, transition structures, and multiple developmental lines. In "The Pre/Trans Fallacy Reconsidered," I alerted the reader to all but one of these exceptions (see notes 3, 5, 11, 14, and 15). We must not forget, however, that Wilber's view is linear in its conception of "normal" (i.e., ideal-typical) development as a movement that climbs a (nested) hierarchy of basic structures without skipping levels or needing to return to lower levels.

In focusing on this basic sense in which Wilber's view is linear, I wanted to highlight his belief that prepersonal basic structures are *merely prepersonal*, as far from spirituality as you can get, as he says, and that transpersonal basic structures are *exclusively transpersonal*, without precursors of a significantly similar sort. I wanted to highlight this belief because I think it unparsimoniously doubles the number of nonegoic psychic potentials. One can explain the difference between pre and trans in developmental terms without having to posit two different pre and trans sets of nonegoic potentials (most of which end up being counterparts of each other). The preoedipal child, I believe, is intimately in touch with energy, the body, affective life, and the autosymbolic imagination. These basic nonegoic potentials experienced by the young child are not, I believe, merely pre, as Wilber's view implies; they are potentials which, once reawakened and *integrated with a mature ego structure*, can express themselves in trans ways. Thus understood, pre and trans are irreducibly different and yet, in many instances, expressions of the same underlying potentials. There is no fallacious collapsing of pre and trans here, as Wilber alleges.

Pre/trans fallacies come into play when one uses an invalid inference to arrive at an account of pre and trans. The two main types of such error are (1) the inference from phenomenological similarity to underlying structural identity, and (2) the inference from phenomenological or developmental difference to underlying structural nonidentity and dis-similarity. What Wilber refers to as ptf-1 (reduction of the trans to the pre) and ptf-2 (elevation of the pre to the trans) are both examples of the first type of fallacy. Both ptf-1 and ptf-2 begin with the premise that pre and trans states are phenomenologically similar in significant respects and then move to the unwarranted conclusion that these states are fun-damentally the same, whether *fundamentally the same* is taken to mean that both are fundamentally pre (ptf-1) or that both are fundamentally trans (ptf-2). The second type of fallacy is what I, following Wilber's con-vention, called ptf-3. This fallacy begins with the premise that pre and trans states are phenomenologically and developmentally different in significant respects and then moves to the unwarranted conclusion that these states are expressions of two dissimilar sets of nonegoic structures or potentials. Wilber, I suggested, in preparing *The Atman Project* for publication, fell prey to just this fallacy. Wanting to distance himself from a naive romanticism and from ptf-2, he overcompensated and fell prey to ptf-3.

Wilber says (p. 360, note 1, in this volume) that he is not guilty of ptf-3: "All I [Wilber] do is infer separateness [of pre and trans basic struc-tures] from separateness." I accept Wilber's word on this. Wilber then says, "even if I did infer separateness from difference, the separateness still might actually be there" (p. 360). There is no issue here. I have always acknowledged that Wilber's view might be correct. I do, however, believe that his view is suspect in at least the following three ways: (1) it is unparsimonious; (2) it is laden with an absolutistic metaphysics (which posits a One, Brahman, or Source that involutes itself as matter and then returns to itself through evolution and spiritual realization); and (3) as I have argued (1995 and elsewhere), it is weak in its accounts of the dynamic, depth-psychological, and relational dimensions of spiri-tual life.

Regrettably, Wilber's exposition of my ideas in his response is marred by egregious misrepresentations. I have space for only three examples:

1. Suggesting that my view prescribes "wholesale infantile regression" (p. 319, in this volume), Wilber asks (p. 318): "Does the adult have to regress to preverbal babbling?" The answer, of course, is no. We do not have to become literal babies to become like babies in spiritually relevant ways. What I call regression in the service of transcendence is a restorative return to nonegoic potentials which were last active during preegoic stages. In this return, ego functions are not lost and are eventually integrated with reactivated nonegoic

potentials. This is why the regression is a regression *in the service of transcendence* rather than a pathological regression to infantilism.

2. Wilber says (pp. 312-13) that I hold that the young ego represses the power of the Dynamic Ground in the form of libido and that I then treat this repression as if it were a spiritual repression so that I can explain spiritual awakening as a spiraling return rather than, as Wilber does, a straight ascent. The problem here is that Wilber formulates my view *backwards*. The ego does not repress the power of the Ground as libido; rather, it is precisely the ego's repression of this power which limits it—except for what circulates as psychic energy—to an unconscious sexual organization, thereby reducing it to libido. Accordingly, the repression of the power of the Ground is a deactivation of a *truly spiritual energy*, an energy which lies dormant until it is reactivated later in life.

3. Treating my view as if it were the same as an earlier view of his own, Wilber says, "The big difference . . . is that Romantic/Wilber-I [which holds that the infant is in contact with spirit] *must* see the infantile preegoic structure as being . . . a oneness with the whole world" (p. 313; Wilber's italics). There are two problems here. The first lies in the assumption that contact with spirit implies a "oneness with the whole world." Why must spiritual power—whether experienced by a child or an adult—be an all-embracing reality? Cannot spiritual power be truly spiritual without being cosmic in stature?

The second problem is that Wilber attributes his own metaphysical assumptions to me. He speaks as if I *must* hold that the infant's contact with spirit is a "oneness with the whole world." He seems not to know that, in my books, I have repeatedly stressed that we cannot know for sure whether the source of spiritual energy—which I call the Dynamic Ground—is an ontological ground or cosmic being of some sort or only an underlying basis of the psyche.

Reference

Washburn, M. 1995. *The ego and the dynamic ground*. Rev ed. Albany: State University of New York Press.

Stanislav Grof

Spectrum Psychology Revisited

IN HIS ANSWER TO MY CRITICAL COMMENTS ABOUT HIS MODEL, KEN FOCUSED primarily on the problems related to perinatal dynamics, which makes sense since that seems to be the main focus of our disagreement. I certainly accept his criticism of the semantic problems connected with the use of the term *perinatal*. It is true that I have occasionally used the term *perinatal* for experiences that did not have an explicit component of biological birth.

To some extent, this reflects the peculiar ambiguity of the perinatal experiences themselves. In most instances, they represent a strange amalgam of heterogenous elements. Some of their aspects are clearly related to the trauma of birth, but others are drawn from the historical and archetypal domains of the collective unconscious or from various areas of nature.

This is further confounded by the fact that, in some instances, people who have typical perinatal experiential sequences show external behavioral and physiological manifestations that link these episodes to birth (such as fetal position, flections, deflections, and ramming movements of the head, rotations of the body, choking, and cyanosis or other vascular changes), but do not themselves subjectively associate their experiences with the trauma of birth.

Most of the time, when I have used the term *perinatal experiences*, the elements of biological birth were present, either for both the experient and the observer, or at least for one of them. However, occasionally, both the internal and external birth-related manifestations were missing and the entire death-rebirth process consisted of a characteristic mixture of historical, archetypal, and natural sequences. However, these experiences were in all other aspects similar to those that usually have various external or experiential concomitants clearly related to birth.

Another reason for the semantic confusion in regard to the term *perinatal* lies in my intellectual history. Naturally, my understanding of nonordinary states of consciousness underwent many changes over the years as I was continuously confronted with new material. When I first observed and experienced perinatal phenomena, I was under the strong influence of my medical and psychiatric traning and thus inclined to explain the symbolic aspects of these experiences from the emotional and physical events of birth. I actually borrowed the term perinatal from obstetrics where it is used only for biological events. At that time, accepting the psychological significance of birth was a very radical conceptual jump. My basic training was in medicine and in Freudian psychology, neither of which recognizes birth as a psychologically relevant event.

Later, as I became more familiar with the transpersonal domain, I realized that the historical, archetypal, and natural sequences that typically accompany the reliving of birth are important phenomena *sui generis*, rather than just derivatives or illustrative concomitants of the biological and emotional trauma of birth. While they often accompany reliving of birth, they can also emerge quite independently of such liaison. At present, my primary conceptual focus is on supraordinated archetypal patterns that can manifest on many different levels and in many different ways. I do not see any reason to give a privileged position to the events in the material world, in general, and in the realm of biology, in particular.

Rather than trying to explain certain archetypes from physiological and emotional aspects of birth, I am now inclined to assume that the archetypal dynamic plays a critical role in creating the experience of biological birth iself. For example, I believe that the fetus trapped and suffering in the clutches of the birth canal (or an adult reliving birth) is experientially under the influence of the archetype of Hell. This certainly makes more sense than seeing the rich and complex archetype of Hell as being a product of what happens in the birth canal. Similarly, when the reliving of birth is associated with images from the collective unconscious featuring other sentient beings who are in a similar experiential predicament, I see both as different expressions of the same archetypal influences.

As I have shown above, my understanding of the experiential domain of the death-rebirth process now reaches significantly beyond the narrow confines of biological delivery. In spite of this fact, I continue to use the term *perinatal*, even for those experiences where the element of biological birth is missing. Ken is certainly right in this regard and I see how this can be confusing.

I am aware of the ambiguities involved, but I have not found a good replacement for the name *perinatal matrix*, and this term also has become part of the therapeutic jargon of hundreds of people who have trained with us. And it certainly is not easy to maintain complete logical consistency over a period of forty years when one explores frontiers of the psyche uncharted by Western science and has to respond to a constant influx of new observations and information. In a sense, this is not dissimilar to Ken's own conceptual struggles, as exemplified by the development of his model from Wilber-I to Wilber-IV.

However, some of the concepts or statements that Ken attributes to me and criticizes me for, have not been part of any stage of my intellectual evolution. I have described how many of the people with whom I have worked have experienced a powerful spiritual opening in connection with the reliving of biological birth. However, I have never claimed that an experiential confrontation with birth is a necessary prerequisite for spiritual opening. I have actually quite explicitly described two major types of spiritual opening, one of them involving the perinatal level, the other based on a direct experiential access to the transpersonal realms.

Similarly, I have described how it is typical to experience an agonizing existential crisis in connection with the second perinatal matrix. At the same time, I have never suggested that every existential crisis is perinatal in nature. And I have certainly never said or written that every experience of death has its source on the perinatal level. I have again quite explicitly described that powerful experiential encounters with death can occur in connection with memories of life-threatening biographical events, with the reliving of birth and prenatal crises, and also with various transpersonal matrices (karmic, phylogenetic, and archetypal).

In conclusion, I would like again to thank the editors for this very unique forum. I feel that the contributions of all the authors and, of course, Ken himself have helped to clarify some of the issues, brought others into a sharp relief, and generally moved us closer to a reconciliation of the differences and a comprehensive vision for transpersonal psychology. I will be looking forward to the continuation of this important dialogue.

Sean M. Kelly

Breaks in the Chain

AS I UNDERSTAND IT, THERE APPEAR TO BE TWO MAIN POINTS TO KEN WILBER'S response to my paper. The first is that my critique is largely irrelevant because it applies to *transitional*, rather than to *basic*, structures. The second point is that transpersonal influxes, when experienced as transient *states*, do not necessarily violate the principle of holarchical integration, since the latter applies only to *enduring structures or traits*.

These are important distinctions. By themselves, however, these distinctions fail to address the very specific problems to which I sought to draw attention. To begin with, what is one to make of such people as Natalie, the eight-year-old Hopi girl (see note 1 of my article) who seems consistently and simultaneously to inhabit two world-spaces—the personal (conop) and the transpersonal (psychic)—at a stage of development *prior* to the emergence of formop? Secondly, if transpersonal (in this case psychic) influxes are possible (even as transient states) at *any* stage of development, should it not therefore be possible for someone at the stage of preop to experience formop? I doubt that Wilber would admit of such a possibility (as it would violate the holarchical principle of "symbols before concepts before rules," etc.). In fact, whenever Wilber admits of apparent deviation from this sequence, not only is it a question (to him) of merely transient states, it is also always *transpersonal* basic structures (and never higher personal ones) to which the individual is said to have potential transient access. Transpersonal basic structures, in other words, seem to be of a significantly different order than, and not continuous with, all other basic structures.

Wilber appears to recognize this to the extent that he postulates the spiritual as a distinct developmental "line" (of "ultimate concern" [p. 331, in this volume]) or axis which runs parallel to, though not necessarily in tandem with, other developmental lines (such as the cognitive, the affective, the moral, and so on). This would be consistent with my view of the transpersonal as the implicate axis of the mandala of consciousness. To adopt this view, however, one has to revision the root metaphor of the Great Chain of Being along with the principle of holarchical integration to which this metaphor corresponds. Wilber himself recognizes that the notion of a distinct spiritual line or axis is incompatible with the view of the spiritual as the "highest" reaches of all developmental lines, and yet he claims that both are probably right. But if the spiritual line, like all other developmental lines, evolves through the "basic levels" of the "Great Holarchy of Being," one can no longer conceive of Spirit as the final term in the holarchical chain: Matter/Mind/Spirit. By the same token, one is no longer justified in maintaining that the sequence Matter/Mind/Spirit corresponds to that of prepersonal/personal/transpersonal.

The other problem to which I drew attention is the fact that the only stages in Wilber's model which seem to satisfy the criteria of holarchical integration are those of the typhon and the centaur. Michael Washburn and I have both pointed out that the stage of the mental ego, in Wilber's own description of it, is constitutionally split off from the body (typhonic consciousness). This split is only overcome with the emergence of the vision-logic of the centaur. Wilber has responded by alerting us to the fact that typhonic, mental (or rational), and centauric all refer to transitional (in this case world views), and not to basic structures, and so are not subject to the principle of holarchical integration. (They are stages in the "weak" sense only.) The first thing that occurred to me while reflecting upon this response is that the whole lower left quadrant (which is said to consist of transitional structures) of Wilber's Kosmic mandala would no longer exemplify the principle of holarchical integration which the mandala is supposed to embody. But neither, for that matter, does the upper left quadrant (which is said to consist of basic structures)—for, as I argued in my paper, it is only with vision-logic that concept (or formop) and symbol (or preop) are truly integrated in a supraordinate holon (the stage of the centaur). When "the self is identified with formop," as Wilber says in his response, "it cannot let go of formop and effect a 'clean' integration of previous levels. . . . The first stage beyond identification with formop is, of course, vision-logic, at which point the formop mind, now basically stripped of self-sense, can be more cleanly integrated with previous levels, including the bodily realms" (p. 361).

The second thing that occurred to me is that, even if it is in some sense a transitional structure, the centaur "includes" vision-logic—that is, the integrated body-mind of centauric consciousness includes the cognitive dimension of vision-logic, as well as the affective dimension of spontaneity, the conative dimension of intentionality, and so on, as constitutive predicates (see Wilber 1980, 61)—but vision-logic does not, per se, include the centaur. The same is true of typhonic consciousness (or the body-ego) relative to preop. In other words, it would appear that the cognitive dimension or "line" is one strand among several which together make up the complex fabric of any given stage of consciousness. It is for this reason, though I had not yet conceptualized it in this manner, that I referred in my paper to typhonic and centauric consciousness as holons. Perhaps Wilber's concept of the Self, or self-system, if suitably reformulated, could serve as the central organizing principle (as with Jung's use of the term) common to all developmental lines. But again, to do so would require revisioning the principle of holarchical integration in keeping with what I have called the principle of complex holism. Such a revisioning would also affect the right-hand quadrants of Wilber's Kosmic mandala. But this is a matter for future discussions.

Reference

Wilber, K. 1980. *The Atman project*. Wheaton, Ill.: Quest Books.

Donald Rothberg
Toward an Integral Spirituality

I WANT TO THANK KEN WILBER FOR HIS VERY GENEROUS COMMENTS ABOUT my work, in his response and elsewhere, and for his contributions in pointing toward a contemporary "integral," multidimensional understanding of spiritual development. Here, I want briefly to address: (1) the definition of "spiritual development"; (2) questions about the ade-

quacy of Wilber's stage model; and (3) Wilber's view of contemporary
spiritual practice.

(1) Wilber helpfully clarifies the meanings of the often vaguely used
term, "spiritual development." His solution is to specify two complementary meanings: first, referring to the most advanced, "transpersonal"
stages of any given developmental "line" (cognitive, affective, moral,
etc.); and secondly, referring to a distinct line of development having to
do with one's "ultimate concern," whether that concern is food (as in
Gandhi's dictum that God appears to a hungry man as food), belonging,
or spiritual liberation.

However, I want to suggest a third, distinct sense of spiritual development as that learning having to do with *any* content of experience of
any developmental line when approached from a transpersonal *perspective*, that is, from an attitude cultivating and/or guided by the "virtues"
or "perfections" of a particular authentic tradition or approach (e.g.,
awareness, love, wisdom, etc.) In the conversations in my "How Straight
is the Spiritual Path?" for example, we find Joseph Goldstein claiming
that the *attitude* toward any given content is more important than the
content itself; Jack Kornfield refusing to distinguish psychological and
spiritual development, when both are seen from the perspective of
addressing places of spiritual ignorance and entanglement; and Michele
McDonald-Smith's most basic intention as a teacher to help her students
to approach *any* experience with openness, compassion, and wisdom.

This rather simple notion of spiritual development may be necessary
in practice to balance the rather awesome complexity of a model of "integral" spirituality involving: a multiciplity of lines of development; "masculine" and "feminine" perspectives on each line; the contemporary need
to explore and express more fully spirituality in connection with body,
emotion, relationships, and the earth; and individual and collective, and
inner and outer, aspects of development (cf. Wilber's "four quadrants").
No wonder that all of the teachers in the conversations emphasize the
practical limits of using theoretical models and their trust in the organic "unfolding" of spiritual development. On the other hand, naming and
identifying the aspects of development that have often been ignored,
excluded, or devalued also seems crucial in order to establish the cultural and personal spaces for such development.

(2) However, the complexity of such an integral spirituality also
leads to questions, still requiring further discussion, about the extent to
which a stage model of spiritual development remains tenable. Given the
questions in my chapter, we can ask whether there indeed really are discrete, coherent, stable spiritual "stages" of "basic structures" or whether
the situation with these structures is much like what Wilber finds with

"transition structures," that is, that at a given moment a person may be operating with an often unstable amalgam of several of these structures. Given the many qualifications that Wilber makes (and may need further to make) to the claims of a strict Piagetian stage model, what exactly is left? How limited or minimal (although still perhaps quite important) is the resulting stage conception?

Some of these same questions, by the way, are also found among the main theorists in the field of adult development, whom Wilber presents as supporting the idea of a stage model, in that most theorists of "higher" or "deeper" development accept some version of a hierarchical stage model (p. 332, in this volume). However, although eleven of the thirteen theories summarized by Alexander, Druker, and Langer (1990, 10ff.), to which he refers, do include some acceptance of a hierarchical stage model, especially for the development of children (and especially for mathematical competences), the majority (seven of thirteen, including those of Levinson and Gardner) do *not* include hierarchical stage theories of "higher" development.

In the context of the conversations with the spiritual teachers, we can ask further questions, which also need additional discussion. How, if at all, can we make sense, in terms of a stage model, of the personal stories from Jack Kornfield, about spiritual development understood as sustained transpersonal exploration followed by "descent" into emotions, relationships, and body, and from Michele McDonald-Smith, about her years of spiritual openings followed by a kind of regression and healing? Can there be sustained and stabilized transpersonal development without the prior achievement of the integrative stage of the centaur?

One way to begin to answer these latter questions is with the help of the earlier model of spiritual development that I suggested. In the particular stories of Kornfield and McDonald-Smith, it was only because of the stabilization of mindfulness through training that they were able to "descend" or "regress." In other words, from a base in transpersonal operations (whether mindfulness, the witness, or love), development on supposedly "lower" levels of various developmental lines occurs as a form of spiritual practice. The extent to which such a base is related to Wilber's transpersonal "basic structures" is a matter for future discussion.

(3) The complexities of considering different developmental lines, and the beginning level of articulation of this aspect of his theory may sometimes lead Wilber to underestimate and misread the spiritual development of contemporary practitioners, as when he claims that American spiritual teachers "will rarely see stages of development of anything" (p. 335). It may require a more sensitive map than we now have, and one not focused so much on nonordinary experiences, to be

able to identify development in a multiplicity of dimensions. Such a map might well guide and inspire a vision of spiritual practice for our times.

Reference

Alexander, C., S. Druker, and E. Langer. 1990. Introduction: Major issues in the exploration of adult growth. In *Higher stages of human development: Perspectives on adult growth*, edited by C. Alexander and E. Langer. New York: Oxford University Press.

Michele McDonald-Smith

Is Anyone Developing Spiritually?

I APPRECIATE THE MANY IMPORTANT INSIGHTS FOUND IN WILBER'S WORK AND find especially important his intention to open up his developmental theory to gender concerns and to a sense of multiple developmental "lines." But I want to respond here to the series of claims stated or implied in the section on "Discriminating Wisdom" of his response. There Wilber mostly questions whether contemporary American spiritual teachers actually observe any spiritual development at all (and thus, I suppose, whether our observations have any relevance to theories of development). Wilber writes (pp. 334-35) that a large number of individuals who come to meditation retreats are at a "preconventional" level of development, that spiritual teachers "constantly find themselves having to cater to these lowest common denominator trends," and that many people's insights are actually getting dragged down by their low centers of gravity in the rest of their psyches. As a result, American teachers commonly have to engage in what Wilber calls "supportive psychotherapy" (p. 335), not transformative or transpersonal spirituality; we supposedly "rarely see stages of development of anything" (p. 335).

I'm drawn in my teaching to use the Buddhist model of the *paramis*. It's actually a model of multiple developmental lines. There's the development of generosity, ethics (*sila*), renunciation, wisdom, energy, patience, truthfulness, resolution or determination, loving-kindness (*metta*), and equanimity. From the perspective of this model and my own observations of meditation practitioners over many years, I see things very differently than does Wilber.

What I see as really important is to help people apply wise attention to every aspect of their lives, so that each of the *paramis* is developed. In coming to a retreat, we take the time to develop wise and compassionate attention and understanding. Then we come home and apply this attention and understanding to all the different dimensions of our lives. But to say that most of what happens is supportive psychotherapy is notably inaccurate.

My sense of many of the people who come to retreats is that they actually are, in comparison with the general population, some of the most highly developed people. Some people are already quite ripe when they come; a teacher only needs to offer fine tuning to help them deepen their practice. There aren't so many obstacles for them in doing the practice; they just do it and they access deep stages of wisdom relatively easily. They may have been developing the *paramis* over lifetimes. Others may come to retreats and access deep stages of wisdom, but still have a lot of work to do in terms of morality or generosity; this is where speaking of multiple developmental lines is important.

Having powerful transcendent experiences, even on a fairly stable basis, may relate to just one aspect of development. Often I find that people are looking for a model which says that certain spiritual experiences will just "do it," that their practice will essentially be done. What I see from well over twenty years of practice is that the map of what needs to be done keeps enlarging. There's such a vastness to spiritual practice; there's so much more for all of us to develop.

Sometimes people come to retreats and think that they're not developing fast enough because they're not like St. Teresa or Ramana Maharshi or the Buddha. Actually, one of the favorite complaints at certain stages of practice in meditation retreats is that meditators think that "nothing's happening."

But often when we think that nothing's happening, it's because we don't have a map that's broad enough to see what is actually developing. Maybe patience is developing, and this is incredibly important—or generosity or lovingkindness or ethics. Wilber seems to be struggling, like many of us, with how to make sense of these different developmental lines.

I think that most teachers try *not* to do "supportive psychotherapy." A lot of the people who come to retreats have done or are currently in therapy. It's really important not to minimize that kind of work while realizing that an impressive number of the people who come to retreats have a strong urge, based in the *paramis*, to touch timeless wisdom. Wilber may also be struggling, as we are, with understanding the connection of therapeutic work and spiritual practice. He speaks, for example, of the fact that many spiritual teachers have only emphasized the "spiritual line" themselves and severely neglected the interpersonal and psychological lines.

Helping people to recognize their own understanding of what the truth is, their own wisdom, is not "supportive psychotherapy." This hap-

pens commonly at retreats, and represents a major shift in consciousness. There are very clear signs of this timeless wisdom as it takes root
in human consciousness. I see that wisdoms develop for people over time;
I've seen it with some people over fifteen or twenty years. I see wisdom
and compassion coming to permeate their beings.

There is tremendous development; there is a vast difference between
the growth within someone who has practiced a lot and someone who has
not. It is absurd to suggest that we don't witness levels of development
of anything! There's just no comparison between a person at the beginning and twenty years later, if the person has really put in time. It's
extraordinary what happens!

Michael E. Zimmerman
On Transpersonal Ecology

LET ME BEGIN BY THANKING KEN WILBER FOR HIS GENEROUS COMMENTS ON
my own writings, some of which clearly show the influence of his
remarkable synthetic vision. In *Contesting Earth's Future* (1994), for
instance, I used his evolutionary model in the context of an attempt to
adjudicate debates among deep ecologists, ecofeminists, and social ecologists. My aim was to show the extent to which these branches of radical ecology could be read as having a progressive orientation. Although
attracted by aspects of deep ecology and ecofeminism, I argued that their
reaction against the nature-dominating aspect of modern rationalism
overemphasizes the immanent and neglects the transcendent. Wilber
rightly calls for harmonizing the Ascent and Descent traditions, instead
of praising one and casting aspersions on the other. Elements of his evolutionary cosmology are discernible in social ecology, but some social ecologists are so wedded to modern this-worldliness that they can neither
appreciate nor adequately define the spiritual. Like radical ecologists,
Wilber seeks to reintegrate the corporeal, natural, and feminine domains
that were largely dissociated by modern rationality, but he also maintains
that many radical ecologists adopt an ecoromanticism that is as ontologically flat as the rationalism of which they are so critical.

In my chapter, I agreed with Wilber that many modernists and ecologists alike share an immanentistic ontology that ignores crucial dimensions of the highly differentiated Kosmos, but I also suggested that he
does not acknowledge that some exceptional radical ecologists, including
Arne Naess, may avoid such a truncated ontology. Perhaps Volume Two

of Wilber's trilogy will persuade me that there are fewer exceptions than I thought to his contention that radical ecologists adhere to schemes that, in comparison with the perennial philosophy, are ontologically impoverished and at least partly reactionary.

Wilber is right that talk of transpersonal ecology is premature, since so few people have attained stable forms of transpersonal awareness. Global consolidation of rational-perspectival awareness, defined as the capacity to adopt the other's point of view, would reduce jingoism, dogmatism, and racism, thereby curbing the militarism responsible for so much ecological destruction. Rational-perspectival awareness would also reveal that economic development that enriches the Northern tier at the expense of the Southern tier is self-defeating, because it is ecocidal (see Athanasiou 1996). Widespread recognition of universal human rights, including the right to satisfaction of basic material needs, would require potentially eco-friendly changes in economic development.

In view of my own appreciation for universal human rights, the evolution of human consciousness, and cosmic teleology, I can understand Wilber's complaint that my warning about totalizing narratives was inspired by political correctness. Recognizing that some grand narratives, however well intended, have been misused, I simply meant that caution must be exercised in constructing and disseminating them. In fact, I think that grand narratives can not only inspire people to rise above those personal and cultural identifications that promote exclusionary (e.g., racist, xenophobic, and sexist) attitudes and practices, but can provide a comprehensive basis for criticizing existing social conditions. Wilber points out that performative self-contradictions are usually involved when postmodernists criticize grand narratives. Far from being a conceptual straightjacket, Wilber contends, his narrative is open ended and flexible. Evidence for or against this contention will emerge as he continues to respond to critics, as he is doing in this forum.

I appreciate postmodern celebrations of cultural difference, but I also know that the most repressive regimes flaunt their right to preserve "cultural difference" whenever international tribunals call for universal democratic rights, and for an end to political imprisonment, torture, and disfiguring cultural practices (see Finkielkraut 1994). Though lacking a God's eye view, I believe that some perspectives give rise to institutions and practices that are better than others. The ideal of respect for human persons (however difficult it may be to specify this term) is better than any tribalism, racism, ethnocentrism, or nationalism, which exclude one or another group from the ranks of humankind.

This same univeralistic impulse animates ecologists who criticize speciesism and the appeal to some allegedly unique or superior human feature (e.g., intelligence or linguistic capacity) to justify heedless treatment of nonhuman life. All forms of life, so many environmentalists insist, are deserving of respect. Despite such laudable inter-species considerations, however, we must not lose sight of differences that make a difference. In this enormous universe, humans are surely not unique either in possessing highly differentiated linguistic-rational abilities, or in being able to achieve more integrated levels of awareness. Even on our own planet, dolphins and whales may have linguistic-rational ability that match or exceed our own. Wilber's central point, with which I am in basic agreement, is this: whichever species happen to possess the powers of awareness with which humans have been gifted, possessing such awareness means that a species "includes" the biosphere, in the sense of containing and going beyond the levels of complexity involved in constituting the biosphere. Far from justifying derelict treatment either of the biosphere or of the life forms belonging to it, this capacity for transcending the biospheric imposes the responsibility of respecting and appropriately caring for all life, human or otherwise. That so many people, modern and otherwise, fail to live up to this responsibility indicates to what extent humankind lacks genuinely integrated awareness, but is instead dis-integrated and thus governed by greed, aversion, and delusion.

References

Athanasiou, T. 1996. *Divided planet*. Boston: Little, Brown.

Finkielkraut, A. 1995. *The defeat of mind*. Translated by J. Friedlander. New York: Columbia University Press.

Zimmerman, M. 1994. *Contesting earth's future*. Berkeley and Los Angeles: University of California Press.

Peggy A. Wright
Difficulties with Integrating the Feminine

WHEN I BEGAN READING *SEX, ECOLOGY, SPIRITUALITY* (*SES*) (Wilber 1995), I was looking forward to a presentation on transpersonal theory that would balance feminine and masculine approaches to transpersonal development. As I continued reading, I became increasingly concerned about how the tone, content, supportive materials, and sources of Wilber's presentation frequently acted against such a balance. I certainly respect the over-arching intent of Wilber's work and agree with substantial portions of his texts as they relate to individual developmental stages and certain epistemological issues. However, it is clear that we have substantial disagreements on a number of gender-related issues. Although it is not possible to cover all the specifics in the space allotted here, I appreciate the opportunity to comment on Wilber's response to my articles (1995, and also earlier in this volume) and to clarify my own position.

DEEP STRUCTURES

Wilber, in his response, claims to "have consistently called for an understanding that carefully balances universal deep structures with culturally variant surface structures" (p. 342). As I (1995) clearly stated, I believe that any such endeavor involves the responsibility to actively identify the cultural assumptions inherent in one's own evaluative framework. This is an area that Wilber has yet to address in detail.

HETERARCHY AND HIERARCHY

As I indicated in my earlier chapter in this volume, I agree with major portions of Wilber's (1995) holarchical theory. However, I am critiquing not just what Wilber presented, but how it was presented, and what was omitted or distorted in this area of his work. Given the generally hierarchical and androcentric nature of our culture, I believe that it is much more important that we explore and better understand the concept of normal heterarchy (what I call "synarchy") than it is to defend the concept of hierarchy. In my earlier chapter in this volume, I consciously reframed Wilber's (1995) presentation in order to highlight these issues, to rectify what I consider to be certain deficits in his presentation, and to bring attention to his questionable generalizations about the views of heterarchists.

GILLIGAN

I am in agreement with much of Wilber's commentary on Gilligan's work, and remain, as always, supportive of the hierarchical aspects of her approach to moral development. Unfortunately, Wilber implies that my use of the term "separate self" is derogatory and the term "connected self" is inappropriately positive. These terms are from Lyons (1988) and emerged from her research work with Gilligan. They originated as descriptive, neutral terms. I have found them to be particularly well suited to representing in a concise, unambiguous, and relatively neutral manner certain concepts about gender-related self-structures that are commonly discussed in the field of women's psychology.

THE PERMEABLE SELF

I am in substantial agreement with the new material that Wilber presents here. Indeed, I (1995) have proposed that the permeable-self involves prepersonal, personal, and transpersonal developmental stages and have described some possible effects of a permeable self-structure on transpersonal development. I haven't encountered any previously published work by Wilber that explicitly acknowledges a connected or permeable self-structure and integrates it into his system. As I've (1995) pointed out, such an omission mirrors the biases of past researchers and psychologists. To my knowledge, Wade (1996) is the first transpersonalist to present a structural model that begins to explicitly incorporate the differing pathways of many women's psychological development. I'm pleased that Wilber is now attempting something similar in his currently unpublished work.

In addition, I do not assume that Wilber (1995) equates the prepersonal stages with permeable boundaries. What I do find, however, is that Wilber often judges what I take to be personal and transpersonal expressions of the permeable self as being prepersonal, much as Western psychology often has done with female expressions of permeable boundaries. As I've indicated earlier in this volume, he (1995) also overlooks the possibility that permeable boundaries engaged at the rational cognitive-developmental stage may actually assist in the development of a mature, less egocentric, ecological self.

HUMAN EVOLUTION

Very simply, I have found Wilber's (1995) presentation in the area of human evolution and development to be at odds with a number of sources that are listed in his bibliography, especially the more feminist sources (see my earlier chapter). I have concerns about Wilber's ability to present these sources accurately; I also question much of his theoretical presentation in this area.

CONCLUSION

In my experience, sifting through the gender and cross-cultural issues that arise in human developmental theory is a task that brings with it a number of thorny methodological issues. As Fausto-Sterling (1985) suggests, "blind spots are an inherent aspect of science and are most frequent and dangerous when one studies socially urgent topics" (11). Essentially, we *all* see through the prism of our own culture and our own usually unconscious agendas. Most often, others are better at identifying our blind spots. To me, becoming consciously aware of our own cultural and gender-related biases and the effect they may have on our own selection and interpretation of materials is an important part of developing a more rigorous transpersonal theory.

References

Fausto-Sterling, A. 1985. *Myths of gender*. New York: Basic Books.

Lyons, N. 1988. Two perspectives: On self, relationships, and morality. In *Mapping the moral domain*, edited by C. Gilligan, J. Ward, J. Taylor, and B. Bardige. Cambridge: Harvard University Press.

Wade, J. 1996. *Changes of mind*. Albany: State University of New York Press.

Wilber, K. 1995. *Sex, ecology, spirituality: The spirit of evolution*. Boston: Shambhala.

Wright, P. 1995. Bringing women's voices to transpersonal psychology. *ReVision* 17 (Winter): 3-10.

Jürgen W. Kremer
Lingering Shadows

1. I WOULD LIKE TO EXPRESS MY APPRECIATION TO THE CONTRIBUTORS TO THIS volume. I find all of their articles thought-provoking because of their constructive critical engagement with Wilber's work. I would also like to express my appreciation for the way in which Wilber pushes contemporary thinkers in the field of transpersonal theory to clarify issues central to our understanding of ourselves and our future. Donald Rothberg and Sean Kelly are to be thanked for the professionalism and patience with which they saw this challenging project to its conclusion.

2. Gregory Bateson pointed out that the lack of response is a significant piece of information (rather than no information). I find Wilber's responses in this discussion disappointing, primarily because they fall short on engagement with the current writings of the contributors, while they are long on restatements of published positions and engagement with previous publications of some of the contributors. The stance that author X "tends to misrepresent my [Wilber's] overall model" seems to be the stimulus for extensive restatements instead of a detailed dialogue with the thoughtful reflections offered by the various authors. Of course, a perceived misrepresentation can mean at least three things: a) an actual misrepresentation and distortion of something clearly stated; b) a misrepresentation of something open to interpretation or unclearly or insufficiently stated; c) something perceived or framed as a mispresentation, which is actually a disagreement based on a correct or at least possible reading of an author's statements. While I can deeply appreciate an

author's concern with the desire to be represented as accurately as possible in the secondary literature, the experience of misrepresentation could at the same time also occasion an introspective exploration of the possible causes that might contribute to such misunderstandings from the author's side. The small amount of space dedicated by Wilber to dialogue about significant issues as they are described and identified by the present discussants results in less of a conversation and much more of a series of monologues than I had hoped for. But then Wilber's vision-logic, and certainly the indigenous mind process I am talking about, calls in part for a different setting and a different kind of interpersonal exchange than a book such as this one can offer.

3. Let me mention some examples of areas where I had wished for more detailed dialogue:

• I find Wilber's lack of "thinking with" Kelly's constructive suggestions disappointing.

• Wright points to a lack of critical political theory in Wilber's writing when she states that he "confuses the issue of who has the *power to set priorities* with the *act of having priorities*" (p. 214, in this volume). Wilber gave no response on this particular, significant issue.

• The three interviews Rothberg conducted potentially present a major challenge to Wilber's assumptions, and they could lead to exciting discussions about the application of various transpersonal models. However, Wilber's response to the actual interviews is minimal.

• It is interesting to notice how Wilber reads McDermott and fails to distinguish between critical disagreements, outspokeness, and level confrontation on the one hand and putdowns, dismissive commentary, and demeaning caricatures on the other hand. (And there is no response to Zimmerman's comments on this topic.) I heartily agree with Wilber's advocacy for honest disagreements and outspokeness. Yet Wilber writes about my article that "I find his [Kremer's] actual argument rather confused" (p. 359) without either saying what his reading of the argument is or why the argument is confused. An equivalent statement would be "I find Wilber's actual writing rather dissociated." Either of these remarks may be true, but they may be stated dismissively or in an engaged level of dialogue; the latter requires different wording and the creation of context through argument and explication.

4. Let me address some more of the specifics in Wilber's reply to my article. Wilber points to my lack of his discussion of Winkelman's reviews of his work. However, Wilber's critique of Winkelman's approach is quite beside the points which I am trying to make—there's no need for me to respond to these criticisms. My model is not one of cultural relativism, and Wilber fails to explain how the performative contradiction identified in Winkelman's work applies to my article. And Wilber has yet to answer the detailed objections by Winkelman and myself regarding available archaeological and anthropological evidence which challenge his model as a whole. (A discussion of cultural relativism, even if valid, is no response to these specific points.)

Wilber's statement about a society's center of gravity is a restatement of his own published work and not a response to the inherent contradictions and unclarity related to Wilber's work that I point out in my article, especially in regard to his contradictory statements about rational societies and the present stage of the majority of their members.

Wilber finds my discussions of the indigenous mind process neither "fair, balanced, [n]or anthropologically representative" (p. 359). This reminds me of debates around racism where one of the defensive responses to discussions of the Middle Passage is: "Well, African peoples had slaves, too." Indeed—but it misses the point of engagement with the complicity in racism and colonialism. Naturally, within the Eurocentered place where Wilber stands he has to find my discussion unbalanced, which is exactly what my critique addresses. The shadow of modernity continues to loom.

Finally, no author can be expected to address all the critical issues raised in this volume, yet Wilber's selection of topics for his responses is disappointingly nondialogical. Wilber's contributions to the field of transpersonal theory are impressive, yet, vision-logic, to my mind, requires a quality of dialogue about these issues which I have yet to see manifested in his response. The groundwork for the emergence of that possibility may have been laid with this volume. I am eager to be engaged in a quality of discourse (which I have called "participatory concourse") which would do justice to the stage which Wilber sees emerging.

Robert McDermott
Toward Transpersonal Philosophizing

IN *SES* WILBER SHOWS THAT HE KNOWS HOW TO "SHAKE THE SPIRITUAL TREE." As he confirmed in his response to my chapter, "The Need for

Philosophical and Spiritual Dialogue: Reflections on Ken Wilber's *Sex, Ecology, Spirituality*," he has no regrets. My article was not solely in response to *SES*, nor addressed exclusively to Wilber, but was focused on the relationship between *SES* and the transpersonal community.

Wilber's response confirms my claim that *SES* (particularly the notes) is polemical: it is, and deliberately so. This exchange has established that we really do disagree. Wilber defends polemics (from the Greek, *polemikos*, war), claims a long list of spiritual philosophers as his models, and insists that the combative and contentious arguments of polemics are consistent with spiritual awareness, equanimity, courage, and honesty.

Wilber says that colleagues tell him "all the time" about "the sad shape the field is in" (p. 356, in this volume). These individuals are reportedly "alarmed by the reactionary, antiprogressive, and regressive fog thickly creeping over the entire field" and encourage Wilber "to stand up and be counted" (p. 356). By contrast, I am hearing from colleagues who are alarmed by the polemics in and concerning *SES*, and by the disparity between such polemics and transpersonal values. My article and this response recommend "discriminating wisdom" and the moral fiber to voice such wisdom ideally joined to interest, humility, and compassion concerning the opinions of colleagues. I believe that this combination would help to create a transpersonal philosophy worthy of the agreement and emulation it seeks.

In this brief response, I make two recommendations: that transpersonal thinkers regard polemics as counterproductive, and that in their writings, particularly in relation to each other, they manifest the ideals characteristic of transpersonal world views, disciplines, and modes of consciousness. Wilber's phrases "discriminating wisdom backed with occasional polemic" and "the wrathful aspect of enlightened awareness" (p. 356) are presumptuous and damaging when addressed to his spiritually striving colleagues. Even if transpersonalism were a tree to be shaken, its spokespersons are not branches or fruit to be pruned and hacked.

The following points are offered both as a response to Wilber and as a plea to the transpersonal community that it not go the way of academic movements which are characterized by factions and *ad hominem* arguments.

1. The best way to clean up a field is to strive for wisdom based on practice, and to express ideas clearly and dispassionately. Self-appointed critics and authority figures can't be too careful about mixed motives and shadows. Attempts to impose improvements on the work of others usually generate defensiveness and scarcely ever better thinking. (By complaining about Wilber in this regard I of course run the same risk and

am subject to the same criticism as I am addressing to his criticisms. I hope that I am performing this task with sufficient caution and respect; others will decide.)

Once polemic begins, thinking on both sides typically fixes on winning rather than on cooperating in an effort to reach a higher or deeper insight. Wilber's references to my position as involving "idiot compassion," "administrative juggling," and "political correctness" are perfect examples of counterproductive polemic. These insulting characterizations are not aids to our dialogue. A polemic does not generate truth; it breeds fear, anger, and further polemics.

2. Wilber misses my point concerning his position as a philosopher and my current position as administrator of an institution of higher learning (as well as a teacher, lecturer, and writer on transpersonal philosophy). I am not confusing philosophy with administration. It was with respect to the responsibilities of a person in a leadership position, a person who wields power and influence, that I consider our responsibilities to be similar. In that context I continue to recommend wise compassion over what Wilber calls "the fiercest of judgments" (p. 356) and polemics.

3. I would not want Wilber or other transpersonal thinkers to "sit by and smile numbly as depth takes a vacation" (p. 356), but neither would I want them to follow the example of Plotinus, which Wilber cites with approval, of saying that the Gnostics had "no right to even speak of the divine." I continue to read Plotinus's *Enneads* for its sublime philosophical mysticism—and despite Plotinus's mistaken attack on the Gnostics. We are only in this century beginning to develop an understanding of the Gnostics after centuries of polemical misunderstandings and attacks.[1]

4. As an alternative to polemics, I think we would do well to join in developing a philosophical method and attitude that is a direct expression of transpersonal values and practices. The spirit of such an approach was well expressed in the concluding portion of Donald Rothberg's introduction to this volume. For a start, for example, we should strive to enter sympathetically into competing positions and to offer suggestions for their improvement. Wilber is like most philosophers in not allowing for the fact that he understands his own position better than he understands and reports the positions of others. One of the aims of a transpersonal world view is an active and insightful imagination, one which can see what lives in positions other than one's own. Admittedly, there has been little of this ability on display in the history of philosophy, but transpersonal philosophy is supposed to be an improvement over the past.

With his vast knowledge, incredible intelligence, and capacity for productive work, Ken Wilber can yet emerge as a model transpersonal thinker. I join with his many readers in gratitude to Ken for taking us as far as he has and for joining in this dialogue. We are also mindful that this dialogue has been made possible by countless hours of facilitation and editing by Donald Rothberg and Sean Kelly. We are profoundly grateful for their *upaya*.

Note

1. In *Ennead* 2.9, "Against the Gnostics; or, Against Those that Affirm the Creator of the Cosmos and the Cosmos Itself to be Evil," Plotinus does not attack individual Gnostics by name but he does attack their ideas with a lack of restraint which suggests the intensity of the competition and the mix of similarities and differences between his teachings and those of the Gnostics—concerning which, see Inge, Henry, Jonas, Brehier, Rudolph, and Willis.

Kaisa Puhakka

A Call to Play

MY RESPONSE TO KEN'S COMMENTS BELIES MY PURPOSE, LIGHTLY AND playfully though I wish to advance it. This purpose is to explore, and invite him to explore with me, the possibility of manifesting, through the very manner in which we speak or write, the dialectical consciousness that we describe in our writing.

To recognize the dialectic of play and purpose and to make room for it in one's theory is one thing; manifesting this dialectic in one's own activity, including writing, is quite another. It is the latter that fascinates me. In my chapter I wanted to try it out and see what happens.

I am delighted to see that Ken recognized what I was doing and was appreciative of it. (I imagine that he might even have been a bit amused by it.) I was hoping that he would like to play as well, with his purposes or mine. But he did not do so. With seeming seriousness, he admonished me for having "completely misreported [his] position" (p. 357). Indeed, I would be remiss had I identified his position with one of the contending camps (the ego as opposed to the eco, the Wilberian hierarchists as opposed to the anti-Wilberian heterarchists), But this was not my intention. Rather, I was concerned with the divisiveness and contentiousness that comes with the narrow and exclusive insistence that "evolution is play" and the equally narrow and exclusive insistence that "evolution has purpose." I did not think of Ken as being guilty of either. Rather, I saw his position as being much bigger and capable of accommodating both. But his theory does endorse directionality in evolution, and thus favors purpose over play. In this sense, I am "identifying" (he says "over-identifying") his theory as purposeful rather than playful (p. 357).

The clarification of my intent regarding Wilber's position hints at a seriousness of purpose on my part, the contemplation of which opens up another turn in the evolving dialectic: The setting forth of any "position" whatsoever—e.g., the one I clarified as mine or the one Ken says I misreported—is an enactment of purpose. Playfulness manifests in the lightness with which the position is held.

Yes, emptiness is neither playful nor purposeful. But it also is playful and purposeful. The Great Cosmic Play, the Dance of Shiva, is neither, and is both. Of course, we live in the world of Form in which play and purpose are opposites and are experienced as a dualism. We may have glimpses of the nondual Play, but, as Ken says, "a glimpse of the nondual is one thing, a stable realization quite another" (p. 358). However, the language of dialectic can remind us of Play and thus perhaps hasten our realization of the nondual. By this I do not mean to suggest that dialectic by itself is sufficient to bring about such a realization. As Ken points out, other forms of contemplative practice are usually needed as well.

But what kind of dialectic are we talking about, and attempting to enact in our talking? Is it the dialectic of Form or of Emptiness? Perhaps it is both, but possibly also neither. The dialectic of Form is dedicated to forms and, true to its mission, quests after the Form of forms. The dialectic of Emptiness shows the lack of form, the no-form, in the very form (and the form in the no-form), thus counseling us to hold all forms lightly. It seems to me that a dialectic of Emptiness does justice to the dialectic of Form when it sees the no-form in the form without a preference for either and celebrates the inherent creativity of forms with a clear view of their emptiness. Perhaps this is Ken's "granddaddy of nonduality."[1] In the world of Form, such a dialectic is a skillful play that avoids getting stuck in its own forms by appreciating purpose as much as it does its own playfulness.

But can one really say anything at all with such dialectic? If by "saying" is meant setting forth a position, proposing a theory, then the answer seems to be "no." Yet, without a theory or a position, there would be no dialectic. One might say that dialectic begins by appreciating a position and the purpose inherent in it. From there it moves to play and to the creation and discovery of further purposes.

Now that Ken has set forth his position, I call on him to play some. It is the magnificence of his position and his skill at play, especially evident in many of the passages of *SES*, that inspires me to do so. But once again, a ring of seriousness in the statements I just made betrays a further purpose in my play. This purpose is to keep Ken's theory truly open-ended and alive—evolving with all of us as we discourse and reflect upon it. Theories of lesser scope can afford to be relatively more rigid and closed without much effect on those who subscribe to them or on the evolutionary process of which they are a part. Such small scale theories are simply amended or replaced in the process of evolutionary change. But a Big View such as Ken's, precisely because it purports to include everything and to stretch all the way to the nondual, must itself remain open and genuinely capable of evolution, lest it become a frozen blueprint to which evolving Spirit is expected to conform. The paradoxes at the edges of a Big View provide the openings, the invitations to a dialectic that at once appreciates and transcends the View. Such a transcendence is vital especially at the higher reaches of human consciousness where Spirit aspires to freedom from identification with any and all views.

From my understanding of Ken, he is fully appreciative of what I just said and intends his theory to be an open-ended, evolving view. But how does it stay open and evolving? And I do not mean open only to the further evolution of Ken's own views but to those of his readers as well. Our critical assessments are usually geared toward acceptance or rejection, which tends to lead to a solidification and closing of one's "position" with regard to the view or theory. Dialectical engagement of the theory, on the other hand, fosters the kind of flexibility and openness that allows for genuine evolutionary change. The deeper purpose of Ken's theory is to be an instrument of such evolutionary change. To honor this purpose, let us play with his theory with a lightness and apprecation that allows further purposes to emerge. Ken has presented a great discourse on play (and, of course, on purpose). I hope that he will also join in a play on this discourse. Such a play, like a dance, can be infinitely more fun when its delights and surprises are shared with partners.

Note

1. The two modes of dialectic that Ken associates with West and East and his attempt to synthesize/transcend their duality, which he considers "the single major message of *SES*," deserve a much more in-depth treatment than space permits here. I hope that these important issues will receive more careful attention in the future than they have thus far.

Part Seven

Final
Reflections

16

Ken Wilber
Afterword

 LET ME BEGIN BY SAYING THAT IT WAS NOT ALWAYS POSSIBLE FOR me to respond as fully as I would have liked—due to time and space limitations—and for this I am truly sorry. It was not out of lack of desire, or lack of respect, or lack of interest. If I could not respond in detail to each criticism, I have nonetheless taken all of them very much to heart. Some exceptionally important issues and criticisms have been raised, a good majority of which I agree with, and if I couldn't work all of them into my response, I most certainly will be confronting them in my future work. This exchange has been an enormous help to me, and my hope is that it was mutual. So I would like to thank all of you for engaging in this discussion—and particularly Donald Rothberg and Sean Kelly for their tireless effort and superb editorship.

Mike Murphy is right that the new canon has immense implications for empirical research in metanormal capacities, and his *Future of the Body* is an excellent introduction to just that topic.

In the long version of Stan Grof's response (privately circulated), he states that, in reference to my explanation of the transpersonal components of perinatal experiences: "I find this explanation perfectly acceptable." In other words, perinatal experiences cannot be reduced to regression to, or mature revival of, preegoic structures, as such experiences are based, in part, on the transegoic "psychic" or "soul" dimension. I think this removes the major source of disagreement between us, and I am glad that, thanks largely to this forum, we have been able to reach a much closer agreement on this crucial issue.

Sean Kelly is quite right that my suggestion to open up the Great Chain by seeing it, not as a monolithic pole but rather as numerous different streams traversing various waves, substantially alters the root metaphor (possibly fatally). We will simply have to see where this line of research leads us. At the same time, if the spiritual is a separate developmental line, then in my model young people (and young cultures) could definitely show a significant spiritual development. As for peak experiences, it is states, not structures, that can be "peaked" (thus, a young girl might easily have a peak or plateau experience of the subtle state, but in the cognitive development line, if she were at preop she would *not* have a formop peak experience). Sean's own suggestion of complex holism is certainly an important idea that will need to be brought to these future studies.

In this regard, so is Donald Rothberg's central suggestion of spirituality as being *any* content of *any* line when approached from a transpersonal perspective or attitude. I think there is much to recommend that notion; it is a central unifying concept that allows us to mitigate the harsher aspects of rigid stage models. And remember, many of the central aspects of my model are *not* stage-like, including the most important of all, the self-system; so I am more than predisposed to this excellent suggestion. My initial question would simply be: Does the spiritual attitude itself come fully formed or does it develop?

Michele McDonald-Smith rightly reacts to my suggestion that American teachers "rarely see stages of development of anything" (p. 335). But I meant specifically when they were dealing with individuals with borderline or preconventional pathology; I was referring to Jack Engler's work, which I still find quite cogent. But aside from that, of course there are numerous cases of genuine transformation! I'm sorry I wasn't clearer on this, and I certainly did not mean to offend any American teachers, many of whom are close and long-time friends of mine. And Michele's overall position—different *paramis* as being "a model of multiple developmental lines"—is actually very similar to mine, so I believe we share much common ground here.

Peggy Wright's response I particularly appreciated, because I feel that we can really begin to work together on these extremely important topics. I believe we got off to a bit of a bad start, but that we can now more readily see and appreciate what the other is saying. Peggy brings a wealth of information, research knowledge, and creative suggestions to this field. If I didn't have time to respond to her positive contributions, I nonetheless learned a great deal, and I hope that I can continue to learn from her in the future. Maybe she'll volunteer to read Volume Two of the *Kosmos* trilogy (*Sex, God, and Gender*) in manuscript and make some positive suggestions; or, at the least, delete the sections where I totally embarrass myself.

I believe Jürgen Kremer thinks I have stopped listening to him altogether, which is not true. It's just that I used to embrace a worldview almost identical to his (I started writing *Up From Eden* to prove that view). But I found it harder and harder to fit the preponderance of evidence into that model, and I had to abandon it. That was part of that very painful transition from Wilber-I to Wilber-II, a transition reflected both ontogenetically, moving from a view similar to Washburn's, and phylogenetically, moving from a view similar to Jürgen's. I now believe that the total web of evidence supports neither of those views, but it cannot easily be maintained that I do not understand those positions or that I have at no time had any sympathy for them. And I am still listening as carefully as I can.

Michael Washburn and I will, I hope, continue to stay on each other's case; I have always found his observations to be cogent, and the ptf-3 is something I will continue to ponder seriously. My old friend Michael Zimmerman and I will carry on this dialogue as usual, as will Roger Walsh and I. And my new friend Robert McDermott has convinced me to tone down the polemic. (But please, it's not *that* characteristic of my writing on the whole; Roger and I actually calculated the percentage of my total writing that has anything resembling a polemical tone. Roger reports it as less than 1 percent; it was actually 0.07 percent.)

As for Kaisa's invitation to play, by all means let us play. As Kaisa says, she takes *seriously* her impulse to *play*—that's the funny part, and that's the fun, the dialectical fun, as she knows—so I hope I can take a lesson from her and hold my views lightly. I'd like to think I do, but it never hurts to be reminded.

My thanks again to all of you for your responsiveness, care, concern, and generosity of spirit.

17

Donald Rothberg
and Sean M. Kelly

Directions for Transpersonal Inquiry:
Reflections on the Conversation

 WE CONCLUDE THIS BOOK WITH GREAT APPRECIATION FOR THE contributors to this forum. Their work has, we believe, touched, often deeply, many of the key issues in transpersonal studies. We thank the participants in this conversation for their hard work, their ability to meet many deadlines, and their many illuminations. We certainly have learned from and with everyone.

We especially want to thank Ken Wilber for his participation, both for his willingness to join in the dialogue and for his hanging in there despite sometimes feeling misunderstood in the face of critical points and perspectives in relation to his work. This was surely not always easy. Most of us would likely have a difficult time facing sustained public scrutiny and even friendly criticism of our published work. It is no doubt a difficult position to be in to have given a pioneering integral vision "of everything," to have theories about many areas where others may have more knowledge, and to engage in dialogue with them.

Despite the limits of the dialogues, we believe we have advanced discussion of a number of core issues related both to Ken Wilber's work and contemporary transpersonal inquiry. Although there was a general recognition of and respect for the significance of Wilber's achievements, most contributors posed challenges to aspects of Wilber's theories. Judging from Wilber's response, it appears that his main adaptive strategy in relation to the challenges has been, in Piagetian terms, *assimilation*. This is no surprise since, as the contributors themselves readily acknowledged, Wilber's comprehensive model is capable of integrating vast amounts of disparate data and theoretical constructs.

Several challenges remain, however. First, the whole notion of discrete, hierarchically (or holarchically) ordered stages and structures of psychospiritual development remains in question, particularly in the context of other *alternative paradigms* of transpersonal theory. On the one hand, there is the matter of seemingly conflictual data—whether from clinical settings (Grof), the observations of meditation teachers (Rothberg, Goldstein, Kornfield, McDonald-Smith), women's experiences (Wright), or indigenous cultures (Kremer). On the other hand, there is the possibility of alternative interpretations of key concepts—such as those of hierarchy/holarchy (Kelly, Wright) and the meaning of spirit or the transpersonal (Washburn, Kelly, Rothberg).

Wilber has for the most part tried to assimilate these challenges to the stage model by insisting on the distinction between structures and states and claiming that his holarchical stage model still holds as far as structures are concerned. He has also stressed the multidimensional nature of development with the notion of distinct developmental lines, some of which—particularly the cognitive—develop holarchically, while others—such as the moral—do not. To the extent that these distinctions require a significant number of qualifications of core elements of Wilber's model—for instance, the root metaphor of the Great Chain of Being— Wilber would seem to be *accommodating* his model to some of the challenges presented, rather than simply assimilating them.

We would like very much to hear further discussion of some of the questions raised that did not get substantial discussion by Wilber. For example, Wilber responded to Washburn's earlier work, but not in significant detail to his main essay (chapter 4) in this book. In particular, it is important to discuss further the extent to which development up to the "centaur" level in many cases does not follow the pattern of "holarchical integration," particularly in the common split of mind and body. Is this normal development? Is it a cultural anomaly? This issue is linked to the question of clarifying how the "developmental lines" relate to one another. We believe this to be one of the most important areas to investigate, both theoretically and practically, and it is an area which Wilber has helped very much to open up. It would be useful to know more about Murphy's Integral Transformative Practices, in this regard, as well as to have further inquiry about the many issues articulated by Goldstein, Kornfield, and McDonald-Smith. We would also like to hear further responses by Wilber to the many questions raised by Rothberg (in chapter 7) about his stage model of individual development.

A second set of challenges also remains concerning Wilber's response to the problems of what we called *the relation of transpersonal theory to the "other,"* problems in part identified by Wilber himself. These problems include: (1) the historical devaluation of body, women, nature, and indigenous peoples in Western and often Asian culture; (2) the over-valuation of "ascent" as opposed to "descent" in spiritual traditions; and (3) contemporary Western individualistic and subjectivistic interpretations of spirituality. In these contexts, we find that there have been some significant explorations by many of the authors that help us to address these concerns. Zimmerman, Wright, Kremer, Achterberg, and Rothberg have raised issues related to the "other," often forcefully and in a way that challenges both Wilber and the transpersonal field as a whole to give more attention to this general area. Wilber himself has been open to rearticulating his theories in an attempt to address these concerns. In his attempt to integrate feminist literature, in his four quadrant model, and in his model of balancing ascent and descent, he has given at least a preliminary response to this whole question area.

However, the *dialogue* around these issues in this book has been less satisfactory, in our view, related no doubt to the often charged nature of these issues. Significant communication in particular between Wilber and Wright, and Wilber and Kremer was not so evident in these pages. Wilber criticized Wright's work at times very harshly in his long response, and only in the footnotes did he treat in depth her chapter from this volume. However, he incorporated her concept of the "permeable self" in his attempt to develop a transpersonal model of "feminine" development, and this may be a testimony to the actual communication that did occur. In Part VI and in Wilber's "Afterword," both Wilber and Wright acknowledged their appreciation for and learning from each other's work, despite differences and frictions.

Wilber's response to Kremer was very short and began only in a very cursory way to respond to what we take to be the very important issues Kremer raised. Furthermore, Wilber's treatment of these issues in *The Eye of Spirit* (1997), to which he refers the reader interested in knowing his fuller response to the issues, represents, in our view, also only the beginning of an exploration and response. Questions persist about the interpretation of the anthropological and archaeological "data" (as well as the data from contemporary indigenous traditions) and whether such data support a stage model. There also remain a host of generally unresolved yet crucial questions concerning romanticism, "regressive" stances, projection, and the examination of what Kremer calls the "shadow" of evolutionary thinking.

On the other hand, Wilber and Zimmerman have carried on, we think, a mostly helpful dialogue around the nature of a transpersonal ecological philosophy, although much of Wilber's response to Zimmerman's questions was promissory, referring to further treatment to appear in Volume Two of his planned *Kosmos*. Wilber has also endorsed the need for "relational" models of spirituality, following Achterberg and Rothberg. His recent theoretical framework provides clear space for such interests to develop. We believe that clarification of relational models in the context of most of the issues of the transpersonal field is a very important horizon for the coming years, having to do with our understandings of individual development, spirituality, gender, modes of knowing, and cultural evolution. Our hope for this general issue, as well as for the other issues having to do with the "other," is that we might see considerably more cooperative exploration and sustained inquiry of these very vital questions.

A third remaining challenge concerns the typically charged and often unclear concept of *regression*. Wilber continues to recognize the potential value of, and even the occasional necessity for, "regression in the service of the ego." However, he remains dubious about the value of many contemporary appropriations of indigenous spirituality, as well as about many expressions of nature-mysticism motivated especially by ecological and feminist concerns. Questions of the extent to which these contemporary forms are exclusively regressive in a pejorative sense, or rather represent "healing journeys" (Wright) still require much more clarification, in large part in relation to some of the other basic issues mentioned above. We would like to urge further careful and open attention to these issues, with considerable attention to data and experience as well as to theory. On the other hand, Wilber and Grof do seem to have come to a better understanding concerning the nature of perinatal experiences through this forum. Wilber and Washburn, however, seem not to have bridged, though they have further clarified, the very significant differences between their two models, especially concerning regression.

We think that a fourth general set of questions has also been addressed, at least in a beginning way, through this volume. We have begun to explore and to some extent exemplify the meaning of *transpersonally inspired dialogue, interchange, and inquiry*, guided by transpersonal values, "vision logic" (Wilber), and an alternative to the common model of discourse as "war" against one's opponents. At times the conversation considered the importance of sympathetic listening to and dialogue with the other, and the place, if any, of polemic in transpersonal inquiry. This occurred particularly through the contributions by McDermott, Rothberg (in his introduction), Puhakka, Wilber, and Kremer (in his final contribution). Not surprisingly, at times in the conversation, there were claims, both by Wilber and by the other authors, of being misunderstood, and seeming examples of war-like discourse and a lack of sympathetic listening to others.

Nonetheless, if we are to judge from the later "Conversation" writings by the participants and by Wilber's "Afterword," some of the breaches in understanding have been apparently mended, and some new understandings seem to have emerged. For instance, Wilber in his "Afterword" commented that he has been convinced "to tone down the polemic." Still, we think that many issues remain to be explored in this area. How to engage (at times clearly and powerfully, yet compassionately) with others with very different views; how to recognize, explore, and work with strong emotions in the context of inquiry; how more fully to understand the dialectical nature of our core concepts and to hold them lightly and playfully, as well as sometimes seriously; how to integrate experiential and practical dimensions with more theoretical inquiry and develop new models of transpersonal exchange—these and other questions call out for theoretical and practical investigations, guided by transpersonal values and principles.

As we see it, there are two main related paths to follow in the further evaluation of Wilber's theories, paths followed, we hope, increasingly in the spirit of transpersonal inquiry, as we come to know what that means. The first involves empirical, historical, interpretive, and phenomenological research, as well as a host of practical and experiential inquiries, which may support, undermine, or suggest further development of Wilber's theoretical positions on specific issues. The data of this research and inquiry will come from a variety of traditions and approaches, including anthropology, comparative religion, social theory, psychology and psychotherapy, and spiritual practice.

However, because all data are theory-laden, a second path will consist in the continued examination of Wilber's theoretical positions in relation to alternative transpersonal models, including those of Grof, Washburn, and other post-Jungians. We will also need to look closely at other contemporary integrative and visionary metatheoretical models, such as those inspired by the work of various ancient metaphysical and spiritual systems, Hegel, Steiner, Whitehead, Gebser, other advocates of the perennial philosophy, feminism, and systems thinking, among others.

Whatever the judgment of future colleagues, there can be no doubt about the great value of Wilber's contributions to the field of transpersonal studies. The *Kosmos* trilogy in particular promises to broaden and deepen such studies, engaging, as it does, critical issues of global concern (we think, in particular, of his treatment of issues of gender, ecology, ethics, globalization, and pluralism). We await with interest the appearance of the remaining two volumes. Perhaps in those volumes, as well as in the further work of our contributors, we will hear many of the voices and dialogues of this book.

Reference

Wilber, K. 1997. *The eye of spirit: An integral vision for a world gone slightly mad.* Boston: Shambhala.

Index

QUEST BOOKS
are published by
The Theosophical Society in America,
Wheaton, Illinois 60189-0270,
a branch of a world organization
dedicated to the promotion of the unity of
humanity and the encouragement of the study of
religion, philosophy, and science, to the end that
we may better understand ourselves and our place in
the universe. The Society stands for complete
freedom of individual search and belief.
For further information about its activities,
write, call 1-800-669-1571, or consult its Web page:
http://www.theosophical.org

*The Theosophical Publishing House
is aided by the generous support of
THE KERN FOUNDATION,
a trust established by Herbert A. Kern
and dedicated to Theosophical education.*